Feb 2018

P9-DFR-798

Kansas City, MO Public Library

THE CADAVER
KING
AND
THE COUNTRY
DENTIST

THE CADAVER KING
and
THE COUNTRY DENTIST

A TRUE STORY *of* INJUSTICE
in the AMERICAN SOUTH

RADLEY BALKO AND
TUCKER CARRINGTON

FOREWORD BY JOHN GRISHAM

PublicAffairs
NEW YORK

Copyright © 2018 by Radley Balko and Tucker Carrington.
Foreword © John Grisham, 2018

Hachette Book Group supports the right to free expression and the value of copyright. The purpose of copyright is to encourage writers and artists to produce the creative works that enrich our culture.

The scanning, uploading, and distribution of this book without permission is a theft of the authors' intellectual property. If you would like permission to use material from the book (other than for review purposes), please contact permissions@hbgusa.com. Thank you for your support of the authors' rights.

PublicAffairs
Hachette Book Group
1290 Avenue of the Americas, New York, NY 10104
www.publicaffairsbooks.com
@Public_Affairs

Printed in the United States of America.

First Edition: February 2018

Published by PublicAffairs, an imprint of Perseus Books, LLC, a subsidiary of Hachette Book Group, Inc. The PublicAffairs name and logo is a trademark of the Hachette Book Group.

The Hachette Speakers Bureau provides a wide range of authors for speaking events. To find out more, go to www.hachettespeakersbureau.com or call (866) 376-6591.

The publisher is not responsible for websites (or their content) that are not owned by the publisher.

Print book interior design by Amy Quinn.

The Library of Congress has cataloged the hardcover edition of this book as follows:

Names: Balko, Radley, author. | Carrington, Tucker (W. Tucker), author.
Title: The cadaver king and the country dentist : a true story of injustice in the American South / Radley Balko and Tucker Carrington.
Description: First edition. | New York : PublicAffairs, [2017] | Includes bibliographical references and index.
Identifiers: LCCN 2017009508 (print) | LCCN 2017011704 (ebook) | ISBN 9781610396929 (ebook) | ISBN 9781610396912 (hardcover)
Subjects: LCSH: Hayne, Steven (Forensic pathologist) | West, Michael (Dentist) | Criminal justice, Administration of—Mississippi. | Judicial error—Mississippi. | Brooks, Levon, 1959—Trials, litigation, etc. | Brewer, Kennedy—Trials, litigation, etc. | Trials (Rape)—Mississippi. | Trials (Murder)—Mississippi.
Classification: LCC RA1025.H38 (ebook) | LCC RA1025.H38 B35 2017 (print) | DDC 614/.109762—dc23
LC record available at https://lccn.loc.gov/2017009508

ISBNs: 978-1-61039-691-2 (hardcover); 978-1-61039-692-9 (e-book)

LSC-H

10 9 8 7 6 5 4 3 2 1

To Kennedy Brewer and Levon Brooks,
and to the memories of
Courtney Smith and Christine Jackson

Shame may restrain what law does not prohibit.

—Seneca

CONTENTS

FOREWORD

It is relatively easy to convict an innocent person. Millions of defendants are processed through our courts each year, so it becomes nearly impossible to determine how many are actually innocent once they've been convicted. No one has the time or resources to examine the facts and backgrounds of those claiming to be wrongfully convicted. Actual wrongful conviction estimates range from 2 percent to 10 percent, but no one really knows. These numbers may sound low, but when applied to a prison population of 2.3 million, they become staggering. Can there really be between 46,000 and 230,000 innocent people locked away? Those of us who are involved in innocence work firmly believe so.

And, practically speaking, once an innocent person is convicted, it is virtually impossible to get them out of prison. I serve on the board of directors of the Innocence Project in New York. In the past twenty-five years, we have secured through DNA testing the release of 349 innocent men and women, 20 of whom had been sent to death row. All told, over 2,000 exonerations, including 200 from death row and including those not involving DNA, have occurred in the United States during that same period. While we are proud of our work, we've only scratched the surface.

Wrongful convictions happen for eight reasons. Not all are neatly defined, and they usually combine with others to produce a bad result. In some of the more egregious cases, the poor defendant unwittingly "hit for the cycle" and got nailed with all eight.

In no particular order of importance, they are:

Bad Police Work. Most cops are honest, hard-working professionals who aren't paid a high salary. However, there are a not insignificant number of cases in which police officers have hidden, altered, or fabricated evidence, lied on the witness stand, cut deals with snitches in return for bogus testimony, intimidated and threatened witnesses, coerced confessions, or manipulated eyewitness identifications.

Prosecutorial Misconduct. Most prosecutors are honest, hard-working professionals who aren't paid a high salary—at least not compared to many other lawyers. However, there have been cases in which prosecutors hid exculpatory evidence, encouraged witnesses to commit perjury, lied to jurors, judges, and defense lawyers, used the testimony of bogus experts, or ignored relevant evidence beneficial to the accused.

False Confessions. Most jurors find it impossible to believe that a suspect would confess to a serious crime he didn't commit. Yet the average citizen, if taken to a basement room and subjected to ten consecutive hours of abusive interrogation tactics by experienced cops, might be surprised at what they would say under extreme duress. Of the 330 people exonerated by DNA from 1989 to 2015, about 25 percent gave bogus confessions after lengthy interrogations. Virtually every one recanted soon after.

Faulty Eyewitness Identification. More often than not, those who witness violent acts have trouble accurately recalling the facts and identifying those involved. Yet police regularly use physical and photo lineups, and these are often manipulated in various ways to focus suspicion on favored suspects.

Jailhouse Snitches. This tactic involves one of the oldest and dirtiest tricks used by police and prosecutors. In every jail there is a career criminal staring at a long sentence. For leniency, he can be persuaded to lie to the jury and describe in great detail the confession overheard from the accused, usually a cell mate. And if he performs well enough on the stand, the authorities might allow him to walk free.

Bad Lawyering. Those accused of serious crimes rarely have money. Most are represented by good public defenders, but too many get stuck with court-appointed lawyers with little or no experience. Capital cases are complex, the stakes are enormous, and all too often the defense lawyers are in over their heads.

Sleeping Judges. Judges are supposed to be impartial referees intent on ensuring fair trials. They should exclude confessions that are inconsistent with the physical evidence and obtained by questionable means, exclude the testimony of career felons with dubious motives, require prosecutors to produce exculpatory evidence, and question the credentials and testimony of all experts outside the presence of the jury. Unfortunately, judges do not always do what they should. The reasons are many and varied, but the fact that many judgeships are elected positions doesn't help. They are conscious of their upcoming reelection and how the decisions they make might affect it. And of those judges who are appointed and not elected, the majority are former prosecutors.

Junk Science. This is a major reason for wrongful convictions. Over the past five decades, our courtrooms have been flooded with an avalanche of unreliable, even atrocious "science." Experts of all varieties and with qualifications that were dubious at best and fraudulent at worst have peddled (for a fee, of course) all manner of damning theories of guilt based on their alleged scientific analysis of hair, fibers, bite marks, arson, boot prints, blood spatters, and ballistics. Of the 330 people exonerated by DNA tests from 1989 to 2015, *71 percent* were convicted based on forensic testimony, much of which was flawed, unreliable, exaggerated, and sometimes even outright fabricated.

University of Virginia law professor Brandon Garrett has studied virtually all of the trial transcripts of wrongful convictions that were later exposed by DNA-based exonerations. He writes: "There is a national epidemic of overstated forensic testimony, with a steady stream of criminal convictions being overturned as the shoddiness of decades' worth of physical evidence comes to light. The true scope of the problem is only now coming into focus."

This book tells the story of two of the most ambitious and daring experts ever allowed in a courtroom. One was a controversial forensic pathologist who once boasted of performing over two thousand autopsies in a single year. The other, his sidekick, was a small-town dentist who brazenly and without formal training or study assumed the role of an expert in many other fields, such as ballistics, gunshot reconstruction, "tool mark" patterns, and the analysis not only of teeth and bite marks but wound patterns, bruises, and fingernail scratches. Together, they tag-teamed their way through rape and murder trials throughout Mississippi and Louisiana, accumulating an impressive string of convictions, several of which have now been overturned. Some are still being litigated. Many others, sadly, seem destined to stand.

This is a maddening story of a broken system, one in which prosecutors allowed—even encouraged—flawed forensic testimony because it was skillfully molded to fit their theories of guilt. Time and again, over two decades, elected judges permitted these two men to take the stand and convince unsophisticated jurors that science was on the side of the state. As professional testifiers, they honed their performances and became thoroughly convincing.

While breathtaking in its scope, the work these two men did within the justice system is also heartbreaking in its devastation. No one really knows the true extent of the damage. No one knows how many innocent women and men have been convicted in trials in which these two testified, nor is the truth likely ever to be discovered. And it seems nearly impossible to think the state of Mississippi will investigate, audit, or take responsibility.

As you turn the pages, you will often be tempted to close this book and either laugh or cry or yell that what happened in Mississippi cannot possibly be true. But it is. It happened in plain view and with the complicity of many who were sworn to uphold the law. It is my hope that this book might inspire those with the necessary will and persistence to finally bring justice for the men and women around the country who have been wrongfully convicted and to fix the system so that nothing like this can ever happen again.

John Grisham

PS: In the spirit of full disclosure, I am compelled to accept my share of the responsibility. As an elected member of the Mississippi legislature back in the 1980s, I remember the struggle to establish and fund the Office of the State Medical Examiner. It was a thorny issue that wouldn't go away, but it was far from the most pressing matters we faced each year. I have no idea how I voted on the various bills, but I do remember being embarrassed by our antiquated system of elected coroners. I recall being frustrated by the state's inability to find and keep a medical examiner. Its failure to do so was a major reason some of the characters in this story were allowed to amass so much power.

AUTHORS' NOTE

The two of us came to this story separately, each after looking into a different case in which we found expert forensic testimony that seemed odd—outside the boundaries of sound science. Then we found other cases with similarly troubling testimony. And then many, many others. It soon became clear that this wasn't about one case, or even several. It was a sprawling, complex affair that spanned decades, that was rooted in history, politics, and law. The story you're about to read took place largely in Mississippi and Louisiana, but the component parts—dubious forensics, innocence, the intersection of science and law, and the structural racism built into the criminal justice system—are issues that find their way into just about every courtroom in America.

RADLEY BALKO

I first traveled to Mississippi in 2005 to report on the case of Cory Maye, a tragic story about overzealous policing and the drug war—a subject that would later become the focus of my first book. While investigating that case, I stumbled onto this much bigger story, one that covers two decades and thousands of trials, several of them death penalty cases.

Cory Maye had been convicted the previous year for killing Ron Jones, a Prentiss, Mississippi, police officer, during a drug raid. Maye, who was home with his young daughter when the twelve-thirty-a.m. raid went down, claimed he mistook the cops who broke down his door for criminal intruders.

The raid on Maye certainly seemed to have been a mistake. Maye lived with his girlfriend and daughter on one side of a duplex. On the other side lived a man named Jamie Smith, who was already facing drug charges. Smith's name was on the warrant. Maye's wasn't, though his address was. The police found a significant quantity of drugs in Smith's home.

Cory Maye had no prior criminal record, didn't know his neighbor, and had no significant quantity of drugs in his home (the police found a single burnt marijuana cigarette in the apartment—which would otherwise have merited a $50 fine). But Maye had just killed a cop. He was black; the cop was white. And this wasn't just any cop: Ron Jones was also the son of the town's police chief.

Maye was arrested and charged with capital murder.

Medical examiner Steven Hayne performed the autopsy on Jones and later testified at Maye's trial. Hayne's testimony was problematic. Based on Hayne's testimony about the trajectory the bullet took through Jones's body, the prosecutor argued to the jury that Maye must have been standing when he shot Jones, not lying on the floor in fear, as he had said he was. The claim made it appear as though Maye had been lying in wait to ambush Jones. In truth, a number of variables can affect a bullet's trajectory through a body, most notably the victim's position when shot. Moreover, bullets found in the door frame of Maye's home had a clear upward trajectory. A bullet's path through a stationary object like a door frame was a much more likely indication of Maye's position than its path through a moving human being.

Given that Maye's guilt or innocence hinged on whether the jury believed him when he said he didn't know Jones was a police officer, the doubt prosecutors cast on Maye's story by way of Hayne's testimony was critical.

Hayne wasn't outright wrong in Maye's case; he was just slippery. He never came right out and said that Maye could only have been standing. Instead, he carefully worded his answers, allowing the prosecutor to weave the testimony into the state's closing argument for the jury, all while still retaining plausible deniability.

Maye was convicted and sentenced to death. He was later given a new trial when the Mississippi Supreme Court ruled that he should have been permitted to argue that he was defending his daughter's life on the night of the raid. In 2011, after ten years behind bars, he accepted a plea bargain in which he pleaded guilty to manslaughter. He has since been released.

Given the way prosecutors were able to use Hayne's testimony to mislead jurors during Maye's trial, I began to wonder if they had also done so in others. So I asked around. I first spoke with Maye's attorney and public defender, Bob Evans, who recalled the case of Tonya Ward, a woman whose skeletonized remains had been found in a wooded area and had been picked at by animals. Hayne testified she had died from strangulation, an improbable diagnosis when there's no soft tissue on the body to examine and no way to tell if any trauma done to her body had come before or after her death.

Other attorneys across Mississippi had similar stories. I called other medical examiners across the South. And then police officials and other forensic analysts. On a couple of occasions, I had barely finished explaining that I was working on a story about a questionable medical examiner before the source would interrupt and ask if I was referring to Hayne. Many wouldn't talk on the record, citing Hayne's reputation for litigiousness.

But some did. Ken Winter, former head of the Mississippi Association of Chiefs of Police, told me that he was most troubled by the sheer quantity of autopsies Hayne performed, which he called "way too many to do . . . in the manner they should be done." One former state official in Mississippi recalled being pressured by district attorneys to change his opinion based on Hayne's analysis. And he could think of two specific murder cases in which Hayne's opinion was "way outside the purview of a forensic pathologist." The official was also aghast at Hayne's sloppy practices. "There were frequently test tubes sent to the lab with the wrong name on them," he said. "I reached a point where we just collected all the trace evidence at the scene." Former Columbus, Mississippi, police chief J. D. Sanders also had stories. Sanders wrote a weekly column in the local newspaper. After a series of columns in which he criticized Hayne and the death investigation system, he received a flood of feedback—both public and private—from coroners and prosecutors across the state. The anger, virulence, and even death threats in some of the responses convinced Sanders that things were worse than he imagined. "There's no question in my mind that there are innocent people doing time at Parchman Penitentiary due to the testimony of Dr. Hayne," Sanders told me. "There may even be some on death row."

In October 2007, I published an investigation of Hayne in *Reason* magazine, along with an accompanying essay in the *Wall Street Journal*. After the story ran, a local TV station confronted Hayne outside his office about the articles. He promised to sue both me and the *Wall Street Journal*. The reporter then asked Hayne if he was board certified in forensic pathology. He said he was. When pressed about what organization had certified him, Hayne replied that he couldn't remember.

In the ten years since, I've written dozens of stories about Hayne. I also began writing about Hayne's sidekick, Michael West, the dentist, bite mark analyst, and—in my view—a person who should not have been allowed in a courtroom. The two men dominated the Mississippi death investigation system for twenty years. West testified in dozens of cases, Hayne in thousands. Until and unless the state engages in a thorough, top-down investigation of their work, we may never know the extent of the damage they may have done. So far, the people with the power to initiate such an investigation haven't shown much interest.

TUCKER CARRINGTON

In 2007, I was hired to found and direct the Mississippi Innocence Project, based at the University of Mississippi Law School in Oxford. I packed up my family and office in Washington, DC, and moved to north Mississippi. On my first day at work, I read through some opinions handed down the week before by the Mississippi Supreme Court. I was startled by the first case I saw. Not only had the state's expert witness given what I considered to be unfounded forensic testimony, the trial court had admitted it in a way that seemed fairly routine. The expert? Steven Hayne. The defendant was convicted, and the Mississippi Supreme Court affirmed.

One of my first tasks as director of a new entity at the law school was to let people know we existed, and to announce our upcoming inaugural fundraiser. The event featured John Grisham—who with his family had provided some of the funding for the new venture—and fellow novelist Scott Turow. We sent a mailer to lawyers, politicians, law enforcement officials, and other prominent figures across the state. After a few days the responses started pouring in, and it was clear that my staff and I had our work cut out for us. Laurence Mellen, the district attorney for several counties in the northwest corner of the Delta, wrote back for proof of my claim—which by then was common knowledge for anyone working in the criminal justice system—that DNA evidence had exonerated more than two hundred people. Somehow that fact, combined with the establishment of the project, meant that many prosecutors across the state, who were graduates of the University of Mississippi School of Law, were "naturally concerned that the law school is impugning our integrity." District Attorney Jim Powell wrote a letter, too. He noted that over the course of America's 230-year history, and among its population of three hundred million, "there is a claim of only 200 wrongful convictions." "Where is the problem?" Powell wondered. He also suggested that instead of an innocence project, the law school should start a "the guilty bastard got off scott free project."

To the extent that these two prosecutors' views were indicative of others', Mississippi's top law enforcement officials seemed unwilling to consider the possibility that Mississippi's justice system might occasionally convict an innocent man. Within a year they'd be proven wrong, though hardly chastened.

Over the next decade or so, as we continued our respective work in journalism and law, Hayne's and West's names and deeds kept showing up. Occasionally our work on these cases would overlap, and we'd find ourselves in conversation about new revelations, old cases, and the state's perpetual obstinacy. It finally occurred to us that only a book could give this story the full airing it deserved.

This book is driven by the stories of Kennedy Brewer and Levon Brooks, two men in eastern Mississippi. Their trials took place in the 1990s, an era that saw soaring violent crime and, in response, increasingly strident law-and-order rhetoric from politicians, pop culture, and the media. In the fifteen years that preceded Kennedy Brewer's arrest, violent crime in the United States increased by 80 percent. John DiIulio, the director of George H. W. Bush's White House Faith-Based Initiatives, warned that society risked becoming infested with "super-predators": young, amoral killers emerging from "the youngest, biggest and baddest generation any society has ever known." In response, lawmakers lengthened prison sentences with mandatory minimums and swelled the ranks of police officers on the streets. In some urban areas governors called out the National Guard. Politicians rushed to outdo one another with ever-more-draconian crime policy. Most importantly for this story, the doctrine of habeas corpus—the mechanism by which prisoners can seek relief from unlawful detention that dates back to the Magna Carta—was rewritten in the wake of the Oklahoma City bombing, making it much more difficult for convicted prisoners to gain relief for erroneous convictions.

Mississippi did not distinguish itself. Or it did, but not well. Governor Kirk Fordice pledged at the time to make the state "the capital of capital punishment." The state's largest newspaper ran regular editorials lamenting the fact that drawn-out appeals were preventing officials from executing more people more quickly. Politicians, columnists, and tough-on-crime activists pushed to expand the death penalty to include rape, child abuse, and drug dealing.

This was the climate in which Kennedy Brewer and Levon Brooks were convicted. But the full context for this story goes back much earlier than the 1990s. Since Reconstruction, Mississippi has executed 809 people, not including extrajudicial lynchings. Of those executed under law, 642 were black. Most were hanged, though the state now kills with lethal injection, as does most of the rest of the country. Noxubee County—where Brewer and Brooks lived, were arrested, and were tried—housed its gallows in the now defunct county jail. It has since been converted into the county library. The gallows trap door is still there, as is the garrote hook—right next to the genealogy section.

Before getting to the Brooks and Brewer cases, though, we'll delve into the historical context that made their stories possible. For decades, white Southerners fought integration and tried to preserve white supremacy with racial violence, most notoriously through lynching. Mississippi's death investigation system evolved into a powerful tool to help cover up those atrocities. By most counts, the state led the country in lynchings. Over and over again, elected coroners deliberately covered up racial violence by convening a coroner's jury of like-minded men who would inevitably conclude that obvious murders had been, in fact, accidental killings, suicides, or natural deaths. When a coroner's jury did occasionally determine that a lynching had been a homicide, little to no effort was made to ascertain the identity of the killers or to bring them to justice.

When lynching became less common, the system that aided and abetted it still remained. Though some states moved on from the coroner system, others, including Mississippi, allowed it to persist. As a new era of public officials assumed power, they used the system for their own ends—to rack up convictions, to manipulate the court system, or simply to make a lot of money. By the mid-1990s, it even became politically advantageous for some state officials to reinvestigate cold civil rights murders and try to bring racist perpetrators of decades-old crimes to justice. Here, too, the death investigation system proved useful. Steven Hayne testified in a few such cases. The point here is not that every official in Mississippi's criminal justice and its death investigation systems was or is motivated by bigotry. Hayne, for example, not only assisted prosecutors in those old civil rights cases but was also married for a short time to a black detective. Nevertheless, the system in which he, Michael West, and the state's coroners operated was built on racism, and the new victims still tended to be disproportionately poor and black, with the effects, though better concealed, just as pernicious.

This badly flawed Mississippi death investigation system was then infused with another problem that has more recently received national attention: dubious forensics. Since the late 1980s, DNA analysis has exonerated hundreds of innocent prisoners. It has also revealed the extent to which unsound forensic science—and improper claims about legitimate forensic disciplines—played a major role in those cases. But exonerations resulting from DNA testing provide only a limited glimpse of the problem. Just 5 to 10 percent of criminal cases involve biological evidence that can be subjected to DNA testing. In the other 90 to 95 percent of cases, DNA doesn't exist, has degraded, or has been lost. But the same unscientific forensic disciplines used in the cases overturned by DNA testing have undoubtedly also tainted non-DNA cases, and probably at about the same rate.

We like to think that our system of justice is unmatched in its guarantees of fairness. Our democracy is too strong, our courts too fair, our prosecutors, judges, and prosecutors too conscientious to allow innocents to rot away in prison or be executed. Judge Learned Hand wrote as much in 1923: "Our dangers do not lie in too little tenderness to the accused. Our procedure has always been haunted by the ghost of the innocent man convicted. It is an unreal dream." That sort of resolute confidence in American justice persisted through the 1990s. For many, it still persists today. To date, the US Supreme Court has denied thirty petitions for certiorari filed by prisoners later shown to be factually innocent. Many of them were victims of faulty forensic science. The record of lower courts around the nation is worse.

The primary antagonists in this story are Steven Hayne, the state's former de facto medical examiner, and Michael West, a prolific forensic dentist. A third is the state of Mississippi itself—not its people, but its institutions. In a larger sense, blame also rests on the courts—both state and federal—the media, and the professional organizations that not only failed to prevent this catastrophe but did very little even after it was clear that something was terribly wrong.

Hayne in particular has maintained that he was merely a bit player in all of this—a hardworking doctor who did what he was asked and had no control over the design of a system decades in the making. That argument plays down the active role he played in preserving the system at various points in this story, but there is at least some truth to it. Certainly no one would accuse Hayne of laziness. He testified all over the state and typically worked seven days a week, often until the wee hours of the morning. It's also true that if Hayne and West hadn't been the central figures in this story, the system and its misplaced incentives would have produced other figures just like them. Indeed, before Hayne's tenure, it already had.

Most of Hayne's autopsy reports were uncontroversial—as was most of his court testimony. And a large majority of people his testimony helped put away were undoubtedly guilty. Moreover, anyone who did the number of autopsies Hayne did was bound to make some mistakes. A defender of Hayne might argue that it's unfair to focus on his mistakes instead of his entire body of work.

But that argument is both a defense of Hayne and an indictment of him. As you continue reading, it's important to remember that this story didn't happen by accident—it happened by design. No one forced him to take on the number of autopsies he did. The death investigation system in Mississippi is designed to allow coroners, prosecutors, and law enforcement officials to use their favored medical examiners. Hayne didn't *have* to be the doctor whom Mississippi DAs and coroners favored for nearly two decades. He emerged as their favorite because of his work product. And for that, he is certainly open to scrutiny.

Michael West is a different story. As a longtime associate of Hayne, he was aided and abetted by trial courts throughout the state that seemed more interested in ensuring the admission of his novel—and often crucial—forensic testimony in criminal prosecutions than they did in rigorously assessing the bases of his claims. For his part, West took advantage of the opportunity, and then some.

Lawyers for Brooks and Brewer have argued that Hayne and West's acts over this period of time were intentional. Recently, a federal appeals court opinion found that while they were mistaken, there was no evidence of an intent to fabricate evidence. It's not our intent—and frankly it would be nearly impossible—to prove whether they acted intentionally or not. But that isn't the point. The point is that courts allowed such unscientific testimony in the first place, regardless of intent.

A few administrative notes: For the last decade or so, each of us has worked not only on but within this story. As the narrative progressed, both of us eventually became a part of it. For clarity and ease of reading, we have avoided the first person in these passages and instead noted our involvement in the endnotes. And because we both have written so extensively about these cases and issues, portions of the book have been adapted from prior publications.

This book also relies heavily on interviews and thousands of pages of source documents—court transcripts, letters, memos, case reports, dozens of books, and newspaper and magazine articles. Between us, we've interviewed over two hundred people. Because of the litigious nature of some of the figures involved, not all of our sources wanted to be identified by name. We've tried to rely on named sources when we can, but that isn't always possible. Because of Tucker Carrington's work as a lawyer, he is or was legal counsel in several cases mentioned in this book, including those of Brooks and Brewer. When we discuss a case in which he or his office was involved, we've disclosed that, either in the text or in the endnotes.

Finally, while this book is a work of journalism, we obviously have strong opinions about what happened in Mississippi and what needs to happen now. Our opinions and analyses (and at times our outrage) appear throughout the book. We hope that expressing our views will not only contextualize the narrative for the reader but also help bring about badly needed reform.

Kennedy Brewer and Levon Brooks were felled by seriously flawed forensics, an anachronistic medicolegal system built on structural racism, and a criminal justice system dependent on both. They were failed by the bar, the media, the state appeals courts, the federal courts, the medical profession, and the field of forensics. But they aren't the only ones. As of this writing, countless people convicted with testimony from Steven Hayne and Michael West still sit in Mississippi prisons. An untold number of murder victims and their families haven't yet received justice because the wrong person was convicted while the culprit remained free, or a homicide was misclassified as a natural death, an accident, or a suicide. While West testified in a range of cases that could safely be called "dozens," Hayne testified in thousands—around 80 percent of Mississippi's homicide cases over the better part of two decades. So far, Mississippi officials have only addressed this calamity one case at a time. Others, in particular federal courts, have skirted the issue by invoking procedural bars to avoid entangling themselves in the facts. The result is a staunch refusal to conduct a systematic review of the thousands of cases potentially affected. Doing so would expose the ugly scaffolding that has propped up the system for decades. It would reveal the deep cracks that run to the very foundations of the state's courthouses.

But that's exactly what needs to happen.

~ 1 ~

THE MURDER OF
COURTNEY SMITH

Our society has a high degree of confidence in its
criminal trials, in no small part because the Constitution offers unparalleled protections against
convicting the innocent.

—Justice Sandra Day O'Connor

SATURDAY, SEPTEMBER 15, 1990

Levon Brooks was dressed and nearly ready when the two McCoy
brothers pulled up and honked outside his trailer in Macon, Mississippi. Brooks checked his modest afro in the mirror one last time.
He pondered his new muttonchops—he was still trying to decide if
he'd actually keep them—and then paused to put a small gold earring in his left ear. In a place like Noxubee County, where "dressed
up" could mean putting on freshly laundered camouflage, Brooks was
something of a fashion maven.

Impatient with their friend's primping, the McCoys honked a second
time. They were anxious to get to their job. All three men worked at the
Santa Barbara Club, a popular nightspot a few miles down the road. It
was a great gig for young, single men like them. It paid well, particularly
for rural Mississippi, and they got to meet women while they worked.
Brooks loved his job. It was tailor-made for his personality. Those
who knew Brooks at the time described him as charming, effervescent, and optimistic. Women found him sweet, playful, and easy on the
eyes. He'd had a lot of girlfriends—and plenty of ex-girlfriends—and
somehow managed to remain on good terms with nearly all of them.

Brooks spent much of his spare time hunting and fishing in Noxubee County's pine forests, hardwood coverts, and isolated ponds. His

1

time outdoors kept him lean and toned. Though thirty-two years old, at six foot one and 180 pounds, he weighed the same as he did in high school.

Brooks had been working at the Santa Barbara since before it opened for business. During the day, he worked as a custodian at the elementary and middle schools in Macon. He had to give up his weekend nights to work at the club, but it wasn't much of a sacrifice. He was getting paid to have fun. The hours were long, but the job was never boring, and it gave him free access to the biggest party in town.

The Santa Barbara sat a few miles off of Highway 45, about twenty minutes from Macon. The early '90s were the club's heyday. Old school blues musicians—such as Willie King from nearby Prairie Point—still played at the older, more established juke joints like Bettie's Place, a shingle-sided shack farther out in the country. But what the Santa Barbara lacked in authenticity, it made up for in accessibility, size, and a regular enough schedule that it advertised on local radio. On weekend nights, two or three hundred people would pack themselves between the building's aluminum sides.

Brooks knew almost all of them, if not as a friend at least by face. He began most nights at the door—a garrulous, welcoming presence as customers lined up to pay the cover charge. Over the course of the night, he'd move to monitor the dance floor or the parking lot. At the end of the night—his favorite time—he'd put on his chef's hat and cook up a feast of fried, artery-clogging food for patrons who stuck around. He'd sometimes sell fish and chicken sandwiches until two or three in the morning.

Eager to get to work that evening, Brooks stepped out of the trailer, skipped down the small set of porch steps two at a time, and trotted toward the truck. Just as Brooks hopped up to get in, one of the brothers gunned the engine on the late-model, cream-and-brown Silverado, leaving the fashionable and effervescent Levon Brooks lying face down in his own front yard.

The McCoys howled with laughter. Brooks took the prank in stride. He bounced up, dramatically slowed up for a moment, and postured for his friends. He could take a joke. He then broke into a jog, hit the rolling truck on a run, and climbed inside.

The Santa Barbara provided the three men a variety of marketable skills and a semi-steady income. On that particular evening, the job Brooks loved so much should have provided one other benefit—a rock-solid alibi. But he'd soon cross paths with Steven Hayne and Michael West. Even an alibi wouldn't save him.

Back in the 1930s, the Works Progress Administration described Brooksville, Mississippi, as "a quiet old prairie town of old-fashioned homes softened by an even spread of shade." Shops lined both sides of the main street back then. There was a grand hotel in town—the three-story Jackson—complete with an ornate lobby and a fancy restaurant. The Mobile and Ohio Railroad ran through town. Residents could take the train seventy-five miles north to Tupelo to shop or, on fall weekends, travel a few miles up the line to West Point and from there take a spur line to Starkville to watch the Mississippi State Bulldogs play football.

Today, what's left of Brooksville sits disconsolate and mostly abandoned. The hotel is long gone, as are nearly all of the old homes and stores. The streets, including Main Street, are bordered by empty storefronts. Appropriately, a lonely Confederate statue stands guard over the railroad tracks that segregate the town. Cross the tracks, and the road fans out into a series of unpaved, graveled lanes that lead to Brooksville's black neighborhoods. Most of the homes are single-story with one or two bedrooms, sometimes clustered several to a lot. Often a single extended family will occupy multiple homes on the same lot. Locals refer to this as "the back of Brooksville." In one of those houses, a single-story blue-clapboard cottage, three-year-old Courtney Smith lived with her mother, grandmother, two sisters, and four uncles.

Courtney and her sister Ashley had spent most of that Saturday with their grandmother Ruby and their great-grandmother Viola. At about seven in the evening, after a supper of hot dogs, watermelon, and rice with tomatoes, they walked back to their house on Phillip's Loop Road. As the evening darkened to night, Sonya Smith bathed her three daughters. She dried Courtney off and dressed her in a faded T-shirt with a duck on the front and the word "Mississippi" scrawled across the top.

Afterward, Sonya went out for the evening, leaving the girls with her mother, Ruby, and her own brother Tony. As the girls fell asleep, Ruby sat out on the porch for a couple of hours, chatting with friends as they passed by. Tony had been working construction all day and had fallen asleep on the couch while watching football. Eventually, a man Ruby had been dating dropped by with some friends and invited her out. She agreed. On her way, she stopped by a neighbor's house where her other son, William, twenty-two, was playing cards. She told him Tony was asleep and asked him to come back to the house in case one of the girls woke up. William agreed but played several more hands of cards before returning home.

As Ruby left at around eleven, Tony was the only adult now at the house, still fast asleep on the couch. He wouldn't wake up until late the following morning. The girls slept in the adjacent bedroom. The only light in the house flickered from the television.

The demons were whispering to Justin Johnson again. It was a late summer evening in Brooksville—warm, sticky, and calm. Johnson typically drank and smoked when he'd start to hear the voices. He usually smoked pot, but also crack if he could find it. Sometimes it helped keep the voices at bay. Sometimes it only made them louder.

Johnson would later tell state investigators that he had always known something wasn't quite right about himself. At the age of five, he had walked into the kitchen and saw his little brother grabbing for a pot of boiling water. Johnson reached out for his brother's arm, but it slipped through his fingertips. Johnson's brother fell into the stove. The pot tipped over, covering him in scalding-hot water. Johnson watched as the boy's skin blistered and separated from his body. The little boy held on for a month before passing away. The incident was Johnson's most salient early memory. He would later say it felt as if he had watched it all happen from a distance, like watching a movie. He'd replay it countless times in his head in the years that followed.

Those around Johnson described him much the way he saw himself—he was slightly off. He was a tad under six feet tall and heavyset. He was usually called by his nickname, Joe Kitty. Neighbors and acquaintances would say he had strange eyes. Even when he was standing in front of you, they'd say, he never seemed to be present. He always seemed to be in the background. He was tolerated—never really invited, but often around, hovering on the periphery. It would be another twenty years before a prison doctor would diagnose him with schizophrenia and mild mental retardation.

Noxubee County law enforcement officials knew the thirty-three-year-old Johnson as a drug user and a sex offender. In fact, it had been just a few weeks since the last time the voices had told Johnson to hurt someone. On August 29, he broke into the home of an elderly woman named Millie Lee Wilborn and attempted to rape her. Wilborn fended him off long enough to call the police. He fled. But Wilborn's description left little doubt about who had attacked her. Johnson found himself in the Noxubee County Jail just a few hours later.

The charges were serious. Mississippi locks up more of its citizens per capita than any state but Louisiana. A sex offense can carry a life sentence. Johnson's court-appointed lawyer was Robert Prather, a local attorney who tended to get some of the more serious indigent cases. Prather told Johnson he'd work to get him a favorable plea offer, and he came through. The prosecutor agreed to reduce the charge to a misdemeanor on the condition that Johnson consent to counseling. Johnson accepted the offer.

As he'd later tell it, on that night, the night of September 15, the voices told Johnson to visit another woman he knew on Phillip's Loop Road. They told him to break into her home and attack her, just as he had tried to attack Millie Wilborn. He tried, but the door was locked. He tried to force it open. He couldn't get in.

Johnson looked around. It was night now. He saw a dim, gently bouncing light coming from the small house across the street. He walked over and jiggled the door handle. The door opened, and he went inside. He walked right by a man sleeping on the couch and entered the first bedroom. There, on the floor, he saw three-year-old Courtney Smith, fast asleep. He picked her up, cradled her in his arms, and walked out. It was that easy.

Johnson carried the girl down a short path between two houses to a hill that overlooked a pond, and laid her on the ground. He would later say that this is when the voices told him to "teach her." He penetrated her vagina with a finger. Courtney awoke and began to cry. The voices then told him to quiet her.

In his confession, Johnson claimed he didn't recall choking the girl, but it seems clear that he did. Courtney Smith's neck showed clear indications of strangulation.

The voices finally told him to get rid of her. According to his own recollection some two decades later, Johnson picked her up, took her over a small hill, and threw her into the shallow pond. He then stood and watched as she struggled to stay afloat. Soon Courtney's head slipped under the water, and she disappeared. Johnson then walked back to his car, climbed in, and drove away.

~

By the time William Smith came home between two and two thirty a.m., Courtney was already gone. He saw his brother Tony asleep on the couch, in front of a television now broadcasting static. He glanced into the girls' bedroom and noticed something amiss, but didn't make much of it. Looking back, he said it probably occurred to him at the time that Courtney was missing, but he added that if that had even registered with him, "I thought she was with her ma—her mamma or something."

William flipped the television to one of the few channels still airing programming and collapsed onto the other couch. Soon he was asleep as well. The night moseyed toward morning.

The McCoy brothers left the Santa Barbara Club before Levon Brooks finished work for the night, so T. C. Phillips, one of the club's owners, offered to give Brooks a lift home. It was between two thirty and three a.m. when Phillips drove Brooks back south to his house in Macon. At the same time, Justin Johnson headed in the opposite direction to his home in Crawford, a small town a few miles north of Macon. The two cars may well have passed one another that night somewhere along Highway 45. By all rights, that's as close as Levon Brooks and Justin Johnson should have ever gotten—two men living two very different lives, passing on a rural highway in the early hours of a warm Mississippi morning. Instead, their lives became hopelessly and inextricably entwined.

SUNDAY, SEPTEMBER 16

After Sonya Smith left the house Saturday night, she eventually ended up at the Santa Barbara Club, arriving a little before eleven. Brooks, an old boyfriend of hers, was working the door. Sonya stayed for the rest of the night, leaving at around two thirty with a new beau. She saw Brooks in the parking lot as she left.

When she awoke the next morning, Sonya went to the home of her grandmother, Viola Davis. Sonya's oldest daughter, Ashley, later came by and told her that Courtney wasn't at home. But Ashley had a habit of telling stories. "Quit playing," Sonya admonished. Ashley demurred. "Yeah, she's at home," she said. "She's still asleep." But she wasn't.

Sonya's mother, Ruby, had also returned home early Sunday morning. When she didn't see Courtney in the house, she, like Tony, just assumed that the little girl was with Sonya.

In fact, everyone thought Courtney was with someone else. It wasn't until seven o'clock on Sunday evening, when Sonya finally returned home, that the family realized for the first time that Courtney wasn't with any of the family. She was missing. They notified nearby friends and relatives. No one had seen her. Soon they fanned out over the neighborhood, calling out Courtney's name. About an hour later they alerted police.

Brooksville police chief Cecil Russell, a white chief in a town that's 80 percent black, received the first call at around eight that evening. Within a few hours, hundreds of people joined in the search. At around one a.m. on Monday morning, Russell, who had assumed responsibility for the search, asked everyone to go home and get some rest. They'd resume at first light.

On the night of Courtney Smith's abduction, Russell never went home. After suspending the search, he continued to look for the girl himself. Exhausted, he eventually returned to his squad car and fell asleep.

MONDAY, SEPTEMBER 17

It was Russell who found Courtney's body a little after dawn on Monday morning. At first, he thought the object a few yards out in the pond was just a trash bag. But as he focused and moved closer, it began to assume the shape of a small child's body. Russell walked down the embankment and eased himself into the water. He floated Courtney to the edge, pulled her up from the pond, and laid her body on the ground. Another police officer had arrived and stood by. Through the thin stand of trees, the two officers could hear car doors opening, and light chatter as volunteers began gathering to resume the search. Russell asked the officer for his jacket. He knelt down and wrapped it around the girl's body.

Deputy Ernest Eichelberger arrived a short time later. Eichelberger, a stocky black officer, had been with the Noxubee County Sheriff's Office for three years and in law enforcement a little over five. Despite his relative lack of experience, he had recently been promoted to chief deputy. He'd previously been a police chief for the tiny town of Terry (population 1,100). Eichelberger looked at the little girl's body. Other than the officer's jacket, she was clad only in the duck T-shirt. She was bleeding from her head and groin. The sheriff's department would soon take over the investigation.

Tales of corrupt Southern police and prosecutors from the bigoted, good-ol'-boy mold are plentiful and well documented. Less clichéd but no less damaging are the inept cops—the well-meaning but badly trained and poorly educated rural sheriffs, police chiefs, and their deputies who rise through the ranks because few others want the job. They're the products of substandard training, they tend to work for departments that are underfunded and neglected by state officials, and they serve poor and vulnerable communities.

Few who are familiar with the Courtney Smith investigation ever doubted that Eichelberger wanted to solve the girl's murder—he wanted to get the right man. It just isn't clear that at this point in his career he had the necessary experience for the assignment. He had only been working at the sheriff's department for about six months. Down the sides of his reports, he sometimes wrote out acronyms from police training manuals that he used to conduct a proper investigation. On his report for Courtney Smith's death, he wrote:

ADAPT:
Arrest the perpetrator if possible.
Detail and identify witness at the scene.
Assess the crime scene.
Protect the crime scene.
Take notes.

Eichelberger began his investigation by getting a positive identification of Courtney Smith's body from her father, Rocky Allen. He then turned her body over to Noxubee County coroner Willie Willie (his real name). Willie then sent the body to be autopsied by Steven Hayne, the state's go-to medical examiner. That night, Hayne determined that the girl had been choked, but likely died of freshwater drowning. He found a large bruise on the top of her head. Her hymen had been torn, and she had lacerations on the inside of her vagina, which he'd later say were consistent with penetration from a finger or penis. Hayne found no semen and no pubic hair. The girl had been sexually assaulted, but it was unlikely that her killer had forced intercourse.

The lack of pubic hair and semen would normally have made it more difficult to definitively identify Courtney Smith's perpetrator. But Hayne also found a few bruises on the back of Courtney's right wrist that he suspected, but was not sure, were human bite marks. Later, after the skin had been excised, he examined it under a microscope, and because it showed no signs of bleeding, concluded that the marks were likely made at the time of death or shortly thereafter. He also found some marks on the girl that he thought might be animal bites. Hayne then called in his frequent collaborator Michael West, a Hattiesburg clinical dentist, bite mark expert, and forensic jack-of-all-trades. West drove up the following morning to examine the marks.

Unfortunately, someone forgot to tell morgue owner Jimmy Roberts and his staff that West was en route, because they embalmed Courtney Smith's body that same night. Ordinarily, that would have made any sort of bite mark analysis extremely difficult, if not impossible. But Michael West was no ordinary bite mark analyst.

TUESDAY, SEPTEMBER 18

On Tuesday morning, West conducted a preliminary examination of the girl's body. He agreed that the marks on her wrist had been made by human teeth. He excised the skin around several of them.

When a section of skin is cut from the body, it typically retracts and then shrinks as it loses moisture. Because of this, when forensic pathologists excise a section of skin for analysis, they first apply a retainer to preserve the skin's shape. Bite mark analysts claim they can find intricate details and unique indicators within bite marks that can be used to identify or exclude suspects. If the alleged bite mark is distorted when the tissue that contains it is cut away, those indicators will warp, change, or shrivel with the skin on which they're recorded. Some might disappear entirely. Michael West did not use a retainer when he extracted the skin from Courtney Smith's wrist. This should have been a red flag.

The fact that Courtney's body had already been embalmed when West conducted his examination should have been another one.

Autopsies are almost always done before embalming, because the process of pushing blood out of the body and replacing it with embalming fluid causes significant physiological changes. West would later claim at trial that embalming can actually preserve the skin. He was correct, in a manner of speaking. The process forestalls the decaying process for a viewing or a funeral. But it does not preserve the sort of details useful to a forensic examiner—it distorts them. West would suggest that, serendipitously, the embalming "fixed" the tissue, thus retaining the integrity of the bite. There's just no medical or forensic literature to support the notion that such intricate data could be preserved by the countervailing effects of a happy coincidence.

After completing his analysis, West concluded that the marks on the wrist were indeed bite marks and that they had been inflicted by a human being. He billed Noxubee County $2,902.12 for his services, and assured Willie Willie that he would make himself available once law enforcement officials had identified a suspect.

Wednesday, September 19

While Ernest Eichelberger's notes included lots of pointers on how to go about investigating a murder—including another mnemonic device that used the letters of the word "homicide"—there were no acronyms to remind him about the constitutional rights of the people he was investigating. Because Courtney Smith appeared to have been sexually abused, Eichelberger's suspicion naturally turned to the men who had access to her home on the night of her abduction. His method of "investigation" in this case was to arrest them—all of them—and then wait for the truth to come out.

Four days after Courtney Smith's murder, Eichelberger began making his arrests. The first was William "Slick" Mickens, a frail, forty-four-year-old man who was married to Ruby Smith's sister Betty—Mickens was Courtney Smith's great uncle by marriage. A heavy drinker, Mickens had a habit of touching women when he talked to them, which sometimes, intended or not, could be taken as a pass. That night, while Mickens was talking to Ruby Smith, her son William thought he got a bit too physical. William came to his mother's aid, and he and Mickens exchanged words. William went to a neighbor's to call the police, but the neighbor wouldn't let him use the phone. Ruby finally asked Mickens to leave. He agreed, and walked home at around eleven thirty that night. According to his wife, he arrived home about an hour later, still more than an hour before the window in which police believed Courtney Smith was murdered.

For Eichelberger, the fact that Mickens was an alcoholic known to occasionally make unwelcome gestures toward women apparently made him a possible child rapist and murderer. As Mickens was talking to some friends on the street in front of his house on the afternoon of September 19, Eichelberger pulled up and arrested him. Mickens would be the first of many.

THURSDAY, SEPTEMBER 20

Late in the morning, the Smith family and friends gathered to say good-bye to Courtney at a graveside service at Brooksville Cemetery. They sang a hymn, said a prayer, and read from scripture. Courtney's mother, Sonya, and her aunt Shamilla each read a poem. Sonya's was short, poignant, and painful:

> *Wherever you go*
> *My love is close beside you*
> *Wherever I go*
> *You're with me*
> *Whoever we are*
> *We're never far apart*
> *Cause we're so much a part of each other.*

After the burial, the family convened for dinner at the home of Freddie Allen, Courtney's great-grandfather. That morning, the Jackson-based newspaper *Clarion-Ledger* reported on Slick Mickens's arrest. Noxubee County coroner Willie Willie told the paper that Courtney Smith had been raped, struck on the head, and cut near her mouth. The paper reported that Slick also coached Little League, which of course made the accusation all the more awful—the monster who had just raped and killed a three-year-old girl had also had unlimited access to children.

In fact, Mickens coached baseball with Courtney Smith's grandfather, Johnny Will Smith, who seemed to be in shock about the arrest. His occasionally inappropriate behavior around women notwithstanding, few thought Mickens was capable of this. Later that day Mickens appeared on the evening news, handcuffed and marched into a jail cell, as the reporter described the heinous act for which he'd just been arrested.

William Mickens suffered from seizures, back pain, high blood pressure, and anxiety. He was on disability. Because he couldn't work, he coached and volunteered. It was a rewarding way to pass the time, and it made him feel useful. Now all of Mississippi had just been told that he had raped and murdered his grandniece.

Friday, September 21

Before he became a police officer, Robert Williams spent eighteen years introducing Woody Woodpecker cartoons and sketching whimsical animals. From 1958 to 1976, the children of Mississippi knew the portly, gentle Williams as Uncle Bunky, beloved host of *Fun Time*, a children's television show broadcast out of Columbus. The "crazy animals" were Uncle Bunky's trademark bit. Between episodes of *Heckle and Jeckle* and *Huckleberry Hound*, Uncle Bunky would stand in front of a large white pad of paper as children in the studio shouted out fantastically mixed-up creatures for him to draw—a cat's face on a giraffe's neck on an elephant's body with the wings of a sparrow. He once boasted that "every kid who appeared on the show left with a teddy bear and a Bible." *Fun Time* hosted both black and white children, reputed the first such television show in Mississippi to do so. When Williams died in the summer of 2015, he was mourned across Mississippi as a beloved icon.

Each *Fun Time* episode featured about twelve kids, all of whom got to appear on camera. Some grew up to become powerful Mississippians. One of them was Forrest Allgood, the longtime district attorney for the state's sixteenth judicial district and the man who would prosecute Levon Brooks.

In the late 1980s, Lowndes County got a new sheriff, Ed Prescott, who had also been in children's entertainment before turning to law enforcement. In fact, for the first few months after *Fun Time* began in the late 1950s, Prescott played the role of a country bumpkin named Cousin Ed, co-hosting the show with his friend Uncle Bunky. Since *Fun Time* was canceled in 1976, Williams had been working with local police as a youth counselor, as a sketch artist, and even in narcotics. But Williams's former cohost and now sheriff suggested a new role. He wanted Williams to interview children who had been victims of or witnesses to violent crimes. "These kids listen to him," the sheriff would later say in a newspaper profile of Williams. "They'll open up to him. And the kids won't talk to just anybody, especially when it comes to something like abuse."

Williams's previous career as a beloved children's entertainer might have made him seem like an ideal figure to console and comfort kids, particularly if it had been in the late 1970s, when many kids were likely to have remembered his TV show. But this new role wasn't about consoling children; it was about getting information out of them. "It's like this," Forrest Allgood said in the same newspaper profile, "if we don't know anything about it, we can't do anything about it. We need the kids to say, 'This man did this to me.' It's fundamental in getting any case started."

As the dozens of wrongful convictions during the "ritual sex abuse panic" of the 1980s and 1990s attest, interviewing children about violent or sexual crimes is a complex undertaking. An interviewer must build rapport with kids, filter fact from fiction, be careful not to introduce known facts, and do it all while protecting the psyche of a traumatized child. A qualified children's forensic interviewer should have a background in psychiatry or therapy. Williams, apparently, had neither. He wasn't a forensic psychologist. He was a guy who drew wacky pictures and introduced cartoons. His methods weren't drawn from years of training or studying academic research, but from seat-of-the-pants intuition. "I'll sit down with them, draw for them," he explained to the *Tupelo Daily Journal*. "And before long, they're telling me everything—who's done what to them. It's amazing sometimes what happens when I sit down and draw a few cartoons."

Noxubee County officials believed the only witness to Courtney Smith's abduction was her five-year-old sister Ashley. So on September 21, Williams made the trip from Lowndes County to interview the little girl. His alter ego was still so well known and beloved that even the official department transcript of the interview refers to Williams only as "Uncle Bunky." No further explanation was necessary.

Ashley Smith's first interview (she was interviewed again a few days later) was a mess, as one might expect from a confused and frightened five-year-old. She frequently contradicted herself. She said things Williams and other investigators knew to be false. For example, she claimed that her uncle Tony had pulled a knife on her sister's abductors. She later changed the weapon to a gun. In truth, he had slept through the abduction. She also made fantastical assertions that couldn't possibly have been true, such as that the man who abducted her sister fled on an airplane.

A skilled interrogator should have concluded from Ashley's mishmash of contradictions, almost assuredly false memories, embellishments, and outright fantasies that she wasn't a reliable witness. Instead, Williams tried to make sense of a traumatized child who was clearly mixing what she may have seen with what she may have heard, all while adding details and enhancements from her own imagination.

It was an understandable inclination. A young girl had been brutally murdered. Perpetrators of such crimes are generally caught quickly, or not at all. It had been nearly a week. As the days went by, Ashley Smith increasingly became the last best chance at catching her sister's killer.

In his interview with Ashley, Williams appears to have seized on various fragments of her answers he found plausible and ran with them, while disregarding the many implausible or false things she said. At times, he even introduced new facts while attempting to get her to clarify. Those new facts then became a part of the narrative.

One example of this proved particularly damning for Levon Brooks. Ashley said at one point during her initial interview that the man who abducted her sister "had a quarter in his ear." Williams suggested to Ashley that she was referring to an earring. He pointed to a photo of someone wearing earrings and asked, "Like the earrings there?" Ashley responded, "Yeah, a earring and a quarter." Later, Ashley would add that Courtney's abductor "took the quarter out and put it up in my sister's ear."

Wearing a quarter in one's ear is a fad that comes and goes in some black and Latino communities. Perhaps Ashley had seen someone wearing one—"Slick" Mickens sometimes did. Perhaps she was referring to a magic trick she had seen, where a magician pulls a quarter from behind a child's ear. Wherever she got it, Williams proceeded with the interview as if when Ashley said "quarter," she really meant "earring." Levon Brooks was one of the few men in the area who wore an earring. This is almost certainly why local law enforcement officials began to look at him as a suspect.

On another occasion, Williams asked Ashley if the man who took Courtney "had a mustache or whiskers on his face." She responded,

"He had a Halloween thing on his face," clearly referring to a mask. Williams then asked, "Was it a stocking or a Halloween thing?" Ashley replied, "Stocking." Ashley had never volunteered that the abductor was wearing a stocking. She only adopted it after Williams introduced it, later adding that the man had taken the stocking off of his face and put it over her sister's head. Only that last detail—the abductor putting the stocking over Courtney Smith's head—made it into the summary of the interview that the sheriff's department then sent to prosecutors. The actual killer—Johnson—wore neither a stocking nor an earring.

Ashley was also wildly inconsistent about the abductor's identity and about what happened after he took her sister out of the room. Among other things, she first said the abductor was a black man named Shavon. She then changed his name to Travon. She then told Williams that Travon went to college with her mother and had a five-year-old son named Travis who often played with her. Later in the interview, Ashley said Travon had an accomplice. Later still, she claimed there were two accomplices, one black and one white. Toward the end she switched again and said the actual abductor was a white man named Clay. She then contradicted herself again by saying she knew Clay, claiming he was her mother's boyfriend and had been to her house. She added, "I ain't saw Travon before," just minutes after claiming she often played with Travon's son.

The problem with Williams's interrogation of Ashley Smith isn't that a scared and confused five-year-old told stories or had difficulty processing what she had seen. It was that after he was clearly aware that Ashley had a propensity to mix fact with fantasy—to confuse what she saw with what she had heard or made up—he not only was still willing to believe the parts of his interview with her that he wanted to believe, he guided her to confirm parts of her story to fit his conception of the crime. Prosecutors then took it all a step further by adopting only the portions of Williams's already-selective account of the interview that fit *their* own narrative.

Even still, it's notable what Ashley did *not* say in that first interview with Williams. She did not say the name "Levon" or "Levon Brooks." In fact, of all of her varied, often conflicting descriptions of her sister's abductor, none of them fit Levon Brooks. The only similarity between Levon Brooks and what Ashley Smith described in that first interview was that Brooks sometimes wore an earring. But it isn't at all clear that Ashley ever intended to describe an earring in the first place.

The same day as that initial interview—the day after Courtney's funeral service—Ernest Eichelberger made a wave of new arrests. He arrested Courtney Smith's uncles, Tony, Ernest, and William Smith. He arrested William McCarthy, the friend of Ruby's who had stopped by that night to visit on the porch, and David Harrison, a friend of McCarthy's who had lent McCarthy his car. He arrested Sonya Smith's boyfriend, John Hodge; Robert Goodwin, a neighbor; and Lee Harris, a friend of Tony Smith's. All of these men, all black, were tossed into the Noxubee County jail. Tony, Ernest, and William had just lost a niece—a young girl with whom they shared a house. Eichelberger wrote the same thing on the arrest paperwork for all of them: "Suspicion of murder."

There was another interview that day as well. Earnest Eichelberger interviewed Sonya Smith. In that interview, he asked her if she knew or had dated any men who wore an earring. She mentioned only one—Levon Brooks. "They call him Ta Tee," she said. "Who?" Eichelberger asked. "They call him Ta Tee," she said again.

Saturday, September 22

When Eichelberger received Uncle Bunky's report from his interview with Ashley Smith, one could see how he might have been discouraged. Of all the men he had arrested so far, none wore an earring, and none had a name resembling "Travon." But now Eichelberger knew that Sonya Smith had once been involved with a man named Levon, or Ta Tee, and that man wore an earring. So he sent a deputy to bring Brooks in for questioning.

When Brooks showed up for work at the Santa Barbara that Saturday night, someone told him that the police had come by the club looking for him. They wanted to speak with him about what he might know about Courtney Smith's murder. Brooks had heard about the child's death, and felt bad for her and her mother, his ex-girlfriend. But he knew nothing about the murder. He thought the wisest and easiest thing to do would be to drive to the sheriff's office in Macon and straighten out the misunderstanding. He told his boss not to worry. Once everything was cleared up, he'd come back and work the evening shift as usual.

He'd never see the Santa Barbara Club again.

Eichelberger began questioning Brooks at 8:47 p.m., nearly a week after Courtney Smith was murdered. Brooks waived his right to an attorney and answered Eichelberger's questions voluntarily. He told Eichelberger that he had briefly dated Sonya Smith several months earlier. She lived with her grandmother at the time. He broke it off because Smith was too "fast" for him—she was seeing other men. He'd occasionally see her and her brothers at the club, and they were all polite and friendly to one another, but he hadn't been to her home in at least five months. Even when they were dating, he had only been inside her home a few times. They usually met at her cousin's place instead. He had never even seen the house where she currently lived.

Brooks then told Eichelberger that for the previous three years, he had worked the door, bused, and occasionally cooked at the Santa Barbara. On the night Courtney Smith was murdered, he said he had reported to work for his typical shift: working the door when the club opened at 8:00 p.m., doing odd jobs throughout the night, then cooking a bit as the night wound down. On that particular night, he said he left at around two in the morning. He provided the names of several witnesses who could vouch for him. In fact, those witnesses would say he left closer to three, or even three thirty. Brooks was so forthcoming, he short-changed his own alibi.

But it apparently didn't persuade Eichelberger. At the conclusion of the interview, he told Brooks he was being detained for Courtney Smith's murder. Under Mississippi law, Eichelberger told Brooks he could hold him for up to seventy-two hours. Brooks would remain behind bars for eighteen years.

SUNDAY, SEPTEMBER 23

Two days after Robert "Uncle Bunky" Williams first interviewed Ashley Smith, Harry Alderson, chief investigator at the district attorney's office, asked him to interview her a second time. According to Williams's subsequent report, shortly before this second interview—which took place in a Comfort Inn motel room—Eichelberger had informed him that Ashley had picked Levon Brooks from a photo array. Williams's task for the second interview was to confirm the identification and to try to collect more details.

It's clear from police records that Brooks was now the central focus of Eichelberger's investigation. Of the six photos Ashley was given, all appear to have been taken recently; the photo of Brooks was old. The men in the other photos had closely cropped hair; Brooks sported an afro.

Other than the earring, there was little reason to suspect Brooks. He had no history of sex crimes. No convictions, arrests, or allegations of abusing children. The suspicion certainly hadn't come from Sonya Smith. In her interviews with Eichelberger, she said she and Brooks were on good terms, and she gave no indication that she suspected him. In January 1992, she would file an affidavit stating that Brooks had never been to her new home, and that Ashley wouldn't have known Brooks, much less known his nickname. As far as she knew, Brooks had no meaningful contact with her children, even when the two were dating.

Eichelberger would later say Brooks had always been his prime suspect—even before Courtney Smith's body was discovered. He claimed to have spoken privately with Ashley Smith the day after her sister went missing, and that during the conversation Ashley identified a man named "Tie-Tee" as her sister's abductor. As Eichelberger explained it, this is why he gave Ashley a photo lineup that included Levon Brooks.

But there was a big problem with Eichelberger's story. If the only witness to the kidnapping told him the name of the perpetrator just hours after the crime, even before the body had been recovered, it's baffling why Eichelberger would then arrest every man who had been anywhere near the house that night—but would *not* arrest Brooks.

In any event, in his second interview with Ashley, "Uncle Bunky" Williams presented the girl with a second photo lineup he had prepared himself. He used the same photo of Brooks that had been used in the first lineup, but picked five different men for the other photos. Once again, all the others were men Ashley had never met, and all had closely cropped hair. She again picked Brooks. Williams then asked if she knew the name of the man she had just picked. According to Williams, Ashley replied, "Tie Tee. I don't know his nickname. I just know his first name. He used to come over to my mama's house and talk to her." According to Williams, Ashley then confirmed that her sister's abductor was wearing an earring, and that he had pulled a stocking over Courtney's head—two details that, again, were first introduced by Williams, not by Ashley.

Ashley also provided a wealth of new information in the second interview. Nearly all of it was wrong. This time around, for example, she said the attackers left after abducting Courtney, but came back later with potato chips and drinks. They then got out of their car and taunted her with, "Na, na, na, I got your sister!" She also told Williams that Tie Tee "had a bag of money in his hand."

At this point, there was little reason to put much stock in anything she had to say about the night her sister was taken. Instead, police and prosecutors again took what they needed and ignored the rest. In its profile of Uncle Bunky that ran the previous June, the *Tupelo Daily Journal* began: "For generations, Robert Williams has been able to get children to say anything." That lede would turn out to be far more accurate than the author could have imagined.

At about the same time Williams interviewed Ashley Smith for the second time, Eichelberger interviewed the man who actually murdered Courtney Smith. Justin Johnson, then thirty-five years old, had dropped out of high school in the ninth grade. He worked at the Bryan Foods meat processing plant in the town of West Point, about thirty miles from Brooksville. When Eichelberger questioned him, Johnson already had a few arrests on his record, at least one for a sex offense. He had been brought in as a suspect in this case because at around the time Courtney Smith was killed, several witnesses had seen his blue and white 1979 Buick Electra parked near the pond where her body was found.

Johnson really didn't have an alibi. He said that after work on Saturday, he had gone to a club in Crawford. He left at around twelve thirty a.m., went home, and went to sleep. Though he said witnesses could verify he was at the club, he had left the club alone, had gone home alone, and was alone during the window of time when Courtney Smith would have been abducted and murdered. Eichelberger read Johnson his rights and placed him under arrest. Next came what should have been a significant clue. Eichelberger asked Johnson if he'd ever been arrested. Johnson replied, "Yes, for a similar deal. Attempt rape." He added that the arrest was "not long ago."

Between the sightings of his car, his weak alibi, and his criminal record, there was every reason for Eichelberger to immediately make

Justin Johnson the focus of his investigation. But despite the arrest, no one ever showed Ashley Smith a photo lineup that included Justin Johnson. His brief conversation with Eichelberger would be the last he'd have with law enforcement about the murder for nearly twenty years. That's because by all indications, by the time local law enforcement interviewed Johnson, they were already pretty sure that Levon Brooks was the killer. They just needed Michael West to tell them they were right.

At around five that evening, West drove to the Noxubee County Jail and took dental molds from twelve people. This is the procedure in which a dentist fills a mouth-shaped tray with plaster, then sinks a patient's upper or lower teeth into it. The dentist creates a model of the patient's dentition from the molds. The procedure is commonly used by orthodontists and cosmetic dentists, but it's also used by forensic odontologists—or forensic dentists.

The suspects from whom West took molds that night included all the men Eichelberger had arrested to date, plus Sonya Smith and a few others who lived or had been seen near the crime scene and consented to the procedure. That night, West examined the dozen dental molds and compared them to the tissue sample he had cut from Courtney Smith's arm. It didn't take him long. The next day, West told county officials that he had "excluded" all twelve people as the source of the bite.

Among those West excluded was Justin Johnson. West was probably right this time, at least about Johnson's teeth not matching the marks on Courtney Smith's wrist. Johnson killed the girl, but his teeth couldn't have matched the bite marks Hayne noted and West confirmed because contrary to Hayne's suspicions and West's assertions, they weren't human bite marks at all. When Johnson finally confessed to killing Courtney Smith nearly two decades later, he made no mention of biting the girl.

Michael West has often claimed over the years that for every suspect he implicates with his bite mark testimony, he "exonerates" many more. In the Brooks case, he claimed to have exonerated a dozen people. But by the time West took those dental molds—between about five p.m. and seven p.m. on September 23—Eichelberger no longer suspected any of the people from whom West was taking impressions. By then, by his own testimony, his chief suspect was Levon Brooks. There's no record of Eichelberger telling West as much, but West frequently consulted with police and prosecutors before performing an analysis.

If West and his groundbreaking forensics had indeed been valid, if his method was really the scientific marvel that he claimed it was, he should have never concluded that the marks on Smith's body were human marks. Assuming West was right about that and subsequent forensic analysts were wrong—assuming they *were* human bites—then West should have implicated Justin Johnson and exonerated Levon Brooks, the man the police would bring to him two days later. Instead, West did just the opposite.

MONDAY, SEPTEMBER 24

On Monday night at around nine thirty p.m., Ernest Eichelberger officially placed Levon Brooks under arrest for the murder of Courtney Smith. Investigator Harry Alderson then interrogated Brooks. Alderson asked Brooks when he was last in the town of Brooksville. Brooks responded that he had been there a couple weeks earlier, when he took his sister to the doctor. Alderson next asked Brooks if he was willing to take a lie detector test. Brooks replied, "Sure will. I will be willing to take the test tomorrow." He then agreed to answer more questions without first talking to a lawyer. Brooks also gave Eichelberger permission to search his home, and his car (a nonoperational Camaro), and have his body examined for any scratches and bruises. He voluntarily provided a hair and blood sample. Crime lab testing would later find several hairs from a black male in Courtney Smith's bed and on her blanket that didn't match anyone in her family. They also weren't a match for Brooks.

Eichelberger then asked Brooks if he had ever been arrested in another state. Brooks replied that he had—in Alabama for "grand larceny." Brooks not only volunteered that information, he overstated his crime. In April 1981 Brooks was convicted of second-degree theft in Pickens County, Alabama. He pleaded guilty and was sentenced to three years, two of which were suspended. In September of the same year he was convicted in Noxubee County of "burglary, accessory after the fact," for helping a friend hide some cash and merchandise that the friend had stolen from a gas station. For that, Brooks was sentenced to two years behind bars. Those were mistakes of youth, committed in his early twenties. He had been clean ever since. Now thirty-one, Brooks had a steady job. He had no ensuing arrests at all, much less for violent crimes, sex crimes, or crimes against children. But Eichelberger and Alderson had pegged him for this murder. They processed the arrest, then drove Brooks two hours to Michael West's office in Hattiesburg to make dental molds of his teeth.

TUESDAY, SEPTEMBER 25

Sometime early to mid-morning on Tuesday, Michael West called law enforcement officials in Noxubee County with the results of his analysis: in his opinion, Levon Brooks was the only person on earth who could have made the (alleged) bite marks on Courtney Smith's wrist. A few weeks later, in a three-paragraph letter to Alderson dated October 18, West made it official. In the second paragraph under the heading "Opinion," West wrote, "The dental structures of one Levon Brooks did indeed and without a doubt inflict the bite mark found on the body of Courtney Smith."

That was probably more than enough for an indictment. But there was still the matter of the lie detector. The Noxubee County Sheriff's Office had neither a polygraph machine nor anyone trained to operate one. So at around ten forty-five a.m., the head detective from the police department in Starkville came to Macon to administer the test to Brooks.

Polygraph machines aren't really "lie detectors," of course, which is why the test results aren't admissible in court. At best they can detect when someone is nervous or uncomfortable. But there could be any number of reasons for nervousness or discomfort, not least of which would include being a suspect in the rape and murder of a three-year-old girl. According to the analyst, Brooks failed the polygraph test. That result was later confirmed by the FBI.

FRIDAY, SEPTEMBER 28

Eight days after arresting him, Eichelberger released William "Slick" Mickens on his own recognizance. On the release form, Eichelberger wrote that Mickens had been "cleared through investigation, of not being number #1 [sic] suspect."

It wasn't exactly vindication, but it did allow Mickens to go home. Mickens never really recovered. His wife, Betty, later said that for the rest of his life, her husband felt as if he lived under a cloud of suspicion. It wore him down. After his arrest, he was told he could no longer help coach the local school's football and baseball teams. He was barred from coaching Little League. In fact, no one in the area would let him work with children at all. Little of that changed even after Brooks was formally charged. It just wasn't worth the risk. Mickens's drinking problem got worse. He ultimately died a broken man.

William Smith also struggled with his arrest. He'd barely had time to mourn his niece before he was arrested for her murder. Many in the family and community never fully bought into Levon Brooks as Courtney's killer. Smith had come home that night right around the time she was killed. He felt their suspicions, even if unstated. He grew despondent. Prior to that night in 1990, Smith had never been in trouble with the law. Afterward, he moved to Columbus and was arrested several times for various low-level offenses. He wound up homeless and eventually lost contact with his family.

But of course Levon Brooks would suffer most of all. A failed polygraph, a stacked photo lineup, a botched interview with a five-year-old, and Michael West's identification of Brooks's teeth were more than enough to seal his fate. Brooks was formally indicted for the sexual assault and murder of Courtney Smith. District Attorney Forrest Allgood announced that he'd be seeking the death penalty.

Shortly after the murder of Courtney Smith, some in the community raised concerns about her surviving siblings, Ashley and Patria. After some complaints to the local social services organization, the two girls relocated to the home of their paternal grandmother, Marion Smith.

Smith also lived in Brooksville. She had a large, clean home and plenty of food. All were enough to convince the social workers that she could provide a better home for the girls. But the transition was hard on the girls, particularly on Ashley, who was old enough to feel the loss of her sister. Whatever she may or may not have seen that night, in the days since then she'd certainly *heard* enough to know to be scared. In order to help the girls cope for the first few nights, Marion Smith gave up her bedroom and moved to the couch in the living room. The children would then beg their grandmother to get in bed with them until they fell asleep. Even then, she remembers, the slightest shift or noise would startle the girls awake, after which they'd cry out for help.

One night about a week after Courtney's murder and just two days after Levon Brooks had been arrested and charged, Smith had finally gotten the girls settled when all three of them heard a terrifying noise. Someone was trying to break into the house. Whoever it was first tried the window. When that didn't open, the prowler moved around to the side door. The girls woke with a start and then froze with fear. Marion Smith grabbed a butcher knife and ran outside. The prowler scurried away. She hurried back inside and called the police. Chief Russell showed up a few minutes later at her door. After reprimanding her for taking matters into her own hands, he circled the house but found nothing.

It was an awful ordeal for the children, but it also made Marion wonder. By then, Levon Brooks was behind bars. What if whoever had murdered Courtney was still out there? Did the prowler target her home by sheer chance that night, or did he know that two young girls were asleep inside?

About a year after Courtney Smith was murdered, Verlinda Monroe fell asleep with her clothes on in the bedroom of her trailer in Crawford, Mississippi. At around two a.m., Monroe woke to the terrifying sensation of someone—or something—touching her stomach. The room was dark, but she sensed a figure hovering over her. She let out a scream and heard the figure bolt toward the door. Monroe's brother woke in the next room and flipped on the lights, just in time to catch a glimpse of a man fleeing the trailer. He gave chase but couldn't catch up to the prowler. When Monroe looked down at her stomach, she saw that her pants had been unbuttoned and unzipped.

Fortunately, Monroe's brother had seen enough of the fleeing man to recognize him. He worked with him at the Bryan Foods chicken plant. It was Justin Albert Johnson.

Johnson was arrested and charged with burglary of an occupied dwelling. He bonded out a few days later.

~ 2 ~

THE MURDER OF
CHRISTINE JACKSON

Beware of false prophets, which come to you in
sheep's clothing.

—Matthew 7:15 (King James Version)

SATURDAY, MAY 2, 1992

Gloria Jackson had gone out to a club—the Santa Barbara of course,
the only game in town. This time, there was no Levon Brooks to take
the cover charge, or to cook at the end of the night. He was three
months into his life sentence for the murder of Courtney Smith. Gloria had left three of her children in the care of her boyfriend, Kennedy Brewer, including three-year-old Christine. For several months,
Brewer and Jackson had been living together in a ramshackle house
on Pilgrim's Rest Road, which wasn't so much a "road" as a graveled
country lane in the further reaches of Noxubee County.

Gloria Jackson wasn't a particularly attentive mother. She was
young, and she'd had some mental health problems. Social services
had been called to the house on a number of occasions to check on
the children's welfare. The kids were often dirty and hungry, and she
sometimes left them unattended. The house wasn't much to look at,
or really to live in. Most of the time, the five residents spent their time
in two rooms, having relinquished the others as too dirty to use. The
front door had no lock. They kept it shut from the inside with a bent
nail. Brewer was the more responsible and capable of the two, but not
by much. He was only nineteen and underemployed. For the most
part, his efforts consisted of bringing the children to his mother's and
sisters' houses from time to time to get them fed and bathed.

Shortly after Gloria Jackson left for the evening, Dewayne Graham and Leshone Williams dropped by the house. The two young men lived just down the road and were close in age to Brewer. Graham's grandmother was Jackson's landlord, and from her house next door, she kept an eye on comings and goings. That night, she noticed Gloria Jackson leaving and was concerned that the children may have been left by themselves. So she asked her grandson and Williams to check on them. At around nine p.m. Graham and Williams went down the road and around to the side of the house—to the bedroom window—in order to get Brewer's attention. The three young men talked for twenty-five minutes or so, until Graham's grandmother yelled at him to come home and wash the dishes. Before they left, they made plans with Brewer to get together later that evening to watch television.

After Graham finished his chores, he left his house and went back to see Brewer. He met up with Williams along the way. The three sat out on the front porch for a few minutes, then went inside to watch *American Gladiators*. Both Graham and Williams remembered seeing all three children asleep on the bed. The three young men hung out until shortly before midnight.

Gloria Jackson came home from the club at around twelve thirty a.m. Brewer had "locked" the door with the nail, and Jackson didn't want to knock and wake the kids. So, just as Graham and Williams had done, she walked around to the side of the house to the same bedroom window where Brewer was sleeping. She called out to wake him. He let her in the front door. Brewer and Jackson had sex and then chatted for a few minutes in the other room before returning to bed and going to sleep. Christine slept on a pallet at the foot of the bed.

When asked to look back on his crimes twenty years later, Justin Johnson said his actions that night felt spontaneous—out of his control. He was out late, walking by himself down Pilgrim's Rest Road with nothing to do and nowhere to go. He'd been staying with his parents since he moved back home from Crawford. They lived about half a mile as the crow flies from Kennedy Brewer, Gloria Jackson, and the kids.

Johnson couldn't say what drew him to that house just off of the road. Nor could he say what drew him to the broken window or what made him quietly lift it up, reach in, and pick up the small girl from her pallet on the floor. But that's what he did. He did it all without waking either her or the adults sleeping on the bed next to her. He then cradled the girl in his arms and carried her into the night.

Johnson walked across the fields behind the house, toward a patch of woods by the creek. That's when the girl woke up. He let her down, and she started walking with him, holding his hand. The voices in his head grew sinister. They told him to "sex molest her, and hurt her, and dispose of the body." He'd later say that he didn't want to harm the girl, but he didn't know what to do.

The two sat down, and the girl fell asleep. Johnson began to cry. He sobbed and beat the ground with his fists. Then he gave in to the voices. He took her clothes off and pulled out his penis. She woke up and began to cry. She told him, "You want my momma." Fearing her cries would be heard, he took her closer to the creek. There the voices told him to "teach her." He penetrated her and quickly ejaculated. She told him she was cold. The voices went away, and his mind began to clear. He'd later say that this is when he realized what he had done, and began to cry all over again.

The two of them sat there for a while until the voices returned and told Johnson to dispose of her body. He obeyed. He walked her closer to the creek, picked her up by the waist and cast her into the water. It was a deep pool, and she quickly slipped under. She tried to climb out, but the sides were steep and slippery. After a few minutes he jumped in, but her body had already washed downstream. Two decades later, investigators would ask Johnson if he kept anything of Christine Jackson's as a souvenir. Of course not, he answered. "I'm not a pervert."

The temperature had dipped into the upper fifties. Johnson was wet, muddy, and cold. Yet after killing the little girl, he stayed in the woods for a long time. He couldn't remember how long. But at some point, he'd say later, the voices finally told him to go home.

SUNDAY, MAY 3

It was an unusually hot and humid day for late spring. Sundays in Noxubee are given to preparing for church and then convening afterward for food and fellowship. In the small church at the head of Pilgrim's Rest Road that Brewer's mother and her family attended, it is often an all-day affair. Annie Brewer, Kennedy's forty-nine-year-old mother, rose early. She had just finished preparing that evening's dinner and was sweeping the covered outdoor porch when the telephone rang. She answered and heard the distressed voice of one of her daughters.

"Christine is missing."

Christine and her brothers and sisters spent a good deal of time with Annie Brewer and her extended family. Christine wasn't Annie Brewer's granddaughter—Gloria and Kennedy got together after she was born—but Annie and the family treated her as if she were.

Christine was small for her age. Though she had a head full of curly hair, she still had her baby fat, much of which remained in her face, particularly in her cheeks. She was tentative and bashful. She spoke quietly, and only to the people she trusted and to whom she was closest. So when Annie Brewer heard the news from her daughter, she felt in her bones that something was wrong. It would have been unusual for Christine to wander off by herself. The girl wasn't bold or assertive enough to do such a thing. Ruby Brewer, Kennedy's older sister who also often took care of Christine, felt the same way. "She would stay up under you," Ruby recalls.

Annie Brewer jumped in the car. When she arrived at the house a few minutes later, a few dozen people from the neighboring houses and trailers had already arrived to help with the search.

Later, there would be a lot of speculation about how Kennedy Brewer and Gloria Jackson acted that morning. It's a common phenomenon to assess guilt or innocence based on a suspect's behavior. It's also fraught with hazard. Innocent people can appear to be withdrawn or disinterested. Guilty people can appear distraught and victimized. These sorts of observations are also necessarily based on eyewitness observations, which themselves are influenced by biases, suggestion, and the witness's own emotional state.

Unsurprisingly, then, some witnesses claimed that Kennedy Brewer and Gloria Jackson were both frantic that morning, worried sick over the whereabouts of the little girl. Others said Brewer kept busy searching while Jackson sat sullenly on a neighbor's porch. Still others said that Brewer acted as though he couldn't be bothered to search in the rising heat and never strayed much beyond the edges of the house. Supporters of Brewer and those allied with Jackson turned on one another almost immediately, and opinions about how Brewer and Jackson acted that morning split mostly along family lines.

Soon, the volunteers had thoroughly searched the small house and surrounding area. They had ruled out any likely nearby hiding places. They then began to fan out across the fields and cow pastures that abutted the house. Others hiked down toward Horse Hunter Creek, a small stream that meandered through the area in a southeasterly direction, carving its way through the pastures. By the time Deputy Sheriff Bud Permenter arrived at a little after eight a.m., at least two dozen people had been searching for Christine for nearly an hour. There was no trace of her.

Because he saw no signs of forced entry, and because the house was "locked" from the inside, Permenter decided early on to focus on the two people who had last seen the girl: Brewer and Jackson. Neither could explain how Christine could simply vanish, so Permenter suspected one or both had to have been involved. If Jackson didn't see the girl when she got home, Brewer was his likely suspect. If Jackson *had* seen the girl, they were both suspects. For the short term, it would be the latter. Jackson told Permenter that she last saw Christine just before she went to sleep, when Brewer picked the girl up off their bed and placed her on a pallet on the floor.

By the time Permenter had finished interviewing the couple, tempers were flaring, both between Brewer and Jackson, and between the two families. Permenter placed Brewer and Jackson in his patrol car—he'd later say it was because he was worried about their safety. He cordoned off the house and checked the interior and exterior, looking for any signs of forced entry. He noticed the bent nail that kept the door shut. The other door to the house was boarded up. The only window that could have offered access to the child was the broken one in the bedroom.

Permenter went into the bedroom and inspected the bed. There was bedding and clothing strewn about, which he recovered and bagged for evidence. The bed itself was still shoved against the exterior wall. The window sat toward the bottom of the bed, along the wall and at about the same height as the top of the mattress. This is where Jackson said she went to wake Brewer up. The window's lower section was broken. There was a gap of about one square foot. Beneath it was Christine's pallet, with the blanket pulled back.

Permenter went back to the patrol car and asked Jackson and Brewer about the broken windowpane. They both told him that the window had been broken when they moved in. He searched the rest of the inside of the house but found nothing of any obvious evidentiary value. On the home's exterior, Permenter found no indication that someone had come in or out—no footprints, and no sign of any kind of disturbance or forced entry.

Permenter was soon joined by Ernest Eichelberger and then Sheriff Albert Walker. Both men also investigated the scene, inside and out, and like Permenter found no sign of forced entry. All of the officers later reported that the plants beneath the window were undisturbed. They saw no footprints leading toward or away from the window. And still no sign of Christine.

MONDAY, MAY 4

A dog team arrived in the morning. Oddly, the handler, a volunteer officer from Newton County, first gave the dogs a piece of Kennedy Brewer's clothing, not a piece of Christine's. The handler would later testify that the first dog was spooked by a large hog and refused to track. The second, he'd say, headed toward the creek and appeared to have been onto a scent before tiring in the heat.

The third dog was the only one to actually track a scent from Christine Jackson's clothes. The handler and dog worked their way down the creek bed, in and out of the vegetation, until they came to a pool of water. At that point the dog tried to go into the pool—"started pawing the water," as her handler described it. The dog then "put her head down in the water and, in other words, she knew something was there, but we couldn't see nothing." The handler would later testify that he could see a small opening from the field leading to the water, and caught a glimpse of a slip mark in the muddy bank on the opposite side. He made a mental note of it, but the dogs were tired and it was getting late. The search was called off for the evening.

Two days had passed, and there was still no sign of Christine Jackson.

WEDNESDAY, MAY 6

On Wednesday morning, Noxubee County brought in a helicopter from the Meridian, Mississippi, naval base to assist with the search for the little girl. Permenter and a couple members of the dog team boarded the helicopter and flew out to the scene. They approached the south end of the creek and flew north to the vicinity of the wide spot in the creek—the pool—that had excited the dogs the day before. Someone on the helicopter then spotted something in the water, but couldn't quite tell what it was. They hovered over the area until the prop wash blew the water off to the side. That's when Christine Jackson's body finally floated to the surface. The deputies recovered her body from the water and turned it over to the county coroner. The coroner then sent it to Steven Hayne for an autopsy.

Permenter had now identified the two people who were with Christine when she was last seen alive, but he was still missing a motive. Why would the couple cover up the abduction and likely murder of a three-year-old girl in their care? Did they play a role in her disappearance?

The similarities to the rape and murder of Courtney Smith couldn't have been lost on him or the law enforcement authorities around him. Less than two years after Smith was killed, another little girl in the same area had been abducted from her bed and was now missing. At a later court hearing, one of Brewer's lawyers asked a law enforcement officer if the abduction and murder of Courtney Smith had any effect on the way they investigated Christine Jackson's disappearance. He answered without hesitation: it had not. And why hadn't they even considered the possibility that the two crimes were related? It was simple: Levon Brooks was the man who raped and murdered Courtney Smith. And Levon Brooks was still under the control of the Mississippi Department of Corrections.

But that answer wasn't completely accurate. Initially, local officials *had* considered a connection. Just as in the Brooks case, local police had gathered everyone who had been in contact with the victim during the previous twenty-four hours: the two young men, Graham and Williams; Gloria Jackson; and another male, James Clayton, an off-and-on boyfriend of Jackson's. They then added one additional suspect: Justin Albert Johnson.

Years later, André de Gruy, now the Mississippi state public defender, would have several conversations with law enforcement officials in Noxubee County about those early days of the investigation. The officials told him they knew that Johnson had been a suspect in the Brooks case. They also knew that within the last few years he had twice been charged and convicted for attempted sexual offenses against women, both of which involved breaking into their homes. They also knew that Johnson lived in a small, green clapboard house less than half a mile from where Christine Jackson lived.

Permenter rounded up all of his early suspects and transported them to Noxubee General Hospital, where they submitted to an examination. A nurse collected blood, saliva, and urine samples from each, as well as body, scalp, and pubic hair. Each suspect was also examined for any lacerations or bruising. Brewer, Jackson, Graham, Williams, and Clayton had no noticeable scrapes or scratches. But one suspect did, all over his arms: Justin Johnson. When the nurse asked Johnson how he got the scratches, he said they were "self-inflicted."

But the authorities had already homed in on Kennedy Brewer. He continued to protest his innocence and insisted that he knew nothing about Christine's disappearance. Permenter told Brewer there was one surefire way to clear his name: he could consent to go with law enforcement to Hattiesburg to see Dr. Michael West, who would make molds of his teeth. If he was telling the truth, Permenter said, West would clear him of any blame.

And so Brewer went with Noxubee County officials to Hattiesburg to see West, along with Graham, Williams, and Gloria Jackson. Justin Johnson was never asked to submit a dental mold.

FRIDAY, MAY 8

As with Courtney Smith, Christine Jackson's body was sent to Steven Hayne. From his autopsy, Hayne concluded that Jackson had been manually strangled. He also found that she had been sexually abused, so violently that she suffered a laceration from the bottom of her vagina to her rectum. Hayne concluded that the injury was most consistent with forceful penetration by a "male penis." More critically, Hayne noted a number of other injuries—abrasions on Christine's arm, forearm, hand, and fingers. The abrasions were small, from between three-eighths of an inch to about five-eighths of an inch long. As with Courtney Smith, Hayne thought these were bite marks, and after he communicated his suspicions, Michael West was brought in to conduct additional analysis. That transfer was easy. West was already at the morgue, assisting Hayne throughout the autopsy and examination.

Less than a week after taking the dental molds from Brewer, Graham, and Williams, West concluded his examination. His findings were definitive. In a letter to Noxubee County law enforcement, West wrote that "the bite marks found on the body of Christine Jackson were indeed and without doubt inflicted by Kennedy Brewer."

WEDNESDAY, MAY 20

Less than two weeks after abducting, raping, and murdering Christine Jackson, Justin Johnson entered a Lowndes County courtroom. He stood accused of the attempted rape of Verlinda Monroe about a year earlier. He pleaded guilty to burglary with intent to commit sexual battery. He was sentenced to ten years in the Mississippi Department of Corrections, with four of those years suspended. He was then taken into custody and transferred to Parchman Penitentiary. He'd serve six years before he was released.

About sixteen months later, in September 1993, Kennedy Brewer was finally arraigned and charged with capital murder for the rape and killing of Christine Jackson. District Attorney Forrest Allgood announced that he would seek the death penalty.

By that time, Michael West had run into a bit of trouble with some professional forensic organizations. The groups had raised questions about the scientific reliability of his trademark phrase, "indeed and without doubt." Because he wasn't allowed to use that phrase anymore, West rewrote his original letter to the law enforcement officials investigating Jackson's murder. The new letter stated that the "dental study models of Kennedy Brewer are found to be within reasonable dental certainty the teeth that inflicted the bites."

The change in wording may have appeased the forensic groups with whom West was in hot water, but it changed nothing about Kennedy Brewer's fate. West didn't conduct a second analysis or seek out a second opinion. He simply changed his letter to express the same degree of certainty, but with different words. He was still claiming that Kennedy Brewer was the only person who could have inflicted the bite marks allegedly found on Christine Jackson.

The state of Mississippi wanted to execute Kennedy Brewer before West rewrote his letter. It still wanted to execute him afterward. And Michael West was still the best route to a death sentence.

~ 3 ~

INVESTIGATING THE DEAD

Gentlemen, you are about to enter the most
important and fascinating sphere of police work:
the world of forensic medicine, where untold victims of many homicides will reach back from the
grave and point back a finger accusingly at their
assailant.

—Jack Klugman as TV character Dr. R. Quincy,
  medical examiner

On March 15, 44 BCE, a conspiracy of Roman senators led by Gaius
Cassius and Marcus Brutus confronted Julius Caesar outside the
Theater of Pompey, ripped off his tunic, and stabbed him nearly two
dozen times. The Roman senate had recently named Caesar "dictator
in perpetuity," and the conspirators feared Caesar planned to exploit
the new title, overthrow the senate, and institute a reign of dictatorial
tyranny. Assassination, they believed, was their only hope to stop him
and restore the Roman republic. Historical accounts vary, but approximately sixty conspirators participated in the assassination, including
at least forty senators. Together they had agreed that each would inflict his own wound on the emperor, a plan that not only promised solidarity but would also make it difficult to determine precisely whose
blade had caused Caesar's death.

After the murder, the eminent Roman physician Antistius examined Caesar's body. What ensued was likely the first recorded postmortem forensic examination in the Western world. Antistius found
twenty-three stab wounds, only one of which he determined was
potentially fatal on its own. He concluded that the wounds had col-
lectively caused Caesar to die from exsanguination—massive blood
loss. Antistius then presented his findings before a public forum.

(This where we get the word "forensic," a relative of "forum," both derived from the Latin *forensis*, which means "to present before the public.")

But while Antistius's autopsy was one of the first for which there is a recorded history—and probably the first in the West—there's good evidence of postmortem physiology dating as far back as 3000 BCE. Unlike societies contemporaneous to theirs, neither the Egyptians nor the Babylonians considered dissection of the dead to be taboo. The Greek physician Galen of Pergamum, who lived in the second century CE, was reputed to be the first to understand the potential usefulness of comparing a living patient's physiological condition with a postmortem examination of the same patient after death.

The first standardized system of investigating suspicious deaths was established in ancient China, predating Antistius by several centuries and other European efforts by nearly a millennium. In the 1970s, archeologists working in China's Hubei Province discovered a collection of engraved bamboo strips titled "Models for Sealing and Physical Examinations" dating back to the Qin Dynasty of the third century BCE. The texts speak not only to postmortem analysis of corpses but also to the investigation of potential criminal conduct, with detailed instructions for finding and preserving evidence, interrogating suspects, ascertaining the identity of perpetrators, and distinguishing suicides from staged hangings. In 995 CE, the Song Dynasty issued a decree establishing the first known inquest system for suspicious deaths. Under it, local authorities were required to alert government investigators after discovering or learning of an unexpected death. The decree mandated something akin to the modern autopsy report, requiring local officials to summarize findings of their investigations, including sketches of the anterior and posterior of the body with annotations to indicate the corpse's condition, the location of wounds, and so forth. The reports were considered public documents. If an investigation revealed that a death was caused by an illegal act, the decree compelled officials in a neighboring jurisdiction to perform a separate and independent investigation.

In 1248, a Chinese criminal investigator named Sung Tz'u authored *Washing Away of Wrongs*, likely the first forensics manual ever published. One of the book's lessons recounts the story of a criminal investigator called to a village to investigate the murder of a local farmer who had been slashed to death. The investigator gathered all of the villagers in a central location and then requested that they bring their sickles forward and place them on the ground. When flies gathered on one of the sickles, presumably drawn to invisible traces of blood, the sickle's owner confessed.

Though not as sophisticated or as organized as the Chinese system, sixth-century Europe saw similar developments in the Justinian Code, which required physicians to assist courts with advice and interpretation of evidence. By the late 1500s, forensic medical texts were spreading throughout Western Europe, gradually becoming a feature of most criminal investigations. By the mid-1600s, medical specialists routinely performed some type of postmortem examination and testified in criminal courts across the continent.

The United States inherited its death investigation system (as well as much of its common law) from the English. It was the English who created the position of *coroner,* a widely overlooked and misunderstood public office that dates back to the Norman Conquest. While there were similarities between the British coroner system and the death investigation systems that had been present for centuries in China and in medieval Europe, those systems—particularly that of the Chinese—were designed from the start for the primary purposes of determining the cause of suspicious deaths and the administration of justice. The English story is quite a bit more convoluted.

The coroner system in Britain began more as a means to an end, and the end was collecting tax proceeds for the king. Most historians credit the creation of the coroner to Hubert Walter, an advisor to King Richard I. Five years into Richard's reign, England found itself in dire financial straits. The crown's claim that the Third Crusade was mostly successful may have been true, but the fight had been funded with unpopular new taxes. The kingdom's financial woes only worsened when, on his way back from the Middle East, Richard I was kidnapped and held for ransom. Hubert Walter paid what the captives demanded, but the steep cost plunged England further into crushing debt.

Desperate to refill the country's coffers, Walter issued a new law in 1194 calling for each county in England to elect three knights and one clerk "to keep the pleas of the crown"—basically, to oversee the crown's exclusive business. These officials became known as "crowners," or agents of the crown. The term eventually morphed into "coroners," after the Latin *custos placitorum coronas,* or "keeper of the crown's pleas."

While coroners didn't have law enforcement powers, they were the only local officials who had the authority to arrest the sheriffs. The latter, charged with keeping the laws in their respective jurisdictions, had become notoriously corrupt, and the king's aides found their thieving and pilfering particularly irksome now that the country was in debt.

The "coroner" concept—and mission—was vague, and probably intentionally so. Walter believed that keeping the coroners' duties loosely defined provided political flexibility. It allowed him to alter the position as needs arose, whether by diminishing the power and influence of the sheriffs, or by improvising ways in which the coroner could collect more taxes and fees.

Initially, the coroner's most important responsibility was to keep records in each county for the Royal Courts of Law. The king levied taxes and fines based on these records. It wasn't long before the tax-happy crown saw revenue potential in life's only certainty: death. Today the terms "coroner" and "death" are inseparable. But coroners came to oversee death investigations really as an afterthought—the by-product of a twelfth-century king desperate to raise some money.

As a result, the early English coroner's main task was not to determine the cause of death, or even identify the parties responsible for untimely deaths. Most English communities at the time were small and close-knit enough that in the event of a murder (which was rare), the identity of the killer was typically known to everyone. The primary purpose of the coroners' death investigations was to levy the appropriate taxes, fines, and surcharges associated with passing away. Walter had also imposed a "death duty," a fee imposed on the family of the deceased, and levied taxes on the deceased's chattel and other property. Not surprisingly, all of this made coroners rather unpopular.

Eventually the crown found new ways to tax death—ways that required someone to figure out how the death had actually occurred. A death resulting from homicide or negligence, for example, allowed the crown to seize the land and holdings of the responsible party through forfeiture. A crime like murder might also invoke the doctrine of "corruption of blood," in which both the perpetrators' property and their inheritance rights were forfeited to the crown. Under the "murdrum" doctrine, a village could be fined for any murder in which it couldn't be proved that the victim was Saxon. That law was meant to protect the Norman aristocracy from reprisal killings by the conquered Saxons. The rules for death investigations eventually became so onerous that some English citizens began ignoring dead bodies or hiding them. In some instances, corpses were covertly deposited in nearby villages as a way to avoid the increasingly expensive hassle.

Given that the office of coroner was never intended to focus on medical issues, early English coroners rarely if ever had any medical training. In fact, the original requirements to hold office were only that one be a knight and that one be affluent. The wealth requirement was meant to immunize against corruption and bribery—coroners were unpaid. (Predictably, this had the opposite effect.) English coroners also had other odd jobs, such as ensuring that the accused showed up for criminal trials at the county courts; taking confessions from criminals who had sought sanctuary in churches; determining the owners of "treasure troves" (money found buried in the ground); investigating shipwrecks and fires; and confiscating any whale or sturgeon caught by fishermen, or that happened to wash ashore (both were considered too valuable for commoners, and thus the property of the crown).

By the late Middle Ages, practices like murdrum fines and death duties had fallen out of favor or been eliminated entirely. Other responsibilities, like tax and fine collections, were transferred to other public offices. What remained—death investigation—became by default the coroners' primary responsibility. Gradually, the position came to be occupied by people with skills better suited for the job, typically physicians and attorneys.

The Industrial Revolution and urbanization hastened this evolution, as the booming population in London brought a surge in violent crime, disease, and factory deaths. Increased attention to public safety prompted coroners to more actively investigate accidental and negligent deaths, as well as homicides. The Coroners Act of 1887 repealed a number of the more antiquated policies and rewrote the powers and responsibilities of coroners to better position them for that role. Today, a British coroner's primary responsibility is to oversee death investigations, although they're still asked occasionally to administrate the proceeds from "treasure troves."

This was the system that the United States inherited. Like their British counterparts, early American coroners attended to death investigations but were also assigned a mixed bag of other responsibilities. (Until the 1980s, for example, Mississippi coroners were responsible for rounding up any stray livestock in the county.) As in Britain, the coroner position was important, though often taken for granted and underappreciated. Most coroners were appointed to the position; others were elected. In some states the position was specifically written into state constitutions, which set forth general duties, qualifications to serve, and certain enumerated powers. Many states also preserved the English tradition of designating the coroner as the only local official with the power to arrest the sheriff—a tradition that persists today.

Because colonial America was mostly agrarian with few large cities, the primary qualifications for coroner tended to be less about training and education and more about practical concerns—such as owning a wagon that could haul bodies. As in early England, colonial American towns were close-knit and fairly homogenous. On the whole, homicides were rare.

When coroners were presented with an unexpected death, they would empanel a coroner's jury—a group of men assembled to investigate. Historical records suggest that early American coroners and their jurors were unlikely to possess medical training or other expertise, and instead tended to rely on common sense and general observation to reach their conclusions.

During the Jacksonian era of populist government in the early 1800s, many public offices that had traditionally been gained by appointment became, instead, elected positions. In most of the country, that included the coroner. "Jacksonian Democrats celebrated the intelligence and integrity of the common man while belittling the attainments of the social and professional elite," writes historian Julie Johnson-McGrath. "Thus, as the western territories were settled and the number of coroners grew, there was no accompanying demand that they possess medical or legal credentials. Political, not professional skills were what was demanded of potential coroners."

As a result, the coroner's office did not evolve into a public service position for doctors and other medical professionals, but instead into an accessible entree into political life. Death investigations suffered as a result. Though nearly all coroners of the era had the authority to convene an inquest into a suspicious death, few had the power or the will to order an actual autopsy. Even if they had wanted to, there weren't many doctors around to give their medical opinion on a cause of death. Some American medical scholars agitated for a system more in line with Europe's, but the country was still sparsely populated and remained largely devoid of the type of specialists required to populate any field resembling modern forensic pathology. Worse, not only was there a shortage of qualified physicians to provide expertise to inquest jurors—even within the limits of the knowledge available at the time—but courts generally deferred to those physicians who were consulted, regardless of their qualifications. And even among the handful of qualified physicians, a coroner with no medical training could frequently trump a doctor's conclusions.

Physicians began to resent coroners, and the medical profession in general began to lose interest in lending its expertise to the criminal justice system. Thus began the adversarial relationship between science and law. The tension between the two would undermine the evolution of forensic pathology for the next two centuries.

Sensing that the problem was just as much about supply as demand, some in the medical community, such as the American Medical Association, began to advocate for making jurisprudential medicine a more prominent part of the medical school curriculum. The group even advocated abolishing the coroner's office. But though it continued to advocate doing away with coroners throughout the latter half of the nineteenth century, the AMA lacked the political leverage to persuade state legislatures, and its reform efforts were stymied by the era's growing distrust of elites.

The medical community offered expertise, practical reforms, and a concern for public health. The coroners countered with protectionism, cronyism, and raw political power. The coroners won out. It was during this period that the institutional structure for the coroner system was built, and along with it came the rise of the factions and interest groups that benefited from its continued existence. It would prove extremely difficult to tear down. The animus between the coroners and the medical community, and the inability of the latter to navigate the politics of the former, explains in part why until relatively recently the scientific community has generally steered clear of the criminal justice system. The resulting vacuum allowed law enforcement interests, politics, and rank charlatanism to fill the void.

By the early 1900s, American public sentiment began to warm to elites. This period saw the rise of progressivism, a political ideology that tended to revere professionals, embrace the pursuit of knowledge, and push for improvements in public health and safety. Breakthroughs in fields like bacteriology, virology, and general germ theory brought the medical profession new prestige. Previously, doctors had merely helped manage illness and death. The country now looked to them to prevent those things.

As progressives positioned themselves as the enemies of corruption and machine-run politics, coroners emerged as a ripe target. The office had become extremely powerful, especially in large cities. In some cities the coroner's office had more investigators than there were detectives in the police department. In other places, the coroner had prosecutorial powers on par with a district attorney.

Coroner's deputies, who were usually in charge of claiming bodies and transporting them to the morgue, routinely collected bribes from undertakers in exchange for recommending embalming and funeral services to the families of the dead. They were also known to loot personal belongings from corpses. The fees earned by coroners and their juries for inquests provided additional opportunity for graft and political patronage. Coroners had great discretion over their juries' conclusions. They could mediate, negotiate, or outright auction off a cause of death. Ample opportunity existed to do just that. The family or associates of a prominent businessman might bribe a coroner to turn a suicide into an accident. The wealthy family of a woman who died of complications from an abortion might pay a coroner to rule that the death was from natural causes. Insurance companies typically didn't pay benefits in cases of suicide, but they might pay double or more for an accidental death. As the country industrialized, factory deaths became an increasingly urgent health concern. Any insurance company able to influence a coroner's jury to find contributory negligence on the part of the deceased could save a fortune in claims.

While the Jacksonian-era push to elect coroners was intended as a check against corruption, party machines rendered the change ineffective. The coroner morphed into a patronage position handed out by party bosses. Some coroners ran on promises to slash budgets by requesting fewer autopsies, a policy that in an era of rising crime, rapid industrialization, and disease from overcrowding could be disastrous for public health.

Most states required little in the way of qualifications to run for coroner. In many places, a candidate needed only to be of voting age and pass some arbitrary test of moral character. The law in

North Carolina was typical: coroner candidates needed only to have renounced atheism and to have never participated in a duel.

The progressives sought to end these problems by moving away from coroners toward a medical examiner system. But the field of forensic pathology (the field in which medical examiners practice) continued to suffer from a familiar problem: there just weren't very many medical examiners around. Most bright, ambitious young physicians went to medical school to save lives, not to work with the dead. As Julie Johnson-McGrath writes, "The popular conception of the coroner's physician was a broken-down, alcoholic wreck unfit to treat the living, or a sociopathic personality who preferred the company of the dead. It was hardly the company a talented young physician would care to join."

In 1911, an Illinois jury convicted Thomas Jennings of murder committed in the course of a burglary. The case would have been unexceptional save for a piece of evidence that had never before been used in an American courtroom, and that was central to the prosecution's case: a fingerprint. According to the prosecution, the print was left on a freshly painted railing. The railing also happened to be near the perpetrator's point of entry. Police analysts determined that the print was a match to Thomas Jennings. It was the only solid evidence against him. The victim's traumatized wife had been unable to pick Jennings out of a lineup, and though Jennings—an experienced burglar who had done time at the state prison in Joliet—had been subjected to a physically brutal interrogation, he never confessed.

The jury convicted. When Jennings's lawyers challenged the admission of the fingerprint evidence on appeal, the Illinois appellate court affirmed the conviction, finding that "the court and jury were properly aided by witnesses of peculiar and specialized experience on this subject." Jennings was hanged.

By the time of Jennings's trial, Europe had been using fingerprint evidence in its courts for several decades. In fact, it was Scotland Yard detectives who introduced it to the American populace at the 1904 World's Fair in St. Louis. That particular World's Fair was in many ways the ideal venue for the birth of American forensics. The fair's theme was all about American achievement in science and technology.

It celebrated the young country's rapid industrialization and the cities' sprint toward electrification.

But the fair's celebration of technological advancement also came with jingoistic claims of American superiority, ugly demonstrations of alleged racial supremacy, and crank theories passed off as science. Among the fair's exhibits, for example, were living dioramas of native "savages" gathered from all over the globe—essentially a human zoo. One featured Ota Benga, a Congolese man who had been captured and sold into slavery, then "rescued" and brought to St. Louis, where viewers could pay admission to see his filed and sharpened "cannibal teeth." Other exhibits touted pseudosciences like phrenology and physiognomy, which posited that trained experts could make broad generalizations about intelligence, criminal proclivity, and morality based on physical characteristics like skull shape and size or the relative ratios of various body parts.

In short, it was a time when it could sometimes be difficult to distinguish legitimate scientific breakthroughs from puffery and dangerous pseudoscientific nonsense. Occasionally the same intellectuals proffered both. Sir Francis Galton, for example, was a Victorian-era statistician, mathematician, meteorologist, and polymath. He is often credited with developing modern fingerprint analysis, an interest he'd nurtured while studying how French police agencies were using biological data to identify and classify criminal suspects. Galton thought anthropometry (the study of measurements of the human body) had uses well beyond mere identification. He believed other physical characteristics could not only be used to distinguish one person from another, but could be predictive of traits like criminality, intelligence, and virtue. Such thinking led to theories that people of a certain nose size, skull shape, or skin tone were inherently more or less virtuous, productive, or intelligent than those who were differently proportioned or colored.

These theories are of course nonsense, and applying them to social policy has proven to be catastrophic. But Galton became one of the earliest and most vocal proponents. In his autobiography, he advocated for the forced sterilization of entire groups of people. "Stern compulsion ought to be exerted to prevent the free propagation of the stock of those who are seriously afflicted by lunacy, feeblemindedness, habitual criminality, and pauperism," he wrote. One of the fathers of modern fingerprint analysis wasn't just a champion of eugenics; he coined the term.

It seems somehow appropriate, then, that the embryonic field of forensics found a home in the progressive movement. Like progressives, early forensics practitioners enthusiastically forged ahead with "science" that didn't always adhere to the principles of scientific inquiry; they embraced expertise but didn't always check the credentials of the experts.

There were exceptions to be sure. One of the earliest adopters of modern forensics was Berkeley, California, police chief August Vollmer. A pioneer of standardization and professionalization, Vollmer also pushed for specialization in policing. He thought law enforcement should be a career, not the patronage position it had become. Led by Vollmer, progressive police departments created police units that solely investigated homicides or only targeted narcotics. Forensics emerged as another such area of specialization. It was Vollmer who created the country's first crime laboratory, including a focus on nascent forensic science.

But more broadly, the newly open atmosphere toward people who claimed expertise presented new opportunities for hucksters and frauds. Everyone seemed to love the experts, but no one was making sure the experts actually knew what they were talking about. Within the justice system, it became the courts' responsibility to tackle the daunting challenge of separating expertise from artifice. "The standard at the time was that if someone had specialized knowledge, and that knowledge seemed to be helpful to investigators, then the court would allow the testimony," says Jonathan Koehler, a behavioral scientist and law professor at Northwestern University. "The problem was that there was no attempt to check the validity of what these witnesses were actually claiming."

By the early 1900s, American medical schools had improved dramatically, as had the standards and prestige of the medical profession in general. This only intensified the antipathy between the profession and the country's coroners. Just as they had with the nascent forensics fields, progressives joined forces with the newly resurgent medical field to push for reform. In some cities, reformers tried to require all coroners to be licensed physicians. In others, they tried to abolish the coroner system entirely and replace it with a medical examiner system.

In most places, the coroner system prevailed. The reasons were mostly institutional. First, many states had enshrined the position in their state constitutions. Abolishing it required a constitutional amendment. Second, by the early 1920s, many former coroners had worked their way through politics and now sat on city councils or in state legislatures, or held gubernatorial appointments. Lawmakers weren't keen to abolish the position that had given them or their colleagues their start in politics. Third, the medical profession itself was not well positioned to take over the job. Though medical schools, certifications, and professionalism in the field had dramatically improved in a short period of time, the field of forensic pathology remained underdeveloped.

But there were some success stories, mostly in large cities. New York City moved to a medical examiner system in the 1910s. That office soon became an example for reformers all over the country. Its success was due to the extraordinary vision of the men who led it, Charles Norris and his protégé, Alexander Getler. The office in Cleveland, Ohio, switched to such a system in 1914. Newark followed in the next decade. The state of Illinois still used the coroner system, but in Chicago, Cook County coroner Peter Hoffman saw the value in utilizing the knowledge and expertise of medical professionals. Hoffman ordered autopsies when investigating suspicious deaths, and he hired only qualified doctors to perform them. He also kept epidemiological statistics and for public health purposes tracked deaths from accidents and negligence.

But overall, coroners were able to beat back the push to make them obsolete, either outright or by fighting to water down reforms. The frequent result of the back-and-forth was a compromise that preserved the coroner system but also created state and local medical examiner's offices, to either oversee coroners or operate alongside them. That compromise, however, often only made things worse.

In 1928, the Rockefeller Foundation and the National Research Council published the first of many damning reports on America's coroner system. It exposed the widespread use of kickbacks and other corruption, found that few states required any qualifications at all for the position, and concluded that inquests tainted by corruption and political influence were reaching highly suspect findings about cause of death. The report recommended that states and cities retire their coroner systems, establish a medical examiner system in their place, reassign the coroner's legal responsibilities to the judiciary, and require medical schools to teach medical death investigation as a full-time specialty. The foundation then followed its own recommendations, sponsoring the first academic department of legal medicine at Harvard Medical School in 1937—a program that soon began graduating qualified forensic pathologists.

Outside of the medical community, though, all of this research and anecdotal data was generally met with silence. As of 1942 just seven states had replaced the coroner system with a medical examiner system. By the end of that decade, only eleven states had attempted any meaningful legal reform. In some parts of the country, the coroners had actually managed to strengthen their position.

Some reformers began to look for a different approach. Chief among them was Richard Childs, a progressive activist from New York state and the longtime chair of the National Municipal League. Childs seized on what would become an enormously effective (if not always honest) tactic to win public support for reform: scare the hell out of people about crime. Childs crossed the country making the case that because of the coroners' ineptitude and corruption, solvable crimes weren't being investigated, and murderers, rapists, and other violent criminals were not only going free, but were ready to strike again. Newspapers loved the angle, publishing series and investigations critical of the coroner system, most with variations of the tagline that their own city or state had become "a good place to get away with murder." Childs had more success than his predecessors. By 1960, about half the states had instituted some type of reform or reorganization of their coroner systems, many borrowing heavily from Childs's model policies.

Childs's chief nemesis was the National Association of Coroners, led by Cleveland's Samuel Gerber, a charismatic, politically savvy coroner best known for leading the 1954 investigation that implicated Dr. Sam Sheppard in the murder of his wife—the inspiration for the movie and TV series *The Fugitive.* The other main obstacles to reform over the years were funeral directors. Between the fees for transporting bodies and the referrals for embalming and memorial services, successful funeral home owners found that good business means maintaining good relations with the coroner's office. Funeral home directors were enormously influential in coroner races in much of the country, either by running for the office themselves or by donating to candidates. In an election for such a seemingly obscure office, even a small donation could give one candidate a huge advantage. At least in this niche of politics, funeral directors proved to be a formidable lobby.

Twelve years after the *Jennings* fingerprint case, the US Court of Appeals for the District of Columbia Circuit became the first federal appellate court in the country to attempt to set some standards for the use of forensic expertise in the courtroom. In the 1923 case *Frye v. United States*, a polygraph instructor had testified that a rise in systolic blood pressure was indicative of a witness's dishonesty. In considering whether to allow the expert opinion, the court ruled that in order for scientific evidence to be admissible it must have "gained general acceptance in the particular field in which it belongs." The court determined that the nascent field of polygraph testing did not possess such acceptance and excluded the testimony. Though it wasn't a Supreme Court case, *Frye* was eventually adopted by every other federal court of appeals, and over time by nearly every state. "That [decision] put some teeth in the law," says law professor Jonathan Koehler. "It looked beyond mere witness qualifications to evaluate the content of a witness's testimony."

But the decision also had at least one ancillary effect that would have an even bigger impact than its core holding: it made judges the gatekeepers of what expertise would be allowed into court. The problem is that judges are trained in legal analysis, not scientific inquiry. These are two entirely different ways of thinking. Nevertheless, for the next fifty years *Frye* remained the model in both federal court and in most state courts across the country.

By 1952, just sixteen of the seventy-two medical schools in the United States offered instruction in legal medicine. Fewer still offered instruction in forensic pathology. Again, the problem was driven by low demand. Evidently, most medical students had little interest in working with the dead, and those who did typically learned on the job. Many (but certainly not all) who chose the profession at the time did so because they weren't skilled enough physicians to specialize in anything else. This presented a significant obstacle to reforming the coroner system. How could reformers convince states to move to a medical examiner system if there weren't any competent medical examiners to take over? Recognizing the problem, reformers set out to professionalize and standardize forensic pathology. By the mid-1950s, the American Board of Pathology—the nation's leading group that certifies pathologists—began creating a specific certification in forensic pathology. The first class of candidates was certified in 1959.

But the effort was far from an overwhelming success. After an initial surge of "grandfathered" certifications of experienced pathologists (though not necessarily experienced in *forensic* pathology), the stream of candidates thinned. Even as a rising homicide rate in the 1960s created an urgent need for additional medical examiners, the field still had to overcome its professional stigma, as well as the comparatively low pay offered by state and municipal governments.

To address the shortage, the American Board of Pathology continued to grandfather certifications, even to applicants with no formal training in the field, despite data showing they performed significantly worse on the board-certifying exam. Morale was low, and new applicants were hard to come by. Opening the door to less-qualified candidates only exacerbated the stigma. The field slipped into a self-perpetuating cycle of mediocrity.

By the early 1970s, over half of the country's traditional coroner offices had been abolished, and just over half the states had implemented some sort of reform. But considering that the reformers had been waging the fight for decades, those advancements were fairly incremental and overshadowed by the continued strength of the status quo. By 1970 the office of coroner remained in some substantial form in thirty-nine states. Even today, just eighteen states have fully abolished the coroner system in favor of a medical examiner system, the same figure as in 1967. And of the thirty-two states in which coroners still serve part or all of a county, twelve require no specialized training for the position at all.

Currently, the United States still faces a critical shortage of medical examiners. The field enjoys significantly more respect than it once did, thanks in part to celebrity medical examiners and high-profile criminal cases, both of which have contributed to public understanding of the job, along with positive pop culture portrayals on television shows like *Quincy* and more recently the *CSI* franchise. But forensic pathology continues to suffer from many of the problems that have plagued it from the beginning. Medical students go to medical school to help the sick. Few enroll to work with the dead. Most medical examiner jobs today are still public positions, meaning they tend to pay far less than medical specialties in private practice. Though medicolegal investigations have at least advanced to the point where autopsies are now standard in most suspicious deaths, the problem persists in that there just aren't enough medical examiners to do them all—or at least to do them properly.

All of which means that despite the relatively low pay of the state positions in forensic pathology, a doctor willing to bend the profession's guidelines to help supply meet demand could make good money. There are quite a few places across the country where that's exactly what has happened—where doctors have willingly performed significantly more autopsies than the field's governing bodies recommend. But nowhere did it happen on the scale it did in Mississippi.

4

AT THE HANDS OF
PERSONS UNKNOWN

We couldn't even count the bullet holes in my
brother's head. But they called it heart failure.

—A black Mississippi woman, 1964

Of all the ways America's coroner system could be—and was—
corrupted, the most damaging and consequential was its deployment
to excuse and cover up lynchings, civil rights assassinations, and other
racial violence during the twentieth century. "The coroner's jury is
often formed among those who took part in the lynching," wrote the
journalist and civil rights activist Ida B. Wells in 1894, "and a verdict,
'Death at the hands of parties unknown to the jury' is rendered." Her
observation was echoed four decades later by the Washington, DC,
publication the *Afro-American*, which editorialized in 1932, "There is
a righteous complaint that officials from coroners' juries to state governors carefully whitewash lynchings in order to keep down public
clamor."

Of course, the coroner system wasn't the *cause* of the hundreds
of lynchings that stained America in the late nineteenth and early
twentieth centuries. They'd no doubt have occurred anyway. But the
system certainly facilitated them. As an elected official in a culture
in which blacks were effectively barred from voting and denigrated
as second-class citizens, the coroner was a powerful ally in preserving the racial status quo. The conclusions of a coroner's jury carried
the force of law. Once an inquest determined that a black man with
noose marks around his neck and riddled with bullet holes had died
of natural causes, or suicide, or by accident, or that, say, the owner

of a sharecropping plantation had shot one of his tenant farmers in self-defense, that conclusion nearly always ended the investigation. There would be no arrests, no charges, no trial. In this sense, the coroner had extraordinary power. Though no coroners obtained the raw power or public notoriety of a George Wallace or a Bull Connor, by persistently thwarting justice for the victims of racial violence they were easily as culpable for the era's worst crimes as any racist lawman or segregationist governor.

As racial violence increased in the 1930s and 1940s, the US House of Representatives passed several different versions of a federal anti-lynching bill. Each time those bills reached the Senate, they were blocked by Southern lawmakers. The argument was as straightforward as it was disingenuous: federal intervention was unnecessary because lynching was already illegal under state law.

Strictly speaking, that was true. Some Southern states had even passed anti-lynching laws as early as the late 1800s. But of course to convict under those laws, someone had to identify the lynchers. Dutifully, coroners inevitably found that the killers' identities were impossible to ascertain. As Stewart Tolnay and E. M. Beck wrote in their history of Southern lynchings, "Potentially severe punishment for mob members was virtually irrelevant when coroners consistently concluded that lynch victims met their fates at the hands of a 'party or parties unknown.'"

Variations on that phrase—"persons, party or parties unknown"—haunt the accounts of lynchings throughout American history generally, and in the deep South in particular. Again and again, reports of lynchings in black publications like the *Chicago Defender* and catalogs of lynchings in the NAACP's annual reports described coroners' inquests that concluded the murders were committed "at the hands of persons unknown." The phrase was so common among coroners and their juries that the author and historian Philip Dray made it the title of his own influential book on the history of lynching in America.

For more than a century, coroners and the juries they convened across the country seem to have had an extraordinarily difficult time identifying members of the white mobs who murdered black people, even when the identities of the people who perpetrated such killings were well known in the community, or even when there were photographs of them carrying out the lynching—even when those photographs were published on the front pages of local newspapers.

The problem was especially egregious in the first half of the twentieth century, when lynchings were often a public spectacle, and the identities of participants weren't just well known, they were celebrated. Lynchings were often organized—even planned—performances. Local newspapers sometimes posted the time and location. They were frequently witnessed by dozens, some by hundreds, of spectators, with the events then reported on and publicized the following day.

The killings were purposeful assertions of white supremacy, a terroristic tool to keep black people docile and subservient. The intended victim wasn't just limited to the doomed soul at the end of the rope, but every black man, woman, and child close enough to be affected by the violence. Publicity was therefore often welcome. In some cases, vendors sold gruesome photos and postcards of lynchings, or pieces of the rope used for the hanging.

In October 1911 in Anderson County, South Carolina, a mob strung up a man named Willis Jackson on a telephone pole and shot him to death. Reporters from the local paper witnessed the entire murder. When the coroner cut Jackson's body down the next day, the paper reported, "his fingers had been removed as souvenirs. Onlookers took home pieces of the rope that strung him up, too." The paper presumably got the scoop on the killing because its editor, Victor B. Cheshire, was part of the mob. So was state representative Joshua W. Ashley. The paper reported that its editor "went out to see the fun, with not the least objection to being a party to help lynch the brute." Even with the names of the lynch mob published in the local paper, the coroner's jury concluded that Willis Jackson died "at the hands of parties unknown."

The investigation into the October 1916 murder of Anthony Crawford in Abbeville County, South Carolina, concluded the same way. Crawford was a successful black cotton farmer who had turned a small field he inherited from his father into a 427-acre operation, making him one of the wealthiest men in the county. That didn't sit well with his white neighbors. After a heated argument between Crawford and a white grocer, one of the grocer's clerks struck Crawford in the head with an axe handle. A mob formed. Crawford was captured, dragged through the county's black neighborhoods by a rope, and hung from a pine tree. White residents then used his hanging body for target practice. A local newspaper reported the incident the next day under the headline "Negro Strung Up and Shot to Pieces." Despite dozens of witnesses, the coroner's jury again invoked the magic phrase, rendering the crime unsolvable.

After the June 1923 lynching of two black men accused of killing Homestead, Florida, town marshal Charles Bryant, the coroner's jury concluded that the victims "came to their deaths as the result of gunshot wounds from persons unknown." But not only did the jury know the men in the posse, the murderers were actually called to testify. Author William Wilbanks writes in his history of law enforcement deaths in the region that the "persons unknown" conclusion was merely a way to affirm the social order. "The coroners' juries may have felt that the killings were justified," Wilbanks writes, "or were afraid to engage in an unpopular 'persecution' of fellow citizens for doing what the (white) community believed to be right (if not legal)." Wilbanks adds that the coroner's jury in Bryant's case also "took the Sheriff 'off the hook,' as he could point to the ruling as justification for not conducting his own investigation."

These are just a few examples of hundreds. Black newspapers, newsletters, and advocacy journals are filled with similar accounts. By the 1930s and 1940s, national sentiment began to turn on racially motivated lynchings, at least outside of the South. Some sympathetic politicians, legal societies, and progressive editorial boards even began to condemn them. Lynchings declined in number, though they by no means disappeared. Instead, the institution underwent a subtle but significant transformation. Where lynchings had previously been conducted as a public spectacle, the murders now became more localized and secretive. The aim was still the same, however: to terrorize the black population into subservience.

Here, too, the coroner system was happy to help. In fact, in some ways it became easier for coroners and their juries to excuse the murders. Those who participated in lynchings were less likely to boast about their crimes in public forums. Killings took place in the woods or on private property instead of the town square. Photos of the lynchers were less likely to show up in the local paper. With participants seeking anonymity instead of notoriety, the coroners' juries' claims to be unable to ascertain their identities were more credible, at least on the surface.

That said, the July 1946 murders of Roger Malcolm, Dorothy Malcolm, George Dorsey, and Mae Dorsey in Monroe, Georgia, demonstrated the resilient power of a coroner's jury to thwart the interests of justice, even in the face of national attention from reporters, federal investigators, and the president of the United States himself. At the time, the country had gone nearly a year without a reported lynching. The incident precipitating the killings had occurred two weeks earlier, when Roger Malcolm, a sharecropper, resisted his landowner's attempt to whip him. The two got into a physical altercation, during which Malcolm stabbed his landlord with a pocketknife. Malcolm and his wife, Dorothy, fled to a farm in a neighboring county, where Dorothy's brother, George Dorsey—a decorated veteran freshly returned from World War II—sharecropped with his wife.

On July 26, a white mob caught up with both couples, dragged them from their car, beat them, and shot all four of them to death. When the coroner and sheriff investigated the crime scene, they found that the surrounding trees had been riddled with buckshot. The women's arms had been broken. The force of a shotgun blast had nearly removed Dorothy Malcolm's face. The earlier altercation was well known to locals, as were the identities of the members of the mob. Yet once again, the coroner's jury made little effort at all to identify them. The local coroner concluded, "Death at the hands of persons unknown."

By the time federal investigators looked into the case, any physical evidence was long gone, and witnesses had been sufficiently intimidated to keep quiet. The FBI got involved, issued dozens of subpoenas, and interviewed thousands of people. *Time* magazine ran a story headlined, "The Best People Won't Talk." NBC led its national radio news broadcast with the opening: "One hundred forty million Americans were disgraced late yesterday, humiliated in their own eyes and in the eyes of the world by one of the most vicious lynchings to stain our national record." President Harry Truman would later say of the murders, "When the mob gangs can take four people out and shoot them in the back, and everybody in the country is acquainted with who did the shooting and nothing is done about it, that country is in a pretty bad fix from the law enforcement standpoint." He was right, but little was done to address it. Coroners' juries would continue to cover up racial violence for decades to come.

Mississippi was in perhaps the worst "fix" of all. The state saw more lynchings go unpunished than any other state. Between 1882 and 1947, Mississippi led the country in lynchings, with 577. And as the black bodies were hanged, burned, and fished from Mississippi lakes, rivers, and streams, the state's coroner system never saw a thing.

In 1931, a Poplarville mob removed Harold "Doc" Jackson from a jail, tied a rope around his neck, and left him hanging from a bridge. The coroner's jury was unable to distinguish if Jackson's fall from a bridge with a rope tied around his neck was accidental or coerced. In 1934, a mob of white neighbors in Lawrence County hunted down black farmer R. J. Tyrone, who they'd decided was "too prosperous" at a time when white farmers were suffering. According to press accounts, the mob then shotgunned him to death. The county coroner ruled Tyrone's death a suicide, and some sources still claim that the case is unsolved. The following year in DeSoto County, a black man was found in a gully with a rope around his neck, his body riddled with bullets. The county coroner called that a suicide, too.

But it wasn't just about covering up racist violence. The same culture that used racial violence to keep blacks in their place also put little value on black lives in general. When black people killed other black people, the coroner often didn't even bother with an inquest. It was less hassle and required fewer resources to simply decide that the death was an accident, a suicide, or from natural causes. A Jackson *Clarion-Ledger* crime report from 1904 captures the prevailing attitude: "Mississippi had the usual number of killings during the week just closed," the paper reported. "Aside from the dozen or so reported in the press dispatches, several homicides occurred which the county correspondents did not deem necessary to report to the public or of sufficient importance to be chronicled in the dispatches."

One of the more well-known examples of this indifference to black lives is the death of the legendary bluesman Robert Johnson. In August 1938 Johnson, then twenty-seven, was playing with his band at a barn dance in Greenwood, Mississippi. By most accounts of his last days, Johnson, a notorious lothario, had been seeing a married woman. Her husband was apparently aware of the relationship. A few nights after the dance, Johnson grew violently ill. Within a few hours, he was on the floor, writhing and howling from excruciating pain in his abdomen. He died on August 16. David "Honeyboy" Edwards, Johnson's band mate and one of his closest friends, was with Johnson when he died. Edwards, who died in 2011 at the age of ninety-six, always maintained that Johnson died from drinking poisoned whiskey. By some accounts, the husband of the woman Johnson was seeing had poisoned the bluesman's drink. In other versions, Johnson's lover poisoned his drink herself after learning that he'd been seeing someone else.

The conflicting stories and ongoing mystery surrounding Johnson's death are the product of the fact that it was never properly investigated. Though Johnson was well known among black musicians, particularly in the Delta, he wouldn't achieve mythology status among white music lovers until decades after his death. (According to lore, Johnson and the devil once struck a deal at a crossroads in Clarksdale, Mississippi. The devil gifted Johnson with virtuosity on the guitar; in return, Johnson forfeited his soul.)

If you were a Greenwood, Mississippi, law enforcement official working in August 1938, Robert Johnson was just another black man in Mississippi. Despite the suspicious circumstances surrounding his death, there was never much of an investigation, never an autopsy. Under "cause of death," the Leflore County coroner wrote simply: "no doctor."

Later, an employee with the state's Department of Vital Statistics added in a handwritten note on the back of Johnson's death certificate that the owner of the plantation where Johnson was staying claimed that the singer had syphilis. But that too was never confirmed.

～

As Mississippi moved into the civil rights era, the racial violence intensified. And as the pile of bodies grew throughout the 1950s and 1960s, the coroner system remained a shadowy conspirator in the carnage. Under state law, the coroner had ultimate authority over the scene of a suspicious death until he or his inquest determined that a crime had been committed. The coroner was the first to examine a body while the evidence was still fresh. The coroners thus had the access and ability to undermine or bungle a prosecution from the earliest stages of the investigation. Local prosecutors usually didn't pursue charges in such cases anyway. But as the civil rights era wore on, federal officials increasingly looked to get involved in cases where they had jurisdiction. A savvy coroner could make it very difficult for them to build a case.

To fully understand the story of Kennedy Brewer, Levon Brooks, and many other similar cases, it's important to appreciate the pliability of Mississippi's medicolegal system—how sheriffs, police chiefs, and prosecutors have manipulated it to achieve a particular end. The system was designed this way. Sometimes it solved crimes, but that wasn't necessarily its chief purpose. Instead, its purpose has always been to facilitate law enforcement's desires as reflected by the prevailing status quo. Sometimes that *is* justice. But at other times it's been something quite different.

Over the first half of the twentieth century, it was about letting racial violence go unreckoned. On several occasions in the twenty-first century, it was about trying to rectify the wrongs perpetrated during the civil rights era. Here too, the system sometimes sacrificed fairness and justice in a particular case to achieve that end. By the time the system got to Brooks and Brewer, it was largely about confirming the hunches and suspicions of local police and prosecutors, regardless of whether those hunches were correct.

The common denominator in these cases is the facilitation of those in power, whether in covering up a lynching, finally bringing to trial a civil rights–era murder case, or merely convicting the man police and prosecutors were convinced committed the crime. In this sense, Mississippi's death investigation system rarely failed. Instead, it tended to perform exactly as intended.

～

In 1955 Mississippi's largest newspaper took notice of the state's woeful death investigation system. It was in the *Clarion-Ledger*'s first such report; many others would follow. The article quoted W. N. Ethridge, a justice on the state's supreme court, who remarked that crime had gone up 20 to 25 percent and, along with others, voiced concern that the state's medicolegal system, including its coroner system, was antiquated and ill-equipped to bring killers to justice.

The evolution of the coroner system in Mississippi—or lack thereof—has largely been a microcosm of the same debates, tensions, political barriers, and alignment of forces that have taken place nationally. But in Mississippi (and in other Southern states), the shortcomings have been magnified by poverty and structural racism, the consequences of the system's failures have been more harmful, and the barriers to reform posed by cronyism and good-ol'-boy networks have been harder to clear. Consequently, medicolegal reform in much of the South has lagged behind most of the rest of the country by decades. On many occasions over the last half century or so, newspapers, medical professionals, and advocates for various causes have tried to call attention to the deficiencies in Mississippi's system. Each time the resulting reforms—if there were any at all—were mostly cosmetic.

So the issues outlined by the *Clarion-Ledger* report will sound familiar. Coroners were incompetent. State law at the time required just two qualifications for the job: candidates had to be registered to vote and "must never have denied the existence of a Supreme being."

Like their counterparts in much of the country, Mississippi coroners and the local medical community had an uneasy, often contentious relationship. On those occasions when the coroner was able to find a physician to perform an autopsy, police and prosecutors frequently had unrealistic expectations for autopsy results, and grew frustrated when a doctor couldn't provide the dispositive evidence to clinch a conviction. In describing an early incarnation of what today is referred to as the "*CSI* effect"—the unrealistic expectations some jurors have because of the way forensics is portrayed in pop culture— one forensic pathologist told the paper, "I am afraid the education of many peace officers with regard to pathologists comes from paper-bound detective books wherein the pathologists make amazing and at times absurd deductions from minimal evidence and with lack of any historical background of the case being studied. These examples, even though complimentary, are gross exaggerations of the actual practice of pathology."

Or at least the *competent* practice. Not surprisingly, the state's doctors bristled at such unrealistic expectations and felt professionally insulted when they were overruled by some funeral home director or aspiring politician exercising the power of a position that was low paid and part-time. As the tension mounted, coroners were increasingly determining cause of death without consulting anyone who possessed any actual medical training.

But the *Clarion-Ledger* investigation had little impact. The system simply served too many powerful interests. This would have been true in just about any era. But the timing of that first investigation was particularly problematic. A year earlier, the US Supreme Court had issued its landmark decision in *Brown v. Board of Education*. That decision—and those that followed in federal courts across the South—reaffirmed and enforced the federal judiciary's determination not only to desegregate public schools but to put an end to Jim Crow. Southern states—Mississippi in particular—responded with defiance.

As *Brown* struck at the heart of Jim Crow, the coroner system— flawed as it may have been in protecting public health and safety—was controlled by the white power structure. It was a critical tool for preserving the racial status quo. The central argument in the *Clarion-Ledger* series was that the antiquated coroner system should be replaced with one run by competent physicians—physicians who in theory would be guided by the Hippocratic oath, a professional code of ethics, and a commitment to public health, not to reelection, serving law enforcement, or preserving the social order. In 1956, that high-minded concept never stood a chance. The state had other priorities.

Just before midnight on May 7, 1955, a convertible pulled up next to Reverend George Lee as he motored down Church Street in the small Mississippi Delta town of Belzoni, in Humphreys County. Lee had just caught up on some work at the grocery store he owned, had closed up, and was heading home. The driver of the convertible pulled out a shotgun, aimed it at Lee, and sent two blasts of buckshot into Lee and his car. One swarm of pellets hit Lee in the head, shattering his jawbone and blowing off the lower portion of his face. Lee lost control of his car, which then jumped a curb and slammed into a frame house. He staggered from the wreckage, collapsed, and died before he could be taken to a hospital.

At the time of his death, George Washington Lee was one of the most successful self-made black men in the South. He was born in Edwards, Mississippi, a small town just east of Jackson, to a minister father and sharecropping mother. After graduating high school, Lee moved to New Orleans to work on the shipping docks. Between shifts he took a correspondence course in typesetting, a trade that would later provide a platform for his activism. In the 1930s, he returned to Mississippi to take a job as a minister in Belzoni, a town that would soon see enough civil rights violence to earn the nickname "Bloody Belzoni."

By the late 1940s, Lee was pastor at four Humphreys County churches, owned a grocery store, and ran a printing press. He was the first black man since Reconstruction to register to vote in the county. In the late 1940s, he and Gus Courts, another black grocer in the county, began a campaign to register the county's black voters. By 1953, Lee and Courts had registered more than ninety black Belzonians for the polls. It had been decades since a black resident had voted in any election. In retaliation, the local Citizens' Council—a "main street" offshoot of the Ku Klux Klan—launched bank boycotts against the two men's businesses. Blacks whose names appeared on voter rolls were threatened. Some were evicted from their homes. Many lost their jobs.

Just a few days before his death, Lee received an explicit threat demanding that he remove his name from the county voter rolls. He refused. Lee's wife would later say that just hours before her husband was killed, two white men had come to their home. Though she couldn't hear what they said, the conversation between the men and her husband sounded tense. She later said she believed George Lee knew he was about to be murdered and left the house that night to spare her life.

After Lee's death, Sheriff Ike Shelton and the Humphreys County coroner convened to investigate. The coroner hastily assembled an inquest jury of white men, all members of the local Citizens' Council. The inquest determined that Lee's death was accidental—that all of Lee's injuries were the result of his car slamming into the frame house. Shelton and the coroner announced that there was no need for further investigation or an autopsy.

Unsatisfied, Lee's family hired two black physicians to perform a private autopsy. The doctors found hundreds of pieces of buckshot in Lee's head. When asked to explain the lead in Lee's skull, Sheriff Shelton responded they were likely pieces of fillings from Lee's dental work, which he speculated must have been jarred loose by the impact of the crash. The press played along. Jackson's *Clarion-Ledger* reported Reverend Lee's death under the headline, "Negro Leader Dies in Odd Accident."

After pressure from Lee's family, the NAACP, and the young activist Medgar Evers, US attorney general Herbert Brownell Jr. ordered the FBI to investigate the matter. FBI agents eventually confirmed what was already obvious to Lee's family and the civil rights community: Lee had been murdered. They conducted tests on the metal found in Lee's head and car and confirmed it to be number 3 buckshot.

Shelton had no choice but to concede that Lee's death may not have been an accident. But he still refused to investigate the crime as racial violence. "If Lee was shot," he told local journalists, "it was probably by some jealous nigger. [Lee] was quite a ladies' man." The Humphreys County coroner convened a second inquest. That inquest changed the original determination about Lee's death. The new cause: "hemorrhage and asphyxiation from a wound." The manner: "murder by persons unknown."

By 1956, the FBI had zeroed in on two white suspects, Peck Ray and Joe Watson, both members of the local Citizens' Council. But the Justice Department decided the case wasn't covered under federal civil rights law because the FBI couldn't definitively determine that Lee was killed for his voting rights activism. Instead, FBI agents presented their evidence to Humphreys County district attorney Stanny Sanders. He refused to prosecute. Sanders argued that the evidence just wasn't convincing, and even if it was, he doubted any Humphreys County grand jury would indict. He said he also feared that trying the two white men for the murder of a black activist "could cause a deterioration of racial relations."

The coroner's role in George Lee's death was a powerful demonstration of just how inseparable the office was from local law enforcement. When Sheriff Shelton proclaimed Lee's death an accident, the coroner and his jury affirmed the sheriff's proclamation, despite ample evidence that Lee had been murdered. When the FBI presented overwhelming proof of a homicide, Shelton changed his mind. The coroner and his jury then changed their opinion to match the sheriff's new theory. All the while, the jury itself was selected from the same white supremacist group to which Lee's likely killers belonged. And not surprisingly, the coroner and his jury made little effort to uncover their identities.

By November 1955, the number of registered blacks in Humphreys County dropped to two. Peck Ray and Joe Watson both died free men in the 1970s. No one has ever been tried for George Lee's murder.

Three months after Lee's murder, a fisherman found the bloated, disfigured corpse of Emmett Till in the muddy Tallahatchie River. The fourteen-year-old boy's body had been weighted down with a cotton gin fan that had been tied to his neck with barbed wire.

Today, the general details of Till's murder are well known, and his story is remembered as a touchstone moment in the story of civil rights in America. But less well known is the role the county coroner and Mississippi's death investigation system played in covering for the men who murdered him.

On August 24, 1955, Till and some neighborhood friends visited the Bryant Grocery and Meat Market. Till, from Chicago, was visiting family in and around the town of Money, Mississippi. Till bought some gum and chatted briefly with Carolyn Bryant, the white wife of the store's proprietor. By some accounts, as he and his friends departed, Till allegedly told the woman, "Bye, baby," and waved. By other accounts, he may have "wolf-whistled." According to Bryant, Till grabbed her and made sexually suggestive remarks.

Of course, even if Bryant's worst account of Till's actions had been true, it amounted at most to harassment or minor assault. But by stepping out of his place, by disrespecting a white woman, Till had broken Southern code. Bryant left the store to retrieve a gun from her car. Till and his friends piled into a car and sped off.

Three days later, Bryant's husband, Roy, and his half brother, J. W. Milam, broke into the home where Till was staying and abducted him at gunpoint. They'd later tell *Look* magazine that they beat Till, shot him in the head, and dumped his body in the Tallahatchie River. The fisherman found Till's body four days later, early in the morning of August 31.

What happened next would later help a jury set Till's killers free. Local authorities knew the teen had been missing for days, so once his body was found, both Tallahatchie County Sheriff Clarence Strider and Leflore County Sheriff George Smith had good reason to suspect the corpse was Till's. Law enforcement summoned the boy's uncle, Mose Wright, to the riverside to identify the body. Wright would later testify that as he approached the body, he could immediately tell it was his nephew. He also saw officials remove from Till's hand a ring that had been carved with the initials of Till's father. Strider called an undertaker to pick up Till's body and take it to a funeral home in Greenwood. The undertaker would later find that the ring had been inscribed with the initials "LT." Till's father was named Louis Till. He had been executed in Italy when he was stationed there with the US Army. The ring was included in the personal effects the army returned to his wife, Mamie, in Chicago. She had given it to Emmett.

Initially, local officials appeared to be outraged by Till's murder. In the days immediately following the abduction, witnesses identified Bryant and Milam as the men who took Till from his uncle's home. Sheriff Strider told the *New York Post* that a coroner's inquest had been scheduled, and that once the inquest determined Till was murdered in Tallahatchie County, "we're going to charge those men with murder."

Yet according to the Leflore County justice of the peace, the ensuing death investigation was "not exactly an inquest" but "more of a post-mortem." No one ever requested an autopsy. In fact, Till wouldn't be autopsied until decades later. Local officials made only the sparest effort to preserve the evidence that would confirm that the body was Till's. C. A. Strickland, a twelve-year veteran of the Greenwood, Mississippi, police department's "collision department," used a low-end field camera to take some snapshots of the body as it lay on a table at the Century Burial Funeral Home. The only physician to examine Till's body was a local doctor named Luther Otken. He was not a forensic pathologist and had no training in postmortem examinations. At trial, Otken was asked whether he had examined Till's body. He answered that he was only asked to "view" it. After describing in some detail the body's condition—"badly swollen, badly bloated" and putting off a "terrific" odor—he testified that the body was "in an advanced state of decomposition."

Within hours of the discovery of Till's body, Sheriff Strider made arrangements to have the young boy buried in Mississippi. Till's mother, Mamie Till Bradley, was still in Chicago. By the time she learned that her son's body had been found, his corpse was already headed to the cemetery. She quickly contacted an uncle in the town of Sumner and asked him to put a stop to the burial. When the uncle arrived at the cemetery, they had already dug Till's grave.

The family had Till's body moved to a black-owned funeral home in the town of Tutwiler. (The boarded-up, run-down remains of that funeral home still stand today, along with a sign memorializing the fact that Till's body had been prepared there.) After preparation, the body was shipped from the depot across the street to Chicago by train.

Till's murder sparked anger and outrage all over the country. NAACP chief Roy Wilkins issued a public statement declaring that "the state of Mississippi has decided to maintain white supremacy by murdering black children." The black activist T. R. M Howard declared that there would be "hell to pay." Editorial boards across the country condemned not only the killing but the entire state of Mississippi.

Such blanket condemnations were understandable, and in many ways justified, but they also provoked a defensive reaction. While Bryant and Milam were initially scorned by local white residents, the criticism from outsiders sparked a backlash. Disgust at Till's murder morphed into resentment of Northerners and integrationists. J. J. Breland, a local lawyer and leader of one of the Citizens' Councils, was initially shocked by the killing and declined a request to represent Bryant and Milam. But as the denunciation of Mississippi mounted, he changed his mind. He began to see the case as a front-line battle in the war against integration. "They're peckerwoods," he'd later tell the journalist William Huie, using a crude term for poor, uneducated Southern whites. "But, hell, we've got to have our Milams to fight our wars and keep our niggahs in line. There ain't gonna be no integration. There ain't gonna be no nigger votin'. And the sooner everybody in this country realizes it the better. If any more pressure is put on us, the Tallahatchie won't hold all the niggers that'll be thrown into it."

Led by Sheriff Strider—the same man who had vowed that Till's killers would be brought to justice—local authorities backtracked and began to publicly question what had previously been a slam-dunk murder prosecution. Strider and the local coroner had locked Till's coffin with the seal of the state of Mississippi and made Till's uncle sign a form promising never to open it. Mamie Till Bradley broke that promise. When she opened the coffin, she discovered that her son's body had been packed with lime, a chemical commonly thought at the time to hasten the process of decomposition. It was a clue of what was to come: local authorities were preparing a defense for Till's killers.

Outraged not only at her son's murder but at the way his body had been handled, Mamie Till Bradley followed the lead of George Lee's widow and insisted on an open-casket funeral. Photos of Emmett Till's corpse ran in *Jet* magazine, sparking more national outrage.

On the day of the funeral, Strider gave Till's killers a gift. He publicly claimed he was never certain that the body recovered from the river was Till's. It was a baffling thing to say. Strider was the official who released the body to Till's family. If he had doubts about the identity of the corpse, he not only may have sent Till's relatives the wrong body, but he would have likely prevented the investigation of a separate murder.

But Strider's comments achieved their intended effect. They set off a host of conspiracy theories, including claims that Till had never been killed at all, but had been secretly sent back to Chicago or was being hidden by his family—all part of a vast conspiracy among Northern agitators to force integration on Mississippi. The local white residents who initially shunned Bryant and Milam later raised over $10,000 for the two men's defense—about $90,000 today.

The trial began on September 19, twenty-two days after the murder. The state's failure to perform an autopsy was a critical part of the defense. Breland seized on that fact, using it to argue to the jury the theory that Sheriff Strider had already advanced in public—that the body recovered from the river was someone other than Emmett Till.

The only doctor to look at Till's body played along. "From the condition that you saw the body in, in your opinion, could anybody have identified any particular person as being that body?" Breland asked Dr. Otken.

"I don't think you could," he responded.

"Now suppose it had been another person's brother, could he have identified it in your opinion?"

"I doubt it."

"Or if it had been a person's son, could a mother have identified that body, in your opinion?"

"I doubt it."

Breland continued to press. "Doctor, from your experience and study and your familiarity with the medical authorities, what, in your opinion, had been the length of time that the body had been dead, if it had been in the open air?"

"I would say eight to ten days." Till had only been missing for three. The defense also argued that the state's strongest piece of physical evidence—the ring—could have been planted. After instilling in the all-white, all-male jury sufficient doubt about Till's body, Breland closed with an appeal to racial solidarity. "I'm sure that every last Anglo-Saxon one of you has the courage to free these men in the face of that [outside] pressure," he said.

And they did. The jury took just a little over an hour to acquit. One juror later reportedly said, "If we hadn't stopped to drink pop, it wouldn't have taken that long."

The following year, safe from state prosecution by the Constitution's prohibition on double jeopardy, Bryant and Milam admitted to killing Emmett Till in an interview with *Look* magazine. They were paid $4,000 for their story.

On June 1, 2005, fifty years after Emmett Till was first pulled from the Tallahatchie, he was exhumed from his grave in Chicago. Surrounded by squad cars, Till's body was taken to the office of the

Cook County, Illinois, medical examiner. The remains were in nearly pristine condition, protected over the years by a glass partition that had been put into place after his mother's demand for an open-casket funeral. The following day, his body was autopsied for the first time. Doctors also conducted a CT scan. The results of the scan showed metal fragments inside Till's cranium, indicating that the boy had been shot. DNA testing then confirmed what had been obvious from the beginning—this was the body of Emmett Till. In 2017, more than sixty years after the fact, Carolyn Bryant told historian Timothy B. Tyson that her account of the precipitating incident—that Till had grabbed her and made crude remarks to her—was not true.

Again and again, black Mississippians disappeared, were abducted and never again seen alive, were murdered in the dead of night, or were struck down in broad daylight. And again and again, the state's compromised death investigation system responded with a cascade of failures—or didn't respond at all. Between 1956 and 1959 alone, at least ten black men were killed by white men in Mississippi in racially motivated attacks. None resulted in a conviction. In other cases, while racism was the likely motivation, it's difficult to say for certain because the local coroner didn't bother to investigate. And those are merely the deaths that were in some way recorded.

Coroner obstruction also played a large but often overlooked role in what is probably the most notorious crime in Mississippi history— the June 1964 murder of civil rights activists James Chaney, Andrew Goodman, and Michael Schwerner. It's one of the most infamous and well-documented incidents of the civil rights era. National anger over the killings moved Congress to pass the Civil Rights Act of 1964 and the Voting Rights Act the following year. The subsequent FBI investigation into the murders is the subject of the 1988 movie *Mississippi Burning*, a 1990 television movie, and a Norman Rockwell painting. But few of the popular depictions of the crime and subsequent investigation have addressed the way the state's death investigation system ran interference for the mob that carried out the murders.

The story begins in the years leading up to the famous killings with several other suspicious beatings and deaths. All of the victims were black, and all involved the same Neshoba County sheriff's deputies later implicated in the Freedom Summer killings. The first incident occurred in October 1959, when Officers Lawrence Rainey and Richard Willis shot and killed twenty-seven-year-old Luther Jackson on the side of the road. After shooting Jackson, Rainey radioed the sheriff's department for help. "Come on down here," he said. "I think I have killed a nigger." Despite two witnesses who said Jackson did nothing to provoke the shooting, the Neshoba County coroner quickly ruled the shooting a justifiable homicide. Three years later, Rainey and Neshoba County Sheriff Ethel "Hop" Barnett shot and killed twenty-seven-year-old Otis Nash as they transported him to a mental institution. The deputies claimed Nash tried to grab a gun from the glove compartment of the squad car, even though he was handcuffed in the back seat at the time. The coroner again ruled the killing a justifiable homicide.

By that time, Rainey had also been accused of harassing and assaulting other black people in Neshoba County, including an allegation he had stripped a black man naked and whipped him with a belt. Yet even as he terrorized the local black population, the white residents of Neshoba County knew Lawrence Rainey for his Stetson hat, his cowboy boots, and his gregarious nature. In 1963 he got a promotion: he was elected sheriff after running on thinly veiled campaign promises to crack heads in the civil rights movement.

In January 1964, Michael Schwerner of the Council of Federated Organizations, a conglomerate of civil rights groups, and his wife, Rita, packed up for Meridian, Mississippi. The young couple planned to set up a community center and a library, and to run a Freedom School to teach black residents how to pass the literacy tests that Mississippi required to vote. A talented organizer, Schwerner quickly had the project up and running. He was so effective that within just a few months of setting up shop, he was already well known to area law enforcement and Klansmen (who were often one and the same). They called him "Goatee." By the spring, Schwerner's abilities had earned him the notice of local KKK leader Sam Bowers, who hatched a plan to have him murdered.

The Meridian school had just started operating when Schwerner began plans to open another Freedom School and was scoping nearby Neshoba County for possible sites. He chose the Mount Zion Methodist Church in the black community of Longdale. Word of the plan got back to Rainey, who then put the church under surveillance. The following June, a group of Klansmen raided Mount Zion. They severely beat several parishioners, then burned the church to the ground.

Schwerner and Chaney were in Ohio at the time to train Freedom Summer volunteers, and had met up with Goodman while they were there. On the morning of June 20, the three men and another activist headed back to Mississippi to check on their friends at the church and to investigate the fire. The following afternoon, Schwerner, Chaney, and Goodman left the Meridian office for Longdale. Schwerner told his fellow activists to come looking for them if they hadn't returned by four p.m. They never came back.

The men were heading home when they got a flat tire just outside of the town of Philadelphia. Deputy Cecil Price, who had been following them, turned on his cruiser's lights and pulled up behind them. He arrested Chaney for speeding and held Schwerner and Goodman for "investigation." All three were taken to the Neshoba County jail.

The men were released around ten p.m., but Price had already tipped off his fellow Klansmen that he had detained them, and about their likely route back. As they made their way back to Meridian, they were pulled over again. This time they were met by a mob of Klansmen. The mob took them at gunpoint to a rural intersection about ten miles south of Philadelphia and shot them to death. According to witness accounts, Klansman Wayne Roberts shot Schwerner and Goodman in the chest. Chaney was beaten and most likely tortured before he was also shot and killed.

The bodies were transported to a nearby farm where one of the conspirators, a heavy machinery operator, was waiting with a bulldozer. The corpses were buried in an earthen dam. Someone then took the station wagon they were driving to the Choctaw Indian reservation, abandoned it on the side of the road, and set it aflame.

When the three activists first went missing, state and local officials echoed the claims made after Emmett Till's murder nearly ten years earlier—that it was all a hoax to slander Mississippi. For the rest of the month and into July, investigators combed nearby woods, fields, and swamps. Incredibly, while looking for the three activists, law enforcement officials found the remains of eight other black men. Two were identified as Henry Dee and Charles Moore, college students who had been kidnapped, beaten, and murdered near Natchez the previous spring. Another, found on September 10, was identified as Hubert Orsby, a fourteen-year-old boy found floating in the Big Black River near Canton, Mississippi. Orsby was wearing a T-shirt with the logo of a civil rights organization when his body was recovered. A coroner's jury ruled his death an accidental drowning.

Federal investigators finally found the bodies they were looking for on August 4, 1964, after acting on an anonymous tip. Under Mississippi law, the Neshoba County coroner should have been in charge of the investigation. But there was concern among federal officials that local authorities might tank the investigation. Eventually, all parties agreed to send the bodies to the University of Mississippi Medical Center in Jackson.

The suspicions about local authorities turned out to be well founded. The victims' families and the FBI had both requested that doctors from the Medical Committee for Human Rights (MCHR) be present to monitor the autopsies. The director of the Mississippi Medical Center also agreed to the monitoring. But when two doctors from the organization showed up at the hospital on the day of the autopsies, they were turned away by officers from the Mississippi Highway Patrol.

The Neshoba County coroner assigned the autopsies to William Featherstone, a pathologist in Jackson. Featherstone was not a forensic pathologist but a clinical pathologist, trained to perform autopsies to determine deaths from disease, not from homicide. What he missed would prove critical to later attempts to hold the perpetrators accountable.

Featherstone concluded that the three activists had been shot but had not been beaten or tortured. The victims' families were suspicious and wanted a second opinion. One of the MCRH doctors then called New York medical examiner David Spain and asked him to perform a second autopsy. Spain was vacationing in Martha's Vineyard at the time, but readily agreed. He hopped the next plane to Birmingham, then drove to Jackson from the Birmingham airport.

Mississippi officials did all they could to prevent Spain from conducting his own examination. They first created a maze of bureaucratic hurdles for the families of the victims. They insisted that Spain could only do the autopsies if the families appeared in person to give permission. When Schwerner's family tried to grant permission over the phone, state officials refused to honor it. Goodman's body had already been sent to his family in New York. That left James Chaney's mother, Fannie Lee, a black woman from the town of Meridian. Despite a barrage of threats, harassment, and intimidation, she agreed to let Spain examine her son's remains. Three weeks later, her home was firebombed.

Spain, too, was harassed from the moment he entered the state. Reports from the Mississippi State Sovereignty Commission released decades later show that state officials tracked Spain's arrival in the state, and presumably tipped off Klansmen and their allies as to his whereabouts and lodging.

Until they could clear all the legal hurdles to permit the autopsy, civil rights groups stationed guards at the doors of the morgue to prevent the theft of Chaney's body. When Spain eventually completed his autopsy, his report was dramatically different from Featherstone's. Spain found that Chaney's jaw had been shattered, his shoulder crushed, and several other bones obliterated. "In my extensive experience of twenty-five years as a pathologist and as a medical examiner," he wrote, "I have never seen bones so severely shattered, except in tremendously high speed accidents, such as airplane crashes." He later told the United Press International, "These injuries could only be the result of an extremely severe beating with a blunt instrument or a chain."

At trial, Featherstone blamed Chaney's injuries on the heavy equipment the FBI used to excavate the bodies. But in 2000, *Clarion-Ledger* reporter Jerry Mitchell obtained access to the full autopsies, along with reports from the Sovereignty Commission. Mitchell also interviewed FBI agent Joseph Sullivan, who was at the scene of the excavation. Sullivan disputed the claim that bulldozers had caused the trauma to Chaney's body. "Some of the digging was actually done by hand," he said. "And I'm not talking about shovels. I'm talking about hands." Based on those reports and his interviews, Mitchell concluded that Chaney had probably broken away from the mob and attempted to flee, an act of self-preservation that likely earned him a thorough beating before he was finally shot. The Sovereignty Commission report also indicated that instead of just one, several people shot at Chaney, and that he was likely struck by bullets fired by more than one gun. But Spain was never able to determine either the number of projectiles that struck Chaney nor their trajectory. By the time he had access to the body, the internal organs had been removed and hadn't been replaced.

When Featherstone heard that Spain had done a second autopsy, he was furious. With the assistance of the State Sovereignty Commission, he filed an ethics complaint with the College of American Pathologists. It isn't clear what ever came of that complaint, but second-opinion autopsies were neither uncommon nor unethical at the time (nor are they now). Featherstone and Mississippi officials claimed that in spite of Chaney's family's request, Spain still needed Featherstone's permission before conducting a second autopsy. That was nonsense. To require the original doctor to give permission for a second opinion would defeat the very purpose of seeking a second opinion.

A few months after the activists' bodies were found, the Neshoba County coroner convened an inquest into their deaths. The inquest jury decided that the cause of the men's deaths couldn't be determined. Therefore, they couldn't recommend that the district attorney move ahead with an investigation or indictment. The men who murdered the activists wouldn't be charged with any crime under Mississippi law. They were later tried in federal court. Most were acquitted. Among the handful who were convicted, none served more than twelve years in prison.

Soon after the inquest closed, the widow of Michael Schwerner received her husband's official Mississippi death certificate in the mail. Under cause of death, the coroner wrote "unknown."

~ 5 ~

SETTING THE STAGE FOR
THE CADAVER KING

We just cut her tits off. She won't be coming here
trying to tell us what to do anymore.

—Former Mississippi state senator Robert
Crook, referring to Faye Spruill, Mississippi's
first state medical examiner

By the mid-1960s, crime was on the rise in Mississippi, as it was in much of the rest of the country. By the end of the decade, political polling would show that crime was Americans' primary concern. In his 1968 presidential campaign, Richard Nixon leveraged fear of crime (or to be more accurate, white fear of black crime) by tying the crime rate to liberal permissiveness. Of particular importance to Mississippi, the Republican Party would exploit crime as a political issue for a generation as part of an enormously successful long-term strategy to turn the South into a permanent party stronghold.

In 1966, a report by Richard Childs's National Municipal League named Mississippi one of the "Best States for a Murder." Childs, an outspoken advocate for medicolegal reform, was right about the need for change, but the way he framed the issue was unfortunate. Most states weren't ready for such drastic institutional changes to their coroner systems. Instead, they tended to react to reports like Childs's with laws that broadened the powers of police and prosecutors, funded more prisons, and expanded the scope of the death penalty. For states with medicolegal systems that acted as little more than a rubber stamp for police and prosecutors, Childs's framing ended up exacerbating the situation.

Mississippi's laws were especially antiquated. For all intents and purposes, the state was still using the system that had been instituted during Reconstruction. Some components of the coroner laws dated back to the late 1700s, when Mississippi was still a territory. The most critical problem was the same as it had always been: authority over death investigations was given almost exclusively to lay coroners.

Though advocates continued to pressure the state government to replace the coroner system with a medical examiner system, they found little success. The state legislature had no interest. But rising crime, or at least the rise of crimes against white people, was a different story. So in 1961 the legislature later considered a bill that would have put physicians in charge of death investigations, expanded their investigatory powers, and scrapped the requirement that coroners convene juries to investigate suspicious deaths.

But a key provision made the proposed changes next to useless: they would only take effect in counties that had elected a physician to the coroner's office. If the coroner wasn't a doctor, the old system would remain in place. At the time, just four of Mississippi's eighty-two county coroners were physicians. Another twenty-three counties hadn't elected a coroner at all. In Hinds County, seat of the state capitol and the most populous in the state, the current coroner was a used-car salesman who ran because he wanted to get into politics. "You've got to start somewhere," he explained to the *Clarion-Ledger*. "I could see where I could win the election with very little effort."

Doctors still had the same uneasy relationship with coroners that they'd had for decades. They weren't paid for their time, the criminal justice system undervalued and underappreciated medical expertise, and most doctors didn't have specialized training in forensic pathology. Save for perhaps an interest in public service, it wasn't at all clear why they'd want to campaign for a part-time, low-paid office that came with significant additional responsibility.

In the state's entire history, only one pathologist had ever been elected coroner in any county. That pathologist, Dr. Lee Scanlon of Natchez, had recently reviewed the coroner system for an article in the *Journal of Medicine of the Mississippi State Medical Association*. In his article, Scanlon pointed out that at the time, coroners were paid $20 for each death they responded to in their county. They were required to be on call twenty-four hours per day in order to respond quickly— whether it was to claim a new body, or to round up some stray sheep.

But for a funeral home owner what the post lacked in salary could in certain circumstances be supplemented with other money-making opportunities. The position had come to be dominated by the owners of funeral homes. The funeral home owners collected fees for transporting bodies, fees that were likely more lucrative than what they were paid to conduct investigations. Potentially more profitable still, the position gave them the opportunity to solicit the family of the deceased for embalming and funeral services. Scanlon found all of this to be ample evidence that the system was a corrupt and broken anachronism.

History indicates that Scanlon's article was mostly ignored. Several years later, the press was back on the story, this time after a death in the town of McComb once again highlighted the need for improvements. When a man was found dead and fully clothed in his backyard, the Pike County coroner convened a jury to investigate. The coroner's jury gave the body a once-over and quickly concluded that the man had died of a heart attack. It wasn't until later, when an undertaker took off the man's shirt, that someone noticed the bullet hole in his chest. His killer was never identified.

Mississippi did finally pass a medical examiner law six years later, in 1974, but that law was also fraught with problems. It created a state medical examiner position that could conduct the occasional autopsy but was primarily tasked with overseeing autopsies assigned by coroners. More problematic, the position was to be appointed by the dean of the University of Mississippi Medical Center. The unusual arrangement may at first have seemed to be a welcome move toward professionalization by keeping the office away from the auspices of police or prosecutors. But the more likely motivation was money. If lawmakers could put the state medical examiner under the authority of the state university, they wouldn't need to fund the position directly.

Shortly after the law passed, Dr. Joseph C. Hupp, the medical examiner in Corpus Christi, Texas, addressed Mississippi state law enforcement officials and explained why a trained medical examiner was critical to ensuring adequate death investigations. Hupp praised the bones of the new law but warned that without sufficient appropriation, it would become an unfunded mandate. He pointed to West Virginia as an example. That state's legislature had created a state medical examiner's office but then refused to fund it, leaving the position vacant for twenty years.

Hupp's warning proved prescient. Mississippi's new office remained vacant for five years. The state legislature never bothered to appropriate adequate funding. Because the University of Mississippi Medical Center was ambivalent about hosting and administrating the office in the first place, it never seriously lobbied for an appropriation.

Edgar Little was elected coroner of Harrison County, Mississippi, in 1975. Upon taking office, he couldn't believe what passed for a system of death investigation in the state. Little told the *Clarion-Ledger* he had found that in some Mississippi counties, the coroners were functionally illiterate. "I've got letters in my files where they put their 'X' at the bottom," he said. The paper reported—once again—that many coroners looked at the position as little more than a chance for some supplemental income. Some had full-time jobs pumping gas. One cleaned septic tanks. Alarmed, Little formed the Mississippi Coroners Association, which he hoped would provide a platform for modernizing the office. It helped, at least for a while. But it would also become a major impediment to reform.

In 1979, the Mississippi legislature finally set aside some money to hire a state medical examiner. It wasn't much. At the time there were only 150 certified forensic pathologists in the entire country. Most worked at modern offices in large cities and earned respectable salaries. It would be difficult to lure one of those 150 medical examiners to Mississippi for substantially less pay and to head up an office that would face staunch opposition from an entrenched system of coroners and their allies.

But Faye Spruill was up for the challenge. A fiery, often combative medical examiner, she had previously worked in Kentucky and in the modern medical examiner's office in Dallas. She had also overseen the conversion of the St. Louis coroner system into one run by a medical examiner. Mississippi governor Cliff Finch offered Spruill the job in 1979. She accepted, becoming one of the first women in the country to be named an official state medical examiner.

But Mississippi's hiring a woman as its first official state medical examiner was less about shattering a glass ceiling and more a matter of Spruill being one of only a few willing and qualified to take the job. From Spruill's perspective, it was an opportunity to obtain a promotion in title, if not necessarily in salary, and to hold a position few other women were likely to get. At the time she accepted the job, she was the only certified forensic pathologist in Mississippi, man or woman.

Spruill immediately began to agitate for change. Echoing Richard Childs's rhetoric, she told anyone who would listen that "our problem is that you can come into Mississippi and commit murder—and get away with it." She found an ally in Edgar Little and his new state coroners' association. The two managed to attract some attention. They proclaimed that the coroner system was a "ludicrous joke." They peppered their points with colorful anecdotes—about the coroner, for example, who had recently been caught mining names off of tombstones, then filling out fake death certificates to collect the $20 fee.

Some of the state's media outlets joined the cause. Columnist James Dickerson wrote in the *Jackson Daily News*, referring to county coroners, "Year after year, Mississippi voters have elected men and women to the office, whom, if the truth were to be known, they probably would not have allowed into their homes." In a staff editorial published in March 1980, the same paper warned that because the coroner was the only public official with the power to arrest the sheriff, the state's more corruptible sheriffs had been "buying off" or even threatening coroners to ward off any possibility of an investigation.

As for autopsies, the state had evolved an ad hoc system whereby some county coroners, frequently with input from the district attorney, sheriff, or police chief, would send bodies to a private doctor for autopsy. Few if any of these physicians were trained or certified as forensic pathologists. This was the procedure that had been in place basically since Reconstruction and that would more or less endure until the late 2000s.

By the early 1980s, there were at least a few states that could be considered models for modernizing death investigations. In Maryland, each county had its own medical examiner (except for the city of Baltimore, which had four), and each was nominated by local physicians and confirmed by a committee of police officials, state and local public health departments, and the medical profession. Maryland had long boasted the first statewide medical examiner system in the country, established in 1939. For much of its early history it was severely underfunded or not funded at all, but by the 1980s it had become a model for the country.

Florida had also moved to a medical examiner system, but a less centralized model than Maryland's. Under a law passed in 1970, Florida used a committee of law enforcement officials, attorneys, physicians, and funeral directors to appoint a "deputy medical examiner" for each of several regional districts.

Maryland and Florida stood as examples of how to modernize in ways uniquely suited to distinct demographics, geography, and political structure. Florida—a more geographically, demographically, and politically diverse state than Maryland—allowed for more local control. Maryland, a much smaller state, sent most of its autopsies to its largest city, which was well equipped for the task. Most importantly, in both states autopsies were performed by qualified forensic pathologists appointed by professionally diverse committees, which kept them comparatively insulated from political pressure and corrupting influences.

Back in Mississippi, Spruill sought a mixture of the two systems. The state was too large in geographic area to send all of the bodies to the medical examiner's office in Jackson. But many of the state's counties were too poor and too sparsely populated to hire and occupy a full-time medical examiner. Spruill proposed breaking up the state into regions of roughly equal population, each with its own medical examiner and forensic pathologist. In 1980 the state legislature considered a bill adopting Spruill's proposals, but the bill failed.

In early 1981, Spruill tried again with a three-tiered system. Her office would be positioned at the top, with oversight responsibility for all state death investigations. Immediately beneath would be three regional districts, each headed by a certified forensic pathologist. But the coroners would still oversee death investigations at the county level and decide when an autopsy was needed. The proposal reflected some political realities, as well as the lessons Spruill had learned from her earlier, failed attempt at reform. She hoped that with trained medical examiners looking over their shoulders, the coroners would take their jobs more seriously.

The new proposal was supported by the state's medical professionals and public health advocates. But there was still formidable opposition. Many coroners were opposed, as was the state's insurance industry. Law enforcement was a mixed bag. While the most prominent prosecutors and police officials supported the idea as a way to help solve murders, some opposed it from behind the scenes. The most likely reason: while the current system wasn't great at solving murders, it was also pretty bad at discovering them. A system run by qualified doctors insulated from political pressure might help solve some homicides, but it would also likely cause a *rise* in reported murders. That could open the local sheriff or prosecutor up to criticism. The current system was a compromise many of them could live with.

Some data uncovered by the *Clarion-Ledger* supported the reformers' cause. In 1977, the most recent year for which state data was available, *nearly half* of reported deaths in the state were attributed to "unknown causes." This meant that each year between one thousand and five thousand suspicious deaths in the state weren't being investigated. Failure to find a cause of death also meant that the state was unable to compile and study statistics on accidents, disease, industrial poisoning, and other matters of public health. As of early 1981, a majority of the state's coroners were funeral directors. All but two worked part-time. Three were doctors, and none were forensic pathologists. Four Mississippi counties had no coroner at all.

Hinds County, the state's most populous, was a good example of the problem. The coroner there was Robert Martin, a former mortician elected in 1979. In his first year on the job, Martin single-handedly oversaw 552 death investigations. Even in the state's wealthiest, most populous county, one man with no medical training or experience in law enforcement was in charge of investigating all suspicious deaths—about 1.5 per day. He told the paper that he handled those investigations with no office, no desk, and no expense account.

In February 1981, a grisly crime brought more support for reformers. Two adolescent girls were found murdered in a field in Lawrence County. Under state law, Spruill couldn't aid in the investigation unless officially requested. No one asked. As days passed and the murders remained unsolved, the case brought new scrutiny to the coroner system. Within weeks the legislature passed Spruill's proposal into law.

Unfortunately for Spruill, persuading lawmakers to approve a new system was a far cry from persuading them to fund it. Here, Spruill faced continued resistance. Legislators balked at giving Spruill any money at all, claiming they couldn't fund a new program while existing agencies were being asked to slash their budgets. By the end of the session, the legislature had refused to appropriate any funds *at all* for the new death investigation system it had just approved.

In 1982, Spruill pled her case to the Senate Appropriations Committee. She highlighted the virtues of a modern medical examiner system, from solving murders to monitoring public health. But her exchanges with committee members grew contentious. Previously, she had clashed on several occasions with state senator Robert Crook, one of the state's more powerful lawmakers.

Crook had been around a long time, long enough to have defeated civil rights icon Fannie Lou Hamer when she ran for the seat in 1971 and to have worked closely with former sheriff and state senator Henry Strider. Strider was sheriff of Tallahatchie County during the Emmett Till murder and trial. He'd made a name for himself in the national media by walking into court each morning during the Till trial and greeting members of the black press the same way each day: "Hello, niggers." In 1966, in response to a tough agricultural market, Crook and Strider cosponsored a bill that would have relocated black farmers from Mississippi to other states in order to free up jobs for white farmers.

This was the man Spruill kept butting up against, the main opposition to her plan. Spruill threatened to resign unless she got the funding she needed to both do her job properly and implement the new system the legislature had already approved. Dr. Lloyd White, who himself would be appointed Mississippi state medical examiner several years later, attended the hearing. He and Crook weren't friends but did have a cordial professional relationship. According to White, Crook approached him after the hearing to vent about Spruill. He seemed enraged that she had taken such a tone with the esteemed appropriations committee—and he seemed particularly offended to have been challenged by a woman. "Well, I'll tell you what we did," Crook told White. "We just cut her tits off. She won't be coming here trying to tell us what to do anymore."

Crook made good on his vow. He wasn't about to let a woman push him around. By the summer of 1982, not only had the legislature still not funded the new system, it had cut off *all* funding to Spruill's office, including her salary. Calls to Spruill's state office phone reached a recording indicating that the number had been disconnected.

Though she had no office, staff, phone, or salary, Spruill was still the state medical examiner. She continued her oversight of the coroners and continued lobbying for funding to restore her office and implement her reforms. Incredibly, she stayed on the job for another thirteen months with no pay. She finally resigned in July 1983, after the state legislature once again refused to fund her office. Asked for comment on Spruill's resignation, state officials said they were "surprised and shocked," despite the fact that she had worked for more than a year without a paycheck or a phone.

Within weeks of Spruill's resignation, the state had returned to the status quo. Law enforcement officials complained that they had to go out of state to find competent forensic pathologists. Clinical pathologists wanted no part of conducting autopsies or testifying in murder cases. Coroners remained untrained, underpaid, and incapable of leading a modern death investigation. And state media went back to describing Mississippi as a sanctuary for murderers. At the time of Spruill's resignation, eleven of the state's eighty-two coroners still couldn't read or write.

The following year, the state legislature passed a bill that placed the medical examiner's office under the authority of the state crime lab, which itself worked under the Department of Public Safety (DPS). The department would have to fund the position from its existing budget. DPS scraped together $150,000. It wasn't nearly enough to fund what the state needed—a qualified forensic pathologist, an assistant or two, and an operational office. But it was something. And it was desperately needed. A study of Mississippi death investigations from 1981 through 1984 showed staggeringly high rates of deaths classified as "undetermined causes." In DeSoto County, for example, the rate was 53 percent. In Benton County, it was 70 percent. The average across the country is around 3 percent.

In spite of all these challenges, in April 1985 Mississippi hired its second state medical examiner. Dr. Thomas Bennett—young, earnest, and mustachioed—had been the state medical examiner in Iowa. His salary would be $67,000, modest for the position. And Bennett began with an office budget of $147,000—a fraction of what well-funded medical examiner offices in other states were allocated.

Still, Mississippi state officials greeted Bennett with a bacchanal of self-congratulation. Police chiefs, prosecutors, and various heads of agencies threw a party when he arrived. Bennett, they declared, was walking, talking evidence that Mississippi was finally upgrading its death investigation system. The elation over such a modest step— filling an office that had been vacant for seven and a half of the nine years it had existed—bordered on parody. Commissioner of Public Safety James Roberts proclaimed, "The potential murderers in Mississippi have been sent a message!"

And yet odd as it was, Bennett's warm Mississippi greeting lasted only a matter of hours. The state of Iowa, where Bennett had just come from, had eliminated the office of coroner in 1959. So Mississippi's

coroners viewed Bennett's hiring as a direct threat to their continued existence. At a luncheon with coroners later that day, the *Clarion-
Ledger* reported that Bennett was greeted with cold stares and blunt
talk. Lincoln County coroner Morris Henderson warned Bennett that
every death investigation must go through him, and him only. He told
the new hire that he was to have no communication with anyone else
in the county. "If I hear you told the sheriff anything, that's it." Another coroner was blunter still. "We're going to be hard on you," he
said.

Despite the uncomfortable welcome, once they were sure he
wasn't going to eliminate the office, the coroners' association—now
headed by Hinds County coroner Robert Martin—warmed to Bennett, at least initially. Martin and Bennett first worked together to persuade the legislature to pass the Mississippi Coroner Reorganization
Act of 1986, the first major change to the state's coroner law in nearly
a century. Under the new law, the state medical examiner would determine who could conduct autopsies in the state, or if necessary, perform some autopsies himself. The law also changed the requirements
to run for coroner. It bumped the coroner's pay from $20 per death
investigation to $50, and did away with the requirement to round up
stray livestock and the requirement that coroners believe in a supreme
being. Finally, the law required that the state medical examiner be
board certified in forensic pathology. That's a pretty standard requirement for medical examiners across the country, but it would become
the source of a lot of controversy in Mississippi.

The law was an improvement, but still left a lot of problems. It
lacked teeth, and in the years since, many of the requirements haven't
been well enforced. And in not doing away with the office of coroner
entirely, the law in some ways reestablished the state's commitment
to coroner-led death investigations. At least one of the state's coroners understood the problem. When the *Clarion-Ledger* asked Marion
County coroner Ed Laird what he made of the new law, he replied,
"Do you think one week's training is going to make a medical examiner out of anybody?"

If Bennett's hiring initially drew the ire of the state's coroners,
his work with Martin on the new law divided them. At one time, the
Mississippi State Coroners Association represented over 60 percent
of the county coroners. By the end of 1986, the relatively progressive group only represented about a third. Many of the coroners who

hadn't joined didn't meet the new requirements (although they would still be grandfathered in) and resented the implication that the office needed modernization. They also resented the notion that they needed oversight. Some told Bennett to stay in Jackson rather than visit their crime scenes personally. They didn't want him looking over their shoulders. Some also fought his attempts to assert his authority when he disagreed with how they were handling an investigation, or went around him when they didn't like his diagnosis.

As Bennett settled into office, he began to see firsthand just how bad the system could be. Even the coroners who had supported him could show astonishingly bad judgment. In 1986, Bennett clashed with Martin over the death of a seventeen-year-old girl. Bennett concluded from his autopsy that while he couldn't rule out death by strangulation, he also couldn't say for sure that it was the manner of her death. It was the sort of careful, nuanced diagnosis that science sometimes demands, but that police and prosecutors find unhelpful. Martin and the local sheriff wanted more, so they took the body to a doctor Martin had used for autopsies in the past—a psychiatrist who had a medical degree but wasn't board certified in forensic pathology. The three men then drove the body to a country road where the doctor performed a bizarre roadside autopsy. According to press reports, after a procedure lasting less than an hour, the doctor told Martin that the woman had definitely been strangled.

The same year, Bennett got into another public fight with coroner Ed Laird after Laird delivered a severed head to Bennett's office. When Bennett asked for an explanation, an investigator in the local DA's office said that he and Laird had decided the body to which the head had once been attached was too smelly and infested with bugs for examination. So Laird simply pulled out a knife and sawed off the head. According to Bennett, Laird had confirmed the story to him over the phone. Appalled, Bennett moved to strip Laird of his position. Publicly, Laird denied the charge and claimed the head had fallen off on its own.

In a well-staffed, well-equipped office, Bennett might have engaged those and other fights, and more firmly established his office's authority under state law. But there just wasn't time for it. He had more than he could handle trying to keep up with the coroners who were cooperating with him. Four months into the job, he was putting in eighty-hour work weeks and had personally performed 104 autopsies. That's a rate of 312 per year. Lamar Burrows, president of the

Mississippi Pathologists Association, remarked in the *Clarion-Ledger*, "That's just about more than any one person can handle." Burrows's comment is notable: within a decade the state would have a medical examiner performing six times that figure.

But Bennett's pace had begun wearing him down after just four months, and he hadn't even yet begun regularly testifying in court, a time-consuming task that required preparation, travel, and waiting around to be called to the witness stand. Moreover, he was forced to perform his autopsies at the University of Mississippi Medical Center, a facility that wasn't equipped for forensic pathology. He was also working with a state crime lab that was frequently backlogged, forcing him to wait on test results before delivering his reports to coroners, prosecutors, and the families of the deceased. Though it was through no fault of his own, that created more tension between him and county officials.

By June 1986, Bennett had not only pushed through the first major reform of the state's coroner system in a century but also reduced the state's percentage of deaths with "unknown causes" from 46 percent to just 2 percent. But he was also frustrated and burned out. He was short staffed, worked untenable hours, and wasn't getting much support from the DPS.

At the end of September 1986, Bennett finally resigned. "I cannot shoulder the burden anymore. I'm just fried," he told the *Clarion-Ledger*. One of the state's more reform-minded coroners worried that Bennett would be impossible to replace. "It would surprise me if they find somebody to come in under the same conditions," said Harrison County coroner Steve Delahousey. "Mississippi doesn't have a very good track record with medical examiners." As Bennett left, the same state officials who had warmly welcomed him a year and a half earlier took potshots at him, accusing him of jumping ship.

When the position remained vacant a month later, DPS commissioner James Roberts played down the importance of having a state medical examiner at all. "I'm not aware of any problem," he said. "Most district attorneys and people who have the need to have autopsies are able to get them. So the system will continue to function."

But most local officials had returned to using clinical or anatomical pathologists, not forensic pathologists. The quality of investigations had undoubtedly diminished. The system had regressed. Faye Spruill was initially encouraged at Bennett's success in pushing through the coroner reform law in 1986. She then watched as he fought and lost the very battles she had fought and also lost. She told a reporter, "I'm really just heartsick."

In October 1986, the Wisconsin Court of Appeals issued a strongly worded, spectacularly flawed opinion in the case of *State v. Stinson*. Two years earlier, Robert Lee Stinson had been convicted of raping and killing an elderly woman in Milwaukee. The only physical evidence linking him to the crime was the testimony of two bite mark specialists: Lowell Thomas Johnson and Raymond Rawson. At the time, Rawson served on the Bite Mark Standards Committee of the American Board of Forensic Odontology. He had also coauthored the organization's original guidelines for bite mark matching.

Johnson performed the initial analysis in the case by placing a mold of the suspect's teeth over photographs of some marks on the victim's body. He concluded that the marks "had to have been made by teeth identical in all of these characteristics" to the teeth of Stinson. Rawson then reviewed those conclusions and confirmed that the marks matched Stinson's teeth "to a reasonable degree of scientific certainty." Stinson was convicted.

On appeal, Stinson challenged the admission of the bite mark evidence. The appellate court shot him down. Based on the testimony from Johnson and Rawson, the appeals court judges went on for paragraphs about how careful and meticulous the two experts had been. Ultimately, the court found the bite mark evidence against Stinson so overwhelming as to "exclude to a moral certainty every reasonable hypothesis of innocence."

A *moral certainty*. Yet in 2009, twenty-three years after he was convicted, Robert Lee Stinson was exonerated by DNA testing. He had never bitten the victim. Nor did he rape and kill her. All of the evidence that screamed guilt—to a *moral certainty*, no less—was unfounded pseudoscience. Yet the court never made any effort to correct its mistake. As of this writing, *State v. Stinson* is still the controlling precedent for bite mark evidence in Wisconsin.

Bite mark analysis, along with fields like tire tread analysis, "tool mark" matching, blood spatter analysis, and even fingerprint analysis, all belong to a class of forensics called "pattern matching." These fields are problematic because although they're often presented to juries as scientific, they're actually entirely subjective. Analysts essentially look at two samples, and determine, using their own judgment, whether or not they're a "match." These analysts aren't subject to peer review or blind testing. There's no way to calculate error rates. You'll rarely find two experts who are diametrically opposed about a victim's blood type or how many DNA markers match the defendant. That's because those are questions of science. In pattern matching, expert witnesses regularly come to opposing conclusions. Juries are simply asked to side with the analyst they find more convincing.

Bite mark matching really grew in popularity in US courtrooms in the 1970s and 1980s, but it can be traced all the way back to the Salem witch trials. It literally began with a witch hunt. In May 1692, the Reverend George Burroughs was arrested in Salem on suspicion of witchcraft. The only physical evidence against him were several alleged bite marks found on some of the girls he was accused of corrupting with sorcery. At trial, Burroughs's mouth was pried open so his teeth could be compared to the marks left on the bodies of the girls. Burroughs actually had a solid alibi: at the time of the alleged attacks, he was in jail. That didn't matter much to his accusers. At the urging of the notorious witch hunter Cotton Mather, Burroughs was convicted, sentenced to death, and promptly hanged.

Two months later, the governor of Massachusetts called for an end to witchcraft trials. He issued a proclamation that prohibited the use of "spectral and intangible evidence" in the colony's criminal trials. Two decades later, Burroughs was posthumously declared innocent, and the colony of Massachusetts compensated his children for their father's wrongful execution. So went the first recorded use of bite marks in a criminal trial.

The most consequential bite mark case in US history occurred in 1974, when a California judge convicted Walter Edgar Marx of voluntary manslaughter based largely on alleged bite marks on the victim's nose. The marks were identified only when the victim's body had been exhumed, more than six weeks after she had been autopsied, embalmed, and buried. After a truly macabre series of experiments that involved a plaster cast of the victim's nose, a frankfurter, and an analyst biting a detective's nose for comparison, three dentists testified for the prosecution. All claimed they could match impressions on the victim's corpse to Marx's teeth. In a ruling that has since become enormously influential, a California appeals court upheld the conviction. Going forward, the *Marx* ruling will be read as a "global warrant" for courts' acceptance of bite mark identification testimony.

The *Marx* ruling was essentially an end run around the *Frye* test, the prevailing standard at the time for determining the validity of scientific evidence. The judges in *Marx* actually *conceded* that there was no scientific research to support bite mark matching. That *should* have been the end of the analysis. The evidence should have been tossed, and the conviction overturned.

Instead, the judges' reasoning took a bizarre turn. Because there was no science to analyze, the court decided a *Frye* test wasn't necessary. Instead, they simply invented their own test for evidence that wasn't scientific but was imbued with what you might call a scientific gloss. They noted that the trial judge had ruled that the bite mark expertise *seemed* sound—and that was good enough for them. In essence, *Marx* introduced a new standard for the admission of forensic evidence: the eyeball test.

Three years later, another California appeals court cited *Marx* in upholding bite mark evidence in a separate case. Strangely, that court explicitly referenced the "superior trustworthiness of the scientific bitemark approach" described in *Marx*, despite the fact that the *Marx* opinion specifically acknowledged a *lack* of scientific research in support of the practice. There would be no going back. There was now an established record of precedent. There would soon also be an established record of wrongful convictions. In the thirteen years following the *Marx* ruling, sixteen court opinions from twelve states either relied on the decision or adopted its "eyeball test." All but three of those rulings noted the "scientific" nature of bite mark analysis, despite the fact that—again—the *Marx* decision itself explicitly acknowledged that scientific research validating the field didn't exist.

It was like an extended exercise in jurisprudential "telephone," the childhood game in which a phrase is gradually corrupted as each kid whispers it to the next. In 1978, the Arizona Supreme Court became the first state high court to hold that bite mark evidence of this sort is an admissible forensic discipline. By 1988 the West Virginia Supreme Court noted in an opinion that bite mark matching had been so "generally accepted" in American courtrooms as sound science that a *Frye* analysis was no longer even necessary.

There still wasn't a shred of scientific evidence to back any of it up. Instead, courts were upholding bite mark evidence based on little more than previous rulings from other courts—stretching all the way back to *Marx*. In some instances, state appellate courts adopted the "eyeball test." In others, the courts erroneously claimed that *Marx* had already validated the science of bite mark matching, thus relieving them from engaging in any analysis themselves. It's been one big judicial echo chamber.

"Most of the time when doing one of these analyses, the only thing a judge will ask is, 'Have other courts allowed this?'" says Arizona State University law professor and evidence expert Michael Saks. "If the answer is yes, then they'll figure out a way to let it in. Or they'll decide that if the government is paying a person to do this analysis, it must be legitimate. That's a far cry from an analysis of its scientific merit. But it doesn't seem to matter."

By 1987, twenty-three state appellate courts had accepted bite mark analysis, without a single dissenting opinion. By 2004, courts in thirty-seven US jurisdictions had accepted it. As of this writing in 2017, no court in America has yet upheld a challenge to the scientific validity of bite mark evidence. And yet the field has been denounced by every panel of scientists that has attempted to assess its scientific validity. Perhaps more pertinent: twenty-five people arrested or convicted primarily based on bite mark matching have been exonerated. Two of them were nearly executed.

~

The late 1980s brought a spike in violent crime, along with a drumbeat of demagoguery from politicians. With more crime came more fear of crime. Cops and prosecutors sought new tools to help them put violent offenders behind bars. Politicians and much of the public itself were eager to give them those tools. DNA testing wasn't yet common, and the more targeted and sophisticated DNA testing we know today was still years away. The country was blissfully unaware of the coming wave of exonerations. The scientific community had yet to take much of an interest in forensics. And most Americans still believed that the criminal justice system was either infallible or pretty darned close.

Given these conditions, and given the courts' reluctance to provide any real oversight of the use of expert testimony, a forensic specialist willing to bend his or her analysis to confirm the suspicions of cops and prosecutors could do very well—financially and professionally. And many did. The exonerations wrought by DNA testing have now exposed too many crime lab scandals to count.

But a truly enterprising showman, one with some charisma and some bravado, might push the boundaries. He might go beyond fudging test results or tweaking lab reports. He might invent new disciplines from whole cloth, concoct new methods of analysis, and claim expertise and powers of observation that only he possesses—all of which he could offer up to help law enforcement officials solve crimes and win convictions. Such a showman could do quite well for himself.

In Mississippi, one man *would* do all of those things. He'd charm police officers and prosecutors with bawdy wit and back-slapping charm, then win them over by providing the scientific-ish evidence that confirmed their suspicions and clinched convictions. He'd also pollute the criminal justice system, help convict innocent people, and help guilty people go free.

His name is Michael West.

Meanwhile, three primary interests drove the evolution of Mississippi's death investigation system in the 1970s and 1980s. First and foremost was the state legislature, a body unwilling to appropriate a budget to build proper facilities and hire the forensic pathologists and support staff needed to run a modern-day state medical examiner's office. It was a body also beset with cronyism; still tainted with old-school chauvinisms like misogyny and mistrust of outsiders, as Spruill and Bennett found out; and populated by lawmakers with a stubborn aversion to change.

Second were the coroners, defenders of a dinosaur institution, fiercely protective of the office, and still powerful enough as a group to beat back any proposed reforms that threatened their authority. Some at least recognized a few of the problems with the system and sought to upgrade the office itself. But no matter how well intended those measures, they served only to perpetuate the status quo.

Finally, there was law enforcement—the state's police officials and prosecutors. Though some law enforcement leaders recognized early on that a real medical examiner system might provide a more accurate read on the crime rate, some also realized that doing so might expose a shocking number of unsolved murders. But for the most part, until the late 1980s the law enforcement community in Mississippi was one of the most reliable lobbies for real, substantive reform. That would soon change.

Faye Spruill and Thomas Bennett were doctors. They tried to create a death investigation system grounded in professional standards and medical science, regardless of how the results of such a system might affect those three main interest groups. When they encountered resistance, they adapted and tried to operate within the state's political landscape. But in the end, their fight was the same fight the medical community had been having with the justice system for decades. Change required some political acuity. Sheriff, district attorney, coroner, and legislator are all elected positions. By running for one of those positions, a candidate has already shown an interest in politics; by winning, he or she has already shown a knack for it. Doctors aren't normally political animals, and the profession is generally incompatible with the character traits that make for successful politicians.

But what if a doctor came along who actually *had* some political acumen? A doctor who could simultaneously please the coroners by making them feel needed and legitimate, law enforcement by helping them get convictions, and state legislators by taking the entire problem—and the problem of funding it—off their plates could very quickly accumulate power, influence, and money. Such a doctor would need to be comfortable with a massive workload—a workload professional medical organizations say would be impossible to maintain without sacrificing quality and professionalism. But so long as all the people in power were satisfied, no one who mattered would complain. He would need to seem authoritative and persuasive to juries. And he'd need to be persuasive even when giving scientifically dubious testimony, or testimony well outside his area of expertise.

Just before his resignation, Thomas Bennett told the *Clarion-Ledger* that the political challenges and strain on his family posed by his workload were just too much to bear. "I wanted to stay here so badly," he said. But the state had asked far too much of him. "You're not going to get some clown to come in here and do the load I've been doing," he said.

With that, the stage was set for Steven Hayne.

~ 6 ~

RISE OF A FIEFDOM

It is certain, in any case, that ignorance, allied
with power, is the most ferocious enemy justice
can have.

—James Baldwin, *No Name in the Street*

Among the witnesses whom Parke Morris has deposed over the
years, Steven Hayne sticks in his memory more than most. In October 2007, the Memphis-based attorney was representing the estate of a man who had died of dehydration in a nursing home. The
family had hired Hayne to do the autopsy before retaining Morris.
The opposing attorneys and Morris had just questioned Hayne in a
deposition.

"I'm a Civil War buff," Morris says. "So as I was in his office talking
to him, I noticed that Hayne had a shelf full of Civil War books. I
pulled a book off the shelf at random. I can't remember what we had
been talking about, but he told me to turn to a particular page, because there was a quote there that was relevant to our conversation. I
turned to the page, and I'll be damned. There it was. The guy had a
photographic memory."

Morris says it was immediately obvious that Hayne was not only
smart, but he seemed to enjoy demonstrating just how smart he was.
Others have noticed this, too. In a 2013 article about Hayne, *New York
Times* reporter Campbell Robertson wryly observed that when he tried
to interview Hayne about the controversy surrounding his work, their
conversation "ranged from the fall of the Roman republic to the folly
of the Vietnam War."

"Brilliant guy. No question," Morris says. "And then I realized:
that's what makes him so dangerous."

Morris had deposed Hayne earlier that day. He found Hayne's answers surprising—and more than a little disturbing. When someone dies of dehydration, Morris says, lab tests should show elevated levels of certain chemicals, such as sodium. "This patient's lab results were off the charts. I've investigated more than 2,500 nursing home deaths before and since, and I've still never seen anything like it."

But despite those test results, Hayne insisted instead that the patient had died of amitriptyline poisoning. Amitryptiline is commonly used as an antidepressant and antipsychotic, but it can be toxic in large doses. Lab tests did show elevated levels of the drug in the deceased patient, but Morris says other tests conclusively showed that the high levels were due to a process called postmortem redistribution—after death, drugs can settle and become concentrated in certain areas of the body. That can skew lab results.

Morris found himself in an ethical quandary. Hayne's claims actually helped Morris's client. But Morris also knew Hayne was wrong. He had previously hired three separate toxicologists, all of whom definitively told him that amitriptyline wasn't a factor in the man's death.

"He's just too smart to not have known. I think he calculated. I remember that he first seemed unprepared for the deposition. But as it got going, he seemed to assess the situation—the attorneys, the parties, what was at stake. Then he tailored his testimony on the fly to fit what he was observing. It was a remarkable thing."

The two men made small talk after the deposition. When Morris mentioned his love of cars, Hayne asked if Morris wanted to see his. Morris agreed and followed Hayne to the parking lot.

"It was an all-black car—I think it was a Dodge Charger—that he had souped up to look like an undercover police car," Morris says. "Here was this short, kinda fat, sixty-something-year-old man, and he's driving a car with decked-out rims, radios, and one of those spotlights that you can control from inside the car."

Morris knew that Hayne frequently testified in criminal cases, almost always for prosecutors. "It looked so out of character. Here's this little bit geeky guy driving around in this muscly, not-so-undercover cop car. It was definitely the car of a guy with a complex."

Morris says he initially couldn't put his finger on what bothered him about it all. The following morning, he read an op-ed in the *Wall Street Journal* detailing Hayne's mammoth workload, questionable methods, and testimony he had given in several cases that other experts said was dubious.

"A chill went down my spine," Morris says. "I thought, *That's it*. I started to see the big picture. Prosecutors in the South—they have this sort of jockish way about them. They're macho. You got the sense that Hayne latched onto them because he liked associating with them. I'm sure he made a lot of money over the years. But he also got to be one of the guys. He got to drive the cool car. And they had a smart guy who would play ball." (Hayne has consistently denied that he would "play ball" for prosecutors).

It was all of that, combined with Hayne's intellect, that Morris found particularly alarming. "I'm not some left-winger. I'm a pretty solid conservative, almost across the board. But I started wondering how many innocent people this guy might have put in prison. It was a terrifying thought." According to Morris, attorneys on both sides of the nursing home case agreed that Hayne's testimony was way off base. The case was settled out of court.

Almost nine years and hundreds of cases later, Morris still remembers that encounter with Hayne. "The guy was brilliant. He also managed to be both insecure and an egomaniac. I remember thinking that seemed like a really dangerous combination in an expert witness."

Steven Timothy Hayne was born in Los Angeles, California, on August 30, 1941. He went to high school in the Bay Area. In 1967, at age twenty-six, he enrolled in Contra Costa College in San Pablo, California. After two years he transferred to North Dakota State University to study agriculture. About his choice of transfer school, Hayne has explained that his decision was simple: "Their application was one sheet, one side, and I decided that's the kind of school I wanted to go to. I liked their attitude." Before completing his undergraduate degree, Hayne transferred to the University of North Dakota medical school in 1972, where he studied for two years before transferring again, to the medical school at Brown University in Rhode Island. This time, expediency gave way to prestige. He would later tell attorneys in a deposition, "I didn't want to graduate with a degree from the University of North Dakota. I wanted an Ivy League degree." He completed medical school in the spring of 1976.

According to his trial and deposition testimony over the years, Hayne's first postgraduate internship followed that same year at the Letterman Army Medical Center at the Presidio in San Francisco, where he specialized in pathology. After completing his internship and rotations at medical institutions in the Bay Area, he was named chief of pathology at the Blanchfield Army Hospital in Fort Leavenworth, Kansas. He then moved around for a few years, from the military hospital in Fort Campbell, Kentucky, to a position as a reference pathologist at Shoals Medical Laboratories in Alabama, then to medical director of Rankin Medical Center laboratory in Brandon, Mississippi, just east of Jackson. He received his Mississippi medical license in 1985 and obtained his certification in clinical and anatomical pathology from the American Board of Pathology soon after.

Hayne began regularly performing autopsies for the state of Mississippi in late 1986 or very early 1987. It was a propitious time to get started. Thomas Bennett had just quit the medical examiner post in frustration, the second state medical examiner in only a few years to do so. The state had reverted to administering autopsies the way it had for decades, but in an ever-increasing atmosphere of need. If the county coroner believed a suspicious death required an autopsy, he or she would hire a private pathologist. At the start of Hayne's career, the fees that came with these referrals were around $400 for the autopsy itself, plus $200 per hour for preparation and time in court. Toward the end, the autopsy fee was around $1,000, and he was charging $350 or more per hour for testimony. He'd also get additional money for lab work and analysis.

Each county was responsible for paying the doctors it hired for autopsies. All the while, the problem of too few qualified medical examiners to handle an increasing number of autopsies wasn't just intractable, it was getting worse. This was the context in which Hayne rose to prominence.

Where other pathologists in Mississippi saw forensic autopsies as a burden that cost them time and money, Steven Hayne found a way to make them profitable. The secret was to do a lot of them. Hayne began his forensic pathology career in Mississippi with just a few autopsies per month, but his workload quickly escalated. In 1988, two years after moving to the state, he did 320. By the early 1990s, he was doing 1,200 per year—about 80 percent of the state's annual autopsy referrals. The number continued to rise from there, peaking in 2007 at 1,857 autopsies. Assuming he worked every day of the year, that's five per day.

To put these numbers into perspective, the National Association of Medical Examiners (NAME), the leading professional organization for forensic pathologists, recommends a medical examiner do no more than 250 autopsies per year. If a physician exceeds 325 in a year, NAME won't certify the lab where that doctor works, regardless of any other factors. In a 2001 deposition, Hayne admitted that in 1998 alone, over a period of just a few weeks, he performed 375 autopsies. He had done more autopsies in eleven weeks than NAME's uppermost limit for a year.

But according to Hayne, performing autopsies wasn't his only job. For most of his tenure in Mississippi, he also held two other professional responsibilities: medical director of the Rankin County Medical Center laboratory and medical director of a kidney care facility and research lab. Over the years he also held titles at various labs and hospitals and consulted in civil cases, including performing private autopsies and testifying in court.

Hayne has tried to explain away his workload by claiming a near superhuman capacity for labor. "I normally sleep no more than two to three hours a day. I also work seven days a week, not five days a week. I don't take holidays. I don't take vacations. . . . So I work at a much more efficient level and much harder than most people. I was blessed with that and cursed with that, but that's what I carry with me, and I do work very, very hard," he said while testifying in a 2003 murder trial. He also testified, "I do not require much sleep. I choose to work." When asked about NAME's claim that after more than 350 autopsies doctors are prone to carelessness and mistakes, Hayne countered, "I have an ability to stay alert. I have an ability to work long hours, and I don't think I make those [i.e., errors], and I think my record stands for itself." He would repeat this claim in other trials throughout his career when questioned about his workload.

Because Hayne held two other full-time positions (or at least positions that were supposed to be full-time), he typically conducted all of his autopsies at night, generally between the late evening and the wee hours of the morning. His penchant for knocking out eight to ten autopsies at hours when most people are sleeping only added a layer of macabre to his lore.

~

Some back-of-the-envelope math shows just how busy Hayne had to have been. Add up even the low estimates Hayne at various points has claimed he spent on continuing education, court testimony, his two salaried jobs, and just a few hours of sleep, and it leaves about three hours per autopsy, assuming 1,500 autopsies per year. That's the absolute minimum most professional groups say is necessary. But that would have left Hayne with no time—zero hours—for vacations, days off, weekends off, or sick days. It doesn't account for meals, commuting, socializing, showering, other personal health and grooming, time with his spouse, parenting, or a single hobby or interest. It assumes he didn't mow his own lawn, watch TV, go to the movies, or take a trip to the grocery store. And it doesn't account for the dozens of journal articles and conference presentations that he claims to have researched and written.

Incredible as they are, even those numbers don't tell the whole story. Hayne also did private autopsies and consulting for civil cases. He has testified in depositions for some of those cases. Beginning in the early 1990s, Hayne also became the go-to medical examiner for several parishes in Louisiana, adding still more to his autopsy total. In fact, in a 2012 deposition, Hayne acknowledged that there were "a couple" years where he topped *two thousand* autopsies.

As for how he managed it all, Hayne claims he simply never took time off. "I guess I am a workaholic," he said in 2012. "I don't go on vacations, don't take weekends, don't take holidays. . . . Just the way I am. I don't go to barbecues and stuff."

Hayne was able to dominate Mississippi's autopsy referrals by being all things to all the important people. Whereas other pathologists in the state reluctantly agreed to perform autopsies, Hayne embraced them and actively sought out referrals. While law enforcement officials found other pathologists reluctant, off-putting, and unhelpful, Hayne made himself available to police and prosecutors, enthusiastically testified in court, and—most importantly—worked with prosecutors to help them win convictions they believed were justified.

Medical examiners are supposed to be impartial finders of fact. But the incentives built into the system are clear. After a suspicious death, the coroner, district attorney, or police official takes the body to a medical examiner for autopsy. In most cases, they then tell the medical examiner what they thought happened. The medical examiner who returns with opinions that back up their hunch earns favor and gets more referrals. The medical examiner who says, "No, that isn't what happened," or—the more likely scenario—"There just isn't enough conclusive evidence for me to say that this is what happened" makes the sheriff's or prosecutor's job more difficult, and perhaps makes them think twice before using the same doctor the next time. There needn't even be any intent to deceive or distort findings. It's human nature; if they have a choice in which medical examiner to use, over time prosecutors and police will gravitate toward the expert who makes their jobs easier. A properly designed system would work to eliminate these sorts of biases and misaligned incentives. The Mississippi system fed them.

The ways in which prosecutors and other law enforcement officials have described Hayne over the years provides further evidence of the problem. For example, John T. Kitchens, a former district attorney, state judge, and longtime Hayne defender, told the *New York Times* in 2013, "I'm sure there's a lot of people that don't like Hayne, but from a prosecutor's standpoint I don't know anybody who didn't like him. He was always so helpful and useful to law enforcement." When Hayne finally came under fire in the late 2000s, law enforcement officials wrote letters to show their support for him. Like Kitchens, many described what a great witness he had been. One prosecutor recalled a case in which, upon hearing Hayne testify, one juror whispered to another, "He must be some kind of genius." The prosecutor also feared that criticism of Hayne would lead to the courts being "overloaded with convicted killers making fruitless claims of wrongful convictions." Another prosecutor noted he was "completely satisfied with Hayne's work," and noted Hayne's ability to make "several court appearances in one day." Still another seemed downright distraught at the prospect of losing Hayne. "It has always been a source of great comfort to me that Dr. Hayne would be a witness in our murder cases," he wrote. "It is a big concern to me that I might have to go through the rest of my career as a prosecutor without Dr. Hayne performing our autopsies."

Prior to Hayne, the perverse incentives in the referral process were less important. There were no forensic pathologists in the state, and the clinical pathologists didn't particularly want referrals. That system still had lots of problems, but they were different problems. Crimes were going unsolved; they weren't being "solved" with questionable expertise. With a little funding, the Mississippi legislature could have followed the lead of Florida, Maryland, and a number of other states by implementing a modern, accountable, well-funded medical examiner system. It was just never a priority.

~

Shortly after Hayne moved to Mississippi from Alabama in the mid-1980s, he visited with Rankin County coroner Jimmy Roberts. After that meeting, Roberts began sending Hayne autopsy referrals. It began a partnership that would last for two decades. The two men would make money together, and they'd become among the most powerful figures in the state.

Roberts was first elected Rankin County coroner in 1981. In an interview with the *Clarion-Ledger* shortly after he was sworn in, Roberts gave a preview of the debate that would unfold in the years to come. At the time, the reform-minded Faye Spruill was serving as Mississippi's first state medical examiner. Roberts, described by the paper as "tall and fragile-looking," insisted that the coroner was still a critical public office. He told the paper that under Spruill's proposed reforms, the counties wouldn't get a good return on the tax dollars they'd be sending to Jackson. "By keeping money in the county, it can be better accounted for," the article read, paraphrasing Roberts. As it would turn out, by "be better accounted for," Roberts meant "benefit Jimmy Roberts."

While working with an established, influential elected coroner like Roberts, Hayne began to get more autopsy referrals from other coroners across the state. The relationship also helped Roberts. In the late 1980s, Roberts opened his own morgue and embalming business in the town of Pearl. As Hayne collected more and more referrals, Roberts would charge the other counties a fee when Hayne used the morgue to do those autopsies. Roberts would also get transportation costs for picking up bodies and bringing them to his facility. One former coroner recalls Roberts getting $150 per autopsy for use of his morgue, plus up to $2 per mile for transporting bodies. Once the body was in his morgue, he also became the practical choice to provide the family of the deceased with embalming services. It was a convenient arrangement.

"After the autopsy, he'd say to the funeral director or family, 'Well, as long as I've got the body, why don't I embalm him?'" says another longtime former coroner. "He made a lot of money hauling bodies all over the state." By 2005, one consultant estimated that Hinds

County alone (the largest in the state) was paying Roberts and Hayne $2 million per year for autopsies, facilities rental, and the transport of bodies.

With Jimmy Roberts in his corner, it didn't take Hayne long to corner the market on Mississippi autopsies. Unlike the reluctant doctors with whom coroners and prosecutors had to deal with in the past, Hayne gladly worked with cops, DAs, and coroners. He was cooperative and agreeable, didn't complain about testifying, and produced results (if not full reports) in a respectable period of time.

Hayne quickly made a name for himself, and it paid off. In June 1987, he was appointed interim state medical examiner. In announcing the appointment, the public safety commissioner touted Hayne's numerous published articles, his time as a pathologist for the military, and his impressive résumé.

There was one problem. The state medical examiner was required by state law to be certified in forensic pathology by the American Board of Pathology (ABP), the discipline's nationally recognized certifying organization. This was part of the recent efforts to modernize the state's death investigation system. Hayne was certified in clinical and anatomical pathology, which deals with determining deaths by natural causes such as disease, heart attack, or stroke. He was *not* certified by ABP in forensic pathology, which concerns deaths that have implications for the legal system.

But the state was desperate to fill the position. And the state officials whose opinions mattered clearly wanted Hayne. The public safety commissioner requested a legal opinion from the state attorney general, asking whether an uncertified pathologist could be appointed state medical examiner if a certified candidate wasn't available. (Faye Spruill was the only board-certified forensic pathologist in the state at the time. She didn't want the job, nor was anyone going to offer it to her.) The attorney general's office answered that it could be done, at least on an interim basis. That's how Steven Hayne became Mississippi's third state medical examiner.

The arrangement didn't last long. In February 1988, eight months after he was appointed, Hayne resigned. He said no one had asked him to step down, but he was doing so in order to clear the way for the appointment of a permanent, board-certified state medical examiner.

With Hayne out of the state medical examiner's office—and the office essentially defunct—the last few years of the 1980s spawned yet another public debate about the state of Mississippi's death investigation system. In August 1988, a legislative oversight group called the Joint Committee on Performance Evaluation and Expenditure Review (PEER) published a study and audit of the coroner system. The group found that the state medical examiner's office was understaffed and underfunded, that the state's autopsy facilities were woefully inadequate, and that county coroners were often unqualified, uncooperative, and deficient in their duties. It described the coroner system as outdated and inefficient, found that thousands of deaths were going uninvestigated or misinvestigated, and concluded that the entire process was corrupting the administration of justice.

The *Clarion-Ledger* followed up with a reported series called "A Skeletal System." The problems outlined in the series had been articulated many times before, and the series quoted several experts and policymakers who advocated scrapping the coroner system for a medical examiner system, as other states had done. One article looked at why Mississippi lawmakers seemed so uninterested in going that route. Most said that funding a proper medical examiner system wasn't a priority for them because the voters who elected them didn't seem to care. One of the more notable opponents of moving to a medical examiner system: Steven Hayne, now in private practice. Hayne told the paper, "Anyone that can talk about building a complete statewide, totally funded system in the medical examiner's office needs to have their brain checked." Of course, a well-funded, statewide medical examiner system would also have scuttled Hayne's burgeoning autopsy business.

By the end of the 1980s, Hayne had significantly increased his share of the state's autopsy referrals. Most coroners embraced him, but he also quickly became the only game in town. Even the handful of officials who had reservations about him felt that their hands were tied. "I didn't like it," says one Mississippi coroner, explaining why he used Hayne for autopsies over the years. "That was the system. I had to use the system because there was no other game." Douglas Posey, now a medical examiner in Houston, said in a 2007 interview that during the 1990s, he had offered to do some autopsies in Mississippi, but was rebuffed. "I remember the Washington County coroner told me that if I wanted to do autopsies in Mississippi, I had to get permission from Steven Hayne first," Posey said. "I thought that was odd, since Hayne didn't hold any office."

Most Mississippi officials either actively encouraged all of this or ignored it. But even among the few who both knew there was a problem and had the authority to do something about it, there was a sense of powerlessness. The late Jim Ingram, a former FBI agent, was the state's commissioner of public safety from 1992 to 2000. Ingram at first defended Hayne, whom he at times called a friend. But he began to worry after Hayne and West clashed with two successive state medical examiners. "We didn't see eye to eye," Ingram said of Hayne in a 2006 interview, "but most of the autopsies went to him. I can't say why. It's just what the coroners and prosecutors wanted."

~

Over the years, Hayne has given conflicting explanations for his resignation as interim state medical examiner. His explanation at the time—that he resigned so the state could begin searching for a certified medical examiner—didn't make much sense. Hayne had been offered and accepted the job despite lacking certification, so it's unclear why he would suddenly be so concerned about that particular qualification. He had also told the *Clarion-Ledger* that he planned to take the certification exam the following spring. A new DPS commissioner, Louisa Dixon, expressed disappointment in Hayne's resignation, as did many of the state's coroners. Even if Hayne had only taken the job as a public service until a more qualified candidate could be found, it made little sense for him to resign before a successor had been identified.

In a 2001 deposition, Hayne offered an alternate explanation: he testified that he resigned because Dixon "wanted another individual," and had selected someone, but that his own lack of certification "was never an issue." In a 2012 deposition, Hayne would claim that he resigned because Dixon had barred him from lobbying the legislature for more money. That too didn't make much sense. Dixon herself has advocated for more funding for the office for her entire career. In 2008 she wrote a long op-ed in the *Clarion-Ledger* in which she declared that having one doctor doing nearly all of the state's autopsies "endangers public safety."

There is one explanation for Hayne's decision that makes a lot more sense: Hayne's brief tenure may have helped him see a way to make a lot of money in the autopsy business. Prior to his appointment, most of Hayne's forensic autopsy work had come from his association with Jimmy Roberts. From his perch in Jackson, Hayne got a view of the entire state. In 1987, coroners and other local officials had ordered autopsies for 836 of the 8,000 deaths in Mississippi. Hayne performed about 107 of those autopsies that year as state medical examiner. The other 729 were split up among other doctors, none of whom were forensic pathologists, and few of whom really wanted to be doing them. A doctor who could take on just half the number of autopsies the state contracted out in 1987 would gross 140 percent more than the $65,000 salary of the state medical examiner. And that wouldn't include the money one might get for lab work and court testimony. Take on more than 400 state autopsies, add in some private autopsies and testimony for plaintiffs' attorneys, and an energetic state medical examiner could easily gross five, six, or seven times his base salary.

But there was a hitch. Just a couple months prior to his resignation, the Department of Public Safety received a complaint that two employees of the crime lab had been moonlighting as autopsy assistants. Commissioner Dixon ruled that DPS employees weren't permitted to moonlight in the same field as their employment with the state. While he was in office, Hayne had seen firsthand just how much money there was to be made from doing autopsies as a private physician instead of as a state employee. If he had any notion of trying to do both, the DPS prohibition on freelancing effectively eliminated that option. But if he resigned, he'd be free to do as many autopsies for county coroners and prosecutors as he pleased.

In an interview with the *Clarion-Ledger*, Thomas Bennett, who had apparently spoken to Hayne about his decision to resign, told the paper that Hayne "made it very clear that he was going to go with his private work, because that was his first love." It was also far more lucrative.

This of course is speculation—it's impossible to say if this is precisely how Hayne's thinking evolved. But it certainly fits neatly with the chronology. Hayne accepted the acting position, where he would have seen just how many autopsies were being done statewide. Then Dixon issued her ban on moonlighting. And then Hayne resigned. Immediately after resigning, Hayne's autopsy load began to increase—rather dramatically.

There's a good reason why stories about Southern injustice, cronyism, and good-ol'-boy politics inevitably come back to racism. And in this story too, there's no question that Hayne and West thrived in a system that was created and honed during Jim Crow, and that for decades was used to reinforce the segregated social order. There's also no question that the system's problems continue to disproportionately affect minority and poor populations across the state. But no one has described Hayne as a racist. He married a black detective in 2006, although the marriage itself was short. In the 1990s, his findings assisted state and federal prosecutors in reopening several cold civil rights murder cases from the 1960s.

Instead, Hayne could be described more as an opportunist. He was quick to accommodate, whether it was a backwater sheriff or prosecutor, or a media-savvy attorney general or US attorney trying to make a name for himself by prosecuting elderly Klansmen.

On the rare occasion when the Mississippi death investigation system would come under fire during Hayne's reign, the major players would claim they were only doing the best they could with a bad situation. Prosecutors and coroners claimed that there were simply no other medical examiners available. Hayne, West, and Roberts claimed they were merely doing what was asked or required of them. But all of that glosses over the fact that the system Mississippi had was exactly the system that all the important players wanted. It's the system they created, and the system they've fought like hell to preserve.

~ 7 ~

THE WEST PHENOMENON

All talents, all gifts that I possess are directed
straightly from God. I feel that the Lord wants me
to work in this arena. It is a good fight.

—Michael West

In 1982, thirty-year-old dentist Michael West attended a lecture by a
Kansas forensic odontologist named Thomas Krauss. In the lecture,
delivered to the annual convention of the American Academy of Forensic Sciences, West heard Krauss explain some experiments he had been
doing with bite marks and ultraviolet photography. The field of bite
mark analysis had blossomed since attracting national attention during
the trial of infamous serial-murderer Ted Bundy six years earlier, but
practitioners had been limited by the fact that bite marks seemed to
begin healing after just a few days. Krauss claimed that ultraviolet photography could detect marks that had been left months earlier.

West, a budding forensic odontologist himself, ran with the idea.
When he returned home to Hattiesburg, Mississippi, West and another local dentist named Felder "Buddy" Wallace conducted an odd
series of experiments. West shaved a patch of skin on his thigh, while
Wallace sedated him with drugs normally used in tooth extraction.
Once West was under, Wallace bit West on the thigh. He had to do
so aggressively, to mimic what forensic odontology textbooks called a
"combat bite"—a bite administered during an attack. Soon, West and
Wallace were paying their assistants, and criminal justice students at
the University of Southern Mississippi, to bite one another. Once the
"bitee" was sedated, the biter would chomp down and then hold the
bitee's skin between his or her teeth for fifteen seconds—until West
hollered, "Time!" From their tests, West and Wallace claimed to have

replicated Krauss's experiment, telling the local paper that they could recreate bite marks left three months earlier on men and six months earlier on women. (West claimed women have an extra layer of fat, which he said preserves the scarring for a longer period of time.) "We've taken a lot of good humor from lay individuals who don't fully understand what we're trying to do," West said.

The following year, West would testify in the first-ever Mississippi criminal trial to include bite mark evidence. In March 1982, a black man broke into the home of a white, thirty-seven-year-old Hattiesburg woman, assaulted her, and raped her. The victim could only describe her assailant as tall, black, and soft-spoken. According to District Attorney Bud Holmes, the woman's attacker had bitten her on the cheek. West noted an alleged bite mark, photographed it, performed his own analysis, and matched it to a suspect. Holmes then sent West's photos of the mark and a dental mold of the suspect to two other bite mark specialists for confirmation. West had not yet been certified by the American Board of Forensic Odontology, so Holmes wanted confirmation from another bite mark analyst in case West wasn't permitted to testify.

One of the bite mark specialists didn't agree with West's conclusion; the other did. The expert who agreed with West happened to be Richard Souviron—one of the forensic odontologists who had achieved some fame in the Ted Bundy trial. On February 17, 1983, Holmes charged twenty-four-year-old Don Horn for the rape. Horn, as it turns out, was a three-year starter and standout wide receiver for the University of Southern Mississippi football team. After the charge, the NFL prospect was suspended from the school.

Prosecutors began looking at Horn after the victim identified him as "one of four black men" she knew. She also shopped at a grocery store where Horn worked as a stock clerk, and Horn was a patient of the dentist where the victim worked as a hygienist. Prosecutors also later pointed out that stock clerks at the grocery store sometimes used box cutters to open shipments, and that the victim said her assailant wielded a box cutter.

Not only was Horn's trial the first Mississippi case to include bite mark evidence, the bite mark evidence was the only real evidence against him. Despite Holmes's assertions to the press, it would turn out to be the *only* physical evidence against Horn. Semen taken from the victim was inconclusive. The fingerprints found in the home didn't match Horn. And lab analysts could only say that pubic hair found on the victim had come from a black man. Horn also had an alibi: on the night of the rape, he had slept at his girlfriend's house after serving as an usher at her brother's wedding.

Horn was tried the following December. It looked bleak for him before the first witness had even been called. The prosecutors had used their challenges to remove all the black candidates from the jury pool, leaving an all-white panel. Then Horn's attorneys objected to letting West testify, pointing out that he had never given bite mark testimony and that he wasn't certified as a forensic odontologist. The judge ruled against them.

When he took the stand, West testified that the mark on the victim was a "dead match" to Don Horn. He relied only on marks from the lower teeth for his conclusion, and in fact didn't even bother bringing his photographs of the upper marks. Richard Souviron also testified that the marks were a match. Norman Sperber, the other expert to whom Holmes had originally sent West's photos, testified for the defense. He told the jury the marks were inconsistent with Horn's teeth. Despite allowing both West and Souviron to take the stand, the trial judge refused to allow a second defense expert to testify about the bite. Remarkably, in spite of all of that, Horn was acquitted.

Horn's trial was both the first bite mark case in Mississippi history and the first in which Michael West testified as a bite mark expert. It resulted in an acquittal. And yet no one seemed chastened by that outcome. West had already been lecturing at state law enforcement conferences about bite mark evidence, and continued to do so. The following year, he and Wallace were slated to give their own presentation on ultraviolet photography at the annual American Academy of Forensic Sciences conference. District attorney Bud Holmes told the *Hattiesburg American* that though he lost, he was pleased to have participated in a case that would be remembered as a milestone in Mississippi criminal law. "It's tantamount to the first time fingerprints or blood type was used," he said, referring to the bite mark evidence. "As it becomes perfected, it will be very useful."

Michael West was born on September 11, 1952, in New Orleans. He grew up in Picayune, a town of about ten thousand people in southwest Mississippi, wedged between the Louisiana border and the Gulf Coast. In 1971 he enrolled at Pearl River Community College and then transferred to the University of Southern Mississippi, where two years later he earned a bachelor of science degree. West earned his DDS from Louisiana State University in 1977 and served active duty in the Air Force dental corps from 1977 to 1981. By 1981, he had set up a dental practice in Hattiesburg, a college town of about forty-five thousand people, ninety miles southeast of Jackson.

A portly man with thick fingers and a drawl as thick as sausage gravy, West was brash, ambitious, and, at times, breathtakingly reckless. His rapid ascent in the world of forensics from the late 1980s through the mid-1990s is a striking example of just how deferential and unskeptical courts, police, journalists, and juries can be when it comes to expert testimony. Many of West's claims about his forensic abilities should have been suspect to anyone willing to give them some serious thought. Yet prosecutors as well as police chiefs, sheriffs, and others in law enforcement rarely thought to double-check them with actual scientists before putting West in front of a jury.

West often portrayed himself as a sophisticated pioneer of forensics but also an everyman grounded in common sense and folksy humility. Juries ate it up. He once told lawyers at a deposition, unprompted, that he had been reading a book on the Gnostic Christians and another on quantum mechanics. But he also wasn't too fancy for a workingman's beer. "While I'm drinking [Miller] High Lifes, I'm working on my magnum opus on why Galileo was wrong," he said. "I've just got to get the pope to read it."

This ivory tower–blue collar dichotomy also appears in West's contradictory descriptions of how he got started in forensic dentistry, which he traces back to his time in the Air Force. In a 2012 deposition, West said his interest in forensics began when an Air Force colonel needed a forensic specialist. So "the colonel came in and he looked around the room. I was the lowest-ranking man. He said I was forensic officer." But later in the same deposition, West claimed he was given the job because he was, in his words, "a boy wonder." "I was a quick study. Whenever a difficult case would come up, Colonel Callaway would assign it to me."

In 1982, West, Buddy Wallace, and West's former dental school classmate Robert Barsley received some local notoriety for their work identifying the remains of some of the 152 passengers killed when Pan Am flight 759 crashed just after takeoff from a New Orleans airport.

It's unclear why West and Wallace stopped working together, but West and Barsley would go on to cowrite numerous articles. In 1991, the two men received a grant from the National Institute for Justice for an experiment similar to the one West and Wallace had conducted nearly ten years earlier: they paid married couples to bite one another, and then examined the resulting wound patterns. According to West, they paid one spouse $100 to be sedated and bitten, and the other $50 to do the biting. The two dentists then used ultraviolet light to examine the marks and photograph the wounds over successive days. According to West, "We were getting better images of the pattern 19 days after it was inflicted than we could an hour after it was inflicted." Though West often cited the NIJ grant as an important credential, the results of his experiments with both Wallace and Barsley have not been duplicated by other researchers.

In one article published in a law enforcement magazine in 1992, West and Barsley took the method to another level. They claimed they had used it to discern what had really happened during an altercation in which a man was killed with a police officer's gun. The man's family believed the officer unjustifiably shot the man; the officer claimed the man had wrested the officer's service revolver away and mistakenly shot himself. West and Barsley claimed that by using ultraviolet light, they found indentations in the man's skin that were invisible to the naked eye. Moreover, the two concluded that those indentations could only have come from gripping the officer's gun. Even if they'd inspected the man's hands immediately after the incident, it was a spurious claim. But they hadn't. Their exam took place well after the shooting. This is the sort of claim West would make over and over again.

Two years after graduating from dental school, West leveraged the publicity he received from the Pan Am crash to start a business, Dental Disaster Squad, which aimed to provide rapid-response dental identification in the event of a plane crash, fire, or other tragedy. In 1984, he received his certification in forensic odontology from the American Board of Forensic Odontology. A year later, he was named "coroner pro tem" for Forrest County, Mississippi. As West has testified, he was offered the position because at the time, the elected coroner for Forrest County "had a problem with drinking." When the coroner's drinking began to interfere with his ability to conduct death investigations, the local district attorney and other law enforcement officials approached West and asked him to take over the job—but informally, behind the scenes. West has said that law enforcement came to him specifically because he was "known to the court and the DA as an individual in forensics."

Over the years, West has also claimed to have been appointed "deputy coroner ranger," "deputy coroner medical examiner investigator," "chief deputy coroner," and "coroner medical examiner investigator"—all titles that describe what is essentially the same position. He was an assistant coroner.

Early on, West won some fawning profiles in the local media. The first was a 1983 piece in the *Hattiesburg American* on the biting experiments he had conducted with Wallace. It ran under the headline, "Taking a Bite out of Crime." In 1988, the same paper ran a big photo of West holding an ultraviolet camera he was given after presenting a paper about identifying wound patterns. That article began, "Most people probably don't think of Hattiesburg as a hotbed of scientific research." The same year, West's hometown paper featured him again, this time in a front-page story about how West and another local researcher had used "video enhancement" to prove that President John F. Kennedy was killed by a lone gunman.

According to his curriculum vitae, between 1989 and 1999, Michael West published fifty-one articles, made fifty presentations, and gave eighty-four lectures. By 1995, he claimed to have given lectures on a tour of China, at the FBI Academy in Quantico, Virginia, and to the detectives at Scotland Yard in England. He has also claimed his research was "monitored by" the Royal Canadian Mounted Police, "Israeli Intelligence," and police agencies all over the world.

West has published articles on a wide array of topics. A sampling of titles from his curriculum vitae include "A New Method for Trace Metal Verification," "A Study of Surface Topography of Footwear and Automobile Pedals," "Serial Mass Murders: A Study of Mass Violence," "Confirmation of the Single Bullet Theory in the Assassination of President John F. Kennedy," "A Second Look at Wax," "The Hidden Danger of Scalding," and "Peanut Butter Aspiration Deaths Among the Mentally Retarded." He and Steven Hayne collaborated on dozens of articles and presentations, often working on them together at the local Waffle House after their nighttime autopsy sessions.

By 2006, West's CV stood at twenty-seven pages. He had testified more than eighty times and claimed to have "investigated 5,800 deaths." (In a deposition just six years later, he put the figure at 16,000.) The vast majority of those cases were in Mississippi, but he has also testified in at least nine other state courts and two federal district courts. West has been permitted to influence juries on a wide range of topics, including bite mark analysis, gunshot reconstruction, wound pattern analysis, pathophysiology, blood stain analysis, gunshot residue, fingernail scratch reconstruction, trace metal analysis, video enhancement, pour pattern analysis, tool mark analysis, and photo enhancement. In civil cases he has offered his analysis about cigarette burns on a nursing home patient and the marks left on a child's arm that had been struck by a ruler. On his CV, he has also claimed to have advised law enforcement officials on the theory of Shaken Baby Syndrome, on child abuse and the sexual abuse of children, and on the detection of accelerants in arson investigations.

Few if any of West's articles and presentations were subjected to robust peer review. Most appeared in law enforcement or forensic publications, not in academic journals. And most were in areas for which he had very little formal training or education. Michael West is either a master bullshit artist or an autodidact for the ages.

$\sim$

In August 1990, serial killer Danny Rolling murdered five college students in Gainesville, Florida. The gruesome manner in which he killed them—they had been bound, tortured, and forced into macabre poses—earned him the nickname the "Gainesville Ripper." He'd later say he had committed the murders because he craved the fame and renown of fellow Florida serial killer Ted Bundy.

The murders certainly attracted national attention. They also attracted Michael West. By the time of the Gainesville murders, the "little ol' dentist from Hattiesburg," as West likes to call himself, had spun his biting experiments into what he called a revolutionary new method of inspecting corpses. By using yellow-tinted goggles and a particular band of fluorescent light, West claimed he could find bites, scrapes, indentations, and other injuries that are invisible to the naked eye. Despite once telling his hometown paper that he first learned of the technique at a presentation by a dentist from Kansas, West would later provide a more exotic origin story. While visiting China, he was told a three-thousand-year-old tale about a Chinese doctor who noticed that flesh wounds looked different when viewed under the light that passed through the panel of a silk tent. According to West, he realized that he could apply the same concept to modern times, and with modern technology. Despite his work with both Wallace and Barsley, he named his procedure "the West Phenomenon."

As the Gainesville murders drew national attention, West headed down to Florida with his specialized equipment to work as a freelance investigator. West touted his ability to use ultraviolet light not only to find marks on the victims, but blood, hair, or fingerprints overlooked by investigators at the crime scene. But his cutting-edge technology didn't do much good in Florida. West generated no leads.

That didn't stop him from offering opinions. West appears to have played the Gainesville murders for maximum exposure. He was quoted often in the newspapers, usually accompanied by glowing descriptions of him as a trailblazing forensics wonder. Ted Bundy's trial in the 1970s had drawn national attention to bite mark analysis and brought acclaim to the specialists who testified for the state, most notably Richard Souviron and New York dentist Lowell Levine. If this killer was the next Ted Bundy, perhaps West could be the next Lowell Levine.

In his media interviews, West recounted his experience in crime scene investigations. He also hyped up the murders, which not only drew more attention to himself but had the unfortunate effect of giving Rolling the renown he craved. West portrayed the then-unknown killer as an evil genius. "I thought I'd seen everything," West proclaimed in the *Gainesville Sun*. But when the full details of the crimes were finally released, he promised, "you'll be shocked and amazed."

~

Portraying the killer as a brilliant butcher served a purpose for West. If his own technology was as revolutionary as he claimed, he might have picked up some previously undetected evidence when he visited the crime scenes. After all, West claimed he could find clues no one else could.

But the giveaway that West's forensic expertise was dubious is that for all the times he was retained, he was almost always of use to law enforcement officials only after a suspect had been identified. West never really generated legitimate leads himself. Once the police had a suspect for whom they already had some incriminating evidence—or even just a hunch—West could swoop in, find telltale marks on the body that others had overlooked, and then find a way to match those marks to the suspect. As an *American Bar Association (ABA) Journal* article noted after interviewing Mississippi defense attorney Armstrong

Walters, "No district attorney in the Deep South stands a chance of re-election if a murder occurs in his or her jurisdiction and somebody does not wind up in prison for it." According to Walters, "West confirms whatever suspicions the police have."

While West was in Gainesville, the police had no strong suspect for the killings, and so West and his alleged cutting-edge technology were useless. Instead, he just praised the killer's methods to the media, telling the Associated Press that he'd never seen such a clean crime scene in all his thirteen years investigating murders.

West's work on the Gainesville Ripper was later mentioned in national publications such as *Vanity Fair*. When *The Phil Donahue Show* came to Florida to cover the killings, West was one of the guests. His contribution: he suggested that Gainesville residents arm themselves. But otherwise, West contributed little to solving the Gainesville murders. However, the whole episode did provide quite a boost to his career. He received adoring press attention, which he'd include on his CV and which undoubtedly earned him favor back in Mississippi. The list of media coverage included, as West put it, "My favorite: *Playboy*." He'd later cite the case in court testimony as one of his "most notable" investigations.

More than a year after West left Florida, Danny Rolling was finally captured and charged. He was executed by lethal injection in 2006.

Steven Hayne and Michael West have given conflicting testimony about when they met and began working together. It was likely sometime in the late 1980s, because by 1990 Hayne and West, operating in Jimmy Roberts's morgue, worked on their first case that ultimately resulted in a wrongful conviction—the Levon Brooks case.

As personally and professionally close as Hayne and West are, they have contrasting personalities. They operated in very different ways but often complemented one another. West can be loud, outgoing, and obnoxious. Hayne is quiet and reserved, but with a hair-trigger temper. On the witness stand, West was cocksure to the point of careless. As one former county coroner put it, West "would always say what he said according to who paid him the most to say it." In the past, West compared his forensics genius to the musical acuity of violinist-conductor Itzhak Perlman and described his error rate as "something less than my savior, Jesus Christ." Hayne was a confident and sometimes arrogant expert witness. He was gifted at giving prosecutors just enough to make their case to a jury without giving testimony that was obviously false. He chose his words carefully. He would often tell juries that a victim's injuries were "consistent with" the prosecutor's theory. Even if that theory was wholly improbable, so long as the victim's injuries were consistent with it, Hayne's testimony wasn't, by definition, completely wrong.

West wrote boastful reports larded with certainty. He used words and phrases like "astronomical," "without question," and his trademark, "indeed and without a doubt." He often claimed to be the best in the country at what he did, and that few others were capable of his forensic wizardry. Hayne, on the other hand, typically wrote vague, malleable autopsy reports. His lack of interest in detail may have been due in part to the sheer volume of autopsies he was performing. But keeping specifics out of his initial reports also had the advantage of allowing him to massage his conclusions in court. Defense attorneys who have opposed him over the years say the vagueness of his reports made it difficult to prepare for questioning him. "He can't be nailed down on his opinions," said André de Gruy in a 2007 interview. "Hayne gives prosecutors leeway to say whatever they want. But he maintains plausible deniability."

Nearly everyone who has known Hayne also acknowledges his intellect, and in particular his social IQ—his ability to read and react to the people around him. Michael West is a different story. Depending on whom you ask, he's either a mad genius or a raving idiot. More importantly for an expert witness, West was very good at *sounding* smart. He threw around bite mark and forensics jargon with ease. He often peppered his testimony with references to art, Latin, classical music, and antiquity. Never mind that those references weren't always accurate. On occasion, when he wanted to be combative with an attorney, West would throw out a Latin phrase or a reference to some book he'd recently read and then say something like, "Do you know what that means?" or "Should I explain that to you?"

The two men were remarkably successful at networking, although they went about it in different ways. West would buy rounds at bars frequented by cops and prosecutors. He'd be the life of the party at sheriffs' association meetings. He was a backslapper, the kind of guy who broke the ice with a raunchy joke, usually before feeling everyone out to be sure all would be comfortable with it. He was the sort who sealed new friendships over rounds of drinks. Hayne also networked, but in starkly different ways. For several years, he threw a swanky annual Christmas party at the University Club in Jackson. Honored guests included state prosecutors, police officials, legislators, and coroners. He also made campaign contributions.

Both Hayne and West seem to have found little time for personal relationships. Both men have had multiple marriages and gone through contentious divorces. Still: "Everyone liked Hayne," one former coroner says, before adding that the same couldn't be said about West.

By the early 1990s, Hayne, West, and Jimmy Roberts would come to dominate Mississippi's medicolegal system. "The Mississippi system was run by the triumvirate for years," says one long-serving former coroner. "Imagine that. A pathologist, a small-town dentist, and a funeral director. . . . The state provided an audience of adoring idiots."

~ 8 ~

ENTRENCHMENT

Never think you've seen the last of anything.

—Eudora Welty

In September 1989, Steven Hayne took a plane to Chicago to take the American Board of Pathology (ABP) certification exam in forensic pathology. His lack of certification had been a factor in his appointment as the interim—as opposed to permanent—state medical examiner in 1987. The ABP is the gold standard in governing organizations. Most states, including Mississippi, require any medical examiner working for the state to be certified in forensic pathology by the organization.

According to the ABP, Hayne failed the test. According to Hayne, he didn't—or not exactly, anyway. Hayne has always claimed that he voluntarily walked out of the exam because he found several of the questions insulting to his intelligence. He has told this story countless times in trial testimony and depositions. But when asked to name specific examples, he has only mentioned a single question that offended him. It allegedly asked candidates to rank several colors in the order in which they're most commonly associated with death.

For example, Hayne provided this explanation in a 2003 deposition: "The questions became so ludicrous, I finally said enough is enough. They gave five different colors. Red, white, blue, green and black. And they asked, rank them in order of association with death. And that became absurd. And I said that was enough."

In a 2001 case, Hayne told the story with a different set of colors. In a 2004 version, he altered the question itself: it no longer asked him to rank the colors but to pick one color most associated with death. In this version, he didn't just meekly walk out: "I got up, handed my paper to the proctor, and said, 'I leave, I quit. I'm not going to answer this type of material.'"

Hayne's explanation for why he never passed the exam has always seemed implausible. Even if the question really was ridiculous, even if there were other, equally ridiculous questions, he had paid a $950 registration fee and bought a plane ticket to Chicago. It couldn't have been the first time he had ever seen a poorly worded question, or an exam that was more of a formality than a substantive test of a candidate's specific area of knowledge. Hayne's explanation for why he was willing to just walk out—that he is a man of certain unyielding principles who has no time for foolishness—seems a stretch. "I've got a temper," he told the *Clarion-Ledger* a few years ago. "I don't put up with crap like that."

Nevertheless, every time he was asked about certification in court, Hayne still claimed to be board certified in forensic pathology. He arguably was. It just wasn't by the ABP, the organization most medical examiners think of when they think of certification. Hayne gave this testimony about both the ABP test and his certification for most of his career. It would be twenty years before he'd be confronted with evidence that contradicted his claims about both.

In June 1990, just a few months before Courtney Smith's murder, Michael West was contacted by Lieutenant Jim McAnnally of the Pascagoula, Mississippi, police department. McAnnally was investigating the death of John Shumock, who appeared to have been smothered in his own bed. The chief suspect was a man named Mark Oppie. McAnnally wanted to know if West could match Shumock's fingernails to the marks on Oppie's body. Thus began one of West's more gruesome adventures.

When West got to the Gulf Coast, he was given police photos of Oppie that showed what West believed to be defensive fingernail scratches on Oppie's neck, arms, and torso. West went to the funeral home where Shumock's body was being prepared and took impressions of the dead man's fingernails. West then went to see Oppie in the county jail, where he compared his replica fingernails to the marks on Oppie's body. After careful examination, West told police that based on his tests "Oppie could not be ruled out" as having been scratched by Shumock's fingernails, but that he'd need to do some additional tests.

In an incredibly ghoulish act, West then returned to the funeral home and *removed the dead man's fingernails* from his corpse. He then mounted them on sticks. West returned to the jail with the sticks and claimed that the victim's fingernails "did indeed and without a doubt" create the scratches on Mark Oppie's skin.

West later admitted that he failed to produce test marks with the mounted fingernails, thus making his procedure impossible for another analyst to reproduce. No one could verify or discredit West's conclusions. Not that the entire episode needed much discrediting—it was transparently ridiculous. And yet the local authorities bought it. After West's positive identification, prosecutors charged Oppie with capital murder and promised to seek the death penalty. Oppie would later plead guilty to manslaughter.

But West was just getting started. On September 7, 1990, less than a week before Courtney Smith's murder, three elderly people were stabbed to death in the rural, unincorporated community of Daleville, Mississippi. The bodies were first brought to Hayne, who performed the autopsies and then consulted with West.

The police suspected a man named Larry Maxwell, who was related to all three victims. They first attempted to arrest Maxwell without probable cause just after midnight on September 8, but backed off when Maxwell threatened to sue. Later that evening, Maxwell was arrested for being drunk and disorderly, though his court briefings suggest the charge was manufactured. Indeed, after the arrest, the police admitted to searching Maxwell's truck for a knife or bloody clothing, but found nothing incriminating.

Maxwell had a solid alibi. He had been working in the kitchen at the Naval Air Station in nearby Meridian at the time of the murder. His alibi was backed by several witnesses at the base. That didn't appear to matter. During their investigation, the police found a knife in a home where Maxwell sometimes stayed. Other than that, there was no particular reason to think the knife was the murder weapon. There was no blood or other biological material on it. Nevertheless, the police handed the knife over to West, who then confirmed their suspicions. He concluded based only on eyeballing the knife next to the stab wounds of one of the victims that the wounds "were indeed and without doubt produced by the butcher knife in question."

Unless a piece of the knife somehow broke off and fell into the body, there's just no way to say one knife was used to create a specific stab wound, to the exclusion of all others. Human skin simply can't record the details of a knife blade in that way. In an affidavit for Maxwell's defense, Chicago forensic pathologist Robert Kirschner called West's conclusions "highly speculative" and "not based on the scientific method." He added, "The fields of forensic science and pathology do not generally accept as scientifically reliable conclusions that a particular knife blade produced a particular knife wound." Another forensic specialist, Michael Bowers, wrote in an affidavit, "I am unaware of any known forensic examination technique involving matching a knife to a wound which would allow a finding that this particular knife and no other was used in the murders."

But West's dubious conclusion merely established the knife as the murder weapon. Because the knife was not found in Maxwell's possession, the police still needed to connect the knife to Maxwell. And so West did. In the first official application of his ultraviolet light wizardry, West claimed to have identified impressions and bruises on Maxwell's hands that were invisible to the naked eye. The knife had a unique handle: it was broken on one side, leaving two exposed metal rivets. West claimed that the rivets made the impressions and bruises he found on Maxwell's hand as he attacked the victims. "The knife in question did indeed and without a doubt make the patterns found on the hands of one Larry Maxwell," West wrote in his letter to local law enforcement. "The patterns on his hands were produced by holding the knife and striking an object or objects several times with each hand. The blows would have been of great intensity."

At a hearing, West then claimed that he had accidentally overexposed the photos he took of Maxwell's hands while examining them under ultraviolet light. The overexposure obscured the very bruises and indentations that only he had observed. This was the only physical evidence implicating Maxwell. West testified that by the time he realized his mistake, Maxwell's hands had healed and no longer exhibited the invisible, inculpatory marks.

Undeterred, West improvised. He made photocopies of Maxwell's hands and then drew in the alleged telltale indentations with a marker, relying only on his memory. Based on this groundbreaking procedure, West declared that "indeed and without a doubt" Larry Maxwell had used the butcher knife to commit the murders.

Maxwell was held in jail for two years before the trial court held a hearing on West's findings. When presented with criticism of his technique by Kirschner and others, West named three other forensic specialists who he claimed had used the same methods. All three subsequently submitted affidavits denying that. One of those specialists was Thomas Krauss, the Kansas dentist who West once claimed inspired his development of the technique. Krauss wrote that West had "no basic understanding" of the tissue he was examining, "nor does he provide an adequate explanation of the 'West Phenomenon.'" He added that West's "only publication on the novel technique has been in a regional police circular," not a peer-reviewed journal.

In the first of just a handful of times a judge would rule against West over the course of his career, Kemper County circuit judge Larry Roberts wrote that West's methods were of "little value, scientifically unproven, and not yet validated or accepted by most of his peers." John Holdridge, who represented Maxwell and had been a persistent and vocal critic of West back then, had hoped the ruling would end West's career. "It just became increasingly clear to me that West was a fraud," he says.

The judge barred West from testifying. And without West, the state had no case. Maxwell was released from jail. By then the case had gone cold. No one has ever been convicted for the murders. In the following years Holdridge would represent several more people implicated by West's magic touch. After the Maxwell case, he began asking forensic experts around the country about some of West's claims. Like Kirschner, who had called West's claims "highly speculative," others gave Holdridge similar opinions.

Maxwell eventually filed a lawsuit against West. A federal district court judge threw out the suit, in part because despite affidavits from Kirschner, Bowers, and other forensic specialists that his theories about the knife and Maxwell's hands were outside the bounds of science, West was able to procure an affidavit of his own from a medical examiner who stated his "confidence that the knife which Dr. West identified as the murder weapon was in fact the murder weapon." The medical examiner added, "I believe that the methods and techniques used . . . was [sic] sound and his opinion was accurate."

Because of that affidavit, the judge ruled, West's conclusions weren't so transparently absurd as to make him liable for Maxwell's wrongful arrest. Instead, it showed that West's conclusions and those who criticized them amounted to a mere "difference of opinion among experts."

That one medical examiner willing to sign an affidavit in support of West's claims: Steven Hayne.

~

In April 1989, Lloyd White became the fourth doctor in six years to be named Mississippi's state medical examiner. Within a few years, he'd also become the fourth to leave the office in frustration.

White, forty-four at the time, was running a private pathology practice in Texas when he was offered the job, which had been vacant for over a year. He immediately struck a diplomatic note, explaining that his hiring didn't mean he'd be assuming responsibility for all of the state's autopsies himself. "As a general rule of thumb, around 300 or 400 autopsies annually is about the maximum one individual can handle to do them effectively," White said.

An editorial in the Meridian, Mississippi, newspaper welcomed White's hiring but feared he was in for a fight. The paper explained that without major changes to the job, White would suffer the same fate as Spruill and Bennett. "The problem is that a single pathologist cannot conduct hundreds of autopsies and, at the same time, make preparations for and give testimony in scores of criminal trials," the editors wrote. "It simply is not physically possible."

Eager to make a good first impression, White tried to relax any fears that major changes were coming. "I want to avoid any suggestions that I'm some sort of reformer who is going to come and fix something that is broken," he said at the time. Asked about that statement in an interview sixteen years later, White said, "I guess I couldn't have been much more wrong than that, could I?"

~

In 1988 Jimmy Roberts obtained a business license to open Mississippi Mortuary Service (MMS) off Highway 80 in the town of Pearl, just down the road from the funeral home where he was general manager. Soon after MMS opened its doors, Hayne began doing his autopsies, forensic and otherwise, in that building. Within a few years, he'd start to get autopsy referrals from coroners, DAs, and police officials from all over the state.

Roberts then persuaded Rankin County officials to designate his business the Rankin County morgue, an act that lent the entire operation the credibility that comes with designation as an official government building, though it was nothing of the sort.

But at least on paper, Central Mississippi now had an "official" morgue. It was a mutually beneficial arrangement: Roberts could help Hayne get autopsy referrals from other coroners, and every autopsy referral earned Roberts a rental fee for his morgue, body transportation fees, plus first crack at pitching his embalming and funeral services to the family of the deceased. Their partnership became more and more lucrative.

The careers of Steven Hayne and Michael West boomed in the early 1990s. With help from West and Roberts, Hayne commandeered the vast majority of autopsy referrals across the state. Few people bothered to ask how a single doctor could do so many. But those who visited Hayne's operation at MMS off Highway 80 got to see the answer for themselves: Hayne was turning out bodies like the state's chicken plants turned out fryers.

"Hayne was constantly looking for any way to cut corners," says one former high-ranking official in state government. "It looked like an autopsy factory. There were no safety precautions." One former police official who butted heads with Hayne referred to the facility as a "sausage factory."

Ken Winter was director of the Mississippi crime lab from 2000 through 2004. "I had to deal with the aftermath of Steven Hayne's shortcuts," he says. "Evidence was frequently improperly labeled. Evidence was tainted because it was improperly packaged and preserved. I once had a case where a woman was raped and murdered in which Hayne had packed all of her undergarments in the same bag. That's a pretty basic thing you never do. When I confronted him, he just shrugged and said, 'Everybody makes mistakes.'"

Winter, who went on to become head of the Mississippi Association of Chiefs of Police, says Hayne's autopsy operation also may have put Hayne and his staff at risk. "They didn't take safety precautions with chemicals or biological materials. Exposure to formaldehyde and other chemicals used with that job can be toxic. I remember one of Hayne's assistants would come by the lab and his hands would be swollen from all the exposure. He could barely bend his fingers."

In depositions, Hayne has angrily refuted such descriptions. "The bodies were treated with respect," he said in a 2012 deposition. "It was not a sausage factory, a sushi shop, no, a slaughterhouse, no. I think that is just outrageous."

The sheer volume of autopsies Hayne admitted to doing also raised questions about how he and a small group of assistants could possibly keep up. Former Columbus, Mississippi, police chief J. D. Sanders said in a 2011 interview with a private investigator, "Often they worked on kind of an assembly line and would have five to eight bodies lined up next to each other. Even my detectives were concerned about cross contamination."

Some former officials have also speculated as to whether Hayne did all of the autopsies himself. "I always found it impossible to believe that Steve did all the autopsies he claimed to have done," one former coroner told an investigator in 2012. "He, even twenty-five years ago, was never in the prime of health. He could not have stood up to the regimen he claims to have followed."

The morgue comprised only one half of the building. The other half was a flower shop owned by Jimmy Roberts's wife. When a body came in that was badly decomposed, Hayne, West, and Roberts would store it in the back of the building. But some bodies were so pungent that they evidently overcame the smell of the flowers—obviously not good for the flower shop business. Those corpses were moved to a separate building. Hayne, West, and the gang called it "the Stinker Room."

As had been the case for much of West's early career, the press was often eager to tout his forensic wizardry. In December 1991, as part of a big series on child abuse in Mississippi, the *Clarion-Ledger* ran a profile of Hayne and West and how their "groundbreaking" ultraviolet light technology was helping solve murders and catch child abusers. It didn't quote a single source who was critical of their work. It almost read like an advertisement for their services.

But attorneys for the people West implicated were increasingly alarmed. In 1992, John Holdridge began filing complaints with several professional organizations. Holdridge's complaints were mostly based on West's testimony in the Maxwell case. He had mixed success. In 1993, the International Association for Identification requested that West relinquish one of his certifications. West resigned instead. In March 1994, two years after Holdridge filed his complaint, the American Board of Forensic Odontology found that West had "materially misrepresented" evidence and data, that the West Phenomenon was not "founded on scientific principles," and that West's testimony was "outside the field of forensic odontology." It suspended him for one year. Shortly after, the American Academy of Forensic Sciences found that West had "misrepresented data in order to support his testimony" in the Larry Maxwell case, and that the term "indeed and without doubt" was unsupported by scientific research. West resigned before he could be expelled.

West's suspension and resignation were not enough to prevent prosecutors from retaining his services. If anything, it all may have burnished his image as a pioneer who was unfairly set upon by colleagues who were jealous of his success. It also didn't stop other courts from allowing him to present his findings in their courtrooms. And it certainly didn't stop West from using the West Phenomenon in criminal cases.

"That's what I found most disturbing," Holdridge says. "The courts were supposed to be the gatekeepers, the entity that kept bad science out of these cases. Instead, these judges would decide that they'd just leave it up to the jurors. But jurors don't have time to educate themselves on the science. They aren't equipped to ask these questions and draw these kinds of distinctions."

That what West was espousing as expertise wasn't grounded in science didn't seem to matter. What mattered was that he was effective with jurors. Judge Roberts's rebuke in Larry Maxwell's case proved to be the rare exception, not the rule. West would go on to be certified as a witness dozens of times over the next decade, and his methods and practices were routinely upheld by appellate courts. "My sense is that judges, especially elected judges, find it very difficult to rule on these issues when it's going to seriously affect the prosecution in a high-profile case," Holdridge says. "They don't want to inject themselves into the case. It's just much easier to let two experts butt heads, and leave it to the jury to decide which one they believe."

As West's business continued to boom, so did the breadth of his alleged forensic abilities. In 1991, he claimed to match an abrasion on a murder victim's body to the laces on a defendant's shoes. He then used his new technique to find a pattern on the defendant's right palm that he claimed "was a match" to the strap on the victim's purse.

The same year, West testified that he had matched marks on a rape victim's vaginal area to the defendant's teeth. He also testified that while using the West Phenomenon, he detected a pattern on the victim's hand—viewable only using his ultraviolet light method—that he said was a match to the handle of a screwdriver police believed the attacker used to threaten the victim. As in the Maxwell case, West was claiming to find patterns on these suspects that had been imprinted by something they'd grasped or squeezed days before. He was not only able to find the patterns, he could somehow distinguish them from any other items the suspect might have grasped or squeezed since.

The following year, West's bite mark identification led to the arrest of a Mississippi man for the rape and murder of an eighty-year-old woman. The police were so confident in West's identification that they didn't bother testing the blood, hair, fingerprints, and skin cells found at the crime scene. The man spent a year and a half behind bars before his attorney demanded the tests, which exonerated his client.

In 1992, West would make another bite mark identification that would earn him national attention. In the summer of 1991, Louisiana couple Anthony Keko and his wife, Louise, were in the midst of a bitter divorce. The couple owned some extremely profitable oyster beds, which had become a point of contention in the divorce. When Louise Keko's body was discovered half submerged in her bathtub, beaten, shot, and stabbed, her sixty-two-year-old husband was naturally the prime suspect. Both Kekos were known to be hot tempered, and Anthony in particular had a reputation for violence. He had previously been acquitted of a separate murder (he claimed self-defense), and several witnesses claimed that he had spoken openly about killing his wife.

Keko had an alibi, although not a great one. His girlfriend said he had been with her on the night of the murder. There were other reasons to suspect someone other than Keko. The crime scene showed signs of a fight and a vicious struggle. When Keko was arrested, he had no injuries—no scratches, scrapes, or bruises. The police were also unable to find any of his hair, blood, or skin or any other biological material at the crime scene.

More than a year after the crime, a new sheriff took office after explicitly campaigning on a promise to solve Louise Keko's murder. The new sheriff brought in Steven Hayne and Michael West to help. In October 1992, Louise Keko's body was exhumed. She had been buried for fourteen months. Using his blue light and yellow goggles, West claimed to find a bite mark on Louise Keko's shoulder. He claimed he could also tell that it had been inflicted near the time she was killed. West then compared a mold of Anthony Keko's teeth to the mark and declared that the mark on Louise Keko's shoulder was from a bite, and the bite had "indeed and without a doubt" been caused by the teeth of Tony Keko.

Unfortunately, West and Hayne then failed to properly preserve the skin they excised from Louise Keko's shoulder. According to West, they put the tissue sample in a solution to keep it intact but had apparently chosen the wrong preservative. Two weeks later, West said the sample had been destroyed. Everyone would just have to trust him.

And they did. Anthony Keko was convicted and sentenced to life in prison. One juror would say later, referring to West's light-and-goggles method, "Well, he impressed all of us. He said it brought the teeth marks out on her where he had bit her at." Another defense attorney who had faced off with West later tried to explain to *Newsweek* how West could charm a jury into agreeing with him, despite obstacles like a body that had been exhumed after fourteen months, or that his own incompetence had destroyed the evidence. "It's like you're in his living room and he's saying, 'Who would ever disagree with me, because I'm so smart and such a nice guy?'"

Two years later, a judge ordered a new trial. As it turned out, at the time West testified at Keko's trial, he was still under suspension by the American Board of Forensic Pathology. That fact was never disclosed. After another two years, and on the eve of Keko's second trial, the judge called a hearing to determine whether West's testimony should be admitted.

In a strange turn of events, one of the detectives who had worked the original case flipped and testified for the defense. He told the judge that he and other detectives had implicated Keko to West. They had told West about the previous murder charge and that the couple had been going through a nasty divorce. And though the police originally had thirteen suspects, they only told West about Keko. His was the only dental mold West analyzed. The judge ruled in Keko's favor, finding that the police had biased West against Keko. Again, it was one of just a handful of times a judge refused to allow West's testimony into evidence. The ruling left the state with very little evidence. In December 1994 the charges against Keko were dropped, and he was freed. Louise Keko's murder remains unsolved.

The Keko case put West back in the national headlines, but this time the coverage was skeptical at best and often critical. The case and

West's role in it were mentioned in *Newsweek*, the *American Bar Association (ABA) Journal*, the *National Law Journal*, the BBC, and a John Stossel special on *ABC News*. Yet none of it had much effect on West's ability to get new referrals or to testify in court. The *ABA Journal*, for example, talked to the Louisiana prosecutor for whom West had helped win a conviction by matching abdominal bruises to a pair of hiking boots. Would the fallout from the Keko matter deter him from using West again? "I'm quite confident in the guy," the prosecutor answered. "I have a lot of faith in him. And I think he makes one heck of a witness." In that article, West dismissed his critics as jealous colleagues and "ACLU types."

In a 1994 article in the *National Law Journal*, West blustered that the groups that had disciplined him were a "joke" and those who voted to sanction him were "vastly ignorant." But he then made a striking admission: he conceded that his testimony in the Larry Maxwell case was "unscientific." Oddly, he excused himself by explaining that this was the first time he had used the West Phenomenon in a criminal case. He assured the reporter that he had since perfected the technique. That West admitted that he had implicated a man for murder based solely on the results of a procedure he had never performed before, hadn't tested, and now knew was "unscientific" seemed to go completely unnoticed. Another Louisiana assistant district attorney told the publication that he still believed in West. "He testifies well and he came with a curriculum vitae that was out of this world. I was sold on his technique. To me he was ahead of his time."

More and more judges were allowing West to testify, even as his testimony moved further and further from anything resembling science. Prosecutors and police still wanted him. The courts still let him testify. And juries still believed in him.

Mississippi officials have often claimed in the years since then that Hayne and West merely filled a yawning gap in the state's criminal justice system. If a coroner needed an autopsy done, there was really no other place to turn. There's certainly some truth to that. The state did suffer (and still suffers) a perennial shortage of certified and credible medical examiners, as did (and still does) much of the rest of the country.

But Hayne and West also aggressively marketed themselves. They wrote articles advertising their methods and then touted their many publications to establish their expertise. Between 1989 and 1994

alone, they published various versions of the same article about using ultraviolet light to observe wound patterns in eight different law
enforcement publications. The articles were often unapologetically
partisan, touting how their novel technology could be used to secure
convictions. At least one article—"Alternative Light Sources for Trace
Evidence Can Lead to Higher Conviction Rates"—featured head shots
of both Hayne and West and closed with a direct appeal: "If you'd like
to find out more about the practical uses of alternative light source
detection, or to ask how you could put it to work in your department,
contact Dr. Michael H. West," followed by West's address and phone
number.

West did most of the in-person promotions. "West was always
hanging out at sheriffs' conferences and events," says Tommy Ferrell,
the Adams County sheriff from 1988 to 2004. (Adams County, home
to Natchez, sits on the Louisiana border in southwest Mississippi.)
"He'd buy everyone drinks, tell dirty jokes, slap a lot of backs." "He
was likable. Friendly. Seemed real knowledgeable about what he did.
At first I found him trustworthy too, in the sense that he seemed pro-
law enforcement."

Ferrell was first referred to West in the early 1990s by a local pathologist, but he says he inevitably would have run into the dentist anyway.
"By—I don't know—the early '90s or so, if you called the state crime
lab to report a body, West would show up to take it to the morgue in
Rankin County. If you sent a body to the state crime lab, West would
show up there, too. He was just everywhere. You couldn't avoid him."

Ferrell eventually grew wary of West but says he understands why
some officials kept using him. "You have to understand the position
we were in," he says. "We're not experts. The state said these guys were
the experts. They were the only people available. So we just went with
what the state told us."

Lloyd White had seen what happened to his predecessors, Faye Spruill
and Thomas Bennett. So when he took over in 1989, he emphasized
diplomacy. He went out of his way to avoid public fights. But he did try
to improve the death investigation system from behind the scenes, with
new rules that required annual minimal competency tests and more
thorough continuing education for county coroners. Instead of relying
on the legislature, he filed his reforms as regulations with the secretary

of state, which allowed him to improve the system without pushback from the coroners. Many of the changes he made are officially still part of the state regulatory code, although in the twenty-five or so years since he implemented them, they have often gone unenforced.

Still, White was concerned about the cozy relationships Hayne and West had developed with coroners, cops, and district attorneys. In interviews, he recalls a typical example: White had just performed an autopsy on a woman found dead in her bathtub. He couldn't immediately determine a cause of death. He suspected the victim had been strangled, but he couldn't yet be certain. He'd need to wait for results from toxicology and microscopic tests. When he told this to District Attorney Forrest Allgood, the DA evidently wasn't satisfied. According to White, Allgood wanted an immediate diagnosis that would allow him to charge his suspect.

The next day, White received a phone call from Steven Hayne. As White tells it, Hayne told him that the previous night, the body had been taken to Jimmy Roberts's morgue in Pearl, where Hayne performed a second autopsy. No one had asked White's permission, and White wasn't present for Hayne's autopsy. Afterward, the body was quickly embalmed and buried.

White was the state medical examiner. By law, he had ultimate authority over any death investigation in Mississippi. In the real world, that authority meant little. Hayne ended the phone call by telling White that he had officially determined that the woman had been strangled. Hayne then suggested it would be in White's "best interest" to issue a report agreeing with him. White refused and told Hayne that what he was asking would be a "deliberate falsification of evidence." Hayne hung up.

"There was a tendency to slant things to favor the people you're working for," White says, looking back. "The politics and power could sometimes run roughshod over people's civil rights."

By the time White took office, Hayne and West were already up and running at Jimmy Roberts's place, an operation that White derisively called "McAutopsies." But White was savvy enough to see that Hayne was already too powerful to take on directly. Disturbed as he was by what he saw, he opted for a more low-key, fight-the-battles-you-can-win approach.

But even that strategy made White enemies. And so as with his predecessors, he didn't last long. In March 1992, he was put on

administrative leave while the Department of Public Safety investigated sexual harassment claims against him. The complaints were
never litigated or made public. At the time, White told local press
that the suspension was just for a few days and that it was an internal matter. But White was fired the following month. At the time,
White vaguely said he was terminated over a disagreement with his
superiors. Some sources have speculated that White was set up because he was preparing to take on Hayne, and because some of the
state's more powerful prosecutors wanted Hayne to have White's job.
Charles Tisdale, publisher of the black Jackson newspaper the *Advocate*, wrote that "Mississippi public officials and employees conspired
to discredit . . . White and banish him from the state." White himself
still hasn't said exactly why he was fired.

But White went out in a fury. He decided to ditch the diplomacy
and raise some hell about what he had seen. He wrote a long letter
to Tisdale and the *Advocate*—a hard-hitting publication that proudly
called itself "the most firebombed newspaper in America." White was
particularly concerned about the death investigation system's impact
on civil rights. In the early 1990s, national media outlets began to
focus on a series of jailhouse suicides across Mississippi. The stories
that got the most attention tended to be about young black men found
hanging in their cells, some of whom had been arrested for crimes as
petty as traffic violations. A familiar narrative began to emerge: Mississippi was killing black people again.

Steven Hayne had done many of the autopsies in these cases and
had determined that nearly all of them were suicides. As the story
gained national traction, Hayne emerged as chief debunker of the
growing fear that black men were being lynched in Mississippi's jails.
"There is no evidence of murder in any of these cases," Hayne said in
the *New York Times*. "None."

White actually *agreed* with Hayne in most of these cases. He
thought the real scandal was that the jails were such decrepit, godfor-
saken places that people arrested on minor charges could be driven
to suicide in the first place. But he was also outraged that Hayne was
being entrusted to make the call in such sensitive, high-stakes cases.
White noted that Hayne wasn't board certified by the ABP, and experiences like the one he'd described with Allgood taught him that
Hayne couldn't be trusted. White also argued in his letter that under
Mississippi law, the state medical examiner's office was supposed to

perform all autopsies on people who die in state custody. Sending the bodies to Hayne wasn't just problematic because of Hayne's credibility issues; it was a violation of state law.

White was also concerned about black people killed by police shootings and beatings. Many of these, he thought, *were* intentional. He worried that the focus on the jailhouse deaths was detracting from "the real problem, a thoroughly corrupt and inadequate system, in which black people and other minorities are traditionally regarded as something less than human." He also worried that those intentional killings were being whitewashed by the state's pliant coroner system. "They want a compliant, easily controllable non-entity who will be subservient to the Highway Patrol, and testify in court the way [DPS Commissioner] Jim Ingram wants him (or her) to," White wrote.

White's letter called the state's death investigation system "a complete sham and a fraud." He called Hayne out by name, noting that despite his lack of credentials and poor practices, "Hayne continues to autopsy jail and prison deaths, as well as persons killed by police or sheriff's deputies, and to generate hundreds of thousands of dollars in personal income as a result of his extremely cozy relations with . . . state employees and officials." White later made even stronger accusations in an affidavit on behalf of the family of a black man who had died in police custody.

In July 1992, three months after White was fired, DPS commissioner Jim Ingram consulted with Hayne and came up with a plan to reappoint Hayne as the state medical examiner. This time, Hayne would serve with no salary or benefits. Instead, he would simply continue to do autopsies as they were referred to him by coroners, prosecutors, and police—and collect the $500 fee from the counties, plus the hourly rate for testifying in court. Ingram argued that this was just too good a deal for the state to pass up. Mississippi would save $125,000 per year in salary and benefits.

Of course, Hayne still hadn't passed the ABP exam, so under state law he still wasn't qualified for the position. State officials were working on a way around that too. They had persuaded state representative Steve Holland, himself the owner of a funeral home, to introduce a bill to do away with the certification requirement.

For Hayne, the arrangement would have been ideal. He'd get the official state title. He'd continue to get paid to do autopsies as a private physician. And there would be no one like Lloyd White trying to impose oversight. He'd be his own oversight. The year before Ingram proposed the idea, Hayne grossed about $500,000 just on state-referred autopsy fees. That didn't include his fees for preparing and testifying in court, extra money for lab tests, or the money he was making from consulting and doing autopsies in civil cases. The state medical examiner position paid less than $100,000 per year.

But a week later, the Mississippi Ethics Commission nixed the idea, finding that the arrangement would raise "suspicion among the public" and "reflect unfavorably upon the state and local government." The commission added that it had a "grave concern as to the practicality and propriety in having a pathologist conducting such a large percentage of the state's autopsies also responsible for the rules and regulations under which he and his professional colleagues perform the public duty."

That the arrangement presented a massive conflict of interest should have been obvious to everyone involved. That it was even proposed was good evidence that Lloyd White was right: state officials didn't want a modern, objective death investigation system. They wanted one they could continue to control.

~ 9 ~

THE TRIAL OF
LEVON BROOKS

I am an invisible man . . . I am a man of substance,
of flesh and bone, fiber and liquids—and I might
even be said to possess a mind. I am invisible, understand, simply because people refuse to see me.

—Ralph Ellison, *Invisible Man*

To enter Macon, Mississippi, you have to take a spur off the main
highway and follow the signs to town. Though Macon is the Noxubee
County seat, the closest highway veers right around it. Macon offers
no Lions Club signs or billboards or catchy slogans to welcome motorists, as similarly sized towns often do.

But as you enter the town, there is one feature that is unique to
Macon, though it's much subtler than a boast about a famous son or
a clever nickname: the spur itself is lined on both sides with embank-
ments of eroded and striated chalk deposits. It's left from long ago,
after tens of millions of years of Cretaceous life, when this part of Mississippi was under the sea. When the sea receded, the calcified remains from an epoch of aquatic life created an alkaline base ideal for
plant growth, giving rise to thick, grassy prairies. Millions of years of
seasonal cycles on the prairie then birthed a black, loamy soil.

It's those piles of dirt that give this part of Mississippi its identity.
Today the region is known as the Black Prairie Belt, a crescent of grassland that starts at the Mississippi-Tennessee border, widens as it swoops
south to Noxubee County, and then takes a hard turn to the east as it
tapers off across south central Alabama. With the exception of a thin
tract of piney hills on its western border, all of Noxubee County is prairie. It features more grassland than any other county in the belt.

While the Black Prairie Belt was first named for its geological history, it has also become a colloquial reference to the skin color of the majority of its inhabitants. When the Choctaw Indians left the region in the 1830s after signing a lopsided treaty with the federal government, white settlers quickly moved in and put the rich new land to the plow. Less than two decades later, Mississippi was producing 194 million pounds of cotton per year, nearly all of it pulled from farmland in either the Delta or the Black Prairie Belt. Virtually all of the Mississippi cotton boom was harvested by African slaves. In 1830 Mississippi had a slave population of slightly more than 65,000. By the start of the Civil War three decades later, the number had ballooned to 436,631. Noxubee County's share at the time was 15,496, almost three times the size of its white population.

The end of the Civil War brought liberation for the slaves under federal law—at least in name—but it also marked the beginning of a decades-long effort by state authorities to resurrect an economy built on forced labor. In 1865, newly elected Mississippi governor Benjamin G. Humphreys called a special session of the state legislature to discuss what he called the "negro problem." His solution, quickly adopted by the state legislature, was the Black Codes, a series of draconian laws that deployed the criminal justice system to enforce de facto slavery. Instead of ensuring justice, this new criminal justice system would traduce it by creating "free" labor in the form of prison inmates.

The Black Codes infected every part of quotidian life. They criminalized black vagrancy, which they defined so broadly that it applied to nearly every poor black resident of the state at just about any time. For black people caught up in this system, a trial on the merits wasn't worth the enmity it attracted among local law enforcement officials. Few lawyers were willing to defend a black misdemeanant, anyway. So most pleaded guilty. The punishment was generally a fine, but because most blacks were too poor to pay, frequently their only option was to hire themselves out to someone willing to pay it for them. For destitute blacks—the Black Codes' intended victims—that invariably meant returning to the plantation.

In 1870, the Noxubee County Census listed thirty-two black people with the last name Brooks. Levon Brooks's ancestors were no doubt among them. As far as he knows, his family has always lived in or very near the county. Brooks and his brothers and sisters were all born and raised on a large farm in eastern Noxubee, where his mother, father, and several uncles all worked for decades.

The same census listed thirty-five local black people with the last name Brewer. Kennedy Brewer's ancestors were also likely part of that population. Brewer's mother, now in her mid-seventies, says she and her family have been chopping cotton in or around Noxubee County for as long as she can remember. She raised fourteen children. Her son Kenny, as she calls him, was her "knee baby"—her penultimate child. When asked how old she was when she began working in the fields, she answers, matter-of-factly, "Just old enough."

In the late 1870s, Congress convened a joint select committee to investigate reports of violence and brutality inflicted as part of the "Mississippi Plan," an effort by the white establishment to overthrow the Reconstruction Republican government. In Noxubee County, one witness described "the whipping of men to compel them to change their mode of voting, the tearing of them away from their families at night, accompanied with insults and outrage, and followed by their murder." There were fifteen such murders in Noxubee County alone.

From the end of Reconstruction through the Depression era, historical records suggest that Noxubee County was isolated from much of the rest of the state. The county not only suffered its fair share of violence, it was too rural and isolated for many outsiders to take notice. One of the few outside organizations to have any consistent contact within the county was the Southern Tenant Farmers' Union (STFU), a Depression-era labor group founded in the Arkansas delta. A few locals had formed a branch of the union in the Black Prairie region. But they may have done so more to establish a lifeline to the outside world than to actually organize tenant farmers. Many of the members' pleas to STFU president J. R. Butler weren't about union matters but read like desperate cries for help. The letters, written mostly in pencil on scraps of paper and on the back of outdated calendars, chronicled tales of raw violence. One archivist of the letters later observed that they seemed to be written merely in the hope "that someone in the outside world would at least care."

Butler quoted one such complaint verbatim in a letter to Walter White, the executive secretary of the NAACP: "Listen, something happened down here in Brooksville with one of our young men. This young man was courting a girl and was attacked by a mob of three white men, one of them castrated him by cutting the whole sack off." Between 1901 and 1927, white mobs murdered at least seven black residents of Noxubee County—there were likely even more victims. The year 1927 was particularly violent. In May, a black man accused of killing a white farmer was shot two hundred times, while two other black men were burned to death in Macon. No coroner's jury indicted their killers, so their names are lost to history.

Boswell Stevens was an influential Noxubee County farmer and land-owner, a local power broker, and an ardent segregationist. In the spring of 1865 Stevens's grandfather, a former Confederate soldier, had come to the eastern part of Noxubee County with little more than "a gray uniform and a poor horse," and settled along its northeastern edge. After two years of hard work, he, his wife, and his father-in-law had earned enough money to buy 25 acres of their own. That 25 acres eventually grew to 1,500, and a small farm swelled to become a thriving plantation.

Stevens was born on that plantation and eventually inherited it. As owner and operator of one of the region's largest farms, he embraced the role of civic leader and joined the local branch of the American Farm Bureau, the nonprofit advocacy group for farmers and denizens of rural America. Noxubee formed its first farm bureau in the summer of 1923 with a membership of about 225 farmers.

As his plantation grew, so did Stevens's reputation. In 1950 he was elected president of the state bureau. It was an enormously influential position. Each year, the federal government gave tens of millions of dollars in subsidies to the American Farm Bureau's various branches. Arch-segregationist and Mississippi senator James O. Eastland, chair of the Senate Agriculture Committee, made sure a huge chunk of that money made its way back to Mississippi. Stevens then got to distribute it. He used the money not only to support the state's white farmers but to shore up the state's defenses against integration.

After the Supreme Court's 1954 decision in *Brown v. Board of Education*, Stevens allied himself with the local Citizens' Council and kept in close contact with the newly created pro-segregation Mississippi State Sovereignty Commission. The commission's director considered Stevens an "enthusiastic" supporter of the agency's goals. One 1959 Sovereignty Commission report noted that "white people were exceedingly hard on the Negroes" in Noxubee County, but the abuse was "necessary to keep them under control." Citizens' Council sources reported zero registered black voters in Noxubee and about the same amount of NAACP activity. A report the next year declared race relations in the area "in very good condition," thanks mostly to intimidation by the Citizens' Council. Of course for blacks, "very good condition" meant full-bore segregation, systematic violence, and no voting rights.

For decades, the Stevens family farm was one of the most renowned in eastern Mississippi. Produce from the plantation perennially collected blue ribbons at the Noxubee County fair, and the Stevens children usually placed in the fair's child beauty pageants. Boswell Stevens eventually moved on from the farm bureau to be elected president of the National Cotton Council, a high honor that brought yet more renown on the plantation.

Today, "Bos" Stevens—Boswell Stevens's grandson—is the postmaster in Brooksville, Mississippi. He sometimes gets lost recalling the olden days. While he's certainly cognizant of the ugly racial oppression that underlies his memories, he speaks fondly of his upbringing. With gray hair protruding from under his Mississippi State baseball cap, he recalls the big iron bell that rang in the morning to wake everyone up. The same bell rang again at noon to announce lunch. Bos would typically scarf down his meal as quickly as possible so he and the boys his age could play an inning or two of baseball before heading back to the fields.

Many of Bos's friends were children of the farm's black laborers. They lived in the tenant houses lining the roads that crisscrossed the fields. Most had their own garden plot. Few had electricity. Almost none had running water. Tenants could buy meat and staples at the commissary, a log structure behind the main house.

Some of Stevens's fondest memories are about the cotton harvest each fall. His family would park wooden wagons at the end of the cotton rows, and the fields would be full of pickers, adults and children, from the Stevens plantation and nearby farms. Workers still picked by hand, even through the mid-1960s, long after most other farms had mechanized. Those who picked the most and the fastest won prizes. Adult winners received a ham. Children got treats. And all of it was laid over with the singing of songs—spirituals, of course, but funny ditties, too.

Stevens is still moved by the nostalgia of those days. "It was what it must have been like a hundred years before," he says. "I mean, it was terrible too. I know that. But there was something beautiful about it."

After his father took over management of the farm, Stevens recalls one afternoon in particular in which he had asked his dad how many people lived on the plantation. His father looked at him with a blank stare. That was a good question, his father said—and one to which he didn't know the answer. So Bos and his father hopped in a truck, drove through the property, and began counting. They counted behind the house toward the dairy barn, and then in the other direction, toward the opposing fields. By the time they finished, they had tallied about 150 black tenants.

Had they stopped at one particular tenant house several hundred yards southeast of the main house, in a field alongside five or six other shacks of the same design, they could have peeked inside and made the acquaintance of Rich and Loretta Brooks, along with their new baby boy. Loretta had already given birth to several other children in that cabin, some at night by lantern light. All had been daughters. The new baby was their first son. They named him Levon.

Some thirty-two years later, a Noxubee County jury will wrongly convict Levon Brooks of raping and murdering a three-year-old girl. Bos Stevens will be the jury's foreman.

~

Shortly after Levon Brooks was charged, a trial judge appointed Robert Prather to be his attorney. Prather had been in practice for a long time and had plenty of criminal defense experience. But there was one significant problem. Prather had represented Justin Johnson after his first attempted rape and was now representing him after his second.

Prather was in a difficult predicament. It's impossible to know if he ever suspected Johnson for the crime (Prather has since passed away), but if he didn't, he certainly should have. At the very least, he should have recognized Justin Johnson as a critical component of Levon Brooks's defense. Johnson was walking, talking evidence that Earnest Eichelberger and Harry Alderson had rushed to judgment, that there were fundamental flaws in their investigation. Johnson was a known sex offender with a modus operandi nearly identical to the one used to abduct and murder Courtney Smith. His car was seen near the pond at the time Smith was killed, and he had no good explanation why. The only reason they'd dropped him as a suspect was because the investigation focused on Brooks long enough for Michael West to apply his forensic methods and seal the deal.

Prather owed a basic duty of care to both his clients, Brooks and Johnson. Central to that duty are loyalty and confidentiality that he couldn't possibly have provided to both. If, in defending Brooks, he pointed the finger at Johnson—or at least pointed out that Johnson was a far more likely suspect—he would have betrayed his ethical obligation to Johnson. And if he didn't suggest Johnson as an alternate suspect, he'd have betrayed his ethical obligation to Brooks.

What Prather should have done was quietly approach the trial judge early on and explain why he needed to withdraw from Brooks's case. Instead, on the day trial began, Prather wrote a vague letter stating that he had represented another original suspect in the case, as well as two probable witnesses. (He represented Sonya Smith after prosecutors charged her with child abandonment for leaving her children at home on the night of the murder. He had also represented William Smith on an unrelated burglary charge.)

According to the trial record, Prather had his cocounsel discuss the matter with Brooks, instead. That should never have happened. It was unfair, unjust, and unethical to put the onus on Brooks. Literally minutes before Brooks's trial was to begin, Prather broached the issue with the court. He told the judge that his prior representation of witnesses and suspects in the case had just "jumped out of the book at me over the weekend." If that was true, he was woefully unprepared for trial. He should have known months earlier that Johnson had been not only a suspect but the strongest suspect.

The judge then asked Brooks if he had read Prather's letter. He said he had. He asked if Brooks had discussed the matter with Prather's cocounsel. He said he had. And he asked if Brooks had any problem with Prather continuing to represent him. He said he didn't. And that was that.

Levon Brooks was about to be tried for murder by the judge who had previously sentenced him for aiding a burglary several years earlier. Brooks's attorney was simultaneously representing another man who was initially a suspect for the murder for which Brooks was being tried, who was by far the more likely culprit, and who in fact did actually commit the crime. And Brooks's fate would be determined by a jury whose foreman inherited the plantation where Brooks was born and where his family had worked as laborers.

∼

In its February 6, 1971, edition, the student newspaper for Columbus, Mississippi's S. D. Lee High School included an interview with eighteen-year-old Forrest "Ox" Allgood. The paper called Allgood the "spokesman" for the school's conservative students. The young Allgood described his politics as "radical right" and feared that though conservatives like him were once a large majority, they were fast becoming a small minority. Allgood railed against student activists who were "burning buildings" and "throwing human excrement at cops." He praised Chicago mayor Richard Daley's infamous order to police to "Shoot to kill!" protesters and rioters after the assassination of Matin Luther King Jr.

Throughout the interview, Allgood portrayed himself as an underdog, even a rebel. He was the conservative fighting for what was right and true, resisting liberalism as it encroached from all sides. (Even, apparently, in Columbus, Mississippi.) "It's hard to be a conservative these days," he said. "If you are not a liberal then you are out."

Today, Forrest Allgood is a Columbus, Mississippi, institution. He was born in the town in 1954, and save for four years of undergrad and three years of law school at Ole Miss (where he briefly played right tackle for the freshman football team), Allgood spent his entire life in Lowndes County. He even appeared as a child on *Fun Time* with Uncle Bunky.

Few prosecutors in Mississippi used Steven Hayne and Michael West more than Allgood. He was first elected district attorney for the counties of Lowndes, Noxubee, Clay, and Oktibbeha in 1989, or at about the same time West and Hayne began working together. Allgood used Hayne often, including in his most controversial cases. He also used West in most of those cases. And he publicly, aggressively defended both men when others began to question their credibility.

At least in appearance, Allgood doesn't resemble the stereotypical Southern prosecutor. He looks a bit like a cross between a tent revival preacher and a roadie for the Allman Brothers. For most of his career, he's sported wavy, surprisingly long hair that dips below his collar in the back, with a cowlick that swoops down to graze the top of his left eyebrow. His slim frame and narrow face strike a skeletal figure, usually adorned with large round glasses, often tinted. He apparently has an affinity for medieval times—his office was adorned with swords, shields, and other paraphernalia from the Middle Ages.

Allgood's colleagues describe him as intensely private, deeply religious, and not particularly congenial. He has never been much for the Southern custom of small talk and exchange of pleasantries, and rarely interacted with other lawyers outside the courtroom. "I don't know if he didn't get humor, or just wasn't interested in it," says one defense attorney who sometimes opposed Allgood. "But I can't ever recall him laughing."

When Allgood speaks, he's careful and deliberate, often leaving long pauses between his words. He rarely gestures, and his mouth doesn't move much when he speaks. It's easy to see how juries might find him persuasive, or at least engaging. You keep listening because he keeps you waiting, if only for him to finish his thought. In its own odd way, his speaking style commands attention.

Allgood joined the prosecutor's office fresh out of law school in 1978, starting as an assistant district attorney. His career tracks closely with the law-and-order movement of the past thirty or so years. His positioning himself as a champion for crime victims, for example, reflects the emergence of the victims' rights movement over the course of his career. "My sympathy is firmly on the side of the victim. It always has been," he has said.

Allgood's politics never changed much from his high school days. One former police chief, who considered himself a personal friend of Allgood's when he was in Mississippi, describes Allgood as "too conservative for the John Birch Society." But more than his politics, it was really Allgood's faith that drove his career in law enforcement. "Allgood has deeply held religious beliefs," says Mississippi defense attorney André de Gruy, who has been practicing in the state since the early 1990s. "He's a fundamentalist, and I think he often acted from there."

For someone so focused on victims of violent crime, Allgood was also an aggressive prosecutor of nonviolent drug crimes. One of his office's last cases involved a seventy-year-old woman given a sentence of ten years in prison for marijuana plants found on her property, even though it was her first offense and no one—including the judge—suspected the woman of distribution, or even of necessarily planting the pot. (The woman pleaded guilty.) In another case from his final few years in office, he prosecuted a woman for "depraved heart murder" because she had miscarried after allegedly consuming cocaine during her pregnancy. That in itself was a highly controversial prosecution, but there was also good evidence that the cocaine isn't what caused the miscarriage.

In a 2015 interview with the *Columbus Dispatch*, Allgood said he believed drug charges were a good way to lock up criminals who had committed other, more serious crimes but were too savvy to get caught. That philosophy of locking up "bad guys" even if the crimes for which they're charged aren't the crimes for which they're most culpable—or perhaps even culpable at all—may help explain how Allgood could seem indifferent when confronted with the possibility that he had convicted the wrong person.

Those who have worked with and against Allgood over the years say he has a formidable intellect. "I always got the sense that he was a bright guy," de Gruy says. "If he had gone into commercial or corporate law, I have no doubt that he'd have been successful at it."

That sort of praise raises a broader question about prosecutors in Mississippi: whether they were really so easily persuaded by Hayne and West—and West in particular—or if they were really persuaded at all. Perhaps it isn't that they couldn't see through some of the more absurd claims; it's that the system gave them little incentive to do so. All that mattered was that the defendant was dangerous or evil.

When confronted with their own testimony that was later strongly criticized by experts, Hayne and West often point to other evidence of a suspect's guilt, or note that the suspect ended up pleading guilty in that case or another. The most likely answer is that it just didn't matter. Forensic experts existed to help convince juries to send bad people to prison. They were a means to a greater good. Whether or not what they said in court was credible and accurate wasn't particularly important.

In the summer of 1991, Levon Brooks was sent to the Mississippi State Hospital in Whitfield for a mental evaluation. The resulting report should have been an additional signal that Brooks didn't present as the type capable of committing a crime as heinous as the one for which he had been charged. The psychiatrists who evaluated Brooks wrote:

> We found no suggestion of a mental disorder in this man. He received a complete battery of psychological tests and these did not suggest impairment in his intelligence, his personality, or his sexual adjustment. We have gotten no suggestion from family members or his girlfriend that he has had mental trouble in the past, nor have we seen any suggestion of mental problems since he has been here.

He has been cooperative, polite, and very pleasant in his interactions with us as well as with other patients and other staff. He has consistently denied commission of the crime.

The staff also noted that Brooks's minimal criminal history wasn't suggestive of a sexual predator. Conscientious law enforcement officials might have taken notice of all of that, particularly when there was another suspect whose criminal history was a much better fit for the crimes. But the system had already decided on Brooks's guilt. He had already been arrested, jailed, and indicted. The only reason for the mental evaluation was to get a doctor to say Brooks was mentally fit to stand trial—and then to be executed. The report stated that he was. Little else mattered.

Brooks's trial began on January 13, 1992. Allgood's opening statement was brief. He set the scene at the Smith household that evening, and then told jurors about the "silent evil cloaked in the shape of a man" that snatched Courtney from her bedroom. Allgood only had one piece of physical evidence, so he hit it hard. "But the man who did this, ladies and gentlemen, left his mark," Allgood declared. "He left his mark in the form of some teeth marks embedded on her arm. The State of Mississippi, ladies and gentlemen, is simply going to prove to you that that man . . . is Levon Brooks."

Allgood didn't even mention Courtney's sister Ashley, allegedly the only person to witness the abduction. Still, his opening salvo was a confident, direct, no-nonsense condemnation of Levon Brooks. His attorneys might have been prepared with a fiery response. Perhaps they'd point out that the only physical evidence against their client was an unidentifiable mark on her wrist, and that the state's expert witness was a controversial figure in an already controversial field. Perhaps they'd point out that they'd be calling two witnesses who put their client at the Santa Barbara at the time the crime was committed. They might have also pointed out how many other suspects were arrested for the crime and how all of them were eliminated based solely on the bite mark evidence.

But they did none of that. Instead, Brooks's attorneys deferred their opening statement until after the state had rested its case. The jury would sit with Allgood's accusation for days without a rebuttal.

The state's first witness was Ashley Smith, who by the time of the trial had turned seven. The judge questioned her first. In an apparent attempt to get her to appreciate the gravity of the proceedings, the judge told Ashley that she must tell the truth. He asked if she went to church and Sunday school. She said she did. He asked her if she knew about God and the devil. She said she did. He then warned her that if she didn't tell the truth, she'd "go to the devil."

Even under different circumstances, threatening a child with the fires of hell seems a bit out of place for a judge. Given that Ashley had clearly been fed false information by either police investigators or prosecutors, the poor girl must have been terrified. If she even partially realized that Brooks wasn't the man she saw, or if she knew she hadn't seen the man well enough to identify him, she had also been told by important men wearing suits and uniforms and badges that he was in fact the man who killed her sister.

There's good reason to believe that Ashley's testimony had been well rehearsed. Her answers at trial were far cleaner and more concise than her interviews with Uncle Bunky. Despite all the time that had passed, her memory seemed to have *improved*. At trial, Ashley immediately said the man who abducted her sister was named "Titee." When Allgood asked her how she knew Titee, she quickly answered, "He was my momma boyfriend."

Again, in her initial interviews she threw out all sorts of other names and only mentioned "Titee" in the second interview, after Levon Brooks had become a suspect. And according to her own family, Ashley barely knew Brooks and wouldn't have known his nickname. This was also the first record of her mentioning Brooks's relationship with her mother.

The transcript of Ashley's testimony reads much cleaner than the transcript of her initial interviews. She saw her sister's abduction. She woke her uncle Tony, who was asleep on the couch, to tell him what happened. Later, everyone realized her sister was gone. The inconsistencies were gone. The wild stories about airplanes, knives, and guns were gone. Nearly everything she had previously said that contradicted the state's theory of the crime was gone.

The defense cross-examination of Ashley went much differently. Prather's cocounsel reminded Ashley that she had told Uncle Bunky that it wasn't one man who took her sister, but three, and that one of them was white. When asked if the abductor had a stocking on his face, she first replied no, and then "I forgot." She reaffirmed that one of the men who took Courtney had a son named Travis, and that she and Travis played together "all the time."

When asked if she told Uncle Bunky that the man went to college with her mother, she said no, she had never said that. (She had.) The defense then asked Ashley about the other things she had told Uncle Bunky, including that her uncle Tony had grabbed a gun or a knife, that the attackers were eating potato chips, and that the abductor was holding a bag of money. She replied *no* to all. She maintained she never told Uncle Bunky any of those things.

It went on like this. Allgood objected a few times, protesting that Brooks's lawyer was repeating the same questions. He was. The problem was that Ashley wasn't giving the same answers.

Allgood must have known how this looked. Ashley's answers to his questions sounded carefully rehearsed. Her answers to Austin's questions sounded like a confused and frightened seven-year-old. On redirect, Allgood asked her, "What did I tell you to tell these people?" That question was clearly aimed at reassuring the jury that she hadn't been coached. Ideally, she'd have answered with something like "nothing" or "only the truth." Instead she replied, "I forgot."

Another of Allgood's attempts to lead Ashley also backfired. Allgood asked, "And this man that you've pointed out in the courtroom as Titee, do you believe—do you really believe that he has a boy named Travis?" This is one of the few things Ashley had said from the start, and it pointed away from Levon Brooks. Allgood needed her to walk it back. She didn't. "Yes," she replied.

Ashley Smith simply wasn't a credible witness, not in her first interview, nor her second, and not at trial. Even if she had actually seen something, she was too young, too scared, too susceptible to influence, and too prone to fantasy to be of value to the investigation, much less to be the only eyewitness at a death penalty trial.

And yet after each of her interviews—whether with Uncle Bunky, the Noxubee County Sheriff's Office, or Forrest Allgood—the adults who interviewed her extracted the vague, contradictory, or ambiguous portions of her answers and deployed them to implicate Levon Brooks. A quarter turned into an earring. "Chavon" turned into "Levon," which turned into "Tie-tee." (Ashley Smith never even uttered the word "Levon.") A white man who went to college with her mother turned into a black man who once dated her. The knife she saw her uncle wield at the abductors turned into a gun—and then just disappeared.

Brooks's attorneys tried to get the recordings of Ashley's two interviews with Uncle Bunky introduced into evidence. Perhaps if the jury could hear those tapes for themselves, they might have noted the stark contrasts between her first interview, her second interview, and her trial testimony. But when the judge refused, Brooks's attorneys' only choice was to ask Ashley about those interviews and her various contradictory statements in order to make sure the jury heard it all. To the jurors, it must have looked as if they were attacking a seven-year-old girl. And that's exactly how Allgood would characterize the questioning in his closing argument.

And yet even for all the ways Ashley Smith's already bad memory had been contorted and co-opted en route to Brooks's trial, Allgood's closing argument took it all a step further.

"From start to finish," Allgood told the jury, "the little girl has never identified anybody else as being the man who came into her bedroom and took her sister away except the defendant. Nobody else. Nobody else. . . . She has said consistently from start to finish this is the guy that took my sister."

That wasn't just wrong. It was brazenly, thoroughly, and indisputably wrong. It's difficult to see how someone could read the transcripts of the original interviews with Ashley and possibly conclude that her story had never changed. But that's what Allgood told the jury. Still today, Allgood insists that this is the case. "Ashley ALWAYS said the man who took her sister was known to her and was 'Tytee,'" Allgood said in a 2017 email interview. "That was the name she had for Brooks. It may or may not be in her initial statement, but she always said that. . . . Just because it isn't in a statement doesn't mean it wasn't said."

Steven Hayne took the stand a couple days into Brooks's trial. Allgood walked through Hayne's qualifications and then tendered him as an expert in the field of forensic pathology. The judge asked Prather if he had any objections. He didn't. The defense made no effort to question Hayne's credibility or qualifications.

Hayne's testimony was pretty straightforward. He said that Courtney Smith likely died of freshwater drowning. She also had other injuries, including bruises on her head and lacerations on the inside of her vagina.

Hayne then testified that he found marks on Courtney's wrist that he believed were left by human teeth. He called in Michael West, who concurred. Hayne also testified he believed the bite was inflicted at the time of death or shortly thereafter, meaning that whoever inflicted it was likely the same person who killed the girl.

Both of these conclusions were problematic. West would later say that the alleged bite marks on Smith's body were only made by a couple of Brooks's upper teeth. These weren't what one might normally picture a bite mark to look like—two arching series of wounds in the shape of a human mouth. They were tiny marks and could have been left by any number of things. Experts who have since reviewed Hayne's autopsy in the case have said it would have been nearly impossible to tell in a body that had been submerged in water as long as Courtney's whether the marks on her body were made before or after her death, much less whether they were made by human teeth.

Because Hayne wasn't the one who implicated Brooks, Hayne's defenders have sometimes claimed that his role in Brooks's conviction was minor and shouldn't cast doubt on his general credibility. But that overlooks these mistakes, as well as others, such as Hayne allowing West to excise the skin around the marks. It also overlooks the history between the two men. Hayne didn't merely bring West on as a consultant and then turn the analysis over to him; he deferred to West in his report. The two were essentially in business together. They advertised themselves to law enforcement agencies in two states. The process they used to tie Brooks to Courtney Smith's murder had become their modus operandi: Hayne would find suspicious marks, conclude they were bite marks, and then bring West in to "match" them to the chief suspect. It's a process they had repeated before, and would repeat over and over again.

During cross-examination, Hayne told Prather that he had assembled a sexual assault kit for Courtney Smith. Hayne was unable to collect any semen or pubic hairs that could be tested for DNA, though he would only say on the stand that he "didn't know" if the crime lab was able to test anything in the kit. Investigators did find male hairs on a blanket, including a male pubic hair that did not belong to anyone in Courtney Smith's family. It also didn't belong to Levon Brooks. Again, this left the bite marks as the only physical evidence tying Brooks to the crime scene.

~

There was one especially odd moment in Hayne's testimony, though more for Allgood than for Hayne. After Hayne described the cuts in the victim's vagina, Allgood asked what could have caused them. Hayne speculated that it could have been a finger or a penis. Allgood then interjected, seemingly from nowhere, "A broom handle for example?"

Allgood would return to the broom handle in his redirect of Hayne, and then again in his closing argument. It isn't clear where this came from, or why Allgood brought it up. It was an oddly specific reference, yet there was no broom found near the crime scene, and no broom handle was ever entered into evidence. We also now know how the crime happened. It didn't involve a broom.

A conscientious medical examiner should have responded that while, yes, it is *possible* that the injuries could have been created with a broom handle, there was no evidence favoring that over a finger, a penis, or any other narrow, bluntly pointed object. But Hayne simply agreed with Allgood. Yes, a broom handle was possible.

Allgood was engaging in a particularly devious rhetorical device, here. Visualization can be incredibly persuasive. The more a prosecutor can get a jury to visualize the defendant committing the crime, the easier it becomes to convince them that he's the culprit. One way to help them visualize the defendant committing the crime is to provide lots of detail. Particularly striking, powerful, or emotional details are especially effective. Allgood knew the jury would be told that there was no semen found in the victim. So getting them to visualize Brooks raping the girl would be difficult. But Brooks, a grown man, raping a small girl with a broom handle? That's a powerfully horrifying image.

Steven Hayne later billed Noxubee County $1,950 for his testimony.

A couple of nights before his testimony, Michael West walked into Roses, a local discount mart. He picked up two packs of cigarettes, a bag of Skittles, mounting tape, tack glides, and a Wispy Walker, a near-life-size doll of a little girl that he'd use in a demonstration for the jury.

West took the stand on January 16, day four of the trial. Allgood had made it clear early on that West would be a critical part of his case. In November 1991, he sent Prather a copy of West's incredibly long CV, along with some purportedly friendly professional advice: "I wouldn't challenge his qualifications."

Prather didn't try to get West disqualified before trial, but he did manage to get some funds to hire his own expert. That expert, Dr. Harry Mincer of Knoxville, Tennessee, had testified against West in other cases, but he wasn't a bite mark skeptic. He was a practitioner. He would prove to be almost as damaging to Levon Brooks as Michael West.

Allgood began by running through West's qualifications. West told Allgood he held the position of "senior crime scene analyst." He noted that he had been on *The Phil Donahue Show* and had testified in thirteen states, and then he named each one. He then ran off the various places where he claimed to have lectured or taught courses on "bite marks or ultraviolet light." He ended, as he often did, with "the FBI academy in Quantico, Virginia."

When it was his turn to ask West about his qualifications, Prather asked just one: whether the American Dental Association recognized the field of forensic odontology as a specialty. West said that it did not. When Allgood followed up, West explained that the ADA only allowed dentists to specialize in one area. So he was glad that forensic odontology wasn't one of those areas, or he'd have to choose between forensics and his dental practice.

"You have to eat, right doctor?" Allgood asked.

"Yes, sir," West replied. They then moved on to the case at hand.

Allgood first asked West about the fact that Courtney Smith had been embalmed before his examination, and what effect that might have had on his analysis. West answered that it would minimize the tendency of skin samples to retract after they've been extracted. Allgood had anticipated that Prather would ask West about the embalming, which would alter and distort the skin. He also knew that West would be asked about his failure to apply a retainer to keep the skin sample in its preexisting shape once it was extracted from the body. West's answer solved both problems. The embalming process's tendency to minimize skin shrinkage had serendipitously counteracted West's failure to use a retainer. Thus, the bite mark and all the minute details within it that he'd later claim were critical to his ability to match it to Levon Brooks had been perfectly preserved.

Allgood next asked West how bite marks could be matched to a specific person. West responded that "everyone's teeth are unique," citing a study from the early 1980s that has since been widely debunked and didn't actually prove the uniqueness of human dentition in the first place. Allgood followed up, "Just like fingerprints or tool marks, then?"

"Exactly," West responded.

Allgood walked West through his "exclusion" of the first twelve dental molds provided to him by the sheriff's office, and then to his analysis of Levon Brooks's mold two days later. This exchange followed:

Allgood: All right. And is that man sitting in the courtroom right now?

West: He doesn't look the way I—the way I—his appearance has changed from when the time I saw him.

Allgood: Okay.

West: This is a photograph of what he looked like the day I examined him.

Allgood: Okay, but is this, in fact, the same man?

West: I—I believe I—I can look at his teeth and tell you if it's him.

(LAUGHTER IN COURTROOM)

One could almost forget that a man's life hung in the balance. The transcript doesn't indicate whether Levon Brooks thought this was funny.

West then began to explain how he could say that Levon Brooks and only Levon Brooks could have left the marks on Courtney Smith's wrist. But before he could get too far into his answer, Allgood needed one more piece of misinformation.

"Now let me back you up just a second," Allgood said. "First of all, Doctor, these examinations, are they generally accepted in the scientific community as being positive for the positive identification of an individual through a bite mark?"

"Yes, sir," West said.

West was wrong. Bite mark analysis may have been accepted at the time in parts of the forensics community (though it has always been controversial even there), but its underlying assumptions have never been verified or accepted by the scientific community.

West then went deep into the details of his analysis. He invoked technical dental terms and interspersed them with the parlance of bite mark analysis. He explained how the "cutting edges" of Levon

Brooks's teeth had "very definite fractures and bevels." He talked about their "L-shaped" curve and how one tooth had "a scalloped-out area with a sharp edge." On the backsides of his teeth, Brooks had "some chips and fractures" and "some wear—what we call wear facets." The "facets" were apparently how West made his positive identification. "When you open and close your teeth and as you get older, the upper and lower teeth wear together so that the cutting edge of the lower teeth actually wears a groove in the back of the upper teeth," he said.

West then talked about the orientation and location of the alleged bite. He first had to determine how the assailant was oriented to the victim to leave the sort of bite he had just analyzed. To demonstrate, West used the Wispy Walker doll he'd bought at the discount mart.

Then there was the skin itself. "Being bit on the skin on your arm is different from being bit on the skin on your stomach or your buttocks or on your legs," West explained. "You have to determine: is this tissue flabby, is it firm, does it have a lot of fat, does it have a lot of give, is it supported, is it tight, loose, et cetera. So what you're actually looking at is if he's in this position and taking into account these anatomical properties of the skin, you try to determine what type of dynamics are going to occur when the teeth grab into the skin and pull across it."

~

The first part of West's answer is unquestionably true. It's one of the main reasons why bite mark analysis just isn't credible. There's simply no way to systematically account for so many variables, along with countless others, such as whether and how much the victim resisted, whether the bite was direct or grazing, which direction the victim may have attempted to pull away, how the victim heals, and the aforementioned problem of skin samples shrinking after excision. Neither West nor any other bite mark analyst has ever offered a calculable way to measure, quantify, or adjust for all of these variables. Instead, they simply eyeball it. They guesstimate. They approximate. That means that the weight of their opinions swings almost entirely on their personal credibility and their ability to persuade. And that means that establishing their credibility with cops, prosecutors, judges, and juries is critically important—far more important than the content of their testimony. This is why West built out a twenty-plus-page CV. It's why he collected titles, and it's why he wrote articles for every magazine, newsletter, and journal that would publish him.

Even given West's typical nonsense about bite mark matching, his testimony in Brooks's case was especially hard to swallow. The marks on Courtney Smith's wrist were tiny and wouldn't be easily identifiable as bite marks to any mere lay person. West needed to account for this. So he posited that Brooks only bit the girl with his two upper incisors, and that only portions of Brooks's incisors actually left those marks. In other words, West was making a positive identification of Brooks based only on two small marks made by portions of just two of Brooks's teeth.

Fortunately, West assured the jury, his pioneering technique with ultraviolet light was perfectly suited for such intricacies. West said the details were too complicated for a lay jury (he added that he was currently involved in a project to "fully describe all of the—uh—biochemical, electrophysical, and optical properties of skin"), but that "for a thumbnail sketch, damaged tissue absorbs UV, healthy intact tissue does not." He said his technique utilized those properties to reveal minute tears and patterns in Courtney Smith's skin that could only have been created by the teeth that bit her.

West next explained that the plaster models he had created of Brooks's teeth didn't provide enough detail for such a delicate analysis. He needed a material capable of capturing more detail. So West revisited Brooks in jail and had him open his mouth again while West pressed Silly Putty—actual Silly Putty—against the back of Brooks's upper incisors. The reason: West said Silly Putty was better for recording the intricate "facets" on the back of Brooks's front tooth that he needed to capture in order to compare the corresponding "bunching" he found deep in the alleged wound on Courtney Smith's wrist.

It's important to appreciate the full scope of West's "creativity" here. He was claiming that the dental substrate he had carefully applied to Brooks's teeth in a controlled environment—a material designed to capture and preserve the unique characteristics of a patient's teeth—was insufficient to convey the level of detail he needed to make a positive identification. Yet somehow, the spongy, fungible skin of a three-year-old girl *was* able to record and preserve those same nuances—this after a bite allegedly delivered outside, as the biter was committing a murder and sexual assault, and after the body had been submerged in water for thirty-six hours, had dried out, and had been embalmed.

Moreover, in his initial analysis of Brooks's teeth, West concluded that they were "highly consistent" with the alleged bite mark, but not a "match." Allgood's office then asked West if he could give them something more certain. That's when West turned to the Silly Putty, the goggles, and the ultraviolet light—just to be certain.

After running through his analysis, West confidently told the jury, "I have no doubt that the teeth of Levon Brooks did and indeed leave the bite mark on the wrist of Courtney Smith."

During cross-examination, Prather got West to admit that bite mark matching was a subjective field, and at the time was practiced by only ninety-two people in the country. He also got West to admit to some pretty embarrassing mistakes. West had actually lost the dental molds taken from Sonya Smith, preventing expert Harry Mincer from analyzing them. More crucially, West had also lost the lower dental mold of Levon Brooks. And as important as he claimed the Silly Putty had been to his analysis, he didn't preserve that either. He sent Mincer only black and white photos he had taken of the Silly Putty after pressing it against Brooks's teeth. There was of course no way Mincer could verify from two-dimensional photographs all those intricate details West claimed to have found. Everyone would just have to take West's word for it.

West also admitted to something that would come up in future cases: one step of his analysis actually involved pressing the suspect's dental mold directly into the alleged bite marks on the victim. This method of analysis has been strongly denounced by other forensic experts, who have pointed out in this and other cases that it distorts the evidence and may even create marks where none existed before. Later, video from two other cases in which West used this method would strongly suggest he did exactly that—he actually *created* the marks he claimed came from the defendant. At the time, however, the "direct comparison" method was deemed acceptable by the American Board of Forensic Odontology, in part because West was so influential in the early years of that organization. The ABFO has since abandoned the method.

In this case, it was especially wrongheaded. Human skin gets increasingly fragile and pliable as it begins to decay. Courtney Smith's body had been submerged in water for thirty-six hours. By pushing Brooks's dental mold directly into the skin, West was distorting the skin, possibly even creating the very patterns he would later say were crucial to his conclusions. He was also altering the skin so that no subsequent expert could analyze the sample in its original condition, making it impossible for anyone to verify his conclusions.

Prather asked West about this. How could he be sure that he hadn't altered the mark itself? West responded, "I did my best to see that that didn't happen."

On redirect, Allgood asked West about how he compensated for distortion. How did he know how to adjust for decomposition, healing, embalming, retraction, variations in skin, and the myriad other variables that could alter a bite mark?

West gave a meandering answer. "Every bite mark or wound pattern has a—a degree of distortion," he said. "Uh—to me the whole technique of being able to analyze wound patterns is actually the ability to compensate for distortion."

Again, he merely eyeballed it. He went on: "When I take impressions of teeth they are not exact duplicates because the word exact means exact. There is going to be a difference of maybe a few microns."

This was classic West—faux humility followed by outlandish boasting. It's also meaningless drivel. A micron is one one-millionth of a meter. The width of a human hair is ten to two hundred microns. The substrate that dentists use to make molds of patients' teeth is thick and gloppy. The process by which the mold is pushed into teeth and then removed is messy and imprecise. The end product is a reasonable likeness of teeth for the purposes of orthodontia or cosmetic alterations, but the notion that it could be an exact replica to within a few microns is ludicrous.

West closed his testimony with a doozy. He said he wanted to make sure the jury knew of his fidelity to his vocation and his recognition of the seriousness of this particular case. On the one hand, he explained, he was well aware that his expert opinion could likely "cost a man his freedom." But he also understood that if he helped implicate the wrong man, it might also "allow an individual to still be loose in the community." For those reasons, Michael West assured the jury, he went "the extra mile on this one."

In the end, West managed to do both. He helped an innocent man lose his freedom *and* helped a killer to remain loose in the community. He then billed Noxubee County $2,902.12 for his testimony.

To make the rest of its case, the state also called Deputy Earnest Eichelberger, Investigator Harry Alderson, Sheriff Cecil Russell, and various members of the Smith family. Brooks's attorneys called several witnesses who put Brooks at the Santa Barbara Club until three or three thirty a.m. The defense also tried to show that Eichelberger's investigation was sloppy and incomplete. No one asked Uncle Bunky to testify.

The most interesting witness for the defense was Sonya Smith, Courtney's mother. Consistent with her affidavit, Sonya Smith testified that when she and Brooks dated, he had never come into her home. At most, she said, she might go out to meet him in his car, but they usually met somewhere else. She verified that they had broken up months before Courtney's death and that Brooks had never been to her current residence on Phillips Loop.

After the defense rested, the judge advised Levon Brooks of his right to testify. He declined. The trial then moved to closing arguments.

In addition to the misinformation he fed the jury about Ashley Smith's testimony, Allgood's closing argument in the guilt phase of Brooks's trial was basically a rehashing of the evidence (or in the case of the fictitious broom handle, nonevidence). Prather had pointed out to the jury that the state had called no witnesses from the crime lab. That's because there was no biological evidence to link Brooks to the crime scene. Allgood countered this by hanging his hat on one of the least reliable forms of evidence: eyewitness testimony from a child. And in this case, Ashley Smith. "You don't get any better evidence than that," he said.

Allgood told the jury that the investigation didn't really "get rolling" until Ashley picked Brooks out of that first photo lineup. "Guess whose teeth marks then wind up on her sister's body but the same man she pointed out?" Allgood asked. "Gee, what a coincident [sic]. Gosh that's funny how that worked out, isn't it?" Of course, it wasn't a coincidence at all. On the witness stand, Michael West had a history of matching bite marks on a body to the authorities' chief suspect.

The jury began deliberations around six p.m. on January 17, 1992. After three hours, the foreman told the judge that they were irreconcilably divided. The vote stood at 10 to 2. The defense asked for a mistrial. The judge refused and told the jury to retire for the night. They would begin deliberations again in the morning. At 2:25 p.m.

the following afternoon, the jury announced that they had reached a verdict. The bailiff brought Brooks in to hear his fate.

The judge warned the courtroom against outbursts or displays of emotion. When he was finished, the court clerk read the verdict:

"We the jury find Levon Brooks guilty of capital murder." Court would resume the following Monday morning to decide if Brooks would die.

That Monday morning happened to be Martin Luther King Jr. Day, which at the time wasn't yet officially observed in Mississippi. As most of the rest of the country paid homage to the civil rights leader, the jury that had just convicted Brooks based on evidence produced by an archaic system designed to cover up lynchings would now decide if he should live or die. A monument to fallen Confederate soldiers stood just outside the courthouse.

During the sentencing phase, Forrest Allgood recalled Steven Hayne, who testified that Courtney Smith likely suffered a lot of pain as she was assaulted and murdered, an attempt to establish that the crime was especially heinous.

Prather called Brooks's parents, who pleaded for mercy and told the jury that Brooks was "a sweet boy." Both stated that they didn't believe he had committed the crime. Prather also called Brooks's girl-friend, Barbara Pippin, with whom Brooks had a one-year-old daugh-ter. She was born shortly after he was arrested. Pippin testified that she had two kids of her own, and that Brooks had always been helpful and kind to them. The defense called Brooks's sister Patricia Rice. She had four daughters and said Brooks often helped her take care of them. They also called a teacher from the elementary school where Brooks worked. She merely testified that Brooks was cordial and punc-tual, but the real intent may have been to get the jury to decline a death sentence by making them doubt Brooks's guilt. Jurors had now heard three separate witnesses say that Brooks had cared for or had access to children, yet Courtney Smith's murder was the first time he had ever been accused of harming one.

The defense also called Sonya Smith. She too asked that the jury give Brooks a life sentence. That the victim's mother requested her daughter's convicted killer be spared the death penalty must have had a profound effect on the jury. It's also clear that Sonya Smith was never entirely convinced that Levon Brooks was guilty.

Allgood then rose to present his closing. He began with three arguments that were unassailable: First, the crime had been committed in the course of a sexual battery. Second, the crime was committed in the course of a kidnapping. And third, the murder was especially heinous, atrocious, and cruel. These were all easy things to prove. There was no question that Courtney Smith was abducted from her home, sexually assaulted, and tossed into a pond to die. And Levon Brooks had just been convicted for it.

Allgood then closed his case with a particularly heartless tactic: he waged a ruthless attack on Sonya Smith, Courtney's mother. He began by telling the jury that Smith had "failed her daughter in life," implying it was her fault that a man had abducted Courtney from her home, raped her, and murdered her. Allgood went on: "Just because she does not believe in the death penalty, just because she does not believe that's the appropriate sentence . . . does that somehow erase . . . the monstrosity of what was done? Does that somehow make it okay—that it's okay to kill little girls in Noxubee County, Mississippi, if their mother agrees to it?"

It's hard to comprehend how Sonya Smith must have felt upon hearing all of that. She had just lost her daughter to an especially heinous murder. Now this prosecutor—who presented himself as the champion of victims everywhere—was accusing her in open court of tacitly approving her own three-year-old daughter's rape and murder, simply because she'd asked the jury to spare Levon Brooks's life.

Allgood then reared back for one last swing. "She was not the best mother to Courtney in life, and she remains so even in death," he said. Allgood wielded the sword and shield for crime victims everywhere—just so long as they didn't stand between him and the execution chamber.

He continued, "You are told that the world is full of cruelty. And it is." Sonya Smith undoubtedly agreed.

To begin their closing argument in the sentencing phase of the trial, Levon Brooks's attorneys asked Levon himself to address the jury. "I know I have been found guilty of capital murder," he said, "but one thing I want y'all to know—I want y'all to have mercy on me and don't kill me because I didn't do it. Thank you." Brooks sat down.

Brooks's attorneys then argued several mitigating factors. They argued that Brooks's crime may have been caused by the fact that he was emotionally disturbed and of limited intelligence. Neither of these things was true, of course; they were trying to save his life. Still, they had already put a psychologist on the stand who claimed Brooks suffered damage to the portion of his brain that governs judgment and restraint. That isn't uncommon in capital cases, but one can only imagine what Brooks must have made of it. Until all of this, he was a cheerful, well-liked man with a great job, a lot of friends, and a baby girl. Now, in the hope of sparing his own life, he had to sit and listen as his attorneys argued in open court about a defect in his brain that made him want to rape and murder little girls.

Brooks's attorneys also pointed to his good behavior in the time he had been incarcerated and awaiting trial, his "Christian background," and the fact that his family had asked for him to be spared. Prather's cocounsel, a black man, invoked the state's history of lynching, though more as a rhetorical flourish than to draw any comparisons between the death investigation system that covered up lynchings and the one that had just convicted Brooks. While they couldn't argue that Brooks was innocent—both attorneys made sure to acknowledge that the jury had already found him guilty beyond a reasonable doubt—they did tell the jury that they could spare Brooks's life if they still had any doubt at all—anything less than reasonable doubt. They then begged the jury to err on the side of caution.

The jury retired to deliberate, and at 7:25 p.m. sent a note to the court that they had reached a decision. Bailiffs brought Brooks from his jail cell back to the courtroom. The foreman passed a slip of paper to the court clerk, who then read it aloud:

"We, the jury, find that the defendant should be sentenced to imprisonment for life in the Mississippi Department of Corrections."

Levon Brooks would live.

~ 10 ~

KEEP THAT WOMAN
UNDER CONTROL

When I go into a courtroom and render an
opinion, it lays me open to savage attacks by
unscrupulous men.

—Michael West

On June 18, 1993, Mississippi got its fifth state medical examiner. Department of Public Safety commissioner Jim Ingram appointed Emily Ward, a native Mississippian, to the position. The thirty-seven-year-old Ward had been a regional medical examiner in Mobile, Alabama. Ingram announced that Ward would also serve as director of the crime lab, the first person to hold both positions. Perhaps as important as anything else, Ward would have use of the state's brand-new, twenty-seven-thousand-square-foot lab and morgue, which had been completed the previous year.

The second woman to hold the office, Ward rose to the position even earlier in her career than Faye Spruill. Both were talented doctors and had thrived in an area of medicine that had proven itself open to women, at least comparatively. As in past searches for a medical examiner, though, there had been a shortage of applicants. The salary was still well below the national average, and after the tenures of Thomas Bennett and Lloyd White, the state had a reputation for being hard on those who took the job. Ward's hiring nevertheless seemed promising. She was smart, board certified, and had experience both in and out of the state. Her roots in Mississippi gave her knowledge (or perhaps forewarning) going into the position that her predecessors didn't have. And her experience in the more modernized Alabama system demonstrated to her that improvements were possible.

Hinds County coroner Robert Martin initially touted the hiring, saying he thought Ward's education, experience, and personality would be an asset to the office. But he'd soon become one of her fiercest critics. And Ward would find out quickly that the men who ran the Mississippi criminal justice and death investigation systems weren't any more ready for a woman telling them what to do in 1993 than they were in 1981.

In September 1993, sixty-five-year-old Texas medical examiner Ralph Erdmann pleaded no contest to seven counts of faking autopsy reports. Erdmann had already given up his medical license the previous month. He was sentenced to ten years of probation and a $17,000 fine.

Since the early 1980s, Erdmann had been performing autopsies on a contract basis for as many as forty rural Texas counties that couldn't afford to hire a forensic pathologist of their own. For the law enforcement officials in those counties who needed an autopsy, Erdmann made it awfully easy. He was willing to come to them, saving them the cost of shipping bodies to state labs. But because most of those counties didn't have the proper facilities, Erdmann had to improvise. He performed autopsies not just in funeral homes but also in garages, alleys, and parking lots. According to true crime author Jim Fisher, who profiled some of Erdmann's work, Erdmann "once performed an autopsy on a door laid across two fifty-five-gallon drums."

Erdmann also had a reputation for producing key evidence that helped authorities crack difficult cases. He called himself the Quincy of the Texas Panhandle, after the popular TV forensic pathologist played by Jack Krugman. But because Erdmann didn't really report to anyone, no one bothered to check just how many autopsies he was doing, or how well he was doing them. The only thing that mattered, it seemed, was that he helped the prosecutors and police officials who hired him.

By the early 1990s it began to catch up with him, in part because his sloppiness began to undermine convictions. In one case, he somehow lost the head of a murder victim. That proved a problem for the state, because the head contained the bullet that prosecutors needed to charge their main suspect. In another case, Erdmann autopsied the body of a man found in a dumpster with a fresh bullet wound to his head. But Erdmann determined that he had died of pneumonia.

On several occasions Erdmann had documented the weight of body organs that subsequent investigations revealed he had never removed. When a panel of pathologists was finally convened to review Erdmann's work, they found that in a third of the autopsies they reviewed, Erdmann hadn't even cut open the body.

Still, as Texas defense attorneys began to complain about Erdmann, prosecutors didn't budge. Instead, they retaliated. When two police officers testified that Erdmann had lied about his results in a case, prosecutors indicted the cops for perjury. One defense attorney who had helped expose Erdmann was himself indicted for witness tampering. The "tampered" witness was Erdmann himself, who complained that the attorney had been threatening him. Even after acknowledging his mistakes, Texas officials at first defended Erdmann, making the argument that he was simply doing his best to help less affluent counties catch up with mounting caseloads.

The parallels to the situation in Mississippi are hard to miss. One Mississippi Supreme Court justice fretted in a 1999 dissenting opinion that after the court's ruling in a bite mark case, "we risk having [Michael] West become the Ralph Erdmann of Mississippi."

There are a couple important differences, but they aren't favorable to Mississippi. When Erdmann was finally exposed, Texas officials convened a panel of pathologists to review his work. Old cases were reopened and reinvestigated by credible and qualified experts. Erdmann was also ultimately held accountable. That still hasn't happened in Mississippi.

There is one other major difference between Ralph Erdmann and what was occurring with Michael West and Steven Hayne. For years after he was exposed, Erdmann was cited as the poster child for bad forensics—a walking, talking argument for more oversight and better checks on expert witnesses. In their 2000 book, Innocence Project cofounders Barry Scheck and Peter Neufeld described the number of autopsies Erdmann did each year as "astonishing." That number?— about 300 autopsies per year. In fact, the most autopsies Erdmann *ever* did in a year was 480.

In his prime, Hayne could pull that off before the magnolias bloomed.

~

For seventy years after the *Frye* decision—the case that set the standard for distinguishing good expert testimony from bad—the US Supreme Court steered clear of establishing any rules for the use of science in the courtroom. In 1993, the court finally addressed the issue in a series of rulings known as the *Daubert* decisions.

The main decision came in *Daubert v. Merrell Dow Pharmaceuticals, Inc.* A group of parents had sued Merrell Dow, the large pharmaceutical company. They alleged that its drug Bendectin, which pregnant women took for morning sickness, had caused birth defects in their children. Ostensibly, the case required the plaintiffs to provide scientific evidence showing that Bendectin caused changes in embryonic development. It became the landmark case in which the US Supreme Court first began to rethink *Frye*, expert witness testimony, and the relationship between science and law.

On one side of the argument were those who believed that *Frye* was too rigid, that it excluded emerging science that was valuable but hadn't yet gained "general acceptance" within its field. On the other were those who believed that the courts needed to reconcile the fundamental epistemological differences between science and law and to adopt a standard that permitted only "settled" science in court.

It was a lot to ask of nine justices, most with very little scientific background. The court ended up attempting to split the difference and may have made things worse. Functionally, the *Daubert* decisions continued what was perhaps the worst but also most inevitable legacy of *Frye*: making judges the gatekeepers. The court instructed federal judges to evaluate expert testimony on factors such as whether an expert's claims are testable, whether the conclusions offered are subject to peer review, whether the methods are governed by standards and protocol, the error rate of those methods, and whether a witness's general testimony has been accepted within a particular scientific community.

It hasn't worked out well. In many ways, *Daubert* exacerbated the problems created by *Frye*. It loosened the standard for the admission of scientific and other technical evidence, but also institutionalized the judge's role as the gatekeeper of such evidence. If that was ever going to work, the Supreme Court should have also required judges to meet some minimum competency in scientific literacy. Of course, it didn't have the power to do that. The fallout has been disastrous: inconsistent rulings about the same type of evidence from district court to district court, and between federal courts of appeals. And to the extent that the courts *have* been on the same page, it has generally been to let bad science in, which essentially delegates the gatekeeping job to juries.

"When I read *Daubert* analyses by judges, it reminds me of what happens when you ask undergraduate students to evaluate the validity of syllogisms," says Professor Michael Saks. "The only thing they know is that they agree with the outcome. And so instead of going through the analysis to reach their conclusion, they begin with their answer, then bluff their way through the analysis. It's mostly for show."

Daubert also exacerbated the ongoing tension between forensic science and science more generally. The former has always seen itself as a tool of the justice system. It was never a product of scientific inquiry. Fields like fingerprinting, arson investigation, blood spatter analysis, ballistics analysis, and tool mark analysis were all developed within the sphere of law enforcement to serve police and prosecutors in solving and prosecuting crimes, not by scientists employing the scientific method. Science is a process of observation, testing of hypotheses, and revision based on the results of those tests. For scientists, being wrong is all part of the pursuit of knowledge. Science is a collaboration. Because forensics was born of our adversarial justice system, it is not collaborative and in fact tends to be contentious—the pattern-matching fields especially. For a forensic analyst, being wrong means a wrongful conviction, or the wrongful exclusion of a guilty party, and serious damage to an analyst's reputation (though not as much as one might think). Less scrupulous analysts adapt accordingly: they just never admit they're wrong. And because most forensic specialties are entirely subjective, it was for a long time nearly impossible to prove an analyst got it wrong. That is, until DNA.

On August 14, 1993, Amy Ware, an elderly woman in Clay County, Mississippi, ate a bologna sandwich for lunch. Sometime that same afternoon, a man broke into her house, robbed her, and murdered her. Suspicion quickly fell on Calvin Banks, who had been playing poker nearby. There was circumstantial evidence to implicate Calvin Banks, but not much. So prosecutors wanted more.

Ware's body was taken to Steven Hayne to be autopsied, and Hayne then consulted West. Local police had found a half-eaten bologna sandwich at the crime scene, and froze it as possible evidence. West wouldn't get around to examining the sandwich for several months, but when he did, he claimed that the bite marks in the sandwich were "consistent" with the teeth of Calvin Banks and "inconsistent" with the teeth of Amy Ware.

There was one problem, which West apparently hadn't realized: in Ware's stomach, Hayne had already documented finding a portion of bologna roughly equal to what was missing from the sandwich that police found in the house. Banks was convicted anyway, but this would become known as the Bologna Sandwich Case, a go-to example of Michael West's excesses.

In 1997, the Mississippi Supreme Court threw out Banks's conviction, but not because of West's testimony. Instead, the court was troubled by the fact that West had discarded the sandwich after examining it. Here again West had "matched" a critical piece of evidence to a suspect, then destroyed it, thus preventing another analyst—and Banks's defense counsel—from verifying his findings.

West claimed he tried to preserve the sandwich by taking photographs—"three pieces of meat and two pieces of bread," he reported—but the bologna began to putrefy, so he tossed the sandwich in the trash. When asked why he didn't freeze it, West said he had considered doing so, but he found from testing other bologna that the freezing dehydrated and shriveled the meat, making it useless for other analysts. Instead, he took photos. Of course, the sandwich had *already* been frozen for months before West himself analyzed it. He didn't explain why the freezing process didn't make the bologna unusable for him but would have made it unusable for any other analyst.

In reversing the conviction, the majority emphasized that their opinion should not affect the ability of prosecutors to use West or bite mark evidence in other cases. In fact, the majority opinion arguably *affirmed* bite mark evidence by finding that it was Banks's inability to have his own forensic odontologist test the sandwich that violated his right to a fair trial. In other words, it wasn't the evidence that was the problem; it was only Banks's inability to test it for himself.

There was a dissenting opinion in that case. Mississippi Supreme Court justice James Smith would have *upheld* the conviction. In his dissent, Smith referred to the court's ruling earlier that year in the case of Eddie Lee Howard. In 1994, Howard was convicted of raping and murdering eighty-four-year-old Georgia Kemp. The victim's body was found in her Columbus, Mississippi, home by firefighters after a neighbor noticed smoke coming from the house. Investigators concluded that the fire had been set intentionally. Kemp's body was taken to Hayne, who concluded that she had been stabbed to death. He also said he found signs of rape, although the rape kit turned up no biological evidence that technology available at the time could test for DNA. Notably, Hayne made no notes in his autopsy indicating that he had found possible bite marks. After the autopsy, Georgia Kemp was buried.

Eddie Lee Howard was unemployed at the time of the murder, lived with a relative near Kemp's house, and had been arrested before for a sex offense. Three days after Kemp was buried, law enforcement zeroed in on him as a potential suspect, and West was brought in to take another look at the case. Kemp's body was exhumed.

West concluded that some marks that Hayne had identified on Kemp's body—but hadn't noted to be suspicious in his autopsy report—were human bites. He then made an impression of Howard's teeth and concluded that the bites could only have come from Howard.

As in other cases, West again made the odd claim Howard had only bitten Kemp with his upper teeth. To claim he could make a unique match based on that was especially suspect in this instance because Howard's upper teeth had actually been replaced with a man-ufactured denture. And yet in 1994, Eddie Lee Howard was convicted and sentenced to death.

Howard represented himself at his first trial. In 1997, the Missis-sippi Supreme Court overturned his conviction. In a 5 to 3 vote (one justice did not participate), the court found that the trial court had improperly allowed Howard to represent himself. But the justices also discussed West and bite mark evidence, and the back and forth was an apt demonstration of just how out of their element judges can be when assessing questionable forensic evidence.

By the time of Howard's appeal in 1997, West had been the subject of several media exposés. He had resigned from two forensics organi-zations and been suspended from a third. West's bite mark testimony was the only physical evidence linking Howard to the crime scene. The police found no blood, semen, hair, or any other biological evi-dence that could be traced back to him.

There *was* some other evidence against him, but in the majority opinion, Chief Justice Dan Lee acknowledged that the state's case was largely reliant on West. He also noted that "numerous scholarly authorities" had called bite mark evidence into question, one of the first court opinions to do so. That welcome bit of skepticism in a majority opinion suggested that at least one time, the Mississippi high court had come tantalizingly close to declaring that bite mark analysis wasn't scientifically reliable enough to be used in criminal trials. But not close enough. Instead, Lee argued that the bite mark evidence in Howard's case was fine, because Howard had been given the opportunity to challenge West in court.

This is precisely the sort of scenario that the Supreme Court's *Daubert* decisions were supposed to preclude. Leaving the interpretation of bite mark evidence to the jury relegated the most critical question—Is this legitimate science?—to the adversarial nature of a criminal trial, in which a jury's decision could be influenced by a wide range of factors not at all related to science. The most relevant such factor was usually the respective charisma and persuasiveness of the opposing experts. To Mississippi juries, West was a hometown hero who gave lectures in China and to the FBI, yet still chose to continue practicing dentistry in Hattiesburg and help put bad guys away in Mississippi. Prosecutors, with West's help, often portrayed defense witnesses and West's critics as hired guns motivated by professional jealousy to tear West down.

In his opinion in *Eddie Lee Howard v. State of Mississippi*, Justice Smith made the arguments that he'd resurrect in the Bologna Sandwich Case a few months later. He pointed out that West had already testified forty times in six states, and that bite mark evidence had been accepted in every court in which it had been submitted. He scolded his colleagues for expressing any skepticism about bite mark evidence at all, writing that the majority had left "an impression that this court does not favor allowing such evidence," and for suggesting that "there is little consensus in the scientific community" to support the claims of bite mark analysts. "This is clearly the minority view nationwide," Smith wrote. He was right about the courts—they had bought into bite mark matching. He was wrong about actual scientists—few had, if any.

Had the court barred bite mark evidence and Michael West in 1997, it seems likely that it would have ended or at least curtailed his career. It probably also would have forced a reexamination of countless cases, including those of Levon Brooks and Kennedy Brewer. But it didn't happen. The Mississippi Supreme Court would revisit Michael West and bite mark matching several times in the years to come. The justices' line on the controversy would get increasingly strident, defensive, and protective of West and his discipline. More people would go to prison. And Kennedy Brewer would nearly be executed.

In the fall of 1994, West made a move that would expand and solidify his position in Mississippi: he ran for coroner of Forrest County. He won. West now held an official state position. For a man who collected titles and credentials, it was a smart move. Of course, West's ability to win an election made him no more credible or knowledgeable than before. But a good chunk of the public doesn't know the difference between a coroner and a medical examiner. They may assume that simply by virtue of the office, coroners must know a lot about forensic pathology. An elected title also gave West power, authority, and bargaining power. It gave him more access to state officials and likely made him more credible still in the eyes of police, prosecutors, judges, and juries. Most importantly, it gave him a platform. He'd use it to protect the status he and Hayne had attained within the state's death investigation system.

Meanwhile, it wasn't long before Emily Ward ran into problems. Soon after taking office, Ward began trying to standardize the way autopsies were done in Mississippi. When she noticed the way Hayne was working, she tried to tell her superiors. She was told to "shut up."

It also didn't take long for the incumbent powers to take notice of Ward. Within just a few months of her appointment, and almost immediately after she tried to impose some oversight onto the autopsy system, Hayne complained about Ward to DPS commissioner Jim Ingram, alleging she had demonstrated professional incompetence. And even early on, some of the state's coroners wanted nothing to do with Ward. In Coahoma County, for example, coroner Charles Scott told his county board of supervisors that he'd keep using Hayne, despite warnings from Ward and his own police officials. The local paper reported that he described Hayne as "just as qualified as Ward, if not more so," and told the supervisors, "When it comes to a difficult homicide, Hayne is going to be my man, whether she [Ward] likes it or not." West and Hayne would later sign a newspaper ad endorsing Scott in his bid for reelection.

Frustrated, Ward contacted George McCormick, the medical examiner in north Louisiana, and Kris Sperry, the deputy chief medical examiner in Atlanta (he would later become the Georgia state medical examiner). The three of them began looking into Hayne's background.

As it turns out, by the time Ward reached out to him, McCormick had already heard complaints about Hayne from other medical examiners in the region. Part of McCormick's motivation was undoubtedly personal. Hayne and West had begun expanding their autopsy empire into Louisiana, particularly in McCormick's part of the state. So he was losing business to them. Local officials said they switched to Hayne because McCormick was slow with his reports. But McCormick told the Associated Press it was because "he sometimes disagrees with police over what led to a death." He added, "I'm not supposed to be a yes-man for the police."

Like Ward, McCormick was troubled by the number of autopsies he heard Hayne had been doing, and he worried about the stories he was hearing about the quality of Hayne's work. So he asked his lab director, Dawn Young, to begin compiling a file.

Young first looked into some of the publications Hayne listed on his CV. Some didn't appear to exist. Many weren't from medical or forensic journals. One other article Hayne had listed as published was actually just a letter to the editor.

Young also found several cases in which Hayne had failed to preserve tissue samples. In many cases, microscopic examination of tissue is a critical part of determining how an injury occurred. In her letters, Young recounted a correspondence with an attorney who wrote about an incident in May 1994, in which he had requested the preserved wet tissue from an autopsy Hayne had performed in a criminal case. In his reply, Hayne told the attorney that federal guidelines only recommend preserving wet tissue long enough to make a diagnosis. Since he had already made his diagnosis in the case, Hayne didn't retain the tissue.

Hayne's explanation was wrong. There were no such federal guidelines. According to guidelines published by the College of American Pathologists, the certifying organization for pathology labs, wet tissue should be retained for six months, presumably to give opposing experts a chance to examine them—which is precisely what this attorney was trying to do. The decedent in that case had died three months earlier.

Young found other cases in which Hayne also refused to produce wet tissue slides. In those cases, too, Hayne claimed he was merely following some federal law, regulation, or guideline. "He has been asked in the past to produce this rule," Young wrote, "but has failed to do so." In a letter to another attorney, Young wrote that Hayne's failure to produce slides was "unheard of in the field of pathology." Other attorneys would complain about this in future cases. "Most autopsies produce 20–30 tissue samples," one Mississippi attorney who has faced Hayne in both civil and criminal cases said in a 2007 interview for *Reason* magazine. "I've never seen a tissue sample from a Steven Hayne autopsy."

In December 1993 Sperry wrote to both the American Board of Pathology and the American Academy of Forensic Sciences to request an ethics investigation into Hayne's qualifications. He argued that though Hayne was not board qualified in forensic pathology as most forensic pathologists understood the term, he was deliberately confusing judges and juries by claiming certification from less credible groups with official-sounding names. He called Hayne a "rather blatant fraud that is being perpetrated on the people of Mississippi, the forensic community, and the medicolegal system."

Neither organization showed much interest. According to Sperry, no one seemed "particularly interested in pursuing any matter that is not, quite frankly, a complete giveaway, and it appears that they will happily rationalize themselves out of any controversial situations, most probably to avoid any litigation that might arise from challenging any but the most obvious trespasses."

This is yet another theme that would resonate throughout Hayne's career. Despite being made aware of his transgressions on multiple occasions dating back to the early 1990s, none of the professional organizations to which he belonged did much about it, at least until 2008. Because of their inaction, Hayne could continue citing his affiliation with those groups when vouching for his credentials in court. "It's a problem," says Vincent Di Maio, a renowned medical examiner and author of several textbooks on forensic pathology. "You have to understand that these organizations are toothless. They publish guidelines, but then don't have the guts to sanction members who violate them. They don't want to be sued. With the exception of the American Board [of Pathology], membership in these groups doesn't mean competence. But juries can be misled into seeing it that way. Too many judges and attorneys don't know to point out the difference."

In August 1995, Young wrote to Sperry again. She claimed to have found two civil cases in which she alleged that Hayne had committed perjury. In one case, Hayne claimed to have formed his opinion after reviewing some microscopic slides. But the doctor who performed the original autopsy testified under oath that not only had he never given the slides to Hayne, the two had never spoken. In the other case, Hayne testified that he had reviewed slides from an autopsy conducted by a doctor who actually worked in Young's lab. Young would have been the person who sent the slides from that case to Hayne. "As the custodian of records and materials for this laboratory," she wrote, "I can and will testify that I have not sent these materials to him, nor has he appeared in our office to review them." (In a subsequent court filing, Hayne's attorney called the perjury accusations "untrue" and "defamatory," and claimed they painted Hayne "in a false light.")

"As you can see," Young wrote, "the evidence is mounting and we are attempting to handle matters on a local level. However, the time is drawing near to have some action on a national scale."

Sperry later alleged to Young and McCormick that he had consulted on a case in which a body Hayne had autopsied was exhumed. In his autopsy report, Hayne claimed to have removed, weighed, and dissected the decedent's internal organs. But when Sperry opened up the body after exhumation, all of the organs were still inside and still intact. McCormick later gave court testimony about a conversation with the Tennessee state medical examiner, who told him Hayne first failed to produce slides in a case in which he had found cancer on a kidney and then produced slides that had nothing on them.

When Hayne got word of the complaints filed against him, he filed notice of his intent to sue Young and McCormick, alleging libel, conspiracy, and "tortious interference with and injury to business and contractual relations." The lawsuit was later dismissed when Hayne failed to serve the summons and complaint. Of course, a lawsuit would have opened his records up to discovery, which could have been damaging for him. But he certainly sent a message: criticize him, and you could expect to spend some time in court.

The lifeless body of twenty-three-month-old Haley Oliveaux lay awkwardly across a metal autopsy table at Mississippi Mortuary Services in Pearl. A red block propped under her shoulders elevated her chest, causing her head to tilt backward and her arms to spill off to the side. The toddler's head hung at an angle that caused her fine blonde hair to fall away from her face, exposing her right cheek, the right side of her forehead, and her hairline. There was light bruising around her ear and right eye, but there were no visible scrapes, cuts, or abrasions on the right side of her face. More importantly, the skin of her right cheek was smooth and unblemished. In a heavy drawl, Michael West's voice announced the date and time: December 18, 1993, 9:35 p.m.

Oliveaux had drowned in a bathtub that morning in West Monroe, Louisiana, while in the care of her mother's boyfriend, Jimmie Duncan. Allison Oliveaux left for work at around eight forty-five a.m. Duncan told police he put the girl in the tub and then went to do some dishes. When he returned to the bathroom to dry her off, he found her in the water.

Haley lived a short and unhappy life. Her parents had divorced, and her father was in prison. She lived with Duncan and her mother in West Monroe. In early November 1993 she was twice taken to the hospital after suffering seizures. That same month, she was again admitted to the hospital. This time, her mother said the girl had pulled a chest of drawers down on top of herself while climbing to reach for a piggy bank. She suffered multiple skull fractures and some bruising on her left elbow. An investigation by the West Monroe Police Department and Ouachita Parish Child Protective Services found no evidence of abuse. Still, to Allison Oliveaux's family, it seemed suspicious. They didn't care much for Duncan. He and Allison both used drugs. At the very least, they thought he was bad for Allison and Haley.

Even a charge of negligent homicide would be difficult to win. Oliveaux was nearly two. Perhaps leaving her in a bathtub for ten to fifteen minutes wasn't prudent parenting, but it was far from clear that it was criminal conduct. But the county's law enforcement officials had recently heard about the two forensic experts in Mississippi who were promoting cutting-edge technology to find bites, bruises, and other wounds that no one else could see. So they turned to Steven Hayne and Michael West. Perhaps they could find the evidence the state needed to put Jimmie Duncan away.

Haley Oliveaux's body was sent 120 miles east to Mississippi Mortuary Services in Pearl. A police chief, a police detective and captain, and two assistant district attorneys went with the body and witnessed the autopsy. That wasn't unusual, but it also wasn't recommended. The National Association of Medical Examiners encourages doctors to maintain their independence—for example, by avoiding interactions with investigating law enforcement officials before conducting exams. Such interaction can bias a doctor's conclusions. In fact, studies have shown that the more details crime lab analysts know about a case before conducting their analysis, the more likely they are to come up with false positives.

A search of court records suggests that the Oliveaux case was one of Hayne's first in Ouachita Parish. Hayne got the job at about the time he and West had begun advertising their services in northern Louisiana. Within a year he was getting nearly all the parish's autopsies.

In his initial examination on the night of December 18, Hayne suspected the presence of possible bite marks on Oliveaux. He called in Michael West. The following morning, West concurred with Hayne, noting bite marks on the girl's elbow and near her ear. In a subsequent examination, West declared that those marks were "consistent" with Jimmie Duncan's teeth. More importantly, he also claimed to have found a mark on her cheek that he said was a "positive match" to Duncan.

For his part, Hayne determined that Oliveaux had been "forcibly drowned" and said he found lacerations on her anus that the state would later suggest were indicative of sexual abuse.

District Attorney Jerry Jones charged Duncan with capital murder, alleging he had raped Oliveaux in the bathtub, forced her head underwater, bitten her, and drowned her. Jones would seek the death penalty.

The video of West's examination of Haley Oliveaux wouldn't see the light of day for another fifteen years, when Jimmie Duncan's post-conviction attorneys found a copy of it in the prosecutor's file. In it, West examined Oliveaux twice. The first five minutes of the video took place on December 18. During this portion of the video, West makes no mention of any scrapes or abrasions on Oliveaux's cheek, and there are no such injuries apparent on the tape. At the 4:57 mark, there's a break in the video, marking the lapse between the two exams. The video picks up on the following day, December 19. The camera returns to Haley Oliveaux's face. Strikingly, where the first video showed no blemishes at all, a conspicuous abrasion now appears to the right of Oliveaux's mouth. West's hand then enters the frame, holding a plaster dental mold taken earlier that day from Jimmie Duncan. West then repeatedly presses the front part of the dental mold directly into the mark on Oliveaux's cheek. Over the next two minutes of the video, he does this seventeen times. At another point, he drags Duncan's mold across Oliveaux's face, beginning near her lips, then scraping the plaster teeth down her face to her jaw. He does this for another minute. West then moves to Oliveaux's elbow and pushes Duncan's dental mold onto an old bruise that, according to Duncan's attorneys, hospital records showed she had suffered weeks before her death, after the chest-of-drawers incident. West would later claim that the mark was inflicted by the back right side of Duncan's upper teeth.

At the 9:32 mark, West asks an assistant in the room to turn out the lights. A fluorescent black light then flickers on. This is the West Phenomenon in action. With the lights out, West continues to jam the plaster cast into the girl's cheek, elbow, and arm. Over the course of the twenty-four-minute video, West pushes, drags, or scrapes the cast of Duncan's teeth into and onto the girl's body at least fifty times.

West had described this method in court testimony in previous cases, but this was the first known time it had been captured on video. Forensic experts who watched the video were astonished. "This is the best documentation I've ever seen of Dr. West's junk bite mark comparisons," said Michael Bowers, a deputy medical examiner for Ventura County, California, after viewing the video in 2009. Bowers was one of the earliest critics of West and later of bite mark analysis in general.

How did Haley Oliveaux get abrasions on her cheek that weren't there the day before? "Dr. West created them," Bowers said. "It was intentional. He's creating artificial abrasions in that video, and he's tampering with the evidence. It's criminal. . . . You never jam a plaster cast into a possible bite mark like that. It distorts the evidence." West would later call Bowers's accusations "a damn lie."

After watching the video, Bowers offered to submit an affidavit for Jimmie Duncan's defense. Several other specialists, including a forensic pathologist and the former president of the American Board of Forensic Odontology, submitted affidavits in Duncan's defense after viewing the tape. Others, like the celebrated forensic pathologist Michael Baden, suggested that the marks may have been caused by the removal of medical tape from Oliveaux's cheek, but still insisted they weren't human bites.

Duncan's post-conviction attorneys found the video in late 2008. It was never shown at his trial. That's in part because West himself didn't testify, either. The years between his examination of Oliveaux in 1993 and Duncan's trial in 1998 were the years during which West had been exposed in media reports and disciplined by three different forensics organizations. By 1995, Duncan's prosecutors concluded that West came with too much baggage. They dropped him from the case and began looking for another bite mark analyst to replace him.

Because even the prosecution had conceded that West had credibility issues, Duncan's attorneys requested that Oliveaux be exhumed so that their own expert wouldn't need to rely on notes from Hayne and West. They were denied. Any expert for Duncan's defense would have to testify based only on the notes of the two Mississippi experts.

Duncan was tried in 1998. Incredibly, the video of West's examination was never shown at trial. Even Duncan's own expert witness never saw it. The state at first had trouble finding a bite mark analyst who would testify from West's work, but eventually brought on Neal Riesner, a dentist from Scarsdale, New York. Using only the photographs West took after his examination of Oliveaux, Riesner concluded that the marks on the girl's cheek were indeed bite marks and that "to a reasonable medical dental certainty," he could say they were made by Duncan. He also said that the marks on the girl's ear and elbow were "consistent" with Duncan's dentition, even though again, according to Duncan's attorneys, hospital records indicated that particular injury was weeks old.

Duncan's defense opted to go after West personally rather than attack the credibility of bite mark evidence in general. They put on the stand Richard Souviron, a well-known bite mark analyst and an evangelist for the field. In recent years, he had also become one of Michael West's most vocal critics. Souviron, who hadn't seen the examination video, testified that the mark West claimed to have found on Oliveaux's cheek wasn't a bite mark at all.

The state also put on a jailhouse informant who claimed Duncan had confessed to him while the two shared a cell. Years later, other inmates would contradict the informant, giving sworn statements that Duncan had always maintained his innocence. By the time he retired, the police officer who solicited that informant's testimony had solicited five murder confessions from three suspects, all of which turned out to be false.

But the jailhouse informant, the anal injuries, and the bite marks were enough to convince the jury of Jimmie Duncan's guilt. In 1998 he was convicted and sentenced to death.

After the video was reported in the press in 2009, West declared that the forensic experts who sharply criticized his work in the case were part of a conspiracy against him. "I'm a little old dentist from Hattiesburg, and I've got the top lawyers in the country coming after me," he told the *Clarion-Ledger*. Oddly, he claimed he was merely following a protocol developed by Bowers himself. (When asked about this, Bowers laughed and said, "Oh, my. That's absurd. That guy is crazy.") "She was raped and sodomized and held under water by this son of a bitch," West told the paper. "Now I'm the bad guy because this guy raped a 2-year-old. . . . I'm tired of being beaten up because of the death penalty."

There were additional problems with Hayne's role in Duncan's case. As he had in other cases, Hayne didn't turn over the slides he had made of the wounds he found around Oliveaux's rectum to Duncan's post-conviction attorneys. He claimed he no longer possessed them. The slides were critical to determine whether or not those wounds were from sexual abuse or, as the defense suspected, Stevens-Johnson syndrome, a condition brought on by anti-seizure medications that can cause blistering and lesions on mucous membranes, including the anus. At trial, Hayne testified that the wounds were consistent with sexual abuse and had been inflicted near the time of death. Since Duncan was the only one alone with Oliveaux before she died, that testimony was damning.

But there was no other evidence of sexual abuse—no semen, pubic hair, or blood from Duncan was found on or in the girl. Hayne should also have kept either the paraffin blocks from which duplicate slides could be made, or at minimum his written record of what the slides showed. He never sent either.

Duncan's post-conviction attorneys also asked Hayne for records related to any other autopsies he had performed that day. Hayne responded that he was under no legal obligation to respond to an out-of-state subpoena—a strange claim, given that Hayne had actively promoted himself to Louisiana's justice system and agreed to participate in Duncan's prosecution. When the attorneys got a Mississippi judge to compel Hayne to turn them over, Hayne said the records had been destroyed. As of this writing, Jimmie Duncan still sits on death row at Angola prison.

∼

Emily Ward had made it clear that she wanted to be consulted in controversial cases, particularly high-profile murders, jail and prison deaths, and deaths in police custody. That just wasn't going to happen. Ward quickly learned what Lloyd White had learned. When prosecutors didn't like what she or one of her staff had concluded after an autopsy, they'd simply take the body to a private doctor, usually Hayne, for an alternate opinion. More likely, they just didn't take the chance, and like Coahoma County coroner Charles Scott, went around her from the start. Ward was barely in office a year before the *Clarion-Ledger* ran an article with the subheadline "State medical examiner often ignored in probes." In fact, the coroners most likely to do an end run around Ward were those near Jackson, right in her backyard—mostly because that also happened to be Hayne's as well.

Ward's efforts to have autopsies done more objectively didn't sit well with the state's old guard. "She is at present undermining death investigations and prosecutions in Mississippi," said John T. Kitchens, the district attorney in Steven Hayne's home county of Rankin. District Attorney Ed Peters added that he had "confidence" in Hayne and another private pathologist he used, and that he found them "reliable." Another district attorney asked, "Why should I forsake him?" referring to Hayne. "I think you ought to dance with the girl who brought you."

In one case, Ward was approached by defense attorneys about her work. As she was ethically obligated to do as both a forensic pathologist and the state medical examiner, she told them what she had found.

This was unthinkable in Mississippi. So in March 1994 the state's old guard brought out the knives. Kitchens was the first to send a letter of complaint to Ward's boss, Public Safety Commissioner Jim Ingram. "It has recently come to my attention that on more than one occasion our State Medical Examiner has unnecessarily rendered aid to the defense of criminal defendants." Kitchens found this unacceptable.

Kitchens argued that the job of the state medical examiner was to assist law enforcement. In a claim that must have come as quite a shock to the state's indigent defense bar—one of the most underpaid and underresourced in the country—Kitchens complained, improbably, that the deck was already stacked against prosecutors. "The list goes on and on where examples can be made of the defendant's advantages," he wrote.

Kitchens argued that defendants were free to hire their own experts, either with their own money or with court funding. He finally insisted that Ingram order Ward not to discuss any case with a criminal defense attorney unless she either was answering questions under oath or had explicit permission from the district attorney whose office was prosecuting the case. On the same day Kitchens wrote his letter, Ed Peters, the district attorney for Hinds County also sent Ingram a similar letter.

~

Kitchens was either posturing or badly informed. First, most criminal defendants in the state were indigent and had no way of hiring their own experts. And it was far from certain that the state's courts would give defendants funding for it. They often didn't.

Second, Mississippi didn't and still doesn't have a statewide public defender system. It mostly relies on local attorneys appointed by the courts on a case-by-case basis. Over the years, national watchdog groups have issued stinging rebukes of the state's public defender system. The idea that defendants in the state had every advantage was laughable.

More importantly, Kitchens had misstated the proper role of a state medical examiner. State-employed forensic pathologists are independent fact seekers, not members of the prosecution or law enforcement team. The guidelines from the National Association of Medical Examiners, for example, instruct doctors to "work cooperatively with, but independent from, law enforcement and prosecutors." The renowned medical examiner Vincent Di Maio stated it more succinctly in a 2010 interview with PBS's *Frontline*. "It's not supposed to be for the police or against the police or for a family or against a family. You're supposed to be impartial and tell the truth. . . . When I was practicing as a medical examiner, I was glad to talk to the defense. I had absolutely no problem talking to the defense."

Ingram passed the letters on to the DPS legal counsel for analysis. The agency's lawyers pointed out that Kitchens was a big defender of Hayne, and that Hayne and Ward had been sparring over control. But the counsel did agree with Kitchens on an important point. The office argued that the state medical examiner should *never* consult with defense attorneys without prior authorization from prosecutors. Again, that was not only contrary to the very concept of an independent medical examiner but also inconsistent with Mississippi law, which authorized the state medical examiner to take control of any death investigation in the state in which she deemed it was necessary.

The tension between Ward and the old guard continued to escalate. Hinds County coroner Robert Martin, who had praised Ward's hiring the previous year, now complained to the *Clarion-Ledger* that Ward was "undermining" coroners and prosecutors. Ward reasonably responded that her job wasn't to help either side win a case but to offer opinions based on reasonable medical certainty, regardless of who was requesting them. "If I didn't," she said, "I would be contributing to the obstruction of justice."

Ward did have at least some defenders. The Alcorn County coroner said he used her for all his autopsies and that she was the best and most professional medical examiner with whom he had ever worked. But it was a funeral director in Jackson who came closest to getting at the root of the problem: "For every [state] medical examiner, there's always been a problem with one of them—at least that's what the coroners say. I just can't believe there is something wrong with every state medical examiner that is appointed by the state."

Later that month, perhaps sensing that yet another good medical examiner was slipping away, the *Clarion-Ledger* ran a strong editorial in support of Ward. The editorial recapped the long and contentious history with the state medical examiner's office, and it took swipes at Martin and his "flimsy excuses" for going around Ward. "Coroners and prosecutors shouldn't be farming autopsies out to private pathologists," the paper opined. "Whatever the reason, whether it's to help cronies, or 'the way we've always done it,' or because they believe they can opinion 'shop' for favorable interpretations, the practice must end." The editorial predicted that unless the counties started to get on board, "we'll be right back where we were, with an empty top slot."

The battle in the press continued, with medical examiners from Alabama, Arkansas, Georgia, Tennessee, and Louisiana writing letters to the editor in support of Ward. But behind the scenes, the old guard stoked resentment. Scott County coroner Joe C. Bradford complained that Ward "doesn't seem interested in building up the local coroner's office as she is in building up her own office." He added, reiterating the complaints of Kitchens and Peters, "Dr. Ward wants us to turn over our death investigations totally to her office and then allow defense attorneys to work with her rather than the local coroners and I don't think that's right."

West in particular painted Ward as power-hungry and authoritarian, and peppered his criticism with personal attacks. One longtime former coroner described a Mississippi Coroners Association meeting West called in Hattiesburg in late 1994 to make his case for a united front against Ward. When the former coroner defended the state medical examiner, West accused him of having an affair with her. A former sheriff, citing West, described Ward as a "bull-dyke" whose do-gooderism hampered criminal investigations. Ward's enemies couldn't decide if she was a lesbian or a floozy. They just knew they didn't want to be taking orders from her.

Jim Ingram was torn. The longtime lawman and former FBI agent had become friendly with Hayne and had vouched for Hayne to be medical examiner before Ward's appointment. But Ward was also his handpicked selection for state medical examiner and director of the crime lab. Now the two were on a collision course. Publicly, Ingram stood with Ward and encouraged the coroners to work with her. But privately, he sometimes sided with coroners in their disputes with her. His inability to pick a side not only undermined Ward's authority, it emboldened her critics.

Finally, in January 1995, Michael West circulated a memo among state coroners that called for Ward's resignation. The petition laid out a series of "grievances," including that Ward was "trying to establish a political power base," was working with defense attorneys, was uncooperative, and was undermining the coroners' authority.

Of the state's eighty-two coroners, forty-two signed West's petition. West typed a memo before releasing the petition to the press. He told his fellow coroners—apparently without the slightest hint of self-awareness—that of the twenty to twenty-five coroners who supported Ward, many did so because they were "afraid of her, as she has shown how vindictive she can be." He then urged them to support a new bill in the Mississippi legislature that would "privatize" the state medical examiner's office. That bill, West wrote, would "remove the politics of the ME's office and place it in the real world that we all must work and live in."

The *Clarion-Ledger* picked up the story of West's petition a couple months later. The paper contacted all forty-two signatories and found that a healthy majority of them used Hayne for all or nearly all their autopsies. They all had backing from their district attorneys to sign the petition. Some of the signatories had never actually worked with Ward, they merely repeated hearsay allegations against her. Others admitted that they only signed the petition out of solidarity with fellow coroners. Most said that the petition was the result of a power struggle between Hayne and Ward. (Hayne had the good sense not to speak out about it, at least publicly.)

West went after Ward with abandon. He told the paper that he had privately complained to Ingram about Ward for months: "He's never been able to keep this woman under control." Forrest Allgood also attacked Ward, accusing her of lying on the witness stand during one of his murder trials. (Ward denied the accusation.) Jimmy Roberts told the paper that in encouraging more autopsies at the state lab, Ward was trying to put him out of business, as if Ward had some obligation to pad Jimmy Roberts's bottom line.

At least some coroners did object to West's petition. Susan Cunningham of Jackson County told the paper that the petition was "baseless" and that "it looked like a group of fifth-graders had written it." L. W. "Bump" Calloway of Warren County, the only coroner in the state who was a certified crime scene investigator, said West didn't even bother asking him to sign because he knew Calloway would tell him off. "I have always found Dr. Ward and her staff to be extremely professional, competent, and willing to cooperate."

Jim Ingram attributed the petition to the usual coroner politics. "No medical examiner has ever been able to survive the system in Mississippi," he told the *Clarion-Ledger.* "Every one has either left the state in disgust or been fired." He told the reporter he supported Ward. But that wouldn't last.

A few days later, the *Clarion-Ledger* ran another editorial in support of Ward. She was "experiencing firsthand the petty politics of having to deal with the 'good ol' boy' system of Mississippi coroners," the paper opined. "They resent having someone—especially a woman—overseeing their work," and the mere fact that the power brokers in that system were attacking her "can be seen as validation that she is doing a good job."

Three months later, Emily Ward resigned. A few days after resigning, she fired back in the *Clarion-Ledger.* She pointed out to the paper that at the same time the state was paying for her office and a state-of-the-art lab, most of the state's autopsies were being done at Jimmy Roberts's privately owned morgue in Pearl. "There is a small faction of people who see an opportunity to make very lucrative income off the taxpayers' dollars," Ward said. "It is just incredibly frustrating to try to run a death investigation system when you are competing with people who want to make money off the system."

In agitating for Ward's removal, Kitchens, Robert Martin, and her other political enemies had argued that she should be replaced by a bureaucrat instead of another doctor. This was also the thinking behind the "privatization" bill West was pushing. The old guard needed a state medical examiner's office to handle paperwork and process records, but they didn't need the hassle of any real oversight. They'd get exactly that. Soon the Mississippi Medical Examiner's Office would be run by a nonmedical administrator. The position of state medical examiner would remain vacant for the next fifteen years.

Michael West couldn't resist gloating about his victory. "She [Ward] has attempted to destroy the death investigation system in Mississippi," he told the *Clarion-Ledger*. "She seems to be a very incompetent individual."

At the time West gave that quote, it had been just three months since his testimony helped send a second innocent man to prison.

~ 11 ~

VESSELS OF WRATH, FITTED FOR DESTRUCTION

It's just another day in America, and we have lost our sense of outrage.

—Forrest Allgood

As in Levon Brooks's case, Forrest Allgood's opening statement in Kennedy Brewer's trial was understated. After briefly recounting the scene on the evening Christine Jackson disappeared, Allgood plainly promised the jury, "The State intends to prove to you simply that sometime either on the late evening of May second, nineteen hundred and ninety-two, or in the early morning of May third, nineteen hundred and ninety-two, Kennedy Brewer choked and killed a three-year-old child, Christine Jackson, after he had sexually battered her."

But even with Michael West's powers at his disposal, Allgood had a couple of problems. Based on the initial investigation by law enforcement, Gloria Jackson was also in the house during the time Christine disappeared, and Jackson told virtually the same story as Brewer: she had no idea precisely how or when the little girl went missing. The only difference was that there was no physical evidence linking Jackson to the crime. (The only such evidence against Brewer came from West.) Allgood could only hope that the narrative would somehow change from the time of the investigation, and that Brewer's defense attorneys wouldn't notice. He was in luck.

When Deputy Sheriff Bud Permenter initially interviewed Gloria Jackson at her house on that Sunday morning, he asked her when she had last seen Christine. Jackson responded that she saw Brewer pick Christine up off of their bed and place her on the pallet before they went to sleep. In the fall of 1992, when Brewer and Jackson were both facing possible capital murder charges, Permenter testified at a preliminary hearing for the case. Allgood asked him about that interview.

"She saw this child being actually picked up out of the bed and put on a pallet next to the bed at that time?"

"That is correct," Permenter answered.

Later at the same hearing, Permenter testified that Jackson had told him that the youngest child, who was sleeping in the bed with the couple, started crying. Brewer got up, retrieved a bottle and diaper for the baby, and came back to bed. Allgood then asked Permenter if Jackson had told him that when she woke up at that point, she again saw Christine sleeping next to the bed. He said she had.

The narrative was clear: Jackson saw her daughter Christine *after* she got home that night. But by the time of the trial two and a half years later, the narrative had changed. Jackson was Allgood's first witness. Early in her testimony, the prosecutor asked her to describe what she saw when she returned home from the Santa Barbara Club and got ready for bed. This time, Jackson said she saw what she "thought" was Christine. Allgood swooped in.

"Now let me stop you for a minute," Allgood said. "You said like you thought it was her. Did you see any arms?"

"No," Jackson answered.

"Did you see any legs?"

"No."

"Did you see her head?"

"No."

"What did you see him pick up, Mrs. Jackson?"

"Nothing really 'cause I really wasn't paying too much attention."

As for the period of time that Jackson had claimed that Brewer had gotten out of bed to get a baby bottle and a diaper, Allgood simply asked, "At any time . . . did you ever see your daughter, Christine Jackson, in that house?"

"No," Jackson answered.

Back when Jackson was still suspected for the crime, Permenter said Jackson seemed certain that she saw the girl. Now that it was just Brewer on trial, she wasn't so sure. There is nothing in the official record of the case to explain why Jackson would so radically alter her story, but there is some compelling circumstantial evidence. Jackson had initially been charged as an accessory after-the-fact. That's because if Brewer committed the crime, according to her initial statements to Permenter, Jackson had to have known about it. But in the years between Jackson's arrest and Brewer's trial, the charges against her were dismissed. After that, Jackson not only changed her story but also offered some new incriminating evidence. She claimed that soon after she and Brewer were arrested, the two of them got into an argument in the jail. As she taunted Brewer about what would happen to him in prison for being a child killer, Brewer allegedly retorted, "It should have been you [Jackson] that I killed."

Jackson claimed that she contacted jail personnel soon afterward to alert them to Brewer's confession. But there's no written record of her having made any such contact, nor did Allgood produce anyone from the jail who could corroborate her claim.

Unfortunately, when Brewer's lawyers cross-examined Jackson, they didn't appear to even notice that the story had changed, much less challenge Jackson on it, or ask in front of the jury if she had struck a deal with prosecutors. They never inquired why the accessory charge had been dropped. Without Gloria Jackson as a suspect, the prosecution could focus solely on Kennedy Brewer.

In his testimony, Steven Hayne noted that after having been submerged in water for several warm spring days, Christine Jackson's body had begun to decompose. He testified that he had observed "skin slippage" and "putrefaction," both of which are common under those circumstances. He determined that Christine had been strangled to death—she hadn't died of freshwater drowning.

As for the other suspicious marks, Hayne "thought that they were bite wounds." That's when he called in Michael West. Anticipating what Brewer's lawyers would later argue, Allgood asked Hayne whether it was possible that those marks had been the result of decomposition or insect bites. Hayne replied that based on his extensive experience, he could distinguish the types of marks that were the result of decomposition or insect activity—the marks on Christine's body were *not* from insect activity, he said.

Once again Hayne allowed West to excise the skin that contained the alleged bite marks, which other forensics experts say is an abrogation of his duties as a medical examiner. At least nine forensic specialists have reviewed the work of Hayne and West in the case, and all nine have concluded that it simply wasn't reasonable for them to have concluded that the marks on Jackson's body were human bites. All have said they were either insect bites or some other injury, but they were definitely inflicted after Jackson's death. Even medical examiner Michael Baden, a friend of Hayne who has at times defended him from critics, concluded, "In my opinion, Christine Jackson's skin damage should have been recognized as, predictably, having occurred after her death given the conditions where and when the body was found. It is further my opinion that it was a serious mistake to misidentify the decomposition changes as being the result of an adult human bite mark."

West's mounting trouble with various professional forensics organizations might have given your average prosecutor pause. Not Forrest Allgood. Neither Allgood nor West even made an effort to keep West's professional troubles out of the trial. Instead, they took a different tack: they would argue that West was right, and all his critics were jealous of him for it.

West admitted on the stand that in recent years, a couple courts had prevented him from giving certain types of testimony, and in other cases charges against a suspect implicated by his analysis had later been dismissed. But he brushed off the investigations and criticisms as being from "vastly ignorant" scientists who were unable or unwilling to appreciate the value of his work because of either envy or their own professional limitations.

West freely admitted that there was no known error rate in the field of forensic odontology. When asked if he knew his own, individual error rate, West answered, "My first marriage ended in divorce. My second marriage is current. So I made one mistake." The court reporter noted in a parenthetical that West laughed. The record doesn't reflect Kennedy Brewer's reaction.

Nevertheless, to hear West tell it, there wasn't a forensic expert around who could match his pedigree. He went through all the usual highlights of his career, adding this time that he'd soon be featured in an upcoming hour-long documentary on the BBC. (The documentary, as it turned out, would be critical of West.)

After the questioning about his qualifications, Brewer's lawyers asked the court to bar West from testifying. "Doctor West has no regard for the standard of reasonable degree of scientific certainty," they argued. They explained that his opinions were entirely subjective, that he had been caught misrepresenting facts in other cases, and that he had called bite mark analysis "as much of an art as it is a science."

Few people disagreed with any of that. Even most bite mark analysts admit that the field is subjective—more opinion than science. It was also well understood by all parties that West himself was a controversial figure. But Allgood and Brewer's lawyers were also only arguing about West personally, not the pseudoscience of bite mark matching in general. This was the position in which the courts often put the lawyers defending those accused by Michael West: they could argue either that West wasn't credible or that bite mark analysis wasn't credible. Both were true. But defense attorneys were usually forced to pick one or the other.

In Brewer's case, as with so many others, neither argument would have been successful. Less than two years before, in the same county, the same court had allowed West's testimony to help convict and imprison Levon Brooks. A few weeks before Brewer's trial began, West had helped secure a murder conviction in the Bologna Sandwich Case. The judge in Brewer's trial was also the judge in that trial. A ruling finding that West or forensic odontology wasn't credible would have undone those and other convictions. It was a lot to ask of a district court judge.

Not unreasonably, then, Brewer's lawyers retained their own bite mark specialist to rebut West specifically. That expert—Dr. Richard Souviron—not only disagreed with West's findings and the rigor of West's analysis, but told the jury that the marks on Christine Jackson weren't bite marks. Souviron also chaired the American Board of Forensic Odontology (ABFO) committee that suspended West. At first blush, that would seem to make him an ideal foil for West. But it would backfire.

Allgood's cross-examination of Souviron was devastatingly effective. It was also incredibly misleading and took advantage of the Hobson's choice that put Brewer's attorneys in a bind. First, Allgood got Souviron to concede that the ABFO had recently approved the same "direct comparison" method that West used in the Brewer case. Then he got Souviron to admit that West was one of the leading bite mark analysts in the country, even a true "pioneer." Finally, Allgood clearly had carefully reviewed the ABFO's guidelines, including the

transcripts of several meetings of the executive board. He got Souviron to admit that the ABFO actually had no hard and fast rules
regarding how bite mark analysts should express probability when discussing their findings in court. Allgood pointed to one ABFO survey
that found that 8 percent of the group's members disagreed with the
language the ABFO recommended (but didn't require) to express an
analyst's most confident conclusions: "reasonable medical, dental scientific certainty."

After getting Souviron to concede all of that, Allgood moved in
for the kill.

"I'm curious, Doctor. Did y'all suspend 8 percent of your membership upon finding that out?"

"Absolutely not," Souviron answered.

"Only Michael West, isn't that right?"

Allgood then drove the point home. He asked if "this business of
forensic odontology is somewhat of an art."

Souviron said it was.

~

Allgood's point was that Souviron and the ABFO had unfairly targeted
West. He was half right. The ABFO *was* singling out West, but not unfairly. What Allgood had demonstrated is that the *entire field* of bite
mark analysis is bogus. At best, the ABFO was a loose confederation
of dentists, most of whom moonlighted as crime solvers. Their techniques weren't uniform, they had no consistent standards, and the terminology they used to describe their findings was bound only by their
own imaginations. West's only sin—at least within this group—was
that his imagination was a bit too flamboyant. He was disciplined not
because "indeed and without a doubt" was any less steeped in science
than the terminology used by any other member of the ABFO; he was
disciplined because his bombast and self-promotion had become an
embarrassment to his colleagues. Michael West was definitely a liability. But the bite mark community also did a fine job of embarrassing
itself without him.

The problem for Kennedy Brewer was that his attorneys had already conceded that bite mark analysis in general was a legitimate
field. If the field itself was legitimate, and West's methods weren't significantly different from those of his fellow bite mark analysts, then
there was no reason to keep West from testifying. So the trial judge

ruled on the motion the same way the judges and appellate courts before him had. West could testify, but Brewer's attorneys could challenge him. Somehow that would make it all fair. Both the *Daubert* and *Frye* rules envisioned judges as gatekeepers who carefully distinguished good science from bad. In reality, judges tend to act more like ushers. Everyone is welcome.

West resumed the stand and didn't miss a beat. He explained to Brewer's jury that he had begun his examination by comparing the unique features of the marks on Christine's body to the unique "class and individual characteristics" of Brewer's teeth. Class characteristics, West explained, are identifying features found in specific groups of objects. As a metaphor, he asked jurors to consider a box of flat-head screwdrivers and a box of Phillips screwdrivers. Though each of the Phillips screwdrivers may be different sizes, they all display the same class characteristic—a Phillips-head shape—which is not shared by the flat-head screwdrivers. According to West, these same class differentiations can be seen in an individual's dentition: the arch, the shape of the jaw, an overbite or underbite, and so forth.

By contrast, he explained that "individual characteristics" arise because of "random wear and tear." They include things like chipped or broken teeth. Sometimes these individual characteristics aren't obvious, such as small cracks or other tiny imperfections on the biting surface of a tooth.

All of that is true. The problem is that West claimed that these distinguishing characteristics are detectable in the marks that individual teeth leave in human skin. There's just no evidence that they are.

Over pages and pages of the trial transcript, West displayed black and white photos for the jury as he walked them through his methods in excruciating detail. This was a man who had invented his own realm. It was a realm in which places most of us have never considered—the surfaces of our teeth—come alive, blown up on slides to reveal otherworldly landscapes of ridges, crevices, elevations, and depressions. According to West, these formations leave signature imprints when teeth rip into human skin. West's jargon must have sounded sophisticated to jurors. The exhaustive manner in which he described his procedures undoubtedly made him seem cautious, careful, and analytical. How could any lay juror find fault with what he was saying?

Unlike the autopsy of Courtney Smith, West and Hayne had recorded their examination of Christine Jackson. So in this case West's "direct comparison" method was on video, though the judge ultimately refused to let it be shown at trial. (The trial judge ruled that because the video depicted the doctors and assistants carrying on unrelated conversations, blaring music, and behaving in a "callous" manner, it was too prejudicial to show to the jury.) Though the video has never been made public, Brewer's attorneys have seen it and have shown it to other forensic specialists. After viewing the video, David Senn, another bite mark analyst, wrote in 2011 that during the examination, "Dr. West placed Kennedy Brewer's dental models directly onto Christine Jackson's body multiple times—with sufficient force to create [visible] marks." This was now the second time a forensic specialist had suggested that West's direct comparison method actually created the very bite marks later used to implicate a suspect.

West wrapped up his testimony on March 23. Earlier that day, the court had been informed of an urgent problem. A rumor circulated that later that night, the TV news program *20/20* would air an unflattering expose of West and his novel bite mark theories. So just before dismissing everyone for the night, the judge gave some unusual instructions to the jury. "Also, it has been my understanding that for this evening and for this evening alone, the television sets have been removed by the management of the hotel from your rooms," he said. There was indeed a news program preparing an expose of West—*ABC News Special Report with John Stossel*. But the episode wouldn't air for another two years.

~

Kennedy Brewer's attorneys had their own problems to address at trial. The first was the state's claim that no one other than Brewer had access to the house during the time that Christine Jackson disappeared. Brewer himself, along with Jackson, had agreed that the locking mechanism on the front door—the bent nail—was accessible only from the inside. And Brewer, from the very first moment he was questioned by the deputy sheriff, was adamant that no one came in the front door that night except Gloria Jackson, whom he let in when she returned from the club.

The window was a different story. The state claimed there was no sign of forced entry at any point near or on the window. The broken windowpane, they discovered from Jackson, had been broken when she moved into the house. It was not the result of someone prying or forcing it open. But ironically, the very certainty with which the state made this point ultimately undermined it. Four law enforcement officers claimed to have inspected the window. All of them said they saw no sign of forced entry around the window and no signs of a prowler on the ground underneath it. But notably, not a single law enforcement officer was aware of the others' prior visits to observe the area beneath the window. Nor, until after they completed their interview of her, were any of the officers aware that Gloria Jackson had also been to the area beneath the window that evening. Later, Leshone Williams and Dewayne Graham said they too had walked around to the rear of the house and knocked on the window to get Brewer's attention before returning to the front door and entering to watch *American Gladiators*. In all, seven people—Williams, Graham, Jackson, and four law enforcement officers—had traipsed around the exterior of the window within a few hours of one another, and evidently not anyone, or any combination of all of them, had left any sign of having done so.

This was a critical point. The state claimed there were no footprints around the window and no signs of forced entry. Therefore, it followed, Christine Jackson's abductor could only have been inside the house. But not only had seven people walked in the area around and beneath the window, Permenter and his assistant had tried to hoist themselves through the window itself. A lack of footprints did not mean that no one could have walked up to the window, opened it, and reached through to grab Christine Jackson. It only meant that either the ground wasn't soft enough to preserve footprints, or the law enforcement officers weren't very good at finding them.

Unfortunately for Kennedy Brewer, his defense lawyers never pursued this hole in the state's case.

The state's narrative of the crime was never tenable. It went like this: Brewer raped and killed Christine while Gloria was at the Santa Barbara. At some point in the night, he carried the body several hundred yards through thick brush to deposit it into the creek. He then returned through the same thick brush to the house, cleaned up any evidence of the rape and murder, and pretended as though nothing was out of the ordinary. By the state's reckoning, he also created a lump of blankets and bed clothes roughly proportional to Christine, put those clothes on the bed, then picked them up from the bed and moved them to the pallet as if they were Christine when Jackson returned home from the club. Once it became public knowledge the following morning that Christine was missing, he for some reason dropped the guise of an innocent. Instead, he acted like a conscience-less sociopath, first refusing to search for the little girl, then later telling Gloria that he should have killed her instead of Christine. It was all rather absurd.

As in every criminal trial, Brewer's prosecutors technically had the burden of proof. But as a practical matter, especially in murder cases, reasonable doubt alone isn't a winning defense. Brewer's lawyers needed a plausible alternative suspect—someone who had the motive and opportunity to commit the crime. Typically, that's a tall order. Law enforcement shapes the initial investigation, and if the investigation quickly focuses on one suspect, as was the case with Brewer, defense attorneys have few alternate leads. Appointed counsel for indigent defendants, like the attorneys who represented Brewer, just aren't positioned to undertake the type of robust investigation that might ferret out another plausible suspect whom law enforcement had overlooked or neglected to consider.

That said, while Brewer's attorneys may not have had the resources to conduct their own investigation, they did have a closed set of potential suspects to consider: Williams, Graham, James Clayton (a former boyfriend of Gloria's), . . . and Justin Albert Johnson.

There were also easily ascertainable facts that should have separated one of those suspects from the others. Up until that time, Noxubee County had experienced one child homicide in its recent history: Courtney Smith. The two murders were of course remarkably similar. Johnson was the only person who at one time was a suspect in both of them. Johnson had been detained and questioned after Smith's murder because a witness had noticed his car in the neighborhood on the night she was abducted. Johnson was also the only suspect who had been charged and convicted of other sex offenses against women—each of which involved entering the victims' homes at night. And Johnson was the only suspect with cuts on his arms, the same sorts of cuts some law enforcement officers must have sustained when walking through the thick brush near the creek while looking for the girl.

Yet Brewer's attorneys never developed Johnson as a possible suspect—at least not in court. The jury was never given an alternative. Either Kennedy Brewer raped and killed Christine, or the killer was still out there and might never be caught.

There is no audio recording of Brewer's trial, but on the written page, Forrest Allgood's closing argument reads like the fire-and-brimstone sermon of a snake-handling revivalist, right down to an altar-call ending. He began with some discussion of concentric circles.

"I know when I was in grade school I learned about concentric circles, that there's a little circle, then a bigger circle, then a bigger circle, and a bigger circle, and so on," he said. "When a body is found, ladies and gentlemen, the immediate world is a suspect. Anybody could have committed the crime. But you can begin narrowing down your suspects, ladies and gentlemen, and I want to do that with you right now."

Allgood did just that, winnowing down the field of possible killers from everyone "in the universe," to the four who were near or with Christine Jackson on the night of her death: her mom, Kennedy Brewer, Leshone Williams, and Dewayne Graham.

"Four; no more. Four," Allgood implored. From there he drew a smaller circle—the number of people locked in the house with Jackson that night. With Gloria Jackson's narrative-changing testimony, that number fell to just one. Kennedy Brewer.

On Friday, March 24, 1995, at a few minutes after four in the afternoon, the jurors in Brewer's case retired to deliberate. At quarter to six on the same day—almost exactly an hour and a half after they began—the jury returned with a verdict. They found Kennedy Brewer guilty. They would wait until morning to decide if he would live.

As in all death penalty cases, to get a death sentence Allgood needed to convince the jury that there were "aggravating circumstances." Allgood first attempted to prove that Christine Jackson had been sexually battered. He then introduced evidence—Hayne's autopsy testimony— to show that the murder was "especially heinous, atrocious and cruel." As in the Brooks trial, neither factor really needed to be proven. The crime itself provided ample evidence. Allgood didn't even bother with much of an opening statement.

Also as with the Brooks case, the defense's task now was to provide evidence of mitigating factors. Mitigation is a critical part of capital defense that's often overlooked in media and pop culture depictions of death penalty cases. The objective is to get the jury to empathize with the defendant—to show that his life is worth saving. It's so important that American Bar Association guidelines call for the appointment of two trial attorneys in death penalty cases, at least one of whom should be proficient in the sentencing phase. Since the early 2000s, the US Supreme Court has consistently found that a thorough mitigation defense is guaranteed by the Eighth Amendment. But it wasn't always that way. Overworked attorneys in indigent cases often failed to introduce any mitigation at all, or saw it as little more than an opportunity to litigate the defendant's character, not to build empathy. It wasn't until the series of decisions in the 2000s cases that the US Supreme Court laid out in more detail what was required for proper mitigation.

Brewer's attorneys' efforts at mitigation weren't necessarily worse than others in Mississippi at the time, but they were further complicated by fact that Brewer had maintained his innocence. The defense first called Brewer's mother, Annie, as a witness. She begged the jury to spare her son's life: "Please, please, sir, and please, ma'am, don't put the death penalty on Kenny," she begged. "Please. I'm askin', please. Don't, please."

When she was done, Forrest Allgood rose and asked Annie Brewer whether there had been "any three year old girls sexually assaulted, killed and dumped in creeks in Noxubee County" since her son had been locked up. She had to agree that there hadn't.

Of course, there was good reason for that. By then, Justin Albert Johnson had already pleaded guilty to the sexual assault of Verlinda Monroe in her trailer in Crawford. In fact, his plea came less than three weeks after Christine Jackson's murder. Annie Brewer had no way of knowing that, but local law enforcement should have. So Allgood was right—there hadn't been any child murders in the area since Kennedy Brewer had been arrested. And he was right that this was because Jackson's killer was behind bars. It just wasn't Brewer.

The defense also called Brewer himself to testify. Given that the jury had found Brewer guilty of the rape and murder of a toddler only hours before, it's hard to fathom how Brewer's attorneys thought this would help. They asked him some rote questions about his background, as well as a few questions that made him somewhat sympathetic, such as how he dropped out of school after his father's death to help support his family.

They then made another critical mistake.

"Kennedy, you understand that the jury has—has to make a decision on sentencing in this case. Is that right?"

"Yes, sir," Brewer answered.

"Are you asking the jury to be merciful within the law?"

"Yes, sir," he answered.

Again, Brewer had just been found guilty of the brutal rape of a toddler. He could maintain his innocence and hope jurors were willing to act on any lingering doubts. But given how quickly they had convicted him, it seems clear that within the jury box, doubt was in short supply. To ask mercy of the same people who just sat in judgment of you is a risky strategy. A defendant would need to demonstrate convincing contrition. And real remorse would require admitting to what he had done. But Brewer was innocent. Having him ask for mercy when he couldn't show contrition couldn't have set well with the jury.

Allgood made the most of the defense's mistake. In his closing argument, he responded to Brewer's lawyer's request for a life sentence by mentioning the possibility that Brewer could escape. "I don't think that any one of you would want to pick up the paper some day and read where this man had done something else to somebody else because in a moment of weakness you did that which you were urged to do." Then in his signature, formalized, folksy patois, Allgood implored the jury to return a death sentence by declaiming, "If we as a society cannot protect our children, if we as a society will not protect our children, then we will not long exist."

For the main portion of his rebuttal, Allgood invoked the Bible. Quoting from or alluding specifically to the Bible—or any authoritative source outside of the evidence or jury instructions—is fraught with problems. Some courts will reverse convictions in almost every instance; others issue reminders or chastise lawyers who try. Jurors' decisions are supposed to be based only on the evidence presented at trial and the jury instructions that guide their deliberations. Attorneys may cite the Bible to illustrate a point or to use as a metaphor, but they're generally prohibited from invoking it as an authority jurors should consult or use for guidance when deliberating.

Allgood often invoked the Bible, and his closing argument in Kennedy Brewer's sentencing trial was a full-blown sermon. Allgood told the jury that he had always wondered about Pharaoh, the cruel ruler of Egypt who had enslaved the Israelites. How, Allgood asked, could God have created someone so cruel, but then at the same time have held that person accountable for his actions? Allgood explained:

One day I was reading along in Romans, and I think it's Chapter 7, I can't be sure, but Paul says this: What if God, wanting to make his power known to the nations made for himself vessels of wrath fit only for destruction—vessels of wrath fit only for destruction. Ladies and gentlemen, I tell you, that there are those among us, they look like us, they talk like us, they on the outside seem like us, but they aren't like us. They are indeed those vessels of wrath fit only for destruction.

The day of Kennedy Brewer's sentencing dawned bright and fair in east-central Mississippi. By noon, the temperature outside edged toward seventy degrees. Brewer sat locked in a cramped jail cell on the second floor of the Noxubee County courthouse. Dressed in an ill-fitting suit, he sat and tried to avoid contemplating his fate. But there was really no escaping what had just befallen him. He had been arrested for something he hadn't done. He then spent four years behind bars waiting for the trial he thought would finally set him free. Instead, just hours earlier, a jury convicted him of capital murder for the rape and murder of a three-year-old girl.

To make matters worse, whatever his shortcomings as a young father, Brewer had come to care a great deal for Christine Jackson. He thought of the girl as his own. Now she was gone, snatched from her home on his watch, then brutally violated and killed. He wanted to be sad about that. He wanted to deal with his guilt for not waking up to protect her. He wanted to mourn. But at the moment, there was no room in his head for grief. Just down the hall from his cell, twelve jurors were deciding if he would live or die.

Just before two p.m., there was a knock from the door leading to the jury room. The clerk walked to the door, cracked it slightly, and received a folded piece of paper. She read it silently and then looked up. The jury had reached a unanimous decision.

The sheriff's deputies ushered Brewer from his cell back to the seat beside his lawyers. The judge returned to the bench, and the clerk opened the rear door. The jurors filed in. The foreperson handed the verdict to the deputy clerk so that it could be read into the record.

"We, the jury find that . . . the defendant should suffer the penalty of death."

As the clerk's voice faded, the judge ordered Brewer to enter the well of the courtroom. He obeyed. Bracketed by deputies, he slowly stepped forward.

The judge began. "Mr. Brewer, the jury of citizens of Lowndes County, Mississippi, has found you guilty of the crime of capital murder. . . . The jury has returned that verdict in open court. That verdict was that you should suffer death. Do you have anything you desire to say to the Court before sentence is imposed?"

"No," Brewer responded softly.

"I am by law required at this time to set a date for your execution. . . . I hereby direct that the sheriff immediately take custody of your body and immediately transport you to the maximum security unit of the Mississippi Department of Corrections at Parchman, Mississippi. You are to there remain in custody until May the 12th of nineteen ninety-five, at which time you will be removed to a place where you shall suffer death by lethal injection," the judge said.

"May God have mercy on your soul."

Between 1976 and 2001, Mississippi executed just 4 people. That statistic may seem surprising. Alabama executed 23 over the same period. Texas executed 166 in the 1990s alone. In fact, in the thirteen years between June 1989 and July 2002, Mississippi didn't execute anyone at all.

It wasn't for lack of trying. In fact, the problem is that the state was trying a bit *too* hard. In 1980, the US Supreme Court ruled in *Godfrey v. Georgia* that Georgia's death penalty instructions to jurors were unconstitutionally vague. As written, the instruction required jurors to return a verdict of death if they found a crime to be "outrageously or wantonly vile, horrible or inhuman." At the time, Mississippi's death penalty instructions included the phrase "especially heinous, atrocious or cruel." Despite the similarly vague language, Mississippi stuck with its law, on the assumption that the inclusion of the word "especially" made its instructions less vague and thus constitutionally compliant.

Eight years later, the US Supreme Court held in *Maynard v. Cartwright* that Oklahoma's instructions, which were identical to Mississippi's right down to the word "especially," were also unconstitutionally vague. That finally moved the Mississippi legislature to change its jury instructions in capital cases. But state lawmakers and judges assumed that the decision only applied to cases going forward, not retroactively.

It wasn't until the 1992 case *Stringer v. Black* that the US Supreme Court formally rebuked the state: Mississippi had to revisit every death penalty case going back to the *Godfrey* decision in 1980. That would take a while. And it's why Mississippi had no choice but to take a long break from its industrious history of executing people.

Another reason for the thirteen-year lack of executions was the work of Justice James Robertson. Robertson was cautious and skeptical when it came to death penalty cases, and he had a knack for bringing other justices along with him. Under Robertson's leadership, the court overturned a number of capital convictions deemed too faulty for the finality of the gas chamber.

But the early 1990s also brought the aforementioned national surge in violent crime, and with it a surge in get-tough-on-crime rhetoric. In 1992, Robertson was voted off the court, defeated by a law-and-order candidate who ran a nasty campaign portraying Robertson as a friend to criminals.

One other big reason Mississippi's executions slowed to a halt: the state consistently refused to fund legal counsel for indigent defendants during their appeals. This was part of the law-and-order crowd's common and most cynical complaint: hardened criminals were routinely "getting off on technicalities." Such outcomes were outrageous enough on their own, the argument went, and it seemed downright insulting that taxpayers should have to foot the bill for such claims.

The reality was that capital defendants weren't getting *any* legal representation after their first appeal. When their cases would then finally get to federal court, either by their own doing, with the help of a "jailhouse lawyer," or through a pro bono attorney, federal appeals courts would find that their legal representation had been unconstitutionally defective. By refusing to fund an adequate public defender system, then, state lawmakers were contributing to the very drawn-out appeals process they were so fond of criticizing.

In 1994, the Mississippi legislature responded to the soaring crime rate with a raucous debate over a bill intended to address prison overcrowding, but that quickly devolved into an orgy of punitiveness. "There was talk of restoring fear to prisons," the *New York Times* reported of the debate in Jackson, "of caning, of making prisoners 'smell like a prisoner,' of burning and frying, of returning executions to the county seat." Governor Kirk Fordice implored lawmakers to "make Mississippi the capital of capital punishment." By the time it was over, the legislature had banned TVs, radios, CD players, and weight-lifting equipment from state prisons. They required inmates to wear striped uniforms with the word "convict" printed across the back. (Said one state representative, "When you see one of these boogers aloose, you'll say, 'I didn't know we had zebras in Mississippi.'")

That summer, Governor Kirk Fordice took some time off to go on a big-game hunting safari in Africa. In his absence, Lieutenant Governor Eddie Briggs filled in as acting governor. Briggs, generally considered to be more moderate than Fordice, took the opportunity to convene a special session of the legislature solely for the purpose of passing laws to expand and expedite the death penalty. Among the bills under consideration: empowering elected judges, not juries, to impose the death penalty; expanding the doctrine of "harmless error" so fewer convictions could be overturned on "technicalities"; and adding a slate of new crimes to those already punishable by death.

In the end, most of the measures never made it into law, but that was mostly due to partisan squabbling over who would get credit for them. When it came to executing more people more often in Mississippi, there was widespread, bipartisan support. By 1997, death penalty fervor even had many clamoring for the execution of a fourteen-year-old girl who had been accused of killing her newborn daughter.

As most in the state saw it, the problem wasn't that Mississippi didn't have adequate protections for the innocent; it was that the protections that did exist were hindering the electorate's blood lust. In 1994, in between the Brooks and Brewer verdicts, the *Enterprise-Journal* in McComb, Mississippi, editorialized, "As an effective deterrent to crime, the death penalty should be swift and certain. Unfortunately, the carrying out of the death sentence in America has been anything but that. Serious wrongdoers are condemned to die, and they often wait five, 10, 12 years or more for the penalty to be carried out."

In 1995, Fordice announced in his State of the State address that he wanted all death row inmates executed within three years of their conviction. The press endorsed Fordice's call to action. Despite the *Clarion-Ledger*'s consistent and admirable demands to hire and support a state medical examiner, the paper also led the charge for speeding up executions. "For the death penalty to be a [*sic*] effective deterrent, it must be carried out quickly," the paper editorialized in October 1995, just a few months after Kennedy Brewer was sentenced to death. "No one wants an innocent person to be executed, but appeal procedures could be changed to shorten the process."

Fordice continued to demand speedier, more frequent state-sponsored killing. In his 1996 State of the State address, he demanded a *one-year* limit on death penalty appeals, and asked the legislature to add high-volume drug dealing to the list of crimes punishable by death. In 1997, he held a news conference in which he was flanked by the widows of two men who had recently been murdered, one of them a former assistant attorney general. Fordice again lamented the state's slow progress with executions, this time with especially dehumanizing language. States like Texas and Arkansas, Fordice complained, "are continually working down their inventory on death row, and ours continues to grow."

Again, the state's press dutifully followed along. The *Clarion-Ledger* ran another supportive editorial in February 1998 that closed with this rhetorical flourish: "There are 58 names on the death row roster. Let's let the sword of justice do its work." At the time that editorial ran, there were eight men in Mississippi's prisons who had been convicted of murder but would later be exonerated.

In fact, there may not have been a more execution-obsessed op-ed page in America at the time than the *Clarion-Ledger*'s. Between 1994 and 1998 alone, Mississippi's largest newspaper ran thirty-eight unsigned editorials in support of the death penalty—calls to speed it up, expand it, or apply it in a particular case. When the Mississippi Supreme Court finally allowed DNA testing for Kennedy Brewer in July 2001, the paper published a staff editorial supporting Brewer's right to have the DNA tested but added, "The existence of DNA does not refute the need for the death penalty."

By the early 1990s, advances in DNA technology allowed for testing that could exclude defendants as the source of biological material found at a crime scene. (The technology enabling DNA scientists to match biological evidence came along later.) By 2001, DNA testing had cleared eleven people who had been wrongly convicted and sentenced to death. In other words, "the existence of DNA" showed that the system could get it wrong, and far more often than most of the public believed. The death penalty didn't cause the system's flaws, but it did cement those flaws with an ultimate and irreversible punishment. By 2001, Kennedy Brewer had been on death row for six and a half years. At one point, he had been scheduled for execution. If the death penalty had been more "swift and certain," as the *Clarion-Ledger*, Kirk Fordice, and a good chunk of Mississippi's politicians and prosecutors had advocated throughout the 1990s, Kennedy Brewer would be dead. If the death penalty across the country had been "swifter" and more "certain," the eleven men cleared by DNA testing across the country by 2001 would be dead, too.

Perhaps the most perverse thing about Mississippi's death penalty debate in the 1990s is that it was only by the grace of petty politics and fragile egos that the state never went on the execution binge that everyone seemed to want. Kirk Fordice's goal to expedite executions and make Mississippi the "capital of capital punishment" was supported by the leaders of both major political parties, prosecutors, most of the judiciary, the state's largest newspapers, and a healthy majority of Mississippians. Certainly, some of Fordice's proposals wouldn't have passed constitutional muster once they were inevitably challenged in federal court. But the main reason most of Fordice's killing agenda was never enacted is that the other power players in Mississippi politics at the time—from Lieutenant Governor Briggs to Attorney General Mike Moore to the leaders in the state legislature—either didn't want to give Fordice a political victory or wanted all the "tough on crime" credit for themselves. You could make a strong argument that Kirk Fordice's likability problems saved Kennedy Brewer's life.

Without oversight from the state medical examiner's office, Steven Hayne was flourishing. By the late 1990s his annual autopsy totals topped 1,500, which meant he was grossing three-quarters of a million dollars per year from county autopsy fees alone. But Hayne was also looking to do more private autopsies, where he often charged $1,500 or more per procedure, plus significantly more per hour for testimony and trial preparation than he got from the state. Around 1995, Hayne joined Investigative Research Inc. (IR) to help facilitate his work in private cases. Initially, IR was a small operation whose main clients were insurance companies that hired it to conduct arson investigations. After bringing Hayne aboard, IR expanded to take on investigations for life insurance companies, plus provide expert testimony in civil litigation, often related to medical malpractice and wrongful deaths.

Meanwhile, two years after Emily Ward left, Mississippi still didn't have a state medical examiner. The coroners and prosecutors who had chased Ward out were fine with that. They both declared victory and pushed to ensure that no one like her occupied the office again.

"All I can say is that Hinds County hasn't missed a beat without [a state medical examiner]," coroner Robert Martin told the *Clarion-Ledger*. Jimmy Roberts agreed: "It seems to me things run smoother when we don't have one." Washington County coroner George Hampton told the paper that when he had a question about the job, he just asked Steven Hayne. "Anytime I have a question, I always call him, and he is able to respond whenever I need him." Karl Oliver, the president of the coroners' association, agreed. "The system is working absolutely fine," he said.

Michael West had done such a convincing job with his public advocacy that his hometown paper, the *Hattiesburg American*, recommended abolishing the state medical examiner entirely. A staff editorial opined, "A competent coroner and pathologist working at the local level are more than qualified to conduct death investigations and render accurate opinions. . . . Mississippi can do without a state medical examiner. As far as we're concerned—pardon the pun—this is a dead issue." For good measure, the editorial also quoted West: "In my 16 years in this field, I've never seen one instance where a state medical examiner was needed. Not one."

For their part, state officials weren't going out of their way to find Ward's replacement. The position was advertised with a salary of $69,000, which would have made whoever took the job the lowest paid state medical examiner in the country. One needn't be a conspiracy theorist to wonder if the Mississippi offer wasn't *intended* to prevent qualified candidates from applying.

It seems clear that most powerful people in the state's criminal justice system wanted the office to remain vacant. Legislators didn't feel particularly obligated to offer more, because no one who had their ear was really complaining. From the legislature's point of view, the state was saving money by not funding the salary and benefits of a state medical examiner and a full office of support staff. From the counties' perspective, the $500 autopsy fee remained the same whether the funds went to the state medical examiner's office or to Steven Hayne's bank account. The former might give prosecutors a more professional autopsy, but the latter often guaranteed a conviction. The coroners were happy. Police and prosecutors were happy. People charged with serious crimes were going to prison.

Yet in reality, even setting aside the problems with Hayne's massive workload, the state was still losing a lot of money. As the legislature was partially funding the medical examiner's office, it was also providing funding for staff and upkeep for the modern state morgue that had been built especially to facilitate autopsies. It went largely unused. Mississippi taxpayers were paying twice for the same government function, once to build and maintain a fancy new state morgue and crime lab, and then again for Hayne's after-hours, assembly-line autopsies at a private morgue. But because the fees were paid by the individual counties, the wasted money wasn't apparent to public officials, much less to taxpayers.

The following year, the *Clarion-Ledger* published another article about the vacant state medical examiner position. This time, it was Michael West who assured Mississippians that he and Steve Hayne had it all under control. Perhaps the state needed a functionary in the state medical examiner's office to handle paperwork, West argued, but nothing more. "We need someone who can help the police and organize the coroners," he said. "What we don't need is a medical pathologist who wants to argue with other pathologists about cause of death, which has happened in the past."

That's *exactly* what the state needed.

~

A few years after Hayne joined Investigative Research, he consulted on two lawsuits against a company called Graco Children's Products. The lawsuits alleged that the company's defective infant rockers had caused two babies to suffocate. Hayne had done the original autopsies on the children and in both cases originally said they had died of Sudden Infant Death Syndrome (SIDS)—a conclusion a medical examiner makes only after excluding nearly everything else. After he was contacted by the attorneys for the parents bringing the lawsuits, he changed his diagnosis to death by positional asphyxiation, which he said was caused by a defect in the rocker. The children's bodies had by then been buried. There is no indication that they were ever exhumed and reexamined.

In a deposition for the case, Hayne claimed that at the time he did the original autopsies, deaths by positional asphyxiation were commonly misdiagnosed as SIDS. Coincidentally, he said that just four months prior to the deposition, just at about the time the attorneys for the plaintiffs in the case approached him, positional asphyxiation had "come to the forefront" of "medical knowledge."

Forensic specialists say Hayne's explanation doesn't add up. "It would be very difficult to change from SIDS to asphyxiation," said James Starrs, a professor at George Washington University and author of several forensic textbooks, in a 2007 interview. "The latter is a more specific diagnosis, one that would require the presence of symptoms Hayne should have noticed during the original autopsies."

That he didn't certainly raises questions about whether he either badly botched the autopsies or concocted the diagnosis for the lawsuit. Investigative Research then invoiced the plaintiffs' attorneys for Hayne's services. His price: $37,000.

John Stossel's *ABC News* report featuring Michael West finally aired in 1997. The segment was part of an hour-long special about "junk science."

Stossel delved into West's analysis and reported that West had been sending a brochure to police departments in Mississippi and Louisiana to advertise his services. In the brochure, West offered to come and explain his methods to any police agency willing to pay him $900—which is to say that for $900, he'd come and tell police departments why they should hire him in future cases. According to Stossel, West's brochure promised that "he can turn cases that were once unsolved into police convictions." The segment also included footage in which West boldly declared, "All talents, all gifts that I possess are directed straight from God."

By 1998, West had been criticized in the *American Bar Association Journal*, the *National Law Journal*, *ABC News*, and the New Orleans *Times-Picayune*. He had been forced to resign from the American Academy of Forensic Sciences and the International Association for Identification, and had been suspended from the ABFO. His testimony had been thrown out in three separate murder cases, and he had caused the wrong man to be arrested and jailed for a year in a murder case in Humphreys County—after which the real killer went on to kill again. It's also the year that the Mississippi Supreme Court officially gave Michael West its endorsement.

The endorsement came by way of Kennedy Brewer's appeal, which the justices were hearing for the first time. In dismissing Brewer's claims about West, the court laid out a litany of excuses and explanations for West's behavior and mistakes. The majority explained away the rising chorus of critics as mere differences of opinion between professionals. The opinion claimed that "the record evidence shows that Dr. West possessed the knowledge, skill, experience, training and education necessary to qualify as an expert in forensic odontology." The court ruled that the "problems he encountered"—a self-serving, antiseptic description of West's history—"went to the weight and credibility to be assigned his testimony by the jury—not his qualifications."

The court then rejected all of Brewer's other claims and upheld his conviction. It ordered his execution to be scheduled within sixty days of the dispensation of his case. There was no dissent.

The next year, the court rejected Levon Brooks's appeal, too. The state's brief in Brooks's case is a study in prosecutorial tunnel vision. It's clear from the brief that its author—who worked in the attorney general's office—made little effort to confirm the veracity of the damning statements Allgood made at Brooks's trial. The meandering, contradictory, often fantastical answers Ashley Smith gave over the course of her two police interviews and trial testimony? Here's how the state characterized them: "Ashley's identification of Brooks was immediate and unwavering, through the first interview, the photo lineup and the trial itself."

This is simply false. It's either a lie or a false statement arising from stunning inattention to the facts. It is of course the job of the attorney general's staff to defend convictions. But the office is also supposed to serve the interests of justice. Here, the state's brief merely parroted Allgood's closing argument. It made no effort to look back to verify if it was actually true.

The brief then addressed the court's denial of Kennedy Brewer's appeal the year before. Its characterization of that decision is chilling:

> Brewer v. State was a case from the same trial court as the case at bar, arising from the murder of another three-year-old in the same small town as in the present case. The facts of the two cases are almost unbelievably similar. Brewer was convicted of murder and an important part of the state's evidence was a bite mark comparison of Brewer's teeth with the marks left on the child's body. The Court found this evidence to be sufficient for conviction. Brewer, unlike the present case, resulted in a death penalty for the defendant. If this evidence passed the heightened scrutiny of death penalty cases, there is no reason why it should be held inadmissible in the present case.

It turns out that when properly motivated, state officials were able to see the remarkable similarities between these two cases after all. They just couldn't take the next step—asking if the same man committed both crimes. That would require considering the possibility that the state got it wrong.

The court voted 8 to 1 to uphold the conviction. With respect to the bite mark evidence, the majority first found that because Brooks didn't object to Michael West's credentials at trial, he was procedurally barred from raising them in his appeal. But the court also went a lot further than it needed to. It ruled that bite mark analysis was now universally admissible in Mississippi courts—a form of evidence just as reliable as fingerprints or DNA. When the *Clarion-Ledger* reached out to Michael West for his reaction, West reported that he was "elated." "It's taken us quite a while to get to reach this point," he said. "For many years I've had to endure the assaults of defense attorneys on the validity of bite marks."

The only dissent came from Justice Charles McRae, at the time the court's most astute justice on these issues. McRae made all of the right arguments—that bite mark analysis in general was entirely subjective, had no scientific support for its underlying premises, and lacked any uniform criteria or methodology for determining a "match." He also included a pretty thorough rundown of West's long and growing list of transgressions.

Unfortunately, just about anything McRae did on the court at that time was overshadowed by a recent drunk driving arrest. A state supreme court justice had just written the most critical and accurate assessment of West by any Mississippi judge to date. But few would hear him.

∽ 12 ∽

PRAYERS FOR RELIEF

Whatever problems our system has, it cannot be as
bad as all that.

—Judge J. Harvie Wilkinson III, Fourth Circuit
Court of Appeals

By 2000, Michael West had lost his position as Forrest County coroner, and Hayne hired him as an assistant. And though at least some
prosecutors began steering clear of West, others, like Forrest Allgood,
continued to use him. In fact, as the public criticism of West mounted,
Allgood's defense of the dentist became strident and unmoored from
reality.

During the second trial of Eddie Lee Howard, the man convicted
of raping and killing Georgia Kemp and then setting her house on
fire, the defense had brought up all of the usual allegations against
West. Perhaps Allgood sensed that momentum was building against
his star witness, and he was growing restless. Perhaps he feared how
that would reflect on his own career. Whatever his motivation, he delivered a closing argument that was the most embarrassing defense of
either Hayne or West ever uttered by a Mississippi public official. By
the time he was finished, Allgood had essentially argued that children
would one day be reading about West in their history books.

"Ladies and gentlemen . . . I expect that much of what you hear
when I sit down will be an attack," he began, anticipating what Howard's attorneys would say in their own closing arguments. "An attack
primarily on one man and one thing, Dr. Michael West." Allgood conceded that West could be brash and evasive, and that he possessed an
ego that probably wouldn't fit into the courtroom—a line that likely
elicited some chuckles. But then came the exaltations.

West, Allgood said, was "also guilty of being a pioneer, a visionary, somebody that has found something new and pushed it to the limits, something that is now accepted throughout his profession as the standard."

The first few items in that list were arguably true, though not in the way Allgood intended. The last line was false. Bite mark analysis was not accepted within or endorsed by the scientific community at large, and even West's fellow bite mark analysts had begun to distance themselves from him.

Allgood went on. "Whether we like to think so or not, the progress of mankind has been carried forward on the backs of people like Michael West," he rhapsodized. "You don't have to look far if you'll look into history. The church threatened to burn Copernicus because he dared to say that the planets didn't revolve around the earth."

Allgood then paused. "So it was with Michael West."

Michael West was no longer merely a credible expert witness. He was an intellect for the ages. He wasn't just a skilled bite mark analyst; he was a martyr, a paladin for truth who had been persecuted for his dogged pursuit of knowledge. (Never mind that in his grandiloquence, Allgood conflated Copernicus with Galileo.)

As for West's suspensions and resignations, Allgood assured the jury, they "hadn't slowed him up one bit. He still testifies as an expert. He still lectures on bite marks. He still lectures on ALI, alternate light imaging, and, yes, he's a leader in his field."

Allgood wasn't wrong here. West did still testify. That was exactly the problem. Not finished, Allgood went on to call West "cutting edge," "a man who wears many hats," and he weirdly praised West's expertise in "ergonomics." Finally, Allgood told the jury that West "is an individual who is very interested in forensic sciences, and has plunged headlong into them with the enthusiasm of a three year old child."

The jury then convicted Eddie Lee Howard a second time. And for a second time, a jury sentenced him to die.

The Supreme Court's *Daubert* decisions of the early 1990s didn't do much to keep bad science out of the courtroom. In fact, they may have made things worse. One effect of the decisions was to create a market for certifying organizations to confer "expert" status on would-be forensic witnesses. As a result, forensics today is awash in a sea of acronyms. Some of these groups are legitimate, but many are pay-to-play certification mills. The net effect is that for a fee, just about anyone who wants to can get "accredited" in a given field of forensics by finding a group willing to sell them a slip of paper to frame and hang on a wall. The courts have essentially ceded responsibility for sorting the sea of acronyms to attorneys.

Steven Hayne is a good example. The organization Hayne most often says has certified him is the American Board of Forensic Pathology. That name sounds suspiciously similar to the American Board of Pathology, a widely recognized certifying organization—and with good reason. Whereas a medical examiner certified by the ABP would say on the witness stand, "I'm certified in forensic pathology by the American Board of Pathology," Hayne would say, "I'm certified by the American Board of Forensic Pathology." The two claims sound virtually the same, but there's a world of difference between them.

When asked in 2008 whether someone should testify in court to being "board certified" without having passed the ABP test, Joseph Prahlow, the then-president of the National Association of Medical Examiners, replied, "When you say you're 'certified,' it means the American Board of Pathology." When told that Hayne routinely says he's "board certified in forensic pathology" despite not passing the exam, Prahlow replied, "That is very disturbing to me. There's definitely a problem with that."

As a result, in the vast majority of cases in which Hayne invoked the organization, judges, jurors, and even opposing attorneys could be confused and not realize that the American Board of Forensic Pathology is an entirely different organization from the American Board of Pathology.

Or to be more accurate, it *was* an entirely different organization. The group hasn't existed since 1996. When it did exist, it was part of a larger Las Vegas–based organization called the American Academy of Neurological and Orthopedic Surgery (AANOS). For years, AANOS issued "certifications" in dozens of medical fields.

If it seems odd that a group of neurological and orthopedic surgeons would be certifying doctors in forensic pathology—an entirely different field—it is. A 1994 profile of the group in the journal *Medical Economics* reported that AANOS offered certifications in more than fifty medical specialties, including "such exotic fields as bionic rehabilitative psychology, ringside medicine and surgery, percutane-ous discectomy, and radiofrequency surgery." The group was founded by Michael Rask, a surgeon, an eccentric, and apparently a devoted fan of Frank Sinatra—he changed his name to Bartholomew Sinatra shortly before he died.

Hayne also claimed certification by another organization with an even odder history. The august-sounding American College of Forensic Examiners Institute (ACFEI) was founded by Robert Louis O'Block, a criminal justice professor who, according to a 2000 *ABA Journal* article, had been terminated from Appalachian State University in 1991 for plagiarism. (In the same article, O'Block insisted that his termination was retaliation for whistle-blowing.)

At his subsequent teaching gig, O'Block developed an interest in the field of handwriting analysis. But when he applied for membership with an existing organization of forensic handwriting experts, they rejected him. So he decided to form his own credentialing organization for handwriting and put himself in charge. In 1992 he founded the American Board of Forensic Handwriting Analysts. *Fraud* magazine reported in 2012 that as O'Block expanded his group to other disciplines, he also hired his first national training director for the organization, a high school graduate with no college experience who claimed he could enlarge women's breasts through hypnosis. (The breast-enlarging hypnotist would later resign as a result of his own doubts about O'Block's credibility.)

And yet, somehow, O'Block continued to collect new members to his organization. In 1995, he renamed the organization the American College of Forensic Examiners. He added the word "institute" after objections from a group already using the ACFE acronym. He formed a board of directors consisting of himself, his wife, and his two minor children. He paid himself a salary just over $50,000 per year and started a hotline to hook his members up with lawyers in need of expert witnesses (1-800-4AExpert).

The *ABA Journal* reported that by the year 2000, the ACFEI offered "boards" in eleven specialties and claimed over thirteen thousand members and seventeen thousand diplomates (a member could be a diplomate in more than one field). Revenues for the group cleared $2 million, and O'Block's salary jumped to $200,000 per year.

Today, the ACFEI claims to be the largest forensic certification organization in the country. It may well be. It boasts celebrity spokespersons from the forensics world, like famed medical examiner Cyril Wecht and forensic analyst Henry Lee.

Hayne, like many other ACFEI diplomates, was grandfathered in for his certification. He had only to provide a résumé and pay a $350 fee. The *Wall Street Journal* reported in 1999 that ACFEI candidates who weren't grandfathered in have to score 75 percent or higher on an ethics test. But the test was largely symbolic. It included questions like, "Is it ever okay to misrepresent yourself?" and "Is it ever okay to stretch the truth?" Failing applicants could retake the test up to three times. Even the test requirement could also be waived entirely if a candidate's application accumulated a hundred "points." Points weren't determined by ACFEI but by applicants themselves, using the honor system. And even that could be waived.

The *ABA Journal* interviewed a psychiatry professor at Washington University in St. Louis who received ACFEI certification without even trying. And a prison inmate named Seymour Schlager was able to obtain a certification by ACFEI's American Board of Forensic Medicine while serving time for attempted murder. In 2002, a woman was able to get certification by using the name of her cat.

Despite awarding thousands of certifications, ACFEI hasn't always been forthcoming about whom it certifies. When asked over the years, the organization has said such information is confidential, seemingly an odd practice for an accrediting group.

Despite ACFEI officials' protestations that the organization is not a "certification mill," in 2012 a journalism graduate student named Leah Bartos was able to get certified as a "forensic consultant," despite having no prior experience in forensics. According to Bartos, no one from ACFEI ever contacted any of her professional references.

In the end, both ACFEI and AANOS allowed Hayne to continue to claim to be board certified in forensic pathology without technically perjuring himself. Most of the time, no one in the courtroom knew enough to ask further questions.

Of course, even properly credentialed experts can still give noncredible testimony. But proper credentials at least establish a baseline. They can define a minimal level of demonstrated competency in an expert witness. Nevertheless, that presumes judges, prosecutors, and defense attorneys will know which credentialing groups are legitimate and which aren't. "Credentials are often appealing shortcuts," Michigan circuit court judge Donald Shelton told Bartos in her 2012

ProPublica report. Fancy titles can have a disproportionate effect on juries. "Jurors have no way of knowing that this certifying body, whether it's this one or any other one, exacts scientific standards or is just a diploma mill."

Ideally, the courts would help jurors sort all of this out. There just hasn't been much interest.

~

In the late 1990s and early 2000s, Mississippi saw an increase in convictions based on Shaken Baby Syndrome (SBS), a controversial diagnosis that holds that if a trio of specific symptoms are found in a dead child, the death could only have been caused by violent shaking, even if there is no corresponding impact to the head. It's a convenient diagnosis in that it provides prosecutors with a method of homicide (shaking), a likely suspect (the last person alone with the child), and intent (built into the diagnosis is the notion that babies only die this way after exceptionally violent shaking).

But over the last decade or so, the diagnosis has come under increased scrutiny. Even the doctor who first came up with the theory has now expressed doubts about it. Recent research has shown that falls, blows to the head, and even some illnesses and genetic conditions can cause the same set of symptoms. It isn't that all SBS cases are wrongful convictions, of course; it's that the trio of symptoms themselves shouldn't be the sole basis of a conviction. A number of convictions have been overturned. Many more are under review.

Defense attorneys interviewed for this book say there has long been a sentiment among some police and prosecutors in Mississippi that when it comes to babies who die unnatural deaths, "there are no accidents." Someone killed the child, either willfully or through criminally negligent parenting. Babies don't die without someone being at fault. Therefore, somebody must be punished.

Steven Hayne testified to SBS in several cases. The *Clarion-Ledger* reported in 2014 that since 2000 there had been eleven such convictions in the state. Because these cases often end with a plea bargain before trial, most don't leave much of a public record. So it's hard to say exactly how many relied on a diagnosis from Hayne. But given the percentage of the state's autopsies he was doing at the time, it seems likely that he was involved in many of them.

In most SBS cases, prosecutors would first file murder charges, then later allow the defendant to plead down to a lesser charge like manslaughter. But there are two cases in which Hayne's SBS diagnosis led not only to a murder conviction, but also a death sentence. The first is that of Devin Bennett, who in 2000 was accused of killing his infant son, Brandon. In an odd twist, Bennett's attorneys actually brought in Emily Ward to rebut Hayne's testimony. Ward, then working for the state of Alabama, was reluctant to testify, given her history in Mississippi. She made her way to court only after an Alabama court ordered her to appear. After she was questioned by Bennett's attorney, the prosecutor aggressively cross-examined Ward about her fights with Hayne, West, and the state's coroners and prosecutors. Ward's efforts to clean up the state had put her under attack all over again; only this time, a man's life was at stake. The tactic apparently worked—the jury convicted Bennett and sentenced him to death. The Mississippi Supreme Court upheld the conviction. The court had no problem with prosecutors probing Ward's "personal feelings about Dr. Hayne and her forthrightness in the reasons for leaving her employment."

"That case was like a lot of others where a baby died, and so someone had to pay for it," Ward said in a 2008 interview. "But I still think about it. I think it was a miscarriage of justice. I still think Devin is innocent."

The SBS conviction of Jeffrey Havard demonstrates as well as any other how without DNA testing, it can be nearly impossible to overturn convictions based on faulty forensic testimony. In many of these cases, the degree to which the courts went out of their way to avoid confronting the obvious problems with Hayne and West isn't apparent until you really dig into the details. Only after reading the court opinions after successive challenges do you begin to see problems, such as how one opinion can directly contradict another but still reach the same outcome, the intellectually dishonest approach courts often take with unfavorable forensic evidence, and how, too often, defendants never really stand a chance of getting a fair hearing.

Havard's case embodies all of these problems. The story begins on the evening of February 21, 2002, when Havard was watching Chloe, the six-month-old daughter of his girlfriend, Rebecca Britt. According to Havard, at some point Chloe had spit up on her clothes and bedding, so he gave the girl a bath. As he pulled her up out of the tub, she slipped from his grip and fell. As she fell, she struck her head on the toilet.

Havard would say that the bump on Chloe's head didn't appear to be serious, so he dressed her in clean clothes and put her to bed. Not wanting to worry Rebecca (or perhaps not wanting to anger her), he said nothing about the incident when she returned. When she did get home, Rebecca checked on the baby, who seemed fine. She and Havard ate dinner and went about their evening.

Later that night Chloe stopped breathing. When Havard and Rebecca couldn't get her breathing again, they rushed her to a hospital. Chloe died shortly thereafter.

When the emergency room doctors examined Chloe, they discovered that her anus was dilated. This isn't uncommon in infants shortly after death. It's also common in infants who are still alive but have lost brain function. Unfortunately, even trained medical staff sometimes mistake it for sexual abuse.

Steven Hayne performed an autopsy the following evening. In his autopsy, Hayne noted a one-centimeter contusion on Chloe's rectum, which he documented in a photograph. But his autopsy report made no mention of any evidence of sexual assault. He also found symptoms he said were consistent with Shaken Baby Syndrome.

Unfortunately, Havard didn't admit that he dropped Chloe until a videotaped interview two days after her death. That meant his story had changed. That, the statements from the ER staff about possible sexual abuse, and Hayne's SBS diagnosis were enough for local officials to arrest Havard and charge him with capital murder. The district attorney said he would seek the death penalty.

Havard was indigent, so the court assigned him a public defender. His attorney asked the district court judge for funds to hire his own forensic pathologist. The judge turned him down, finding that there was no need for a separate pathologist when Dr. Hayne was available. Havard's jury would hear from Steven Hayne and only Steven Hayne.

Though he had no prior history of abusing or molesting children, by the time Havard's trial began ten months later, word had spread around Adams County that he was a pedophile and baby killer. Studies have shown that not only can eyewitness memory change over time, it can be significantly altered with the acquisition of new information. That appears to be what happened in Havard's case, as some witnesses' memories grew considerably more vivid by the time of his trial. Jurors heard the sheriff, the coroner, and the medical staff at the ER describe "tears," "rips," "lacerations," and other injuries to the child's anus. Some claimed to have seen blood. Two nurses said it was the worst example of anal trauma they had ever witnessed.

Yet once the infant had been cleaned off, Hayne's own autopsy photos showed there were no rips, tears, lacerations, or similar injuries anywhere on the girl's rectum—only the dilation and small contusion.

Despite his own photos, and the fact that he made no mention of sexual abuse in his autopsy notes, Hayne played up the contusion at trial. He told the jury that it was an inch long, not a centimeter, as he put in his report. While he conceded that he had found no tears or lacerations, he speculated that rigor mortis (the tightening of muscles after death) could have caused the girl's rectum to close, hiding any tears or cuts from his view. But if that was the case, Hayne should have accounted for it in his autopsy and looked more closely for tears. He did neither.

Hayne also testified that because he found the symptoms of Shaken Baby Syndrome, he could conclude that Chloe had been "violently shaken" to death. To emphasize the point, Hayne and the prosecutor exchanged the phrase "violently shaken" an additional six times.

Havard's defense attorney wasn't exactly aggressive. The prosecution called sixteen witnesses, whose testimonies comprise 261 pages of the trial transcript. Havard's attorney called a single witness, a nurse at the ER. His testimony takes up three pages. The state didn't even bother to cross-examine. It's hardly surprising, then, that the jury convicted Havard and sentenced him to die. The entire trial, deliberation, guilty verdict, sentencing trial, deliberation, and death sentence took two days.

After Havard was sentenced, his case was taken up by the Mississippi Office of Capital Post-Conviction Counsel, which had been set up by the state supreme court to guarantee that indigent defendants in death penalty cases received adequate legal representation. That office had funding to hire its own experts. Havard's new attorneys asked former Alabama state medical examiner James Lauridson to review Hayne's autopsy and trial testimony. Lauridson found a number of problems. Most notably, he found no evidence of sexual abuse at all.

But for Havard's direct appeal, Lauridson's opinions didn't matter. In a 2006 ruling, the Mississippi Supreme Court delivered a brutal one-two punch. The court first upheld the trial judge's decision to deny Havard funds to hire his own forensic pathologist, finding that

Havard's trial attorneys had failed to show why an independent medical examiner was necessary. The justices then explained that because Lauridson's affidavit wasn't submitted during Havard's trial, they were barred from considering it on appeal. The court upheld his conviction and death sentence. The ruling was unanimous.

Havard's first post-conviction appeal came two years later. In post-conviction, a defendant has more leeway to introduce new evidence, but the bar for a new trial is set much higher. This time, the court had to at least consider Lauridson's affidavit. It did, but not all that carefully. For example, in his report Lauridson referred to medical literature documenting the fact that the anus often dilates in infants shortly after death and that this is often mistaken for sexual abuse. He disputed Hayne's contention about rigor mortis, and speculated that the ER staff likely mistook the exposed lining of the girl's rectum for blood. Like others before him, Lauridson also had difficulty getting the tissue slides from Hayne, but when he finally did, he found nothing on them that suggested sexual abuse.

The majority opinion roundly dismissed Lauridson's report—and also appears to have badly misread it. Justice George Carlson wrote that Lauridson "opined in his affidavit 'that there is a possibility that Chloe Madison Britt was not sexually assaulted.'" Carlson then wrote, "Taking this statement to its logical conclusion, this leaves open the possibility that she was."

That isn't necessarily the logical conclusion at all. Worse, the phrase "there is a possibility," which Carlson put in quotes, doesn't actually appear anywhere in Lauridson's affidavit. Lauridson actually wrote: "The conclusions that Chloe Britt suffered sexual abuse are not supported by objective evidence and are wrong." Lauridson did write that he couldn't *definitively* say there were no signs of sexual abuse because that would require examination of Hayne's tissue slides, and at the time of his original report, he still didn't have access to them. When he finally saw them, Lauridson was much more conclusive.

Justice Carlson continued to mischaracterize Lauridson's report throughout his opinion. It was arguably a more forceful brief for the state than those submitted by the prosecutors themselves. Havard's appeal was denied, and his conviction and sentence upheld. The vote this time was 8 to 1. The lone dissent was from a justice named Oliver Diaz, though Diaz didn't write an opinion. That dissent would come back to haunt him.

In March 2012, the Mississippi Supreme Court again denied Havard relief. His attorneys had asked for a new trial because in the intervening years even Steven Hayne had changed his opinion—sort of. In a declaration for Havard's attorneys, Hayne wrote, "Based upon the autopsy evidence available regarding the death of Chloe Britt, I cannot include or exclude to a reasonable degree of medical certainty that she was sexually assaulted." Hayne also acknowledged, as Lauridson had pointed out, that a dilated anus is not in itself evidence of sexual abuse.

Even here, Hayne was typically hard to pin down. He managed to reframe his trial testimony without directly contradicting it. At trial Hayne had never definitively testified that Chloe Britt had been sexually assaulted; he merely said her injuries were consistent with that possibility, then speculated that one possible method of assault could have been "penetration of the rectum by an object." The prosecutor did most of the heavy lifting to advance the assault narrative, often by citing the observations of the ER staff, sheriff, and coroner. For most of his testimony, Hayne merely acquiesced, despite the fact that he knew he'd found no biological material from Havard on or in the child, and that the only anal trauma was the small contusion.

Forensic experts say a credible and conscientious medical examiner should have said at trial what Hayne stated in his declaration a decade later. A credible medical examiner wouldn't have let the jury be misled, and wouldn't have allowed a prosecutor to use his own testimony to do so, even if his own testimony wasn't *technically* false.

Three months later, the Mississippi Supreme Court rejected Havard once more. Justice Carlson again wrote the opinion. Carlson first argued that Hayne's declaration and deposition in 2012 weren't substantially different from his testimony at the trial. Hayne hadn't *explicitly* testified at trial that Chloe had been sexually abused, Carlson argued, so his 2012 declaration stating he had found no evidence of abuse wasn't really new evidence. Yet in his 2008 opinion, Carlson himself wrote that Jim Lauridson's conclusion that the girl's dilated anus was not indicative of sexual abuse "was . . . *contrary to that of Dr. Hayne*" and that of emergency room personnel. Hayne may not have explicitly testified that the dilation was caused by sexual assault, but his testimony was so suggestive of it that even Carlson at the time seemed to think that this was Hayne's position. The jury obviously did, too.

In two rulings handed down just four years apart, then, Justice Carlson had found that Hayne's testimony supported the jury's finding of sexual assault *and* that Hayne had never explicitly testified that a sexual assault had taken place. Hayne could make a state supreme court justice argue two self-contradictory points without realizing that they were contradictory. It's little wonder why prosecutors loved him.

Carlson closed his opinion with one last and especially absurd contradiction. Carlson first claimed that Hayne's 2012 declaration wasn't new evidence because it was "duplicative" of the Lauridson affidavit that the court had rejected in 2008. Yet, as noted, in that 2008 decision Carlson himself wrote that Lauridson's opinion was "contrary to that of Dr. Hayne." Between his 2008 and 2012 opinions, then, Carlson asserted that (a) Lauridson's affidavit *contradicted* Hayne's trial testimony, (b) Hayne's 2012 declaration *was "duplicative"* of that affidavit, and yet (c) there was *no substantial difference* between Hayne's trial testimony and his 2012 declaration.

Logically, these three things can't possibly all be true. Two affidavits can't at the same time be both duplicative of and contrary to one another. And yet Carlson stated exactly that. So did his fellow justices. Again, the court denied Havard's petition. This time, the vote was unanimous.

Over the next few years, the state's case against Havard continued to deteriorate. First, two more forensic pathologists reviewed the case and wrote scathing reports deriding Hayne's work. Then in January 2014, Hayne appeared to walk back his trial testimony even more. In an interview with the *Clarion-Ledger*, Hayne said he *never* believed Chloe Britt had been sexually assaulted at all. The following July he filed another affidavit with Havard's trial attorneys, this time claiming he had explicitly told prosecutors on more than one occasion that he could not support a finding that Chloe had been sexually assaulted. Havard's attorneys said this information was never turned over to them.

At Havard's trial, the prosecutor told jurors that Hayne would "testify for you about his findings and about how he confirmed the nurses' and doctors' worst fears this child had been abused and the child had been penetrated." Now, all this time later, Hayne claimed he explicitly told prosecutors precisely the opposite.

If true, that would be a major violation on the part of state prosecutors. Hayne's statement to them would have been exculpatory information, and they would have been obligated to turn it over. Moreover, Hayne was the only medical examiner to testify, and the alleged sexual assault was not only a major part of the state's case but the aggravating factor that allowed prosecutors to seek the death penalty.

While it now seems clear that Chloe really *wasn't* sexually assaulted, Hayne's latest attempt to rehabilitate his role in the case is hard to comprehend. Although it's true that he never explicitly testified that Chloe Britt had been sexually abused, his testimony did plenty to help prosecutors convince the jury she had.

"A medical examiner has an ethical duty to clarify whatever point is being made, whether by the prosecution or the defense," says Jaime Downs, a medical examiner who has served on numerous forensics ethics committees and recently edited the book *Ethics in Forensic Science.* "If someone is putting words in your mouth, or manipulating your testimony to give a false impression, you have an obligation to speak up and say, 'That's incorrect.'"

If Hayne knew all along that the state had persuaded a jury to convict Jeff Havard of an assault he never believed happened, why did he wait thirteen years before speaking up? Why did he speak up only after three other forensic pathologists filed affidavits?

In 2015, Jeffrey Havard finally caught a break. It was a modest win, but it at least put his execution on hold. In April of that year, the Mississippi Supreme Court gave Havard's attorneys permission to request an evidentiary hearing on the scientific validity of SBS. The court still rejected Havard's claims challenging the allegations of sexual abuse. The ruling wasn't an exoneration, and it wasn't a new trial. It was a three-paragraph order giving Havard permission to ask a trial court judge to hold a hearing to determine the scientific validity of SBS. In June 2016, the judge granted permission for the hearing. If Havard could convince the judge that Shaken Baby Syndrome is no longer a scientifically reliable diagnosis, he'd finally get a new trial.

It took Havard's jury less than two days to deliberate, convict him based on bad scientific evidence, hear evidence on appropriate punishment, deliberate again, and sentence him to death. It took thirteen years for the courts to admit that a small portion of the bad evidence *might* have been scientifically unsound. It took another fourteen months for the trial court judge to agree to hold a hearing on the matter. It will be another fourteen months from that decision until the hearing itself.

It's often said that the wheels of justice grind slowly. That isn't always true. When it comes to convicting people, they can move pretty swiftly. It's when the system needs to correct an injustice—admit its mistakes—that the gears tend to sputter to a halt. For now, Havard remains on death row.

The Havard case is also illustrative of the way Mississippi state officials have neglected their duty to look into Hayne. Beginning in the late 2000s, media exposés and groups like the Innocence Project had finally begun to single Hayne out for criticism. For the most part, Mississippi prosecutors and coroners continued to defend him. One of the more important of those officials has been Mississippi attorney general Jim Hood, who himself used Hayne back when Hood was a local district attorney. By 2013, Jeff Havard's case had attracted a lot of attention. The *Clarion-Ledger* and the *Huffington Post* had both published articles about Havard, and a website and Facebook page maintained by his friends and family has been marshaling supporters.

The fact that Hayne was now arguably contradicting his own testimony in a death penalty case made it hard for officials like Hood to continue to defend him. By that time, Havard's case was in federal court (he had exhausted his state appeals). So in August 2013, Hood's office filed a motion in federal court asking for a gag order. Hood wanted to prohibit the public from seeing any further filings or proceedings.

The state claimed the motion was sparked by a Facebook post from one of Havard's lawyers who had complained that the state didn't "want to be bothered by actually responding to his [Havard's] claims of innocence." But the state's brief itself revealed the real motivation: Havard's case "had become a public spectacle." The attorney general's office argued that it had received letters from Havard supporters and expressed concern that the letters were similarly worded, which suggested the letters' authors had all gotten their information from the same source. Why this was of such grave concern isn't exactly clear. A federal judge ruled against the motion.

Hayne's testimony in yet another Shaken Baby Syndrome case was more controversial still, and provides an even more egregious example of the lengths to which state officials have gone to defend him. Christopher Brandon was convicted in 2009, well after the concerns about overdiagnosing Shaken Baby Syndrome had been documented in both medical literature and the popular press. But Hayne also cited a textbook that actually states the precise opposite of what he claimed at trial and cited a study that doesn't appear to exist.

Brandon claimed that his girlfriend's fifteen-month-old son died after falling and hitting his head on a toy. (There was an external bruise on his head.) Hayne claimed the infant had been violently shaken, despite the absence of any signs of neck trauma. As in other cases, the trial judge had refused to give Brandon funding to hire his own pathologist to review Hayne's work.

Brandon's attorney asked Hayne if he was aware that some researchers had begun to question the basis for the SBS diagnosis. Hayne said he was but countered by first citing a forensic pathology textbook written by Vincent Di Maio. "There are disagreements in the field," Hayne answered, "but, the standard text, *Di Maio and Di Maio*, they list shaken baby syndrome as a cause of death and they go into the explanation of the different variables that constitute shaken baby syndrome. So the preponderance of the experts in this country do believe an injury like this to be shaken baby."

Hayne was then asked about a recent study showing that the injuries commonly attributed to SBS can occur in a short-distance fall. He replied, "That would be in disagreement with the vast preponderance of the literature." The attorney followed up—but had he read the study? Hayne replied, "Yes, counselor. That has been roundly argued against that position by that particular physician. I think the . . . most important article that has come out recently, [is] the Alperi study by Harvard University in the Mass General, and they disavow that position."

With no one to counter Hayne's testimony for the defense, Brandon was convicted. After his conviction, another medical examiner reviewed Hayne's work and concluded that the child did not die from being shaken, and that his medical condition had been affected by an advanced case of pneumonia.

Even when defendants were given funding to hire their own experts, Hayne's testimony often won the day. But as with Jeffrey Havard, the Brandon case shows how, when there was no one to counter him, Hayne could be absolutely devastating. A defense expert well-versed in the SBS literature, for example, might have pointed out that the Di Maio textbook Hayne cited on the witness stand actually states the *precise opposite* of what Hayne claimed. From the textbook: "The authors [of *Forensic Pathology*] have grave reservations as to the existence of SBS. This was expressed in the first edition of this book. Since then, we have no reason to change this opinion but rather to solidify it. There is just no conclusive evidence that this entity exists."

If that isn't clear enough, Di Maio himself also said in a 2014 interview that Hayne had misappropriated his text. When asked if it was possible Hayne's testimony could have been mistaken but well-intentioned, Di Maio replied, "No, I don't think it's possible. Look, that passage about SBS begins with a quote from *Alice in Wonderland*. You would think that would be a good indication that we are skeptical of the diagnosis. I don't know how he could have honestly misread it."

Then there's Hayne's mention of the "Alperi study by Harvard University in the Mass General." That study doesn't appear to exist. "A search through databases dedicated to SBS scholarship, as well as the entirety of the Westlaw and LexisNexis databases of literature dedicated to SBS, reveals that no such study exists," Brandon's lawyers from the Mississippi Innocence Project wrote in a post-conviction petition. "Furthermore . . . counsel have consulted with both legal and medical experts in the field of SBS who have [n]ever heard of the [study] or anything like it." They added, "In short, the circumstances suggest that Dr. Hayne simply conjured up a scholarly journal article."

Both these examples from Hayne's testimony would likely have been exposed had Brandon been permitted to have his own expert in the courtroom. Even a defense attorney well-versed in SBS cases isn't likely to have a thorough enough grasp of the literature to recognize a nonexistent study, or to know when a textbook has been misquoted. But an expert in the field likely would. Without an expert, Hayne was able to give bad information to the jury without rebuttal.

In his closing argument, the prosecutor doubled down on the misinformation by misleading the jury about *why* Hayne's testimony went unrebutted. Referring to Brandon's claim that the infant died from a fall, the prosecutor told the jury that "*every doctor in the world* says it [Brandon's story] is impossible. It's impossible." Incredibly, he then argued that Brandon's defense team couldn't call an expert witness to contradict Hayne because no such experts existed.

Brandon's story was not impossible. There are plenty of doctors who would say so, and there were plenty at the time. The defense didn't call any of them to the stand not because they didn't exist, but—again—because the court didn't provide Brandon with the funds to hire one of them.

The state's reaction to Hayne's testimony was even worse. In July 2014, the office of Attorney General Jim Hood filed a response to Brandon's motion for a new trial that's almost too absurd to believe. After first conceding that they too could not find the mysterious study that Hayne had mentioned at trial, the state did point out that in 2012, the Alpert Medical School of Brown University hosted a conference on Shaken Baby Syndrome that included a panel discussion about short-distance falls. Because the name of the school sounded vaguely similar to the name Hayne mentioned as the author of his mystery study, "It is more likely that Dr. Hayne was recalling these studies than it is that he entirely fabricated a study," the state wrote.

That sounds like a plausible explanation until you consider that Hayne *attended* Alpert Medical School at Brown. It seems unlikely that he'd mistake the name of his own medical school for the author of a study.

But there's also a much more profound problem with the state's attempt to rehabilitate Hayne's testimony: The Boston conference was held in 2012. Christopher Brandon's trial took place in 2009. By the laws of physics, Hayne couldn't possibly have "recalled" a presentation from a 2012 conference during testimony he gave in 2009.

The state also added that the same medical school hosted a similar conference in 2010 and posited that perhaps *that* was what Hayne was recalling. We're at least getting closer. But we're still faced with the fact Hayne couldn't possibly have recalled a 2010 conference during testimony he gave in 2009.

For years Mississippi state officials have argued that Hayne could competently perform 1,800 or more autopsies per year, all while testifying in court, completing his continuing education, and holding down two full-time positions. In the Brandon case, they either were alarmingly careless about fact-checking their arguments or suggesting that Steven Hayne could slip the bounds of time.

It's odder still that instead of merely asking Hayne to submit an affidavit clarifying his testimony, the state resorted to such wild speculation about what he actually meant. In August 2014 the Mississippi Supreme Court ruled in Brandon's favor on every claim and ordered the Lee County Circuit Court to hold an evidentiary hearing.

That same year, the Mississippi Supreme Court overturned another conviction that was due in part to Hayne's SBS testimony. The court in that case didn't explicitly criticize Hayne, but ruled that the trial judge was wrong to deny the defendant funding to hire his own expert.

Mississippi elects its judges at all levels, from local justice courts to the Supreme Court. Over the years, the campaign and election process has produced a lot of scandals and even a few indictments. But one noticeable effect has been to weed the state's highest court of justices with an inclination to protect civil liberties and the rights of the accused. And that has produced a court that for the most part remained reliably unskeptical of Hayne and West.

The two factions that have poured the most money into judicial elections in recent years are the plaintiff's bar (more commonly called trial lawyers) and pro-business groups like the Chamber of Commerce. The judicial candidates who rise out of the plaintiff's bar tend to be more friendly to regulation and civil liability for corporations accused of wrongdoing. But in a state as conservative as Mississippi, Democrats tend to compensate for those positions with aggressive law-and-order policies on issues like policing, the death penalty, and due process rights. Mississippi's two most recent attorneys general—current AG Jim Hood and his predecessor Mike Moore—are good examples. Both have been heavily supported by the plaintiff's bar, but both are also adamantly pro–death penalty.

This sort of political splintering benefited Hayne and West. Many of the state's criminal defense attorneys are also trial lawyers. They get paid a few thousand dollars per month to be the official "public defender" for some county or town but make the larger part of their living as plaintiff's attorneys. Civil liability cases in areas like medical malpractice or product liability often involve allegations of a wrongful death. Those cases require an autopsy. For someone like current Mississippi attorney general Jim Hood, Hayne was the only game in town. He also served a dual purpose: he helped many of Hood's supporters win wrongful death cases, and he helped prosecutors like Hood win convictions.

The few justices on the court who have shown proclivity to, say, protect the constitutional rights of criminal defendants, or to criticize the application of the death penalty in capital cases, have come under heavy scrutiny when they run for reelection. That's how James Robertson—perhaps the closest thing the state has ever had to a civil libertarian justice—was defeated in 1992.

"It's complicated," says the longtime Mississippi defense attorney André de Gruy. "I've spent my entire career here, so I've only known a system in which judges are elected. But my sense is that whether you appoint them or elect doesn't make much difference at the local level. But at the appellate level, you probably get better judges if they're appointed."

John Holdridge, the defense attorney who was an early critic of Michael West, says his bigger worry is how the fear of losing a bid for reelection can bias an incumbent. "My sense is that elected judges find it very difficult to rule on these issues when it's going to seriously affect the prosecution in a high-profile case."

"I think that's why James Robertson may have voted with the state in the Tracy Hansen [case], when he otherwise may not have," says de Gruy. "There were protests outside the supreme court at the time. You don't want to be known as the justice who turned a killer loose." Hansen was convicted of killing a Mississippi state trooper in 1987. There wasn't much doubt about his guilt, but there were some problems with his trial, and he was sentenced to death under the vague death penalty jury instructions later struck down by the US Supreme Court. The Mississippi Supreme Court voted unanimously to uphold both the conviction and the sentence, and Robertson wrote the opinion. Hansen was executed in 2002, ending Mississippi's thirteen-year dry spell. Robertson lost his election anyway.

A 2013 report by the liberal group the Center for American Progress found that spending on the 2000 Mississippi Supreme Court elections surged by over three million dollars. In fact, a single group called the Law Enforcement Alliance of America (LEAA) spent more on Mississippi Supreme Court races than all of the candidate campaigns combined. There's some evidence that all of that spending has affected how the court rules. In its next term, the court ruled against criminal defendants in 90 percent of the cases it heard, a 20 percent increase over the previous term.

Perhaps that was due more to the facts of the cases the court considered in those terms, but the report found a similar correlation in other states where supreme court justices are elected. As spending from outside groups went up, so did the frequency with which the courts ruled against criminal defendants.

In the early 2000s, Mississippi was ground zero for all of these interests. By the early 2000s trial lawyers, pro-business groups, and law-and-order groups were all spending furiously to seat their preferred justices in Jackson. For the most part the trial lawyers backed one candidate, while the pro-business and law-and-order groups backed the other. (There really weren't any well-funded interest groups to promote civil liberties or protections for the accused.)

But it didn't always line up that way. In the 2000 Supreme Court elections Justice Lenore Prather, who had become the state supreme court's first female justice in 1982 and its first female chief justice in 1998, was heavily favored to win reelection and had strong backing from the Chamber of Commerce. Toward the end of the campaign Prather's opponent, a little-known municipal judge named Chuck Easley, began attacking her for being "soft on crime." Prather was a moderate conservative. She had occasionally voted to overturn convictions but rarely went out on a limb. (She voted to uphold Kennedy Brewer's conviction and death sentence in 1998 and then to deny him DNA testing in 2000.) Easley won in an upset that surprised much of the state.

The Mississippi justice everyone expected to lose in the 2000 campaign was Oliver Diaz, an affable, mop-haired former state legislator from the Gulf Coast. Diaz made his jump to the judiciary in 1994, when he was elected to the Mississippi Court of Appeals. In March 2000, Governor Ronnie Musgrave appointed him to the state supreme court to finish the term of a justice who had recently died. But the term to which Diaz was appointed expired later the same year. He'd barely had time to zip up his robe before he had to start thinking about reelection. The Chamber of Commerce spent $800,000 trying to defeat Diaz, including TV ads accusing him of supporting "baby killers and drug dealers" when he sat on the court of appeals. Somehow, Diaz still won. But in winning he had to raise a lot of money in a short amount of time. That would eventually present problems for him.

Diaz later affirmed that the ads affected how his fellow justices handled criminal cases, and that it was causing opinions based more on politics than on the law. "A fellow member of the Mississippi Supreme Court . . . actually saw those ads, and after that point, he refused to vote to overturn criminal cases," Diaz told *ThinkProgress*. "Judges who are running for reelection do keep in mind what the next 30-second ad is going to look like."

By the end of his first and only complete term, Diaz would emerge as the court's toughest critic of Steven Hayne. He'd also have some personal experience with the criminal justice system that would make him better equipped than his colleagues to talk about the perils of letting the political process run roughshod over the judiciary. But his outspokenness would eventually get him voted off the court.

The next justice to feel the wrath of law-and-order groups was Charles "Chuck" McRae. By the end of the 1990s, McRae was really the only justice willing to take a skeptical look at Michael West. To that point, he was the only judge in the state who had actually criticized West in an opinion. (No judge—McRae included—had so much as batted an eye at Steven Hayne.)

McRae seemed more like the protagonist in a Hemingway novel than a state supreme court justice. He was more brash than bookish, more insouciant than stuffy. In 2003, *Forbes* described him as "a colorful, cocky figure who drives a motorcycle to the courthouse and dresses in cowboy boots, blue jeans and lots of leather." The same year, the *Franklin County Times* noted that McRae had run with the bulls in Pamplona, climbed Mt. Kilimanjaro, and enjoyed scuba diving in the Bahamas. The *Clarion-Ledger* noted that he sometimes swam in public while wearing only a thong.

McRae grew up poor and orphaned on the Gulf Coast, but moved to Pennsylvania just before graduating high school. He returned to Mississippi after college to teach and coach high school, then went to law school. Despite his criticism of West, McRae was hardly a bleeding heart on criminal justice. While he was a former president of the Mississippi Trial Lawyers Association, he had also served as counsel for the Pascagoula Police Association.

But McRae *was* an outspoken opponent of tort reform, and by the time he was up for reelection in 2003, it was a hot issue, nationally and especially in Mississippi. That put him squarely in the crosshairs of pro-business groups like the Chamber of Commerce.

McRae didn't do himself any favors. In 1995 he had crashed his sports car just outside of Jackson and then refused to take a breathalyzer. He was sentenced to a two-hour meeting with victims of drunk drivers, which sparked (probably accurate) accusations of special treatment. In 1999, his behavior on the roads again put him in the headlines when he and a friend were pursued by a Mississippi Highway Patrol officer while riding their motorcycles. The friend stopped;

McRae didn't. He sped up, taking the officer on a chase through Jackson, during which McRae at times exceeded a hundred miles per hour.

Despite all of that, one of the more damaging blows to McRae's reelection hopes was over what in retrospect was perhaps his finest moment on the court. During the 2003 campaign, the LEAA bought a round of TV ads touting McRae's opponent, Jess Dickinson, whom the ads called "a strong leader who supports the death penalty." The ad then ominously shifted to McRae. "When a three-year-old was sexually assaulted, the Mississippi Supreme Court upheld the murderous conviction. Only Judge Chuck McRae voted to reverse it." A similar ad delivered the same ominous message: McRae "was the only judge to reverse the conviction of the murderer of a three-year-old girl."

The "murderer" to which both ads referred was Levon Brooks. McRae lost his reelection bid by thirty points.

∾

No one really thrives or flourishes in prison, but Levon Brooks did better than most. His charisma and optimism served him well. So did the fact that at thirty, he was a little older and perhaps wiser than most of the men in his cell block.

"It felt like a dream," Brooks says, reflecting back to the first days after his sentencing. "I remember I questioned God. 'What have I done to deserve this?'" Brooks at first thought he'd have to harden. "Everyone I knew who had been in prison came out so doggone mean," he says. "I figured it would turn me, too."

But he quickly changed his outlook. "My momma told me, 'You do what you gotta do in there, but don't change who you are. God's gonna get you out.'" Brooks pauses after he says this, then lets out a soft laugh. "She was right. It sure took Him a while. But I got out. And I didn't get one write-up [for disciplinary problems] while I was in there. I'm proud of that."

Brooks's experience cooking at the Santa Barbara helped him get a spot in the prison kitchen. That was critical. It made him feel productive, gave him something to do. More importantly, it gave him access to food, which he could occasionally distribute outside the rules. It would become powerful currency for him: first to carve out some independence and space for himself, and then to help out his fellow inmates. "You'd be surprised what you can get done with extra sandwiches," he says.

Brooks also helped guards and other prison staff with their paper-work. Having always had some talent with a pencil, he began drawing greeting cards and selling them to prison staff. That earned him both some spending money and additional favor. He then put that favor to use in the kitchen, where he'd sneak in indulgences like fast food for his fellow inmates. Sometimes he even got unofficial permission to prepare fancier meals on holidays. Ever the opportunist, he also used his kitchen access to sell sandwiches to guards and other prison per-sonnel on the side.

Brooks says his dominion over the kitchen provided him with some protection. Despite the conventional wisdom about what happens in prison to people convicted for hurting or sexually abusing children, Brooks says he was largely left alone and was able to avoid the pris-on's gangs. Over time, his lack of affiliation positioned him to become something of a broker between the gangs, and between the gangs and the guards. He says he once helped a man get out of a prison gang, get into protective custody, and eventually get transferred to another prison. He stopped another man from hanging himself.

"You just have to keep your humanity about you," Brooks says. "That's how I got by. You do little things for people, you make their lives better, and it comes back to you."

He kept his eye out for new inmates in particular. "It's lonely when you first get in," he says. "It goes a long way if you think you have an ally—that there's somebody on your side. It can be the smallest thing." Brooks would typically reach out to new inmates with the only thing he had the power to do—he'd give them an extra half sandwich or an extra piece of meat. "I just tried to look out for folks," he says.

One story in particular still moves him. A few weeks before Brooks was released from prison, a white man came to visit him. The two had been in the same cell block, but Brooks never really got to know the man. "I do remember when he first got in, though," Brooks says. "He was a bad case. He was hurting. He just had this broken look about him that said, 'What am I going to do?'"

The man was released several years later. Soon after he got out, he came back just to see Brooks. "So he came back to visit me," Brooks says. "He had . . . he had tears in his eyes. Said he just wanted to come back and thank me.

"I didn't know what he was talking about. I asked him, 'What'd I do?' And he said to me, 'You gave me extra food. I never forgot that.'"

Brooks gets choked up himself as he tells the story, so he stops and collects himself. "No matter what color you are, we all serve one God," he says. "Like I said, you just have to humble yourself. You just have to keep your humanity."

In 2000, well after Michael West had been widely criticized in both the media and the forensic world, Dunn Lampton, a long-time district attorney in central Mississippi, sought West's help in his prosecution of Leigh Stubbs. The story begins in March 2000, just after Stubbs had successfully completed rehab at a drug addiction center in Columbus, Mississippi. She checked out of the facility with Tammy Vance, a friend she met in rehab, and Kim Williams, the woman Stubbs and Vance would later be accused of assaulting.

The three women first drove to the home of Dickie Ervin, whom Williams had been dating. Vance and Stubbs left and later met back up with Williams, who by then had stolen some of Ervin's oxycontin. Vance and Williams began drinking and taking the oxycontin while Stubbs stayed sober and drove them around. The three eventually ended up at a Comfort Inn in the town of Brookhaven. By evening, Vance and Williams had passed out. Stubbs checked the three of them into the hotel. According to the motel clerk's trial testimony, Stubbs didn't seem drunk, high, or otherwise intoxicated—only tired. (She would pass a drug test the next day.)

By Stubbs's account, she then helped the other two women into the room, and the three went to sleep. The next day, Stubbs and Vance went to get some food, leaving Williams in the room, still sleeping. Later that afternoon, Stubbs and Vance noticed that Williams still hadn't woken up and was having trouble breathing. They called an ambulance. Williams had suffered a drug overdose and had fallen into a coma.

At the hospital, doctors found a number of injuries on Williams, including swollen breasts, a swollen and bruised vagina, and some marks across her buttocks. The attending physician estimated the injuries to be two to four days old. A rape kit was inconclusive. Another doctor later found an additional injury to Williams's head. The police opened an investigation. A few days later, Lampton called in Michael West to examine Williams's injuries. (Williams, who ultimately recovered, was never able to remember the event.)

West initially didn't find any bites on Williams. It was only five days later that he claimed to have found a mark on her hip. During that exam, West also claimed to have found injuries to Williams's vagina that he described to be consistent with "sucking." He deduced that these injuries had been inflicted during "severe oral sex."

West then compared the alleged bite mark on Williams's hip to dental molds that had been taken from Stubbs, Vance, and two other suspects. That took a few days. By the time the plaster impressions arrived, Williams's alleged wounds had faded. So West performed his analysis based on photographs he had taken of his findings several days earlier. He would later testify that he had determined it was a "probability" that the bite mark he claimed to have found on Williams's hip had been inflicted by Stubbs. (In a rare display of humility, West did concede that he wasn't "100 percent" certain of the match—only that it was likely.) Stubbs and Vance were arrested and charged with assaulting Williams.

At trial, as West showed the jury a photo of the alleged injury to Williams's hip and told them, "I must admit to a novice, this may not appear to be a bite mark by any means." But he assured them—it was in fact a human bite mark.

But West didn't stop with bite mark analysis. He had a lot more to say. On the night of the alleged attack, the Comfort Inn had a security camera trained on the parking lot. Lampton had obtained a VHS tape with grainy footage from that night and sent it to the FBI for analysis. The agency found nothing incriminating in the footage. In fact, the FBI report repeatedly pointed out that the quality of the recording was too low to even say for certain how many people are depicted in the video, much less determine their identities or what sort of clothing they're wearing.

Unsatisfied, prosecutors sent the video to Michael West. The Copernicus of forensics then morphed into a "video enhancement expert," and claimed that by using off-the-shelf Adobe software he'd bought for his computer, he was able to enhance the video and capture still photos from those enhancements that implicated Leigh Stubbs and Tammy Vance in Williams's injuries. Though obligated by law to do so, state prosecutors never turned over the FBI report or the correspondence with West to Stubbs's defense attorney.

The ability to enhance security camera footage beyond its original resolution is a fictional Hollywood trope so common that mocking it has become a running internet meme. Yet where the FBI determined that the video was too grainy to even make out how many people were in the frame, West confidently told the jury there were two. He claimed he could also tell that one of the people was wearing shorts and the other blue jeans—two details that matched neatly with police reports of what Stubbs and Vance had worn that night. Where the FBI could only determine that someone had removed an object—possibly a bag or suitcase—from a toolbox in the truck bed, West claimed he could make out hair, legs, and another pair of jeans, leading him to conclude that the object was obviously a body. "She takes a body out of this toolbox," West conclusively told the jury. "That's what I see."

He didn't stop there. West also claimed he could actually *read the body language* of one figure in the footage. He said he could tell that the figure appeared "anxious" and was exhibiting the sort of adrenaline-fueled "fight or flight" response one shows after having committed a crime.

The video showed none of these things. It was grainy, flickery, and dark. At best, a viewer might make out a truck, and perhaps the vague form of a few other cars. It's possible to make out human figures walking out to and back from the truck, but they have all the detail of an eight-bit video game, only in black and white, and with the brightness turned to low.

West apparently knew that the jury wouldn't be able to see any of this, so he conditioned them to unquestionably accept his expertise. "What I see isn't what everybody else sees," he said. "There are interpretations." As for the bite mark, West again used his "direct comparison" method, and just as in the Kennedy Brewer and Jimmie Duncan cases, forensic specialists who have reviewed the case say West likely created it himself. A video of his "examination" surfaced years later on the blog of forensic experts and bite mark analysis critics Michael Bowers and David Averill. The video depicts West repeatedly jamming the mold of Stubbs's teeth into Williams's thigh, just as he'd done in other cases. The alleged bite mark doesn't appear until after West does so. (In this case, West's subject was alive but comatose.) On the blog, Bowers—a longtime West critic—writes, "West then proceeds to tamper with the evidence by actually imbedding a stone cast of Leigh Stubbs' teeth into the comatose victim's hip resulting in a fabricated bite mark on the skin of the victim." In a 2011 interview, Bowers offered this opinion: "The tampering with the evidence on the skin is likely a crime. But to create those marks on a woman who was comatose, and who hadn't given consent, is also an assault," he said.

Still not finished, West then donned his "tool mark expert" cap and claimed to have found marks on Williams's head and thigh that "matched" the shape of the latches on the tool box in the truck bed. He added, "those two latches are 37 inches apart. And if you look at Kimberly [Williams], from the head injuries to the thigh injury is 37 inches." West elided the fact that the distance between Williams's head and thigh would vary a great deal depending on how she was positioned. Even if she had been put into the tool box, there's no way West could have known her positioning, much less have replicated it, to the inch, while she lay unconscious in a hospital bed.

Police investigators also found no biological material from Williams in the tool chest. No blood, no hair, no skin cells. West explained that biological material can be wiped away with a good scrub and some chlorine. But there was a problem there too. Investigators did find some hair, but it didn't belong to Williams.

For his final act, West transformed himself into a behavioral psychologist—or perhaps just a bigot. After hinting that Stubbs may have been a lesbian, Lampton asked if one might be especially likely to find bite marks in an assault perpetrated by a homosexual. West, who was no more credentialed to be giving jurors an expert opinion on how lesbians quarrel than he was on "severe oral sex," replied that "it wouldn't be unusual." Lampton pushed further, asking West if bite marks after an altercation between homosexuals "would almost be expected."

Yes, West replied. "Almost."

Years later in a deposition, West would refer to the Stubbs trial as "the case of the two lesbians that bit the girl's vagina lip off."

Once again, the jury bought it. In 2001, Leigh Stubbs and Tammy Vance were both convicted of assaulting Williams and stealing oxycontin and methadone. The only evidence against Stubbs for stealing drugs was that she happened to be with Williams and Vance when the drugs were taken. Stubbs, who had no prior criminal record, was sentenced to forty-four years in prison. In 2003, the Mississippi Supreme Court upheld both the convictions and West's testimony. The ruling was unanimous. The court had already stated that it had accepted bite mark evidence as scientific and credible—in the Levon Brooks case. As to the various other areas of forensics in which West testified, the court found that either Stubbs's trial attorney failed to properly object or that they were satisfied that Stubbs had the opportunity to both cross-examine West and to call her own expert witness to challenge him. The court added, "This does not mean that Dr. West can indiscriminately offer so-called expert testimony in other areas in which he not even remotely meets the criteria. We caution prosecutors and defense attorneys, as well as our learned trial judges, to take care that Dr. West's testimony as an expert is confined to the area of his expertise." Given the wide-ranging fields in which West testified in the case, it's hard to imagine what the court could possibly find outside of his expertise.

By the time the Mississippi Innocence Project took up the case in 2008, even Mississippi prosecutors were no longer using West. Yet while Mississippi attorney general Jim Hood has admitted that West isn't a credible witness, Hood and his staff have nevertheless continued to fight to preserve convictions won on West's testimony. Typically, these cases are in post-conviction, which usually means that the defendant at some point has already argued that West should not have been permitted to testify—and almost certainly lost that argument. Instead of arguing for West's credibility, the state now argues in these cases that the defendants are procedurally prohibited from reraising West's testimony as an issue.

Legally, they're on shaky ground. There has been a sea change surrounding forensic evidence nationally, and bite mark matching has come under particular fire. But morally, it's reprehensible. If he wanted, Hood could drop the charges in all of these cases—or at least agree to a new trial without testimony from Hayne or West. Instead his office argues about procedure.

That's exactly what Hood's office argued to keep Leigh Stubbs and Tammy Vance in prison. And they were succeeding, until Stubbs's father tracked down the FBI report on the surveillance video that Lampton never turned over to the defense—along with the correspondence between West and Lampton that referenced the report. He then handed the report over to Stubbs's new lawyers.

That finally did the trick. In June 2012, a district court judge threw out the convictions of both Stubbs and Vance, citing the state's failure to turn over exculpatory evidence. The following year, Hood's office backed down and offered the women a plea bargain. If they pleaded guilty to the drug charges, the state would dismiss the assault charges, agree to a sentence of time served, and let the women eventually expunge all the charges from their records. The women agreed.

Dunn Lampton used West and his preposterous testimony well after West's exploits were well known. In an ideal world, that should have ended his career as a prosecutor. Instead, in 2001, President George W. Bush nominated Lampton to be US attorney for the Southern District of Mississippi. Lampton died in 2011.

Christopher Plourd was furious about what happened to his client, Ray Krone. And rightly so. Krone had *twice* been wrongly convicted of murder and was nearly executed. Thanks to bite mark testimony from a local dentist and renowned bite mark analyst Raymond Rawson, Krone was convicted of murdering a cocktail waitress in 1992 and again in 1996.

Over the strenuous objections of prosecutors, Plourd eventually persuaded a court to allow DNA testing on biological evidence from the crime scene. In 2002, the testing showed that Krone was innocent. It provided a match to a man named Kenneth Phillips, who should have been a suspect from the start. After ten years in prison, including two on death row, Krone was exonerated and released from prison.

Plourd, offended and angry that his client could have been convicted not once, but twice, based on quackery that had been presented in court as science, decided to conduct his own "blind proficiency test" on some unknowing and prominent bite mark expert. By chance, Plourd chose Michael West for his test.

In October 2001, Plourd and his friend James Rix conceived the plan. Rix called West and introduced himself as "Phil Barnes," a private investigator who was looking into the unsolved rape and murder of an Idaho college student (the crime was fictitious). He asked if he could send West some crime scene photos and a dental mold of the teeth of his "prime suspect." West agreed.

Rix then sent West the photos of the bite mark on Kim Ancona's breast, the one used to convict Ray Krone. The dental mold was from Rix's own teeth. He also sent a check for $750—West's retainer.

Two months later, West sent back a letter and accompanying twenty-minute video. In the video, West meticulously explains the methodology he used to match bite marks to dental molds. Using the photo of Ancona's bitten breast and Rix's dental mold, West walks the viewer through his process, eventually reaching the conclusion Plourd and Rix suspected he would: the mold and the photos were a definite match.

"Notice as I flex the photograph across these teeth how it conforms to the outline very nicely," West explains. "The odds of that happening if these weren't the teeth that created this bite would be almost astronomical." West adds that the "matching" patterns he found between the photo and the dental mold "could only lead an odontologist to one opinion and that [is] these teeth did create that mark."

To watch the video without knowing the context, it's easy to see how juries found West convincing, at least when it comes to bite marks. He intermingles dental and forensics jargon with ease. He's confident, as if he's done it all a hundred times before. (And he had.) He really appears to know what he's doing. But to watch the video while knowing the story behind it shows how frighteningly easy it was for West to convince juries of things that simply weren't true.

Over the next fifteen years, defense attorneys in Mississippi repeatedly tried to bring Plourd's sting to the attention of Mississippi courts—to persuade them to finally stop certifying West as an expert witness. It still wasn't enough.

Kennedy Brewer spent twenty-three of every twenty-four hours isolated in a cell on Mississippi's death row at Parchman. It gave him plenty of time to worry about his appeal. He had heard nothing from his lawyers or the courts. So he wrote a letter to his attorney. "I just been wondering," he began, "since I haven't heard nothing in a while it would be good for me to no if everything the same or have anything change?"

Brewer's lawyer wrote him back, but only to tell Brewer that he was no longer handling the case. The trial court had appointed two different lawyers to draft and file Brewer's appeal, but neither had been in touch. Several months later, Brewer still had heard nothing from his new appellate attorneys. So he wrote his trial lawyer again to see if he had any information.

"I hope that I am not worrying you," Brewer wrote, "it just that sense I been over here a guy almost got executed all because his attorney didn't file this certain motion in court and . . . all I want to no is where my case stand because I don't want that to happen to me."

The trial court had appointed Brewer a lawyer to handle his appeal—or at least gone through the formality. The first lawyer the court appointed had never participated in a jury trial, nor had she ever worked an appeal. Shortly after her appointment, she became ill and requested the aid of another attorney. The trial court obliged, this time appointing an attorney who had limited experience practicing criminal law, and after reading the trial transcripts "and considering the severity of this matter and the consequences . . . if the trial court's decision was affirmed" asked to be removed from the case. With both of Brewer's initially appointed appellate attorneys out of their league, the court finally turned to a more senior attorney who had experience in both trying and appealing serious cases: Richard Burdine.

Burdine's legacy is a complicated one. He's a black lawyer from Mississippi who for decades has willingly accepted appointments to represent indigent defendants when few others would. In 2014, the Mississippi legislature publicly commended Burdine. The House commendation was titled, "A Resolution Commending the Historical Legacy, Reputable Iconic Career and Esteemed Service of Mr. Richard Burdine as a Distinguished Member of the State of Mississippi's Legal Community and One of the State's Most Illustrious and Oldest African-American Attorneys."

But Burdine's name is also well known to Mississippi courts, and for less laudatory reasons. By the time he was appointed Brewer's appellate counsel, Burdine had already been subjected to disciplinary action by the state bar on numerous occasions.

In 1988, he represented a nineteen-year-old high school senior involved in a fight that led to a fatal shooting. Burdine made no effort to request that the state turn over its evidence to him prior to trial, didn't subpoena any witnesses, and then failed to file a timely appeal after his client's conviction. The Mississippi Supreme Court later reversed the case, writing that Burdine had failed "to perform any act basic to the defense of the accused." In 1996 Burdine failed to file a burglary defendant's appeal on time, despite two reminders from his client; Burdine's failure cost the man his chance to appeal. In a 1996 death penalty case, Burdine's opening statement in the penalty phase was just eight lines long. The Mississippi Supreme Court did not find his actions constitutionally deficient. That client was sentenced to death.

So perhaps it wasn't all that surprising when Kennedy Brewer's first attempt to appeal his conviction and sentence failed. The

Mississippi Supreme Court denied every one of his arguments, including his claim that West should not have been permitted to testify. Brewer next sought to have his case heard by the US Supreme Court. They declined to hear the case. Two days later, the State of Mississippi filed a motion to set Brewer's execution date once again.

Brewer returned to the Mississippi Supreme Court in 1999. He wanted permission to perform DNA testing on the sperm that had been found in Christine Jackson. Shortly after Brewer's original trial, his lawyers had been given access to the DNA for testing. But at the time, DNA technology was too primitive for such a small sample to be useful. They feared that if they tried to test it, they might destroy the evidence for future analysis.

By the turn of the century, the technology had improved. Brewer's legal team sought to have the evidence tested. The Mississippi Supreme Court initially turned them down, although to be fair, Brewer's attorneys at the time hadn't made the best legal arguments. But even in declining Brewer, the court did leave the door open to a future challenge. After another challenge from Brewer, the court reversed itself and ordered the trial court to hold a hearing on the issue of testing.

In April 2001, Brewer was finally granted permission by the trial court to test the sperm evidence. They sent it to a lab in New Orleans, which found that the sperm belonged to at least one—and perhaps two—unidentified males. Neither of them was Kennedy Brewer.

To that point, in almost every instance in which a defendant had been given results excluding him from DNA found in a rape victim, the defendant was promptly released from prison. Not in Brewer's case. When Brewer returned to the Mississippi Supreme Court, this time to ask that the court dismiss the charges against him, the justices turned him down. Though the court agreed that the results of the DNA evidence were compelling, it also found that "the DNA evidence does not prove conclusively that Brewer did not murder the victim" and there was "sufficient evidence in the record . . . indicating Brewer's involvement." The evidence the court was referencing—the only physical evidence in the case—was West's bite mark claims. The court then remanded Brewer's case to the trial court.

To his credit, Forrest Allgood didn't object to the DNA testing. But he also didn't seem particularly moved by the results. Not only was Allgood determined to retry Brewer, he planned to put Michael West back on the stand as the star of that trial. He had to. It was the best evidence he had. In a just world, the test results would have prompted Allgood to reopen Christine Jackson's rape and murder investigation and immediately free Kennedy Brewer. Instead, the case became a murder prosecution in search of a theory. Under one of Allgood's theories, Brewer, Leshone Williams, and Dewayne Graham all participated in Christine's rape and murder. Allgood had what he believed to be solid evidence: A jailhouse informant allegedly told Allgood's office that while he was in the Noxubee County Jail, Brewer "confessed" to him that he was forced at gunpoint to bite Christine while Williams and Graham raped her. The claim was baffling and implausible, but Allgood apparently thought it had some merit so asked Williams and Graham to submit to DNA testing. They were promptly excluded as the sources of the sperm. This too wasn't enough to persuade Allgood of Brewer's innocence.

Kennedy Brewer had been arrested within hours of Christine Jackson's disappearance. When he was excluded as her rapist some fifteen years later, no one seemed in much of a hurry to try the case again. Brewer would languish in prison for nearly six more years.

The initial DNA test results may not have freed Kennedy Brewer, but they did again thrust Michael West into the national spotlight, bringing yet more negative media exposure. In 2001, *Newsweek* profiled West, calling him a "clutch witness" who was "affable and supremely confident," but also noting West's growing number of critics, who West said were driven by "ignorance" and "personal jealousy."

But the article also provided space for the broader argument against bite mark evidence in general, an issue that to that point had been less discussed. *Newsweek* referred to a recent proficiency test given to twenty-five bite mark analysts (including West). Each analyst was given four sets of bite marks and asked to match them with seven sets of dental molds. The experts who made a positive "match" had an astonishing error rate of 63.5 percent. This was the same field whose practitioners had compared their proficiency to fingerprint or DNA evidence. It wasn't just West. These analysts were putting people in prison.

Parroting the party line, West told *Newsweek* that he still believed Brewer to be guilty. "Just because the DNA isn't his doesn't mean the bite marks aren't his," he said. He then told the reporter to "stop bothering me."

After the story was published, West complained about it to local media, insisting that the national criticism was inaccurate and likely orchestrated by well-funded death penalty opponents. "The national interest is not in my work; it is in the death penalty," West told the *Clarion-Ledger.* "In a murder trial when the death penalty is not involved, there is very little interest. When the death penalty is, it is amazing the money and interest that comes into play. Opinions are based on science or who wrote the check. My opinions are based on the science."

The following year, West was profiled on the CBS news program *60 Minutes.* Though the profile was far from flattering, West speaks of the profile as a professional accomplishment. Steve Kroft interviewed John Keko's attorney, who called West "a dangerous, dangerous witness." When Kroft asked West how bite mark evidence compared to DNA or fingerprint evidence, West didn't stop at calling them similar; he claimed that his field was actually superior. "If you look at bite marks, you don't walk into a woman's house and borrow a phone and accidentally bite her on the arm," he said. "You have to be in a violent contact with that individual to deposit a bite mark. In that light, bite marks are better than fingerprints, because they not only show that you were present, they show you were in a violent confrontation with that individual."

West told Kroft that he had testified seventy-three times in nine states, resulting in convictions that had only been overturned three times because of his testimony. "I'll take that percentage rate of error," West said. As John Holdridge pointed out to Kroft, West was *boasting* about an error rate of 6 to 7 percent—far too high when the consequences are life in prison or the death penalty. But even that figure wasn't quite right. West only counted the cases in which a judge had determined that his testimony wasn't based on sound science. It didn't include wrongful arrests or cases where prosecutors had decided to drop the charges on their own. It also didn't include Kennedy Brewer and Levon Brooks.

As Hayne's autopsy load continued to pick up, so did criticism of his work, including in cases where he appeared to have taken shortcuts and made questionable findings. Ken Winter, who served as crime lab director in the early 2000s, says that every year he would allocate part of his crime lab budget to hire a new state medical examiner. Every year, the legislature took it out. "You have to understand, the coroners and prosecutors loved Hayne," Winter says, "and with the counties paying his fees, the legislature didn't have to fund a state office and staff."

In October 2002, a grand jury indicted a man for the murder of a woman whose partially clad, skeletonized body had been discovered on the side of a road in Rankin County. Hayne did the autopsy. Under "Cause of Death," he wrote, "Changes consistent with Suffocation/ Strangulation." Two years later, the defendant's attorney sent Hayne's autopsy report to Harry Bonnell, a forensic pathologist in San Diego who at the time sat on the board of ethics of the National Association of Medical Examiners. In a preliminary letter back, Bonnell called the quality of Hayne's report "pathetic," adding that "the failure to obtain specimens and perform toxicology testing in this type of death borders on criminal negligence." In November 2004, Bonnell sent his full review of Hayne's work. It was more scathing still. He wrote that Hayne's favored cause of death was "near-total speculation." Because the body was in an advanced state of decomposition, the description of the remains in Hayne's report would have been consistent with nearly any cause of death. The defendant eventually pleaded guilty to manslaughter. When asked about the case in a deposition years later, Hayne claimed that the defendant's plea vindicated his work in the case.

Hayne had made similar claims about a partially skeletonized body in another case. In 1999, after the remains of Tonya Ward had been found in a wooded area of Jefferson Davis County, Mississippi, Hayne testified that she had been strangled to death. But there was no neck tissue left on Ward's body to examine. In that case, the defendant was acquitted.

As Hayne did more and more autopsies, testified in more and more cases, and gained more and more influence, the courts seem to give him more latitude to testify outside his area of expertise. In murder cases like that of Tavares Flaggs, he took full advantage of the opportunity.

In April 2005, Flaggs was accused of murdering a man during an altercation. Flaggs never denied killing the man, but said he had done so in self-defense. At trial, Hayne testified that blood spatter patterns at the crime scene supported the prosecution's theory that Flaggs was the aggressor—and he hadn't been defending himself.

There are multiple problems with Hayne's testimony. First, blood spatter analysis in general is a controversial field. It has been roundly criticized by scientific bodies like the National Academy of Sciences. But even if one were to accept blood spatter analysis as scientifically sound, Hayne was never presented as a blood spatter expert at the trial, only as a pathologist. Nothing about the skills and experience required to be a medical examiner would automatically qualify someone to give an expert opinion about blood spatter patterns. Nevertheless, over Flaggs's lawyer's objection, the trial court allowed Hayne to testify. He then told the jury that given the pattern of spatter, the victim was "moving in a backward position away" at the time of his injuries, and that the spatter was produced as he raised his arm and hand in a manner that was "consistent with defensive posturing injury."

There was another, more severe problem with the blood spatter testimony. As Flaggs's attorneys from the Mississippi Innocence Project wrote in their petition to the court, "Dr. Hayne provided testimony concerning the discolorations on the hallway walls that were presumed to be—but without any evidentiary support—blood spatter," adding, "the 'blood spatter' was never tested in order to determine whether it was in fact blood; nor, it follows, was there any determination about whose blood it was." The only evidence for the alleged blood spatter were crime scene photos the state introduced into evidence, and Flaggs's attorneys argued that the state offered no evidence Hayne even examined those. If the state *did* test the discolored portions of the walls to make sure that (a) it was blood and (b) it was the victim's blood, one would assume it would have introduced those tests into evidence. It didn't. Even in its response to Flaggs's petition, the state didn't contest that the alleged blood spatter had never been tested, instead arguing that even if Hayne's testimony had been admitted in error, it was "harmless error"—that is, the remaining evidence was sufficient to find Flaggs guilty.

When Flaggs appealed his conviction and life sentence, the Mississippi Court of Appeals summarily dismissed the blood spatter controversy and Hayne's testimony by finding that "our supreme court has indicated that forensic pathologists are qualified to give opinions regarding blood spatter. . . . Therefore, while there was no mention of blood spatter analysis during Dr. Hayne's expert qualification, we cannot say under the circumstances of this case that the trial court erred in allowing Dr. Hayne to testify regarding blood spatter." George Washington University law professor Jonathan Turley wrote about Flaggs's case in 2014: "No one reading this record could come away with anything but disgust for the handling of the prosecution." Turley also criticized the "dismissive ruling" in one of Flaggs's later appeals. Yet the conviction has been upheld by three Mississippi courts and a federal court of appeals. Flaggs is still in prison today.

Cleared by DNA testing—but still locked in a cell and condemned to die—Kennedy Brewer finally decided to take it upon himself to save his own life. He wrote yet another letter to his lawyer. "Could you send me about $60.00 to get me a type writer," he asked. "What I am doing is fixing to get involve in learning the law because I just can't spend my life in prison for nothing that's why I try to learn more and about the law each day."

Brewer's lawyer never sent either money or a typewriter. But Brewer continued to learn everything he could about the law, devouring any legal-related newspaper articles or magazines he could get his hands on. In the back of one of those magazines, he saw an ad for an organization that seemed promising. So Brewer pulled out a piece of lined notebook paper and a pen and began writing another letter.

"Dear Mrs. Greene," he began in careful script, "how are you today? I know you probably don't know me but the reason am writing is can you . . . help me out concerning my case? I really, really, really would highly appreciated."

Four days later, Brewer's letter arrived at the Innocence Project in New York.

～ 13 ～

THE UNRAVELING

And the horrible thing about all legal officials,
even the best, about all judges, magistrates, barris-
ters, detectives, and policemen, is not that they are
wicked (some of them are good), not that they are
stupid (several of them are quite intelligent), it is
simply that they have got used to it.

—G. K. Chesterton

Sometime around 2006, Steven Hayne and Jimmy Roberts had a falling-out. One former Roberts staffer said the spat had been building for a while but came to a head when Roberts started billing Hayne for supplies and Roberts's staff began complaining about the hours they had to work to accommodate Hayne's schedule.

In a 2012 deposition, Hayne offered a different take. He said Roberts's monopoly on the business of transporting dead bodies for the counties had begun to fray. Some counties had purchased their own hearses. Other, wealthier counties had bought several and had begun transporting bodies for neighboring counties for a fee. New private competitors had also sprung up. According to Hayne, Roberts was losing money, which created friction between Roberts and the other coroners. That friction could have threatened Hayne's relationship with those coroners, too. So Hayne parted ways with Roberts.

But Hayne already had a new plan in the works. In 2006, Commissioner of Public Safety George Phillips offered Hayne a contract that gave him the noncompensated position of chief state pathologist. That specific title didn't exist anywhere in Mississippi law. It was invented. But it certainly sounded official. Under the contract, Hayne would continue to teach training classes to coroners. And he could continue his private autopsy practice.

More importantly, the contract allowed Hayne to use the state crime lab for his private autopsies, at a low rate of $100 per procedure. The state of Mississippi would also foot the bill for his supplies and give him use of an office. Hayne now had the title and the facility, and was doing more autopsies than ever. He was no longer reliant on Jimmy Roberts. He was at the height of his career. Soon, it would all begin to unravel.

The years 2000–2008 were the busiest years of Hayne's professional life. And it's probably safe to say that a day in Steven Hayne's life at that time was unlike a day in the life of just about anyone else. In 2008, an opposing attorney in a civil case subpoenaed Hayne's autopsy and testimony records for an eighteen-month period in 2007 and 2008. Those records give a more complete picture of Hayne's jaw-dropping schedule. On September 10, 2007, for example, Hayne testified for a case in Jackson and performed four autopsies. The next day, he traveled 160 miles to Marks, Mississippi, testified, traveled back to Jackson, and performed three more. The following day, he again testified in Jackson and completed five autopsies. The next day, it was 118 miles to Greenville for court testimony, then 90 miles back to the town of Marks for testimony in a separate case, 170 miles back to Jackson, and four more autopsies. The four-day total: five court appearances, sixteen autopsies, and over 700 miles of travel. The following day he did six more autopsies.

According to these records, as well as a review of Hayne's court testimony, over one forty-eight-hour period on January 22–23, 2008, he testified in Clarksdale in the Delta, Magnolia and Columbia in the far south, and Forest in central Mississippi, and knocked out seven autopsies. But Hayne's most impressive two-day stretch during that eighteen-month window came on April 3 and 4, 2007, during which he testified in Jackson, Hazlehurst, Tunica, and Yazoo City, and also performed nine autopsies.

Recall that through all of this Hayne was also working a job at a kidney research lab and another at a local hospital, each of which paid him over $100,000 per year.

Not surprisingly, Hayne made some particularly egregious mistakes during this period. One Mississippi attorney, for example, recalls a murder case in which Hayne noted in his report that he had removed and examined the decedent's ovaries and uterus. The problem? The victim was male. (The defendant in that case still pleaded guilty.)

In 2007, Mississippi Department of Corrections inmate Randy Cheney was exhibiting signs of sepsis. He had been complaining about a worsening infection but had instead been given medication for an irregular heartbeat. When his condition worsened, he was transported to Parchman Hospital at the Mississippi State Penitentiary, and then to Greenwood Leflore Hospital. He died of septic shock the following day.

When Hayne performed the autopsy on Cheney, he determined that Cheney had died of hypertensive heart disease and coronary artery disease, and ruled the manner of death to be natural. In his autopsy report, Hayne indicated that he had weighed Cheney's spleen and that it was within the normal range of an adult man. Hayne added that after removing and examining it, he found the spleen capsule "intact," with no contusions. It could perhaps be dismissed as a careless but forgivable oversight by a busy medical examiner if Hayne had merely failed to note that Cheney's spleen was diseased as he removed it, weighed it, dissected it, and commented on its appearance. What actually happened is far less forgivable: Cheney's spleen had been removed four years earlier. This wasn't a frivolous oversight—a diseased, compromised, or missing spleen can increase the risk of sepsis.

Then there's the sad case of Hattie Douglas. In August 2006, Douglas, a resident of Camden, Mississippi, fell asleep with her eleven-month-old son, Kadarrius, asleep on her chest. When she woke the next morning, Kadarrius was unresponsive. He died before he got to the hospital. Hayne's original autopsy report on the boy indicated no signs of alcohol poisoning. He then sent blood samples off to a Texas-based lab called ExperTox for testing. When the tests came back, it showed Kadarrius had an off-the-charts blood-alcohol level of 0.4. A child of Kadarrius's size would have had to ingest five to six ounces of pure alcohol to reach that level. Based on the toxicology results, the local coroner concluded that Kadarrius died of ethyl-alcohol intoxication.

Hattie Douglas was arrested, charged with murder, and held without bond. She faced a possible sentence of life in prison. Her remaining five children were taken from her, and local law enforcement officials pilloried her in the press. Douglas and her family had maintained from the start that the child had been sick and she had given him only cough medicine. She had even taken him to a medical clinic three days earlier for coughing and congestion.

In July 2007, Douglas's attorney asked former Alabama state medical examiner Leroy Roddick to review Hayne's autopsy and the toxicology reports. Riddick found that Hayne had ignored or overlooked evidence in his autopsy that clearly conflicted with elevated alcohol reading. For one, with such a high level of intoxication, Hayne should have noted a strong stench of alcohol during the autopsy. He hadn't. There were no other signs of intoxication, either. Just the lab report. Moreover, ExperTox had actually run several tests on the sample from Kadarrius Douglas. One test showed a concentration as low as .02— about what one would expect after a dose of cough medicine. The alcohol concentration then increased with ensuing tests. Hayne and the authorities ran with the highest one.

Hayne and local officials blamed ExperTox. But a spokeswoman for the company told the *Clarion-Ledger* that the results were likely because someone in Mississippi had stored the sample at the wrong temperature. Another tube of the child's blood had been contaminated. In fact, the company had actually stopped taking lab samples from Mississippi in 2006. "We didn't feel as comfortable with samples coming from that state as we did from other states," a company official said.

But even if the faulty test were solely the responsibility of ExperTox, a conscientious medical examiner should have noticed such an abnormally high result and consulted his autopsy notes before agreeing to change his conclusions to support a murder charge. Hayne didn't, and an innocent woman who had just suffered the loss of her son then lost custody of her four other children and spent eighteen months in jail.

On May 9, 2003, Kristi Fulgham, age twenty-six, picked up her half brother, Tyler Edmonds, and brought him to her home in the Longview community in Oktibbeha County, Mississippi. Edmonds, age thirteen, spent every other weekend with Fulgham. On this particular weekend, he thought she was taking him to see their father. Instead, she took him to the house she shared with her husband, Joey.

Kristi and Joey Fulgham had a volatile marriage. Kristi told her family that Joey sometimes beat her and her three children. But acquaintances also said that Kristi could be manipulative and was seeing other men. She had previously moved out of the house, but then moved back in, believing she was the beneficiary of her husband's $300,000 life insurance policy.

Tyler Edmonds adored and idolized his half sister. She often took advantage of that, using him to run interference on the various men in her life. Before she picked him up that weekend, she asked Tyler to bring her an old rifle from his stepfather's closet so she could shoot a stray dog that had been bothering her and her kids. She had also previously asked a couple of neighbors for a gun, using the same story. But according to her father, Kristi wanted the guns for another reason: she planned to kill her husband to put an end to his abuse, after which she and her kids would live off his life insurance policy.

On that particular night, a Friday evening, Tyler, Kristi, Joey, and the three children had dinner, watched a movie, and went to sleep. At around four a.m., Kristi woke Tyler and told him she was leaving. She asked him to help her put the three kids in the car. According to Tyler, as he was waiting in the car, he heard a "pop," but didn't think much of it at the time. Kristi rushed to the car, carrying a computer and jewelry box. At that point, she told Tyler that they weren't going to visit their father after all. They were going to Jackson to pick up her boyfriend, and then to Biloxi on the Gulf Coast. They did just that. The five of them spent that Saturday night at Biloxi's Beau Rivage casino and resort.

When they returned to Jackson the following afternoon, Joey Fulgham had been found dead, shot once in the head as he slept. According to Tyler, that Sunday evening Kristi confessed to him that she had killed her husband. She also told him that they'd likely give her the death penalty, and that his only chance to continue seeing her and her kids would be for him to take the blame for the crime. She told him to tell the police that it was all an accident—that he had mistakenly shot Joey while playing with the gun. She assured him he wouldn't go to prison because he was still a juvenile.

After dropping Tyler back off with his mother, Kristi was interrogated at the Oktibbeha County jail. She blamed her husband's death on Tyler.

The police asked Tyler's mother to bring him in for questioning. While he was still in the presence of his mother and with a camera rolling, the police questioned him for three hours. Tyler repeatedly denied any involvement in Joey Fulgham's death. He was then separated from his mother and questioned alone. That's when the police interrogators told Tyler that Kristi had already blamed him for Joey's death. He didn't believe them. Then they turned off the camera and brought Kristi into the room. Kristi took Tyler's hand and told him to tell the truth. As she did, she slipped him a note. The note instructed

Tyler to tell the police that he shot Joey by accident. If he didn't, she wrote, "they want to see me fry."

The police then turned the camera back on, and Tyler confessed, but with an odd and contradictory narrative. He claimed he and Kristi had decided to carry out the murder together, by holding the old rifle and pulling the trigger simultaneously as Joey slept. Tyler said he didn't even think the rifle would work. He said he had closed his eyes before they pulled the trigger, then opened one eye after he heard the shot. He said he saw specks of blood on a pillowcase. (There was no blood at the crime scene.) He said he then confessed to Kristi's boyfriend while they were in Biloxi. Her boyfriend later denied it.

Three days later, after talking to his mother and other relatives, Tyler recanted his entire confession. He said he had falsely confessed because he thought that by taking some, but not all, of the blame, he could save his sister from getting the death penalty. Forrest Allgood's office filed murder charges against both Tyler and Kristi and announced that Tyler would be tried as an adult.

The only real evidence against Edmonds was his confession. But he had recanted it. So the prosecution needed jurors to believe the confession over the recantation. That's where Hayne came in. At trial, the prosecutor in the case, one of Allgood's assistants, asked Hayne if he had viewed Tyler's videotaped confession. He said he had. She then asked if in light of that confession he had considered the position of Joey's body. He said he had. She then asked, "Based on the path of the projectile and everything that was viewed," if Hayne thought "the defendant's version of the events is consistent with what you found in Mr. Fulgham?" In other words, she asked, were the wounds in Fulgham's body consistent with Edmonds's initial confession, the one in which he and his sister held and fired the gun simultaneously?

Edmonds's attorney objected, arguing that to answer that question would require knowledge "outside of anything in his report and also outside of anybody's expertise." He requested a *Daubert* hearing on the scientific bases, if any even existed, to suggest it was possible for a medical examiner to conclude from a victim's wounds whether there was one or two people holding the gun used to commit the crime. The judge refused to even hold a hearing.

The prosecutor then asked the question again. Did Hayne find that the crime scene evidence, his autopsy, and the other forensic evidence were consistent with Tyler's videotaped confession? Hayne answered, "Within a reasonable medical certainty, it's consistent with the scenario provided to me and would be in compliance with the facts that I saw."

The question was absurd, and so was Hayne's answer. There's simply no way a medical examiner could have known such a thing. Tyler's attorneys undoubtedly knew exactly what Hayne had just done. He had found language that allowed the jury to hear an opinion that wasn't really defensible, while permitting him to avoid stating that indefensible opinion explicitly. So on cross-examination, the defense provoked Hayne to be more explicit. They asked straight up if he believed the evidence suggested that two people fired the shot. He said it did. They then asked if he thought just one person could have fired. He answered, "I could not exclude that; however, I would favor that a second party be involved in that positioning of the weapon." That answer would prove to be the beginning of the end of Hayne's stranglehold on Mississippi's autopsies.

Later in the trial there was another battle over expert testimony that provided a striking contrast to the debate over Hayne's two-hands-on-the-gun theory. Edmonds's defense attorneys had planned to question Allison Redlich, a trained experimental psychologist who has conducted research into false confessions, particularly among children. Redlich was prepared to testify that Edmonds was a prototypical candidate for a false confession. In addition to his being separated from his mother and pressured by his sister, a court-ordered psychological evaluation had found that Edmonds was emotionally and psychologically immature for his age—all common factors among those known to have falsely confessed.

The state preemptively objected. Despite allowing Hayne's absurd gun-holding testimony without even so much as a hearing, the trial judge set aside an entire day for a *Daubert* hearing on whether Redlich's research was scientifically credible. After the hearing, the judge ruled that it wasn't. His analysis was a case study in the folly of asking judges to be the gatekeepers of science in the courtroom. For example, one of the judge's self-selected criteria for determining whether Redlich's research was valid was how often other courts had permitted expert testimony about false confessions. His own research showed that about half had allowed it, and half hadn't. This, he decided, meant that Redlich's opinions hadn't yet been accepted in the scientific community.

It was a revealing bit of analysis. Whether other *judges* had allowed a particular field of research into evidence said little to nothing about whether that field had been accepted in the *scientific* community. The judge also claimed that the number of researchers in the field of false confessions was too small for the field to be considered scientifically accepted; he claimed only six were doing work similar to Redlich's. But the actual number was around sixty, and one review of published research on false confessions in 1992—more than a decade before the Edmonds trial—found eight hundred different peer-reviewed studies. Of the three experts the judge *did* cite who had questioned the frequency of false confessions, one had never published a peer-reviewed study on the topic. Another is a former federal judge, victims' rights and death penalty advocate, and conservative legal commentator, not a trained psychiatrist or social scientist.

For nearly twenty years, Mississippi's courts had permitted the testimony of Michael West without so much as a single *Daubert* hearing to entertain the possibility that his methods and practices may have lacked scientific merit. For twenty years, they had allowed Steven Hayne to testify despite his lack of certification and absurd workload, and in areas well outside the parameters of forensic pathology, including blood spatter on walls, the positioning of shooters based on bullet trajectories, and tool mark identification. But it was on the subject of false confessions that this particular court suddenly grew skeptical.

The jury found Edmonds guilty. In October 2003 he was sentenced to life in prison. He was sixteen years old at the time. He wouldn't be eligible for parole until he turned sixty-five. In a separate trial, Kristi was also convicted. She was sentenced to death.

Hayne's preposterous testimony in the Edmonds case was later upheld by the Mississippi Court of Appeals. The majority of that court, along with Hayne's defenders, pointed to the fact that in his confession, Edmonds said he closed his eyes before shooting. They argued that Hayne wasn't claiming he could tell there were two hands on the trigger, but merely that if Edmond's eyes *were* closed, it would only make sense that Kristi Fulgham's hand helped guide the gun—otherwise, Edmonds would have missed. That's certainly one interpretation of his testimony. On its own it seems plausible, if unlikely. But it's more easily dismissed by the state's own opening argument, in which the prosecutor explicitly told the jury, "You're going to hear how Kristi stood behind him and held him and you're going to hear how *they both put their finger on the trigger* and you're going to hear how they both shot and killed Joey Fulgham."

In a surprise decision handed down in January 2007, the Mississippi Supreme Court granted Tyler Edmonds a new trial. More surprising, for the first time ever, the court overturned a conviction because of testimony from Steven Hayne. The majority explicitly ruled that Hayne's two-hands-on-the-gun testimony wasn't supported by science. The vote was 7 to 1.

But even in tossing out Hayne's testimony in the case, the majority went out of its way to emphasize that its criticism of Hayne was limited only to the case at hand. It was not a comment on his general credibility, much less a suggestion that he should no longer testify in court. The majority also upheld the trial judge's exclusion of the evidence from Allison Redlich about false confessions.

Two justices would have gone further. Oliver Diaz wrote a concurring opinion, joined by Justice James Graves, in which he explicitly called on his colleagues to pay rigorous attention to experts like Hayne and others when they attempt to testify in Mississippi's courts. Diaz cited Hayne's enormous autopsy workload, as well as the fact that he wasn't properly certified. Diaz also wrote that he would have admitted Redlich's testimony about false confessions and would not have admitted Edmonds's taped confession.

Justice Charles Easley, who had defeated Chief Justice Prather in 2000 by accusing her of being soft on crime, was the lone dissenter. He would have upheld Edmonds's conviction. But even that wasn't the case at first. It was later revealed that the justices had initially voted in favor of upholding Edmonds's conviction. Diaz responded with a dissent so blistering and persuasive that several justices reversed their votes.

Forrest Allgood decided to try Edmonds again. That trial took place in 2008. This time, without Hayne's two-hands-on-the-gun testimony, the jury quickly acquitted.

~

The Edmonds case brought national attention to Mississippi, but nearly all of it focused on the fact that Edmonds was being tried as an adult for a crime he had allegedly committed at the age of thirteen. That was certainly worthy of attention. It seemed like an especially cruel decision. Edmonds had no prior criminal record, and his teachers, relatives, parents of his friends, and his school counselor all testified that he was a gentle and good-natured kid. He was well-behaved and got good grades, and had never been prone to violence. Even if Allgood and his subordinates truly believed Edmonds helped his sister kill her husband, there was every reason to think he had been emotionally manipulated into doing it. At worst, this was a boy who came to the aid of the sociopathic older sister he adored and saw as a maternal figure.

But as with the jailhouse suicides in the 1990s, despite the national attention from media outlets and various activist groups, the ongoing problems with the state's death investigation system still escaped much scrutiny, at least in the short term.

The Mississippi Supreme Court ruling in Edmonds's case was a different matter. That decision started a chain of events that would ultimately lead to Hayne's termination as a designated pathologist who could perform autopsies for prosecutors. It not only drew attention to his egregiously awful testimony in that case (which in itself should have spurred a thorough review of all of Hayne's work) but renewed the suspicions and criticisms of Hayne that had percolated among his critics and colleagues for years. Hayne's reign was coming to an end.

After receiving Kennedy Brewer's letter, the attorneys at the Innocence Project in New York agreed to represent him. Shortly after Brewer had been cleared by DNA testing, but well before he had been exonerated, his attorneys from both Mississippi and New York paid a visit to Forrest Allgood in Macon. The prosecutor had already announced that he planned to try Brewer again. The legal team wanted to make a personal plea to Allgood to drop the charges. What happened next, as recounted by André de Gruy and Peter Neufeld, was remarkable.

The attorneys, along with Brewer himself, were to meet with Allgood in the jury room of a Noxubee County courthouse. Only after Brewer left the room did Allgood agree to talk. He then brought them back to an office in the courthouse and took a seat behind a desk. He leaned back, propped up his cowboy boots, and crossed his feet.

Neufeld carefully explained the science behind DNA testing, why the science in this case proved Brewer's innocence, and why the US Constitution compelled Allgood to drop the charges.

When Neufeld had finished, Allgood slowly looked up from the floor, paused, and said, "You really believe in this science stuff, don't you?"

Stunned, Neufeld replied that, indeed, he really did believe in DNA and in science. Allgood shrugged, took his boots off the table, and said, "Well I guess everybody's gotta believe in something."

When asked about the conversation, Allgood denied making the first comment. "I have never disbelieved in DNA," he wrote, adding that he does sometimes object to how DNA test results are interpreted. He does recall making the second comment.

"We had multiple experts saying this guy was innocent. We had two labs confirm the DNA tests. We were thinking: we just need to round up as many scientists as we can. More confirmation, more tests, eventually we'd convince Allgood that our client is innocent," de Gruy says. "That conversation was such a revelation. The fact is, none of it mattered. We were dealing with a guy who thought science was just another set of beliefs, just another religion that wasn't his. You can see how a guy like that . . . how once he's convinced someone is guilty, he just isn't going to stop."

The core problem with the medicolegal system in Mississippi is that it's easily manipulated—it serves those in power. Historically, it has served as a means of preserving the state's white power structure. But that's only because those in power wanted it that way. At some point between the early 1980s and the mid-2000s, the respectable politics on the race issue in Mississippi shifted from defending the past, to apologizing for it, to trying to reckon with it in order to move beyond it. As the state's politicians positioned themselves over the course of that shift, the state's death investigation system evolved to serve them. The cold case trial of James Ford Seale is a good example of how the system changed to accommodate the new era.

By late June 1964, state and federal authorities found the bodies of Henry Dee and Charles Moore while looking for the missing Freedom Summer workers. Dee was a nineteen-year-old sawmill employee; Moore, a twenty-year-old college student at Alcorn State. They lived in Meadville, Mississippi, a small community about thirty miles east of Natchez, along the northern border of the Homochitto National Forest. The area also happened to be the home of one of the most violent factions of the state Ku Klux Klan, known as the Silver Dollar Group. Immediately after the bodies were recovered, an aggressive investigation got under way. Unlike similar investigations of that era, this one held promise. There were witnesses, and they were talking.

On May 2, 1964, James Ford Seale picked up Dee and Moore as they hitchhiked near a gas station in Meadville. He posed as a federal revenue agent investigating local moonshine activity. Seale then drove them deep into the Homochitto National Forest to a waiting group of Klansmen, who tied Dee and Moore to trees and repeatedly lashed them with bean poles. The two men's bodies, alleged to be badly beaten but not yet dead, were then driven a hundred miles west to a boat launch by an isolated part of the Mississippi River. Seale and a fellow Klansman were arrested in November 1964. They would later successfully convince the local white community that they had been beaten by federal law enforcement during their arrest and brief imprisonment. Instead of a pretrial hearing in January, the district attorney moved to dismiss the indictments.

The murders were not likely Seale's first. He was believed to have killed another Klan member who was trying to get out of the organization and was suspected of providing information to the FBI. Six months later, he was believed to have murdered a seventy-four-year-old black man, one of the few black residents of Franklin County brave enough to have registered to vote. The coroner's jury failed to bring charges in either case.

In 2007, after years of pressure and activism by Charles Moore's brother Thomas, Seale was charged in federal court with one count of conspiracy to commit kidnapping and two counts of kidnapping. But the federal prosecutors would need to surmount a number of problems with the case. Witnesses had died, and there was at least some residual resistance to pursuing a case that would potentially reopen old wounds and stir up racial strife. But the most critical problem at first seemed intractable: jurisdiction. In order to get jurisdiction for federal kidnapping charges, the government had to show that a living victim—in this case Dee or Moore, or both—had been transported across state lines after being kidnapped. They would have to prove that Dee and Moore were killed *after* they were taken from the Homochitto Forest into Louisiana and then back again into Mississippi— that they were still alive when they were thrown into the river.

The evidence for this was thin. None of the witness statements at the time indicated as much. The only witness willing to say decades later that the men were alive was himself a former Klansman with a history of lying about the case. What prosecutors needed was a medical examiner willing to review old records, autopsy Dee's and Moore's remains, and determine that they had died of drowning. The old autopsies, however, offered no help. Drowning is a difficult diagnosis even with a fresh body. But the indications of drowning—water in their stomachs or lungs, changes to the blood vessels in the eyes—wouldn't be discernible in the remains of two bodies that had been cut in half, submerged in the river for weeks, and buried for more than forty years.

As part of the initial forensic investigation in the 1960s, the bones had been sent to one of the preeminent forensic anthropologists in the country, Dr. J. Lawrence Angel at the Smithsonian National Museum of Natural History. Angel could make no determination about cause of death. At best, freshwater drowning was not inconsistent with the available evidence. That wouldn't be enough to establish jurisdiction. Decades later, as a new prosecution was being considered, federal prosecutors consulted Steven Hayne.

Hayne wasn't nearly as circumspect as Angel had been. He found that "to a reasonable degree of medical certainty the cause of death was consistent with freshwater drowning," but testified that the condition of the body precluded a definite conclusion. Still, that was what federal prosecutors needed to establish jurisdiction. In August 2007, James Ford Seale was convicted and sentenced to three life terms for his role in the 1964 murders of Dee and Moore. He died in the federal penitentiary in Terre Haute, Indiana, in 2011.

James Ford Seale wasn't a sympathetic figure. He was an unapologetic racist and a Klansman, and he almost certainly committed multiple murders. He should have been tried locally in 1964. There was plenty of evidence and plenty of witnesses who were still alive. But in 1964 Mississippi wasn't ready to try a white man for murdering two young black men. And the sad fact of the matter is, forty years later, there still wasn't much of an appetite for it. "In truth," as Harry N. Maclean writes in his book about the murders and trial, "if it had been solely up to the authorities, this latest act in Mississippi's redemption drama would not" have been prosecuted.

Seale's trial could only be conducted by the federal government—in Jackson, away from Meadville. When the United States decided to prosecute Seale in 2007, the entire endeavor was largely symbolic. There were at least seven Klansmen who were involved in the abduction and murder of Dee and Morris. In the end, only one ever stood trial, and by the time he did he was a doddering old man. At its heart, Seale's trial was about declaring that the rule of law was alive in Mississippi—that it could bring the worst among us to justice, even if that justice was considerably and inexcusably delayed. But as federal judge Harold DeMoss wrote in a dissent to the appeals court decision upholding Seale's conviction, "Our treatment of those accused of the most heinous and despicable acts is a measure by which we mark our adherence to the rule of law."

The failure to bring Seale and his co-conspirators to trial in the 1960s was a failure of the rule of law. But while his conviction some forty years later was well intentioned, it too was a failure of the rule of law. For decades, officials in Mississippi exploited the death investigation system to whitewash racial violence. In 2007, they exploited it to give an old racist what he deserved.

It could be argued that Hayne's assistance in the Seale prosecution was evidence that he was on the side of right. Indeed, many would agree that the state's pursuit of cold civil rights cases is an expiation of sorts. Certainly few would question that Seale finally received some sort of justice—karmic, perhaps. But it's also true that prosecutors had to go to Hayne in order to shore up what otherwise was a fatal problem with its forensic evidence. The stakes seemed different: an old, unrepentant racist and a chance for the state to make a name—a good one this time—for itself in an arena that mostly featured failures. But in the final analysis, the state's death investigation system was open to manipulation. Nothing had changed except the times.

14

REDEMPTION AND
INSURRECTION

Power concedes nothing without a demand. It
never did and it never will.

—Frederick Douglass

"Kenny's a shy guy," says André de Gruy. "He doesn't have a lot of words." De Gruy speculates that police, prosecutors, or jurors likely mistook that shyness for the clichéd "quiet loner" label often attached to child predators and killers. "I think it could have hurt him with a jury," he says.

When Forrest Allgood had Brewer's IQ tested, he scored a 65, generally considered borderline mentally disabled. But IQ doesn't always tell the whole story. "I remember there was a point after the DNA tests that Allgood had made Kenny a [plea] offer," says de Gruy. "He still thought Kenny was guilty, so his theory was that there were other people involved in the crime. He made Kenny a deal. If he gave up the names of the other attackers, Allgood would let him out with time served."

By then, Brewer had been in prison for over ten years. De Gruy took the offer to his client. After Brewer finished listening, he asked de Gruy, "So all I gotta do is give you a name, and they'll let me walk out?" That's right, de Gruy replied. Brewer thought for a moment. "But if I give you a name, they'll do a DNA test on that person, right?"

De Gruy nodded. Brewer said, "So I gotta give you the *right* names, don't I?" Again, de Gruy nodded. Brewer paused and then said, "Don't they know that if I knew the right name of the killer, I'd have given it up a long time ago?"

Brewer doesn't show a lot of emotion. He rarely gets angry, rarely gets upset. That, too, may have made him look cold to police, prosecutors, and jurors.

"I've always said Kenny's mother was angry enough for the both of them," de Gruy says. "I used to tell Kenny after talking to him, 'Now I'm going to go get yelled at by your mother.' I mean, she wasn't yelling at me. She just needed someone to yell at. But that wasn't Kenny. It just wasn't his way."

According to de Gruy, the closest he saw Brewer come to anger was when he once said of Allgood, "I can see how maybe you screw up a case, but you could at least apologize." (Allgood still has never apologized to Brewer.)

Because Brewer so rarely got emotional, de Gruy remembers vividly one of the few times he did. It was in 2007. Brewer had been released on bail but had yet to be formally exonerated. There was still talk of trying him again. *New York Times* reporter Shaila Dewan had come to Macon to write about Brewer's case. "We were talking to Kenny at his mom's house," de Gruy recalls. "Shaila started asking Kenny about Christine Jackson, the little girl who was killed. And Kenny began to cry. I guess I just wasn't prepared for that. After all that time, it came out of nowhere. But there it was. He told Shaila that she wasn't his daughter, but he still cared for her. He started talking about how because he had been taken to jail so quickly, he never got to go to her funeral. All these years had gone by, and he still hadn't had a chance to visit her grave."

De Gruy says that's when he realized something important that he and Brewer's other attorneys had been overlooking. "We were so busy trying to get Kenny out of prison, we had never really talked to him about Christine. It hit me that Kenny wasn't just a victim of a wrongful conviction; he was a victim of Justin Johnson, too. He was a victim of this crime just as much as anyone else in that little girl's life. And after all that had happened to him, he never really got the chance to heal."

It wasn't just the timing of the emotion that stuck with de Gruy, but the impetus for it. "Here's a guy who had never gotten angry over being wrongly convicted for killing this little girl. Never got angry about being put on death row. The one time he really broke down, it was because he never got to grieve for that little girl."

∼

When Brewer's lawyers asked the jury not to execute their client back in 1995, one of their pleas was that the jury allow Brewer to live—to return a sentence of life in prison—so that he might have the chance to someday test the biological evidence in the case. DNA testing, particularly in criminal cases, was at the time a relatively new concept. The technology was still young.

"Give an opportunity for technology to catch up," Brewer's lawyer pleaded with the jury. "If technology confirms your decision, he will remain in prison for the rest of his life. If technology decides that the sperm that were inside that little girl were not his, then he may be released."

The jury wasn't persuaded, but despite the best efforts of Governor Kirk Fordice, the *Clarion-Ledger* editorial board, and a good portion of the Mississippi legislature, Kennedy Brewer did live long enough for the technology to catch up.

But two critical, unrelated events separated by more than a decade had to occur for Levon Brooks and Kennedy Brewer to win their freedom. The first came in the spring of 1983, when Kary Mullis, a scientist at a California biotech company, was on his way to spend a weekend at his mountain cabin in Mendocino County, three hours north of San Francisco. Around mile marker 46 on Highway 128, Mullis had an epiphany. He pulled over and grabbed a pen and paper from the glove compartment. His girlfriend, Jennifer, was sleeping in the seat beside him. She woke up and wondered, somewhat annoyed, why they had pulled over in the middle of nowhere.

The drive had gotten Mullis thinking. Specifically, he had been thinking about oligonucleotides. Exactly what he was thinking about them isn't as important as what happened next: Mullis was on his way to discovering a process called polymerase chain reaction—PCR for short. It would revolutionize the field of DNA study. It would win him a Nobel Prize. And it would save the lives of Brooks and Brewer.

The second event occurred on June 13, 1994, with the murders of Nicole Brown Simpson and Ron Goldman in Los Angeles. Nicole's ex-husband, former professional football star O. J. Simpson, was eventually arrested and charged with the killings. DNA evidence found at both the crime scene and later at Simpson's house connected him to the murders. Simpson's attorneys reached out to Barry Scheck and Peter Neufeld, two former New York Legal Aid attorneys who had become leading legal experts in a niche practice area—what they referred to as the "intersection between science and the law." This was the newly emerging science of DNA testing.

After arriving in California to become part of Simpson's legal team, Scheck and Neufeld brought in Edward Blake, a DNA analyst in Richmond, California, to help with the blood evidence. It was the first of many times that Blake would help the two men exonerate an innocent person. Neufeld would later describe Blake's analytical prowess in baseball terms. "There are a bunch of .300 hitters, and then there's Ted Williams," Neufeld would say. "Ed Blake is Ted Williams."

DNA was first used to help solve crimes in the mid-1980s, when a British geneticist named Alec Jeffreys developed a technique to match a strand of DNA to a specific person. His technique was known as the "restriction fragment length polymorphism," or RFLP. But RFLP had some problems. The first was that there had to be a lot of DNA available for an RFLP test to be effective. But even under optimal conditions the procedure itself was cumbersome. Even with enough blood, it could be difficult to get consistent, conclusive results.

Kary Mullis's side-of-the-road revelation was about a process that would allow scientists to essentially take trace amounts of DNA, or DNA that had degraded, and reconstruct and reproduce it so that it could be analyzed. Ed Blake was a colleague of Mullis's in California. The two men began working with the FBI to explore how PCR could be used to analyze criminal evidence. They debuted their new technique in the late 1980s in Pennsylvania, in a macabre case in which a couple was accused of holding a man captive and starving him to death.

From there, PCR revolutionized the field of DNA science and its use in the criminal justice system. DNA testing would soon be used both to add certainty to new convictions and to free hundreds of people who had been wrongly convicted. It would also expose critical flaws in numerous fields of forensics once thought to be foolproof.

The primary mission of Brewer's attorneys in New York was to redo the DNA tests on the sperm. Analysis from the lab in New Orleans had cleared Brewer years earlier, but oddly suggested that two other men had raped Christine Jackson. After getting court permission to pursue additional DNA testing in 2007, Brewer's new legal team turned to Ed Blake.

Noxubee County law enforcement officials sent several boxes of physical evidence to Blake's lab in California. The lab began by retesting all of the evidence. The state's case began to crumble almost immediately. The police had found fecal material and semen on one of Christine's dresses recovered from the bedroom. Forrest Allgood had claimed at trial that this was evidence of a sexual assault, and referred to the bedroom as a "killing ground." Blake's tests showed that the material was indeed semen and fecal matter, and the semen was Brewer's. The fecal matter, though, was not from Christine. Instead it was from Gloria Jackson. This was consistent with Jackson's story—she had used the dress to wipe herself off after she and Brewer finished having sex. For some, that may have been evidence that Jackson and Brewer weren't model parents. But it was not evidence that Brewer had raped Christine Jackson.

Blake's lab tested the sperm sample next. It quickly discovered a mistake in the original testing from 2001. While they confirmed that the DNA profiles did not match Kennedy Brewer, Blake discovered that the earlier analysts were wrong to suggest that there were two male contributors. There was only one.

Brewer's lawyers were stunned at the news, but also knew they needed more. The state was still determined to try Brewer again. In the fifteen or so years of forensic DNA testing to that point, no one who had been excluded by DNA had ever been retried for the same crime. Forrest Allgood's determination was historically unprecedented. Other authorities were just as adamant, if not completely clear on what had happened. Deputy Earnest Eichelberger told the *New York Times* in 2007 that he hadn't used DNA to investigate and convict Brewer, seemingly suggesting that DNA couldn't therefore exonerate him.

While Allgood had tested the DNA profile from the crime against Brewer's two friends and several of his male relatives, he had yet to run it through the state's DNA database of criminal offenders. That seemed odd, given that a match not only might clarify whether Brewer played a role in the crime but might help apprehend one or even two child rapists and killers. Allgood told the *New York Times* he had never run the sample through the database because no such database existed in Mississippi. He was wrong. There was a database, and it had been up and running for years.

Fortunately for Brewer, by that time Allgood was no longer on the case. In March 2006, Allgood's office had hired one of Brewer's former attorneys. That presented a conflict for Allgood that forced him to remove himself from the case. Ben Creekmore, a district attorney from northwest Mississippi, took over as special prosecutor.

The only way to shake Brewer free from state prosecution once and for all would be to identify Christine Jackson's real killer. Ed Blake figured the most obvious place to start would be with whatever biological evidence might exist within the boxes of material included in the shipment from Noxubee County. When county law enforcement had transported the suspects to a local hospital back in 1992, a nurse swabbed their cheeks and preserved the swabs. Blake went to work on the swabs, extracting DNA profiles from each. After locating and isolating the useable DNA, he began his analyses. It didn't take long for him to match the profile developed from one of the swabs to the sperm found in Christine Jackson. The sperm belonged to Justin Johnson. After sixteen years, Christine Jackson's murder was finally solved.

The evidence boxes from Noxubee County also included a rape kit from Levon Brooks's case. Unfortunately for Brooks, what little DNA remained had degraded to the point where even Blake couldn't generate a usable profile. For now at least, Brooks was out of luck.

Brewer's lawyers bypassed Allgood and Noxubee County law enforcement with the news and, instead, approached the state attorney general's office. On February 5, 2007, state investigators traveled from Jackson to the Pilgrim's Rest community in Noxubee. They drove past Gloria Jackson's old house and took a left. Less than a quarter mile later they pulled up beside a small, green clapboard cottage. Several agents covered the rear of the house while two knocked on the front door. Justin Johnson answered. They confronted him with the DNA test results and placed him under arrest. He confessed to the murder and agreed to return with the investigators to the crime scene.

At Brewer's old house, Johnson showed the investigators how he walked up to the bedroom window, quietly opened it, saw Brewer asleep, reached in and lifted Christine, and removed her from the house. He then described how he sexually assaulted her, strangled her, and threw her, still alive, into the creek. He said he had acted alone.

The investigators then asked Johnson if he remembered committing any similar crimes. He did. It happened in Brooksville a few years before he murdered Christine Jackson. He remembered driving his car and parking near a pond. He described spotting Courtney Smith's house, opening the unlocked door, walking past a man sleeping on a couch, and entering the bedroom. He described abducting the little girl, assaulting her, killing her, and disposing of her body. He never bit either girl. Brooks was back in luck.

Ten days later, swarms of friends and family, state and local officials, and reporters packed the Noxubee County courthouse. Satellite trucks parked on the surrounding streets. Out front, someone dressed as Smokey Bear handed out saplings as part of a campaign to reforest the county.

Kennedy Brewer returned to the spot where he had once been condemned to die, surrounded by his new attorneys. Forrest Allgood sat off to the side, by himself, in the well of the courtroom. Peter Neufeld addressed the court at length about the case's many twists and turns, but the next day's *Clarion-Ledger* headline summed it up best: "Without DNA, He'd Be Dead."

Once he'd been informed of the results from Ed Blake's lab, special prosecutor Ben Creekmore raised no objection to the defense motion to exonerate Brewer. At court that day, he apologized to Brewer and his family: "Nothing I can say will give you back the time and loss."

With that, the judge turned to Brewer. The most recent exchange between the two men had been thirteen years earlier, when the same judge had set Brewer's execution date, following that with the words, "May God have mercy on your soul." This time, the judge said simply, "You're hereby discharged. You are free to go."

Levon Brooks's exoneration followed a month later, on March 13. Cumulatively, the two men spent over thirty years in prison. Though they had known one another before all of this, they never communicated in Parchman. Until the very end, neither knew that the same man had committed the crimes for which they each had been convicted.

Four years later, on April 9, 2012, Justin Johnson pleaded guilty to two counts of capital murder for killing Christine Jackson and Courtney Smith. He was sentenced to two consecutive life terms without the possibility of parole.

Ed Blake's rigorous work had saved Kennedy Brewer's life. His insistence on testing the remaining biological material—he felt that as a professional matter, "it just simply was something that had to be done"—also ended up saving Levon Brooks.

"There's the theory of how our criminal justice system should operate, and then of course there's the practice," he says. "Cases looked at individually can teach us things. Whether they do teach us anything is the debate. The Kennedy Brewer case can teach things. You can't say—it's not logical to say—that simply because the situation got corrected that that shows the strength of our system."

Blake's view is not widely shared, particularly by those who are best positioned to take stock, learn, and offer a sensible path forward. Forrest Allgood has said on numerous occasions that although the system failed in the Brooks and Brewer cases, it also worked. What he means, of course, is that all things considered, the net result was what the process aspired to in the first place: the identification and apprehension of the real perpetrator. In a 2008 letter to the editor defending his prosecutions, Allgood argued that the fact that Brooks and Brewer combined spent nearly three decades in prison for crimes that they didn't commit was nothing more than truth being the "daughter of time."

Allgood isn't alone in his thinking. The late Supreme Court justice Antonin Scalia believed the same thing. In a 2006 opinion discussing the intersection of an inmate's claim of factual innocence and the death penalty, Scalia wrote that "the possibility that someone will be punished mistakenly . . . is a truism, not a revelation."

For Scalia, Allgood, and many others, the moral hazards inherent in that position are worth the risk. But the risk is not an abstract one. It means people like Levon Brooks and Kennedy Brewer must spend time in prison—for Brooks, eighteen years, and for Brewer twelve, five on death row. Brooks was thirty-two when he was incarcerated, fifty when freed. Brewer was just eighteen when he was arrested; he was thirty-two when he got out. The two men spent their time in one of the most notorious penitentiaries on the planet. They missed births and deaths, graduations and weddings.

Both men missed their kids' entire childhoods. Shortly after his conviction, Brooks told the mother of his then-infant daughter, "Just go on with your life. Just go on with your life." Kennedy Brewer had a little boy at the time he was convicted. When Brewer was finally freed, his son, now a young man, drove his dad home from the courthouse.

It's worth noting that Forrest Allgood still believes in Kennedy Brewer's guilt and still seems to have a tough time stating definitively that Levon Brooks is innocent. In a 2017 email interview, he wrote, "Just because Brooks' or Brewer's DNA wasn't found in the victim's vaginal vault doesn't mean they didn't participate in the kidnapping/killing."

By the time Justin Johnson confessed, Allgood had been recused from Brewer's case but was still the prosecutor in Brooks's. In the same 2017 email interview, he explained why he didn't retry Brooks. "I made the decision not to retry Brooks only after talking to Ashley. Of course, it was 20 years after the fact and she was a young lady. She told me, 'Sometimes, I know exactly what I saw; then at other times, I'm not so sure.' That's not proof beyond a reasonable doubt, and that's why I didn't retry Brooks."

Brewer is another matter. "In short, they believed in DNA. I believed in my case," Allgood writes, referring to the courts and Brewer's attorneys. "The circumstances of the child's disappearance were powerful, and I would have retried Brewer had I been able to remain in the case."

Brooks's and Brewer's incarcerations spanned the better part of Forrest Allgood's time in the district attorney's seat. When asked in a 2011 documentary to reflect on the cases, Allgood pondered for a moment and then said, "No one died."

He of course was referring to the fact that neither Brooks nor Brewer was executed. But for a man who had claimed to be the voice, the shield, and the sword for victims of violent crime for his entire career, Allgood's comment was strikingly short-sighted. *Two* people died. Two little girls. And at least one of those deaths could have been prevented.

In May 2008, Mississippi governor Haley Barbour appointed Steve Simpson to head up the Mississippi Department of Public Safety. Privately, some of Hayne's critics in the state were optimistic about the appointment. The Brooks and Brewer exonerations prodded the legislature into finally budgeting money to hire a state medical examiner and staff—half a million dollars. Part of the money would come from the fee the state charged motorists who wanted NASCAR-themed license plates. Despite the funding, given the state's history with medical examiners, there was good reason to think that the most qualified candidates might be wary of the job.

Simpson was a Republican. A perch at DPS made him a possible future opponent of popular Democratic attorney general Jim Hood, one of Hayne's biggest public supporters. Perhaps most importantly, Simpson was from the Gulf Coast, where he had previously been a prosecutor and circuit court judge. The Gulf Coast was one of the few parts of the state Hayne never penetrated, likely because of geography—it's a three-hour drive from Bay St. Louis to Jackson.

That meant Simpson hadn't used Hayne when he was a prosecutor and probably hadn't seen him very many times as a judge, if at all.

Consequently, Simpson had little to lose in going after Hayne. And he may have had something to gain: it was an issue he could potentially leverage against Hood should he decide to challenge Hood for attorney general.

Simpson delivered, though at first reluctantly. On August 5, 2008, he removed Hayne from the list of doctors who could perform autopsies for Mississippi's prosecutors. Among Hayne's critics, there was some hope that Simpson would also announce a review of the doctor's thousands of cases. Instead, flanked by Mississippi lieutenant governor Phil Bryant and several state legislators and county coroners, Simpson announced that his main priority was to hire a new state medical examiner—the first in thirteen years. Until he could fill the position, the state would contract most of its autopsies to a private pathology firm in Nashville, Tennessee. The rest would be handled by a list of approved pathologists designated by Simpson's office. Simpson didn't mention Hayne by name in his opening statement, and during the question-and-answer period went out of his way to say that none of this was in reaction to the criticism of Hayne, or to the Brooks and Brewer exonerations. Later, he was quoted in the *Clarion-Ledger* thanking Hayne for his service. But it was obvious to anyone who had been paying attention what had just happened. On that list of designated pathologists, only Steven Hayne's name had been removed. Prior to the announcement, Simpson had sent Hayne a letter informing him that his name had been removed and that he could no longer perform autopsies in the state lab. He was the only person to receive such a letter. After twenty years, thousands of court cases, and upward of twenty-five thousand autopsies, Steven Hayne had just been fired.

Yet, Simpson publicly insisted that this *wasn't* what he was doing. Hayne would no longer be doing autopsies for state prosecutors, Simpson said, but "he has not been terminated." The next day, he invited Hayne to apply for the state medical examiner position. (Though Simpson surely knew that under state law, Hayne wasn't qualified to hold it.) Still there's no mistaking what had just happened. Prior to Simpson's announcement, Hayne had been doing about 80 percent of the state-ordered autopsies. After Simpson's announcement, he'd be doing none.

And yet Simpson's move still didn't bar Hayne from Mississippi's courtrooms. He would still be allowed to testify for the state in his backlogged cases, as well as any prior cases in which an appellate court might order a new trial. He could also continue to testify in civil cases and, should he want to, for criminal defendants. Two weeks later, the *Clarion-Ledger* reported that Hayne still had yet to issue reports for four hundred to five hundred autopsies. His *backlog* was twice the number of annual autopsies recommended by the National Association of Medical Examiners.

~

Hayne and West haven't been the only sources of forensic controversy in the United States. The problems with expert testimony have manifested in scandals all over the country. In Oklahoma City, crime lab analyst Joyce Gilchrist had earned the name "Black Magic" for her uncanny ability to find damning forensic evidence to link a suspect to a crime scene. She sent twenty-one people to death row, eleven of whom were executed before she was exposed in 2001. One of the men she had helped convict was later exonerated by DNA evidence. A subsequent investigation showed that Gilchrist had provided false evidence in a number of cases.

In West Virginia, crime lab analyst Fred Zain became a darling of the state's prosecutors with his ability to produce matches in difficult cases and then sell juries on those matches. Like Michael West, Zain won a reputation that soon landed him referrals from out of state. Zain was exposed when DNA testing cleared Glenn Woodall of a series of sexual assaults. It was the first ever DNA-based exoneration in the United States. Zain was later shown to have lied about his credentials and to have faked evidence in countless cases. A West Virginia Supreme Court report concluded that Zain may have caused the wrongful convictions of as many as 134 people.

In 2005, the state of Tennessee found state medical examiner Charles Harlan guilty on twenty counts of misconduct that included incompetence and tampering with evidence. He was stripped of his position and his medical license. The state's chief witness against Harlan was Bruce Levy, who replaced Harlan as state medical examiner and whose Nashville-based company inherited the bulk of Hayne's work in Mississippi. Incredibly, Levy would later be arrested in Jackson, Mississippi, on drug charges. He had allegedly received a package of marijuana while staying at a hotel. (Levy was put into a diversion program for first-time offenders, and his record was expunged. He's now back doing pathology work and is a respected medical examiner.)

In the years *since* Hayne's firing, more crime lab and forensics scandals have erupted all over the country, including at some of the most prestigious labs in the world. Since 2015 alone, there have been crime lab controversies in Houston; Austin; Orlando; Santa Clara County, California; San Francisco; Broward County, Florida; three different state police labs in Oregon; a state police lab in New Jersey; and a state lab in Ohio.

Some cities, states, and government agencies have reacted admirably, calling for immediate, thorough, and well-funded investigations to both uncover the extent of the damage and seek out and reverse wrongful convictions. In April 2017, for example, the state of Massachusetts threw out more than twenty-one thousand drug convictions after it was revealed that a lab analyst had been faking results for years. Others have been far less forthright and transparent. Few have implemented the sorts of changes needed to minimize cognitive bias, to ensure that incentives for analysts are structured to reward neutral fact finding, and to root out corruption.

For the better part of twenty years, Hayne performed approximately 80 percent of Mississippi's state autopsies and testified in a similar percentage of its homicide cases. In that sense, what happened in Mississippi may be the most wide-reaching scandal to date. Few states have encountered revelations that strike as forcefully at the very foundation of its criminal justice system. And few states' public officials have shown less concern or taken less action after having learned of the problem.

In fact, part of the problem may just be *how* profound it really is. Even for a judge or prosecutor who never used Hayne, to concede that it was a mistake to let him dominate the autopsy referrals all these years would be to acknowledge that the system to which they've dedicated their careers is profoundly and fundamentally flawed. Who would review all of those cases to see which may have been tainted? Who would be set free? Would every Hayne case be retried, or only those in which his testimony was crucial to the outcome? What about all the civil cases? What about the cases in which his autopsy results cleared cops or jail guards of deaths in their custody? Who would bear the expense for all of these reviews? To admit to the full extent of the problem would also potentially open up the state to massive liability, likely in the hundreds of millions of dollars, possibly more, never mind the collateral damage to the state's justice system generally.

Still, at least some officials have called for that. Ken Winter, the former director of the Mississippi crime lab and head of the state's police chiefs association, said so in a 2013 *Huffington Post* article. "I've been telling Jim Hood for years that this calls for [an] investigation into Steven Hayne and Michael West," Winter said. "At the very least, we need a bona-fide cold case unit that looks for cases like this. And it needs to be done by people with some integrity, people who are willing to look for open murders, but who will also look for cases where an innocent person may have been convicted."

But voices like Winter's have been rare, particularly when it comes to police and prosecutors. "This is a political problem, not a medical problem," says Vincent Di Maio, the renowned medical examiner and author of several forensic pathology textbooks. "The government needs to do the right thing. But doing the right thing could hurt political careers, subject people to lawsuits, and force people to admit to making mistakes. Governments are made up of people. And people don't like to put themselves in those positions."

By 2010 Mississippi Supreme Court justice Oliver Diaz had emerged as one of the most prominent critics of Hayne, and he did so from his perch on the state's highest court. In *Jones v. State*, he rejected Hayne's claim that the angle of bullet trajectory in a murder victim's body was consistent with being shot by someone across the street where police had found a beer can containing the defendant's DNA. As Diaz pointed out in his opinion, Hayne was not an expert in ballistics, and there were far too many variables for him to have reached that opinion. It wasn't the first time Hayne had offered such speculation. Diaz was the lone dissenter in that case.

The talkative, "proper Southern" Justice Diaz came to the court from the Gulf Coast, where a large portion of the state's plaintiff's bar is headquartered. After his election in 2000, he took some loans from a Democratic operative to pay off the debts he had incurred responding to attack ads. There was nothing illegal in that. But once judges are elected, they're supposed to recuse themselves from any cases involving a party with whom they have a personal or financial interest. In a state as small as Mississippi, it can be difficult to discern where to draw that line. That also can make it easy to draw connections to make a judge appear corrupt.

In 2003, Dunn Lampton, then a US attorney, indicted Diaz on allegations that he had tried to influence the court in a libel case involving the father of the man who gave him the campaign loan. As it turns out, the vote in that case was unanimous, and there was no evidence that Diaz had exerted any influence with other justices. Diaz was acquitted of the charges in 2005. But six days later, Lampton indicted Diaz again, this time on charges of tax evasion. The following year, Diaz was acquitted of those charges too. Lampton then filed a complaint against Diaz with the Mississippi Commission on Judicial Performance. That too was dismissed.

The charges against Diaz fueled existing allegations that the Bush administration was running a politically motivated Department of Justice. They also came during the national backlash against trial lawyers. And in this instance, they may have also been personal: the man Diaz beat in the 2000 campaign was Dunn Lampton's mentor. The late prosecutor's crusade against Diaz would later serve as the inspiration for John Grisham's book *The Appeal*.

Diaz was up for reelection in 2008. Even though he'd been twice acquitted by a jury and cleared by the judicial commission, he was still running as a justice who had been twice indicted. Fighting those charges also forced him to sit out a good portion of his term. The law-and-order group the LEAA pounced. They ran a ghastly TV ad accusing Diaz of voting in favor of two "baby killers" and a man who was later executed for beating a woman to death. All three allegations were gross distortions. One of the cases should sound familiar. "When a six-month-old child was raped and murdered," the menacing voice-over sneered, "Supreme Court Justice Diaz was the only one voting for the child's killer." The ad was referring to Jeffrey Havard.

The LEAA ad was condemned by a committee set up by the Mississippi Supreme Court to review judicial election procedures. Several television stations eventually pulled it off the air, although by then it had run statewide for at least a week.

Diaz eventually lost the election by sixteen points. His loss slowed any momentum that may have been building toward a proper review of Hayne's tenure in Mississippi. Diaz's last opinion was a dissent in a death penalty case. In it, he reflected on capital punishment and his own experience on the receiving end of the criminal justice system.

"My unique life experiences have shown me—to a greater degree, I submit respectfully, than any other justice voting today—the potentially oppressive power of government prosecution," he wrote. "Innocent men can be, and have been, sentenced to die for crimes they did not commit. In 2008 alone, two men—both black—convicted of murders in Mississippi in the mid-1990s have been exonerated. . . . One of these men, Kennedy Brewer, spent an astonishing six years on death row. Just as a cockroach scurrying across a kitchen floor at night invariably proves the presence of thousands unseen, these cases leave little room for doubt that innocent men, at unknown and terrible moments in our history, have gone unexonerated and been sent baselessly to their deaths."

Each year, the various innocence projects around the country gather together to discuss their work, learn about developments within the field, and socialize with colleagues. The group also invites all the exonerees from the previous year to attend, with all expenses paid. Levon Brooks and Kennedy Brewer received their invitations in 2008.

It was a surreal moment for both men. The conference was in Santa Clara, California, and neither had ever been on an airplane. In fact, with the exception of west Alabama, which borders Noxubee County, neither had ever been outside the state of Mississippi. Levon Brooks almost didn't make it. When Brooks returned home from prison, he had a difficult time tracking down his personal records, not an uncommon problem among exonerees who have spent years behind bars. Because the conference was just a couple of weeks after his release, Brooks hadn't had time to get a new photo ID. The Mississippi Department of Motor Vehicles refused to make an exception for him.

Fortunately, American Airlines was more forgiving. When notified of his predicament, the airline sent gate agents to meet Brooks at the airport. He presented them his Parchman Penitentiary identification badge—now expired—and they welcomed him onto the plane.

The two exonerees marveled at California. Neither had ever seen the ocean, so they gingerly waded into the Pacific—but not too far. They gazed in awe at the towering trees in Big Basin Redwoods State Park. They toured an art museum with the Innocence Project's Peter Neufeld. They bought new clothes. Brewer bought mirrored sunglasses. Brooks sported jeans still lined with the crease from the store shelf. They looked at sushi, then opted for something else. They politely tried craft beer, but quickly returned to their old standby: Bud Light. At one point they ran out of their favorite brand of tobacco dip and spent the better part of a morning hitting up convenience stores across Santa Clara until they found it. They also met Ed Blake, the man who helped set them free.

The entire adventure took place in Kary Mullis's backyard, just miles from where he had once pulled over along a stretch of Pacific Coast highway to ponder the thoughts that—all these years later—ignited the chain of events that ultimately brought Brooks and Brewer to California.

Outside the courts, Steven Hayne began to face mounting criticism from others in his profession. In 2008, members of both the College of American Pathologists and the National Association of Medical Examiners investigated complaints against him. The Innocence Project of New York also filed a complaint with the Mississippi Board of Medical Licensure, requesting that the board revoke Hayne's license. Dwalia South, the new president of the Mississippi State Medical Association told *Reason* magazine, "I don't know why Dr. Hayne is still a member of our organization. I'm going to try to get him booted. I can't believe he is allowed to take the stand and use our organization's name to boost his credentials. That isn't right. . . . What he's doing is unethical and unprofessional. It's malpractice."

There was more. The newspaper in Hattiesburg, the state's fourth-largest city, called for a comprehensive review of the cases in which Hayne had testified. And Louisa Dixon, the former public safety commissioner and crime lab director, wrote a long op-ed in the *Clarion-Ledger* criticizing Hayne and explaining why the state's death investigation system needed both a state medical examiner with a full staff and a dramatic overhaul.

One might think that after such criticism from such varied sources—not to mention the Brooks and Brewer exonerations—the state's prosecutors would be a bit chastened, and perhaps be reviewing their case files for other questionable testimony from Hayne or West. Perhaps, as had happened in other jurisdictions, they'd even work *with* a group like the Innocence Project to help uncover other possible wrongful convictions.

Not in Mississippi. In March 2008, the Mississippi Innocence Project and the Innocence Project of New York sent an open records request to every prosecutor in the state, asking for copies of reports of any autopsies Hayne had done for that office at the state crime lab. The attorneys for the organization weren't demanding that prosecutors reopen these cases; they were only asking for the records so they could conduct a review themselves.

The next day, Mississippi Prosecutors Association president Ben Creekmore—the same man who had apologized to Kennedy Brewer in the well of a Noxubee County courtroom—said he'd be advising all members of his organization to refuse the request. He told the Associated Press, "There are families all across the state of Mississippi who would be affected by the wholesale release of information related to the death of their loved ones."

Taking advantage of Mississippi's stingy open records law, the state's prosecutors followed Creekmore's advice. The rejection letters poured in. None of the state's twenty-two district attorneys complied, and sixteen sent letters denying the request. Most of the letters included boilerplate legalese about privacy, burdensomeness, and how their work product was exempt under the state's open records law. The latter, even if true, didn't bar them from turning over the reports; it only gave them the option to refuse.

Like nearly all the other district attorneys, Twelfth Circuit DA John Mark Weathers, whose jurisdiction included Michael West's own Forrest County, said he was unaware of any wrongful convictions in his circuit. However, he wrote, if the Innocence Project was aware of such a case, they should forward him the name of the victim, the name of the defendant, the date and place of the crime, the case number, and all other factual information so his office could investigate. He missed the point entirely. The purpose of the request was to review old cases to find possible wrongful convictions. If the Innocence Project lawyers had already been aware of a wrongful conviction, they'd almost certainly already have the autopsy report.

In 2010, two years after Weathers stated he was "unaware of any wrongful convictions" in his circuit, three men—Philip Bivens, Larry Ruffin, and Bobby Ray Dixon—were exonerated by DNA testing for a 1979 rape and murder in Forrest County. The DNA matched a man who had committed a similar crime in the county two years earlier. Ruffin died in prison in 2002. Dixon was released on medical parole in August 2010 but died a month before he was exonerated. Only Bivens lived to see his name cleared. Of course, Weathers had no role in those cases, nor did Hayne or West. And Weathers himself didn't oppose the DNA testing that cleared the three men. But that the exonerations came so soon after Weathers declared he knew of no such cases in his district only underscored how easily injustices could slip through the cracks.

In February 2009, the National Academy of Sciences released a long-awaited report on the state of forensics in America's courtrooms. The report was a broad denunciation of many fields of forensics commonly thought to be reliable. But it was particularly critical of bite mark analysis. The report found that bite mark analysis "is introduced in criminal trials without any meaningful scientific validation, determination of error rates, or reliability testing to explain the limits of the discipline." Analysts were too often provided with only a suspect and a few alternatives, which created the potential for "large bias." Blind comparisons were rare, and once law enforcement officials got the match they wanted, they rarely turned to a second analyst for confirmation.

The report's final paragraphs were its most critical. Despite the fact that practitioners felt that human skin could register and preserve enough detail from a bite to match it to someone's teeth, "no scientific studies support this assessment." The report added that its authors found "no evidence of an existing scientific basis for identifying an individual to the exclusion of all others."

The NAS report was widely expected to be a watershed event in forensics. But those predictions underestimated the intransigence of the status quo. Prosecutors continued to use and defend bite mark evidence around the country.

In the years since the NAS report, more reports from the scientific community have criticized bite mark evidence with increasingly strong language. In February 2016, the Texas Forensic Science Commission, which was formed after revelations that the state had executed an innocent man based on bad arson science, recommended a moratorium on bite mark evidence. And in September 2016, the President's Council of Advisors on Science and Technology (PCAST) not only found no scientific research to support bite mark comparison but also found "the prospects of developing bitemark analysis into a scientifically valid method to be low."

As of this writing, no court in American has upheld a challenge to the validity of bite mark evidence. Every defendant who has tried has lost.

While these reports have aimed their heaviest criticism at bite mark analysts, they've generally been critical of all the pattern-matching disciplines. The law enforcement community hasn't taken the criticism well. After the PCAST report was published, US attorney general Loretta Lynch dismissed it out of hand, and the Justice Department released a statement declaring that it had no intention of implementing the group's recommendations. This put President Barack Obama in an interesting position. His council of science advisors had strongly recommended reforms that his attorney general had just disavowed. The following December, Obama touted the PCAST report in an article for the *Harvard Law Review* about his administration's successes in criminal justice reform. What the article didn't mention: when it mattered most, Obama had sided with Lynch. The PCAST recommendations were never implemented at the DOJ.

This was particularly unfortunate because although the FBI crime lab has a reputation as one of the most elite labs in the world, the agency has its own troubled history with bad forensics. Only recently, the FBI admitted that its hair fiber analysts had been overstating their findings in courtrooms for two decades and over thousands of cases. To make matters worse, those analysts had trained hundreds of analysts at state and local crime labs across the country. Even after the FBI admitted its mistake, federal prosecutors did only the bare minimum to notify defendants whose convictions may have been affected by the tainted testimony.

Prior to that, the lab admitted that it had been wrong about bullet analysis. For years, the agency claimed that every batch of manufactured ammunition has a unique chemical signature. Therefore, if a bullet found at a crime scene matched the signature of bullets found in a suspect's home, the bullets could only have come from the same box. The theory was bogus.

The FBI had also botched its investigation of the anthrax attacks in 2001, leading to the wrongful arrest and persecution of Steven Hatfill, and had mistakenly matched a partial fingerprint taken from the 2004 Madrid train bombings to Oregon attorney Brandon Mayfield.

Given all of that history, Lynch's assertion that the DOJ didn't need to implement the PCAST reforms because the FBI had internal procedures to ensure it was using good science wasn't particularly reassuring.

Recent investigations, exonerations, and studies have also revealed scientific shortcomings in ballistics comparison, tire tread analysis, shoe print analysis, handwriting analysis, and even fingerprint matching. Shaken Baby Syndrome has come under scrutiny. Drug field test kits have been shown to have scandalously high rates of false positives, as have drug-sniffing dogs and dogs used to identify suspects based on scents taken from clothes or from the air.

One study published in 2013 found that, incredibly, crime lab analysts in many states *are paid per conviction*. Many labs are funded partially or even entirely by fees assessed to defendants, but only upon conviction. No conviction means no fee, and no fees mean less funding. In North Carolina, judges assessed defendants a $600 fee "upon conviction" to fund state and local crime labs. In Kansas, defendants were charged $400 for each conviction that required the use of the crime lab. Washington charged $100. In all, the study found that at least seventeen states (including Mississippi) at least partially funded their crime labs with money assessed upon conviction. Needless to say, funding crime labs with money assessed only after convictions is a dangerous way to get sober, objective analysis.

All of these could be classified as mistakes involving analysts who were well meaning but mistaken. Then there's another entire class of scandals involving analysts who faked their credentials, "dry-labbed" (a euphemism for faked) test results, or otherwise knowingly deceived jurors. A 2010 investigation of the North Carolina state crime lab revealed analysts' year-end reviews were conducted by prosecutors, who evaluated them on their ability to help win convictions.

Steven Hayne may have been fired, but he was far from finished. The Innocence Project's complaint against Hayne with the state's board of medical licensure was unsuccessful. The board said it was concerned that Hayne was performing too many autopsies, but it declined to take any action against him. The College of American Pathologists sealed its own investigation into Hayne—the entire process was conducted in secret. When it was over, the organization essentially punted. The group did send Hayne a "letter of concern" about the volume of autopsies he had been doing, but the ethics committee ultimately concluded that it lacked "sufficient evidence on which to base a finding that you are deficient in moral character or professional competence or guilty of professional misconduct," and therefore would take no further action. Hayne's attorney, Dale Danks, told the *Clarion-Ledger* that the group had "absolved" his client of "wild accusations."

The National Association of Medical Examiners (NAME) investigation went a little differently. According to a source involved in the investigation, Hayne was given a choice: either stand for an ethics inquiry or resign from the group. He chose to resign. According to Hayne, after a complaint was filed with the group, he demanded to know who filed it. NAME refused to tell him, so he resigned.

Perhaps emboldened by these professional organizations' decisions not to discipline him, Hayne and Mississippi's prosecutors and coroners began to fight back. In April 2009, Hayne filed a defamation lawsuit against the Innocence Project of New York and two of its attorneys. After a contentious deposition in that suit in 2012, Hayne accepted a settlement that was less than it would have cost to litigate the case. The Innocence Project of New York didn't retract its accusations against Hayne but cited the contract with its insurer. Danks again claimed vindication for his client, and this time said that Hayne "deserves credit" for helping exonerate Brooks and Brewer because Hayne had preserved the DNA from those cases.

That same year, Yazoo County coroner Ricky Shivers asked Mississippi attorney general Jim Hood to issue an opinion about an antiquated state statute that allowed adjoining counties to form their own "districts" for the purpose of administering autopsies. The old law was intended to help poorer counties pool resources to conduct murder investigations. Shivers wanted to use the law to allow adjoining counties to create such districts for the purpose of hiring their own medical examiner. Shivers later admitted—boasted even—that it was all an attempt to circumvent Steve Simpson and bring back Steven Hayne. On June 26, Hood's office issued an answer: go for it.

Just days after Hood's office released that opinion, Hayne began faxing copies of the opinion to sympathetic coroners around Mississippi. He followed up with a packet of information, including a copy of the legal forms necessary to form the new independent districts. Shivers said in an interview with *Reason* that eleven different coroners explicitly told him they had already taken steps to create renegade districts, solely so they could rehire Hayne, and that around twenty others indicated that they planned to do the same. "I've already done the paper work for Yazoo County," he said. "And it's already been approved by my board of supervisors."

DPS commissioner Simpson was livid at Hood for issuing the opinion. The ruling "is contradictory to a 1992 attorney general's opinion that says medical examiners must be approved by the Department of Public Safety," Simpson said in a 2012 interview. "I had heard that Hayne was soliciting coroners to set up these, 'independent districts' I guess they're calling them. . . . I would say to the coroners, this is not wise. Where are you going to do these autopsies? They won't be allowed to use the state lab."

Hood's move seemed to irritate Simpson so much that he started speaking more freely about Hayne. "To me, the most troubling thing about this is that these coroners and prosecutors want to use the services of a medical examiner who isn't board certified, who does way more autopsies than he should, and who wouldn't be subject to minimal standards and protocols," Simpson said at the time. "I would caution the district attorneys that whoever they get to do these autopsies, that person isn't going to be subject to any state law or oversight, and they're going to have to defend the results in court."

Of course, the lack of oversight was precisely the point. It was also the arrangement under which Hayne had operated for most of his career.

State representative Robert Evans, who had introduced the legislation to fund and hire a new state medical examiner the previous year, was also irritated by what Hood and the coroners had done. He warned that if the coroners' plan came to fruition, he'd seek new legislation to stop it.

Over the next few months, Hood and Governor Barbour began receiving letters of support for Hayne from law enforcement officials across the state. The overarching theme of the letters was that there couldn't possibly be any truth to the allegations against Hayne, because the prosecutors who wrote the letters had never heard complaints about Hayne—from other prosecutors. The president of the Mississippi Sheriffs' Association wrote to declare his support for Hayne as "an invaluable tool to law enforcement." Forrest Allgood wrote Barbour, too, though he confessed that he couldn't understand why his effort was even necessary. "Many accusations have been made against him of late," Allgood wrote, referring to Hayne. "It seems he works too hard, sleeps too little, and testifies too much. This is Mississippi. We are a poor state and we are all under staffed. I know I am. Consequently, we all have to do more."

District Attorney Jim Powell fretted over what he would do with all the homicide cases in his district for which he was preparing to call Hayne as a witness. Now defense attorneys were going to ask questions about Hayne's competence and credibility. Powell urged Barbour to reinstate Hayne. He also denounced the "propaganda" from the Innocence Project and expressed his displeasure that the taxpayers had to continue to fund it—a reference to the organization's affiliation with the University of Mississippi.

A few years later, attorneys from the Mississippi Innocence Project would help *solve* a grisly murder that had haunted a town in Powell's district for fifteen years. Through some diligence and communication with the state crime lab, the attorneys helped find the man who killed Kathy Mabry—a crime law enforcement had never been able to solve. In the late 1990s, the decision by local officials to ask West to examine Mabry's body had led to the arrest of the wrong man. That man remained in jail for a year before he was cleared by DNA testing. The case then went cold until the defense attorneys solved it in 2012.

At about the same time these letters arrived at the offices of Barbour and Hood, defense attorneys across Mississippi also received a letter from a newly formed company called Pathology Consultations Inc. The letter began: "We are pleased to announce that Steven Hayne, M.D. will be available immediately to assist criminal defense attorneys in the state of Mississippi."

Among his many other qualifications, the letter noted that Hayne is "board certified" in "Forensic Pathology."

⌒ 15 ⌒

NO RECKONING

The truth does not change according to our ability
to stomach it emotionally.

—Flannery O'Connor

⌒

Steven Hayne has maintained that most of the criticism directed at him is just cherry-picking. His defenders argue that he did tens of thousands of autopsies in Mississippi, and in the vast majority of them, no one complained about the quality of his work. Likewise, in the vast majority of the cases in which he testified, his testimony wasn't at all controversial. Even for those cases in which his testimony was challenged by other medical examiners, his conclusions were rarely dispositive of guilt. There was often plenty of other evidence against the accused.

There's a good deal of truth in all of these points. There's also a lot of truth in Hayne's contention that he was providing a service for Mississippi—that the state faced a critical shortage of medical examiners, and he was only doing what was asked of him. No one would doubt that Hayne put in long, hard hours of work, over many years. His schedule was grueling and would have quickly worn out just about anyone.

But it is also important to remember that all of this was by design. Hayne did approximately four out of every five autopsies in the state because that's the arrangement that Hayne and most of the state's DAs and coroners wanted and fought for. And as this book has shown, the workload itself was a huge part of the problem. Every medical examiner consulted for this book said that it's simply impossible to perform anywhere near that volume of autopsies with the care, precision, and best practices required of the profession. When confronted with these opinions, Hayne has simply insisted that he isn't your average medical examiner. In the past, noted medical examiner Michael Baden, a personal friend of Hayne's, has criticized Hayne in individual cases, but has defended Hayne's professionalism and credibility in the press and in affidavits.

Yet in many of the cases documented in this book, cases where Hayne's testimony *was* critical to the outcome of a case, his approach to the work appears to have been less, rather than more, rigorous, and was at times characterized by a willingness to testify outside of his expertise, and to draw conclusions that have little basis in science.

Hayne has also pointed out in testimony that some of his critics have themselves been embroiled in scandal. After his death, for example, Louisiana medical examiner George McCormick was shown to have signed off on autopsies he didn't do. Thomas Bennett, the second state medical examiner in Mississippi, has come under fire after a series of Shaken Baby Syndrome diagnoses in Iowa and Montana. (Bennett preceded Hayne, and was a critic of the Mississippi system, not of Hayne in particular.) Georgia state medical examiner and longtime Hayne critic Kris Sperry retired in 2015 after a newspaper investigation found he was billing the state for time he spent testifying as a private consultant. (Interestingly, among the criticisms of Sperry were that he had a caseload that ranked "among the highest in the country." But that investigation found that between public and private, Sperry had performed or reviewed 366 autopsies over a four-year period—a total Hayne regularly cleared in a month.)

Hayne views his role in the Brooks and Brewer cases as minimal. In filings for the lawsuit filed against him by the two exonerees, Hayne's attorney argues that Hayne is not responsible for either conviction—that he never stated that the marks on the victims were human bites (he only suspected as much), and that it was West, not Hayne, who made the identifications that implicated Brooks and Brewer. In his 2012 deposition for his own lawsuit against the Innocence Project of New York, Hayne made similar comments. He said he was "suspicious" that the marks on the girls were human bites, he said, "but that was beyond my expertise." But Hayne's autopsy report on Courtney Smith clearly stated that there were bite marks on the girl.

Likewise, Hayne's testimony in the Brewer case belies his claim that only West—and not he—ever stated that the marks on the girl were human bites. At Brooks's trial, Forrest Allgood asked Hayne to draw on his training and expertise after having examined "thousands of bodies" to state "to a reasonable medical certainty whether or not these marks that you found on this child's body that you perceive could very well be bite marks, [or] whether or not they were the result of insect activity?"

Hayne replied, "I did not think that they were insect bites."

Hayne has also tried to further distance himself from Michael West more generally. In his 2012 deposition for his lawsuit against the Innocence Project of New York, Hayne said he thought the "West Phenomenon" was "a little excessive." He also claimed that he tried to convince West that the ultraviolet method needed to be proven effective and reliable by a scientific study. West wouldn't comply, so "I stopped using it. I wanted to see a scientific study." Yet at the same time, he insisted, "I didn't have doubts" about his prior uses of the technique, because "it's an old process," but he added, "but I think if you introduce in a court of law, you have to have a scientific study where you can show error rates." Those statements are hard to reconcile. Hayne's efforts to distance himself from West are also hard to reconcile with the fact that the two men coauthored articles together on the technique, marketed the technique, and that Hayne employed West well after West's methods had been widely criticized. Hayne has also admitted that he himself has used West's highly controversial method of pushing a suspect's dental mold directly into the victim's skin.

Hayne also said in that deposition that he no longer trusts bite mark analysis in general. "I would be very reluctant to call in a forensic odontologist to do a bite mark comparison study," he said. "It's not a fingerprint. It's not DNA." With these statements, and his statements in the Jeffrey Havard case, Hayne seems to acknowledge the use of bad science during his time in Mississippi, and that injustices may have occurred as a result. But other than conceding in Havard that he (and a lot of others) may have been wrong about Shaken Baby Syndrome, he has yet to acknowledge his own culpability in any of it.

~

As the rebelling coroners and prosecutors planned their mini-coup against the Department of Public Safety, state representative Robert Evans made good on his promise of a legislative response. In early 2010, he and other state lawmakers introduced a bill that required any doctor performing an autopsy for the state of Mississippi to be both board certified in forensic pathology by the American Board of Pathology and deemed qualified by the Department of Public Safety. When the bill unanimously passed the state senate, Hayne and Hood sprang into action and began lobbying state representatives to defeat it.

Hood disseminated an email calling the bill an "Innocence Project bill which threatens cases which involved Steven Hayne," and promised, "Our office is working diligently to stop this potentially harmful legislation." Among other things, Hood's lobbying clearly suggested that so long as he was in the attorney general's office, there would be no serious review of old cases to find other potentially innocent people Hayne's testimony may have helped convict.

In public, Hood's office insisted that he took no position on the bill. He couldn't support the bill: it thwarted his behind-the-scenes effort to bring back Hayne. But to oppose a bill requiring that doctors who perform state autopsies be certified by the group widely recognized as the gold standard in forensic pathology might raise some eyeballs. So Hood remained neutral on the bill in public, even as he privately lobbied to kill it.

The Mississippi legislature passed the bill anyway, by a vote of 91 to 31. Governor Haley Barbour signed it into law.

Several months after the new bill passed, Hayne received a letter from his old friends at the American College of Forensic Examiners Institute (ACFEI), congratulating him on his newly achieved status of "Certified Forensic Physician," a position that, according to the group's website, "holds an integral role in determining the outcome of many important court cases." The cost for the new certification: $869.

In what appeared to be a last-gasp attempt to get back in the game, in May 2010 Hayne sent a letter to the Mississippi attorney general's office inquiring whether his new ACFEI certification (which was still pending at the time), along with his "re-certification" from the "American Board of Forensic Pathology," fulfilled the requirements of the new law. A state legislature could and should require some minimum qualifications before allowing someone to perform autopsies paid for by the state. Here, the legislature had made its intent pretty clear. Hood's office had no choice but to tell Hayne that his request would ultimately be answered by the Department of Public Safety. And DPS commissioner Simpson had already made his intent clear. All of which meant that the challenges, schemes, and appeals had come to an end. Hayne was finally finished doing autopsies for the state of Mississippi.

A more daunting task remained: a thorough accounting of the damage and persuading state officials to fix it.

"I wish now that I had been more courageous," says Edwin Pittman, the former chief justice of the Mississippi Supreme Court. "A couple of those old cases embarrass me now. We should have been less accepting of Hayne and that culture."

Pittman, now in his early eighties, retired from the court in 2004. He has likely held more high state offices than anyone in Mississippi's history. Before joining the court in 1989, he had been a state senator, state treasurer, secretary of state, state attorney general, and brigadier general in the Mississippi National Guard.

Pittman's tenure on the court began just as the careers of Steven Hayne and Michael West were taking off, and lasted through all but the tail end of their dominance of the state's death investigation system. As a justice, he reviewed forty-six cases in which Hayne was a witness, second only to justices Chuck McRae and James Smith. He didn't throw out Hayne's testimony in any of them.

To be fair, Pittman was on the court as Hayne became ingrained in the state's criminal justice system, and he retired before there had been much public criticism of Hayne. Defendants had only challenged Hayne's testimony in a few of the cases Pittman heard while he was on the bench. Still, Pittman himself relied on Hayne while he was attorney general. He defended convictions that had been won based on Hayne's testimony. He now says he wishes that he and his colleagues had been more skeptical: "There could be a herd mentality on the court—there was always a strong majority of justices that were just always accepting of prosecutors and expert testimony."

"At the time," he says, "Mississippi had no state medical examiner, so there was no one backing up, verifying the work Hayne and West were doing. All the DAs believed in Hayne. We probably had more confidence and trust in the DAs than we should have—more than I do now."

After retiring, Pittman grew increasingly alarmed as additional information came out about Hayne's record—and Mississippi officials' reaction to the revelations. His thoughtfulness and willingness to speak out are as courageous as they are rare. "What ultimately shocked me were the numbers of autopsies that Hayne was doing. When you see those kinds of numbers, you realize that they're impossible." He adds that Hayne's personality is probably why he was able to elude criticism longer than West.

Pittman bears more responsibility for his role in enabling West. The feisty dentist was directly challenged several times while Pittman was on the court. In fact, Pittman heard eight cases involving West's testimony. Only two other justices heard more.

Pittman upheld West's testimony in all but one of those cases, and in that case (the Bologna Sandwich Case), he voted with the majority, who faulted West not for claiming he could "exclude" or "include" people as sources of the bites in the partially eaten sandwich, but for destroying the evidence. Pittman most regrets his 1997 majority opinion in the Levon Brooks case, which upheld West's testimony, Brooks's conviction, and the life sentence. "Looking back, I can't believe that I bought into all of that—that I believed West's 'science' was really science. I wish I had voted differently."

Pittman says there was a strong pro–death penalty culture on the court in the 1990s. Part of that culture was driven by ideology. "There was a sense that if a death penalty case came to us, that that was the jury's decision, and it ought not be interfered with," he says. Since then, he has learned how bias can limit how authorities view those cases. "Experience eventually taught me that it really began with the DA. Once the DA decided he was going to seek the death penalty, it was really all downhill from there."

Pittman recalls a couple of DAs who were careful about when they sought death for a murder suspect. But others sought death in nearly *every* murder case. The death penalty wasn't being applied based on the merits of the case or the seriousness of the crime, but on the politics and aggressiveness of the local prosecutor.

Five years after retiring from the court, Pittman, now a lawyer, filed a post-conviction petition on behalf of a man who had been convicted partly as a result of questionable testimony from Steven Hayne. In the brief, Pittman made the same arguments many others had before him. Pittman's former colleagues unanimously rejected the petition.

$\sim$

"I'm not a finance person," Steven Hayne once said in a deposition. "I'm a physician and I never paid that much attention, you know, to the finances."

If Hayne was doing around 80 percent of Mississippi's public autopsies over the span of fifteen to twenty years, he grossed well over $10 million from taxpayers during that span. To complicate matters, in 2014 Hayne's former business partner Cecil McCrory was indicted for a bribery and kickback scheme involving officials at the state's Department of Corrections. McCrory has held a number of public offices in Mississippi, including state representative, county commissioner, sheriff's department investigator, school board chairman, and local justice court judge. Hayne wasn't implicated in the investigation that ultimately sent McCrory to prison, but his longtime partnership with a man now serving time, their unusual business arrangement, their opaqueness about the business, and McCrory's contacts in state government raise some legitimate public interest questions.

In 1991 McCrory started a company called Investigative Research. McCrory himself had been certified in fire investigations (another area of forensics heavily criticized in recent years as it has been subjected to scientific scrutiny), and most of his early clients were insurance companies that hired him to investigate claims for possible arson. At the same time, he was serving as a state legislator and was chairman of PEER, the legislature's oversight committee structure that investigated official corruption. It was also the committee that issued reports critical of the state's death investigation system in 1988 and again in 2008, reports that urged the state to stop contracting autopsies out to private doctors—though neither report was published while McCrory was on the committee.

When Hayne joined Investigative Research around 1995, the company started taking on pathology consultations as well. (The word "company" might give the wrong impression—the staff usually consisted of McCrory, Hayne, and perhaps an administrative assistant or two.) McCrory processed the money Hayne made from consulting in civil cases. Once the arrangement had been set up, when opposing counsel would ask Hayne questions about his income in such cases, he'd often simply defer to McCrory. In criminal cases in particular, defense attorneys rarely had the time or the inclination to follow up by subpoenaing McCrory or his records.

After losing his seat in the legislature in 1996, McCrory also began lobbying his former colleagues on behalf of both the coroners' association and the sheriffs' association—two groups whose members had enormous influence over the assigning of autopsies, and thus would have been of particular interest to Hayne.

It's difficult to ascertain the exact nature of Hayne and Mc-Crory's business relationship, except to say that it was odd. According to sworn testimony from both men, McCrory handled all the money, did all the paperwork, and kept all the records from Hayne's consultations in private cases. He then deposited the money from Hayne's clients into a slush fund, from which he wrote checks at Hayne's request. While the money was Hayne's to do with as he pleased, according to McCrory, Hayne never had access to the account himself. He always had to go through McCrory. According to McCrory, at any given time, the account balance would be around $50,000 to $60,000.

It also isn't clear what position Hayne held at IR. For most of the 1990s, Hayne testified that he was a partner at the firm. In 2001 he testified that McCrory owned 100 percent of the company—meaning that his testimony in who knows how many cases until that point had been mistaken. In 2003, Hayne went back again. When asked who owned the company, he replied, "Technically, Cecil McCrory and myself." McCrory testified in 2012 that Hayne didn't own—and had never owned—a stake in the company.

According to McCrory, during Hayne's most lucrative years in the early 2000s, he was bringing in $250,000 per year for Investigative Research, although in a 2005 deposition Hayne claimed he was billing half that much.

Yet McCrory and Hayne have insisted in sworn testimony that Hayne made almost no money from his civil cases. Testifying at a deposition, for example, Hayne claimed that "zero percent" of his income came from civil cases. (Odder still, he said in the same deposition that just "5, 7, 8 percent" of his income came from criminal cases.) Hayne repeatedly made similar claims. He has often said that he made no money from IR, save for $1,000 every five years. He has claimed his accountant told him the IRS requires this minimum amount so that his consulting isn't classified as a hobby. It isn't clear what Hayne meant by that. When McCrory was asked about this alleged IRS rule in a 2012 deposition, he replied, "I don't know what he's talking about."

Despite Hayne's claims, McCrory at times paid him sums much larger than $1,000. When asked about a $25,000 check he received from the company in the 1990s, Hayne said it was reimbursement for a conference room that a local hospital had been letting him use. But McCrory also cut him four more checks of $25,000 to $34,000 in 2007 and 2008. Hayne has never been asked about those. When McCrory was asked under oath, he replied, "I don't have a vague recollection of why I did that." Hayne has testified that he left Investigative Research in the "early part of two thousand." McCrory has testified that Hayne left in 2008.

When asked where all of the money went, if not to him, Hayne has repeatedly testified that he gave it all away—to pay for office equipment and salaries, to students, and to various charities. But when asked to produce records of all of these transactions, he has claimed that they've been destroyed or that he entrusted all his record keeping to McCrory, to his accountant, or to his ex-wife.

Though both Hayne and McCrory have claimed that Hayne was enormously generous, both say he also gave away his money in ways that didn't create a paper trail. Hayne frequently claimed to give lots of money to charity, but he rarely named any specific charitable organizations. Instead, he has said that he engaged in more individualized charity, the kind that leaves no public record. According to McCrory, about "90 percent" of the "charitable donations" Hayne made were to "kids going to college." How did Hayne find these kids? "They seemed to find him. Once somebody tells that they got a contribution or donations for books . . . word gets around. He had more requests than he had money."

In 2012, Hayne and McCrory claimed that Hayne sometimes even paid these students' full tuition. Both claimed that Hayne once bought a student a car and sent another to Europe. McCrory testified that Hayne also often gave money to someone simply because McCrory requested it. "I actually have asked him to donate to some people who I would come across who just, you know, were—didn't have any food or whatever in the house. And he—he never questioned it. He was always supportive of that," McCrory said.

All of this certainly seems extraordinarily kind. Yet between them, Hayne and McCrory couldn't remember the names of a single recipient of such generosity. When asked in 2012, Hayne had vague recollections of his connections to at least two students he had helped, but couldn't recall their names. And yet some have said he has an incredibly precise, almost photographic memory.

Hayne did remember that he always made checks out to the students themselves, not the educational institutions. He said the reason for this was that he didn't want the students to think he didn't trust them. That also meant that the college or university would have no record of his check. When asked in 2012 to name the last time he had made such a gift to a college student, Hayne hesitated, then said it was probably in the late 1990s. He was later shown a 2004 deposition in which he claimed that at that time he was putting a student through college.

Hayne also periodically paid West to work for him, sometimes at Jimmy Roberts's morgue, sometimes at Investigative Research. Hayne at one time loaned West a lot of money, apparently to help pay off a tax bill, and may have asked West to work it off by assisting him with his autopsies. Over the years, Hayne has often claimed he netted very little money from his autopsies, citing his obligation to pay for administrative staff and supplies. But when challenged on exactly *who* paid those expenses on his behalf, he has said he isn't sure. He isn't even sure who sent his staff their tax forms.

One former coroner said he didn't know what "the fiduciary deal was between Hayne, West, and Roberts," but "Mike West was always around when Hayne did autopsies. . . . Once, Hayne brought West over when he did an autopsy for me here. Then I got a bill from West for consulting. I refused to pay it, and I told Steve never to let that happen again." Another coroner says he refused to work with Hayne so long as West was present at Hayne's autopsies. "I was always pretty sure that West was hiding in the back room at Mississippi Mortuary. . . . I knew he was there even if you couldn't see him."

Hayne has often testified that for most of his career, he didn't worry about money because his wife handled all of their financial affairs—personal and business. "My wife, Ann, was a meticulous person with all the finances," he said in 2012. "She could tell me how many socks I bought each month for the last 15 years."

When Ann Hayne herself was asked about her ex-husband's finances by a private investigator for the Innocence Project in 2012, she said that while she was certain that Hayne, West, and Roberts had some sort of financial partnership, "you won't find it in writing. I looked."

By his own testimony and that of his business associates, then, Hayne made little to no effort to track who owed him money, how much money he made, whom he paid to help him (and how much), and to whom he lent and gave money. All of his financial affairs were apparently handled by either his wife, Ann (until they divorced), Cecil McCrory, Jimmy Roberts (though both deny they ever had a business relationship), or his accountant. But all of those people to varying degrees have disagreed with both Hayne and one another on the specifics of how Hayne's finances were handled.

Figuring out Hayne's total income over the years can also be a difficult task. But it's possible to at least make some estimates based on his testimony. Hayne has testified that he made about $170,000 per year from his position at the renal lab, and that his compensation for his work at Rankin Medical Center ranged from $140,000 a year when he started to $200,000 a year when he left. He was also bringing in $150,000 to $300,000 per year from his consulting work on private cases. Of course, the bulk of Hayne's income came from state autopsies and the work associated with them, and at the height of his career he was grossing well over $1 million per year from those. Taken together, Hayne's work grossed in the neighborhood of $1.5 million to $2 million per year, not including what he made for serving on various boards and holding various titles at hospitals, medical research facilities, and start-ups.

Hayne's lifestyle certainly reflected that sort of income. According to divorce records, when Hayne and his second wife, Tonia, split in 2008, the couple owned several nice automobiles and three properties, including a six-thousand-square-foot house valued at $1 million, and eighty-one acres in Rankin County. Over the course of their short marriage, Hayne spent over $317,000 at the Lee Michaels jewelry store. After his divorce from his first wife, Ann, Hayne began paying her $150,000 per year in alimony.

And then there are the records themselves. Hayne, West, and McCrory have apparently lost or destroyed most of their financial records, personal records, autopsy records, and correspondence with police and prosecutors over the years. Hayne said in his 2012 Innocence Project deposition that most of his records from civil cases were destroyed when a pipe burst and flooded his home. As for his autopsy records from criminal cases, he said he had transferred all of those to the state crime lab.

Michael West has had similar problems. When asked in recent depositions to bring all records he still had from all of the cases in which he had consulted or testified, West brought in only his CV. According to West, some of his records were destroyed after he stored them in a friend's barn and the barn subsequently burned down. Others were destroyed by Hurricane Katrina. Any that remained had been thrown out by his wife. West also said he kept no backup files of the photographs he took for his cases. He has said he failed to back up any of his data and lost more of his records when each of his three hard drives crashed. Like Hayne, West also dismissed his foggy memory about finances by citing his lack of interest in such matters. When asked a question about Jimmy Roberts's finances, West replied, "If you look in this CV, you will never see the word *accountant*."

It's a similar story with Cecil McCrory. When deposed by the Innocence Project in 2012, McCrory said he had only kept documents from Investigative Research going back to 2009, one year after he says Hayne left the company. As for the donations Hayne had made to students and charitable organizations, McCrory said the only record he made of them was in the registry for the checkbook for Hayne's account, and he had thrown that out years ago. McCrory also had none of Hayne's tax returns, nor any of the company's tax records from the years of Hayne's employment. He also had no transcripts of Hayne's trial testimony in the cases for which Investigative Research had been paid for Hayne's services.

McCrory was indicted by federal prosecutors in 2014. According to the initial indictments, McCrory had started several new companies, and through them had paid nearly a million dollars in bribes to Mississippi Department of Corrections commissioner Christopher Epps in exchange for Epps awarding no-bid contracts to McCrory's clients and businesses, including Investigative Research. The indictments later expanded to include more people and allegations of fraud affecting over $800 million in corrections contracts. According to federal officials, Epps and McCrory were the two central figures in the massive scheme. In February 2017, McCrory was sentenced to eight and a half years in prison.

Hayne wasn't implicated in any of his former business partner's shady dealings with the state's prison system. But he has said that he was personally affected by McCrory's indictment. "I feel just horrible that this has happened," he told the *Clarion-Ledger*. "It makes me sick to my stomach."

Hayne may have finally been barred from doing state autopsies in Mississippi, but with just a few exceptions, the state's public officials seem uninterested in revisiting his old cases. Attorney General Jim Hood has arguably possessed the most power to order a thorough review of Hayne's previous work. At the very least, Hood could have told his staff to halt pending prosecutions until he could find other medical examiners to review Hayne's testimony and autopsy reports. After all, we now know that two men have been wrongly convicted of rape and murder. One of them was nearly executed. And a little girl died whose death might have been prevented. Perhaps *some* introspection was in order. Instead, within weeks of the Brooks and Brewer exonerations, Hood took to the press to defend Forrest Allgood. Hood called Allgood a "straight arrow" who "always played it by the rules." That comment didn't age well. Two years later, Allgood and Judge James T. Kitchens were upbraided by a federal judge for allowing false testimony in a separate death penalty trial.

Hood also continued to publicly defend Hayne. In 2010, he tried to refute the allegation that Hayne shilled for prosecutors by telling the *Sun Herald* that Hayne had testified for the defense in some cases Hood had personally prosecuted. But the public record of cases for which Hayne had testified for the defense prior to his termination *at all* is spare. And there's no appellate court opinion in any case in which Hood was the prosecutor and Hayne testified for the defense. That doesn't necessarily mean that it never happened, but if it did, it was rare. When Hood's office was asked for a list of such cases, no one responded.

Hood later took a slightly different line on Hayne and West. In a 2011 interview with the *Jackson Free Press*, Hood claimed he had never publicly defended Hayne. He also told the paper that Michael West "is someone we have investigated, and I don't support him in any matter."

He was being duplicitous. At the very same time that he made those statements, Hood's office was arguing in cases like Leigh Stubbs and Eddie Lee Howard that the defendants were procedurally barred from challenging West's credibility. Publicly, Hood was admitting that West wasn't a credible witness. Less publicly, his office was simultaneously arguing legal technicalities to keep people in prison—and on death row—who had been convicted because of West's testimony.

Hood has steadfastly refused to consider a task force or any broad review of Hayne's work. In a 2011 TV interview, he did claim that his office had opened an investigation into twenty cases involving Michael West. But when asked for a list of those cases, or even the name of the attorney who was heading up the investigation, the office responded, "We can not release any of the information you are requesting at this time." Hood is one of the most PR-savvy attorneys general in the country. He has never been shy about trumpeting his accomplishments. He often holds press conferences to announce new initiatives and major investigations. Yet here, his office has been suspiciously quiet.

A few months after Hood's statement about investigating West, in a hearing for the Leigh Stubbs case, an assistant attorney general from Hood's office was asked who was running the alleged investigation of Michael West. The assistant attorney general replied that *he* was. When asked about the status of the investigation, he replied that he had done no more than a Westlaw search on West's name—the legal equivalent of a Google search. As of this writing, Hood's office has offered no new information about any investigation into Michael West.

Still, Hood's obstinacy about Hayne and West has never hurt him at the polls. In January 2011, DPS commissioner Steve Simpson announced that he'd challenge Hood for attorney general. By the time the campaign was in full swing, Simpson had not only fired Hayne but also appointed Mississippi's first state medical examiner in sixteen years—Mark LeVaughn, a forensic pathologist from Buffalo, New York.

"I hired Mississippi's first state medical examiner in more than a decade. Jim Hood fought me on that," Simpson said in the August before the election. "I'd be delighted for this to become a campaign issue."

In the end, it didn't matter much. Simpson didn't really push Hayne, West, and death investigations as a campaign issue, and neither did the press. As a Republican running for statewide office in Mississippi, calling for a review of thousands of murder convictions was probably never going to be a winning campaign issue for him. By Election Day, most of the press and public were more interested in a mini-scandal over Simpson's request to be reimbursed for a $400 dinner he and some colleagues had eaten at a steakhouse two years earlier. Hood went on to clobber Simpson by twenty-two points.

The courts were more of a mixed bag. In the 2011 case *Gause v. State*, the Mississippi Supreme Court finally showed some signs of movement when it came to Hayne, but these were still only the tiniest of fissures. The justices found that while the court had previously found Hayne to be qualified to testify as a forensic pathologist, "that should not be taken as eternal, nonexpiring judicial anointment of Dr. Hayne as an expert pathologist for all of time and in every case in which he might thereafter be tendered to offer expert testimony."

That at least was something. Yet when it was time to vote, the court still rejected the challenge to Hayne in that case, too, because it found that the defense attorneys hadn't sufficiently challenged Hayne's credibility at trial.

In March 2013, the court finally threw out Hayne's testimony for a second time. In a unanimous decision, the justices ordered a new trial for David Parvin, a former Mississippi State University professor, who had been convicted of killing his wife. In that trial, Hayne testified that he could tell by the shot pattern in Joyce Parvin's skin that the gun that killed her was fired at shoulder height, not at waist height as Parvin had claimed. Despite never inspecting the gun, or even knowing what type of shotgun it was, Hayne also said he could tell by the shot pattern in Joyce's skin that the gun had been fired from four feet away, again contradicting David Parvin's story.

The state supreme court didn't buy it. With unusually pointed criticism, the court ruled that Hayne's testimony was "woefully short of the requirements for admissibility." Furthermore, the court ruled that "the speculative 'expert' opinions" should never have been put before a jury.

The court also seemed to be onto Hayne's tactic of writing vague autopsy reports, then elaborating on the fly at trial. Quoting Parvin's brief, the court noted that the measurements in Hayne's autopsy report were made "without comment, explanation, or support," and none of these measurements could be "determined by the autopsy report or any of the related scientific tests." Hayne had waited until trial to spring those details on the defense, as he'd done many times before. This time, the court called him on it.

Hayne and a few of the prosecutors who regularly used him often engaged in a misleading and manipulative use of hypotheticals. This isn't uncommon, but Hayne and some prosecutors were particularly deft at it. A prosecutor might ask Hayne if a crime *could* have happened in a way that contradicted the testimony of or otherwise implicated the accused. Hayne would reply in the affirmative. The prosecutor would then tell jurors in his closing argument that Hayne's testimony was proof of the defendant's culpability or evidence that the defendant's version was implausible. If challenged during cross-examination or later criticized, Hayne could always point out that he was merely responding to a hypothetical, or that he had merely said his findings were "consistent with" the hypothetical, not that he thought the crime could only have occurred that way. How prosecutors then used his answer in their closing arguments, in other words, wasn't his responsibility.

The majority opinion in *Parvin* points out that using Hayne's measurements and observations, prosecutors concocted a "possible scenario" of how the shooting occurred. Though there was no scientific evidence to suggest that particular scenario was certain—or even probable—the jury was nonetheless shown a detailed computer animation based only on Hayne's approximations—which Hayne then affirmed in his testimony. The court noted that "the only scientific method or principle appearing in the record was the *ipse dixit* or self-proclaimed accuracy of Hayne."

~

In the few years leading up to the *Parvin* decision, the Mississippi Innocence Project had been compiling a long and comprehensive dossier on Hayne, which attorneys for the organization then used to file appeals or post-conviction petitions. Parvin's case was one of those still on appeal. But for those who had exhausted their state appeals, the federal courts were the only remaining option. The problem is that absent a DNA test, it has become nearly impossible to get a federal court to order a new trial.

Under the 1996 Antiterrorism and Effective Death Penalty Act (AEDPA), in order for a federal court to order a new trial on the basis of new evidence, a defendant must show that (a) there is new evidence, (b) that evidence could not have been discovered at the time of trial, (c) the petition has been filed within one year of when the new evidence could reasonably have been discovered, and (d) the new evidence would likely have altered the jury's verdict.

It's an exceedingly high bar, and the Tavares Flaggs case illustrates just how high it is. After the Mississippi Supreme Court denied Flaggs's post-conviction relief, his lawyers with the Mississippi Innocence Project went to federal court, backed by their new dossier on Hayne. (Flaggs is the case in which Hayne had contradicted the defendant's self-defense claim with speculative blood spatter testimony based on photos of discoloration on a wall near the crime scene.) In January 2014, a three-judge panel for the US Court of Appeals for the Fifth Circuit turned Flaggs down with a curt, four-paragraph opinion.

Flaggs had based his claim on revelations from the 2012 deposition that Hayne had given in his lawsuit against the Innocence Project. The court wasn't impressed. The judges wrote that Hayne "had been widely and publicly criticized for several years before the 2012 deposition and certainly before the filing of Flaggs's first application in 2011. Indeed, the deposition merely revisits the facts compiled in the Innocence Project's letter."

That was all true. Yet it was also true that both state and federal courts had been rejecting challenges to Hayne's credibility throughout that period of time. Nevertheless, the panel ruled that Flaggs had failed at part (c) of the AEDPA test—he hadn't filed his petition within one year of when the new evidence could reasonably have been discovered. For good measure, the panel added that even if he had made the deadline, Flaggs hadn't convinced them that Hayne wasn't a credible witness. "Moreover, Flaggs does not show that Hayne's testimony at trial was false or unreliable," they wrote. "Nor does he show by clear and convincing evidence that no jury would have convicted him but for the allegedly unconstitutional admission of Hayne's opinion testimony."

Ten months after that ruling, a three-judge panel from the same court of appeals issued a stunning decision in a separate challenge to Hayne. That ruling was also short, and might have been easy to overlook. But it included one critically important sentence. It was a damning sentence—damning for the court of appeals and damning of the criminal justice system in general. When taken with the ruling ten months earlier—which again was issued by the same appeals court—that single sentence illustrated as well as anything could how the courts and AEDPA have made it next to impossible for those wrongly convicted by bad forensic testimony to even be heard, much less find their way out of prison.

Here's what happened: In the second case, a panel from the same Fifth Circuit unanimously denied a new trial for a Louisiana man named James Koon, who had been convicted in 1996 of killing an infant. Hayne was the state's expert witness. In his petition, Koon claimed that the recent revelations about Hayne's credibility were newly discovered evidence. As in *Flaggs*, the panel unanimously rejected that claim. As with the previous panel, this panel ruled that Koon should have discovered allegations made by Hayne's critics years earlier. But this particular opinion included two important words that proved Koon and appellants like him never really stood a chance: "The evidence shows the witness for Louisiana, Dr. Steven Hayne, a *now-discredited* Mississippi coroner, lied about his qualifications as an expert and thus gave unreliable testimony about the cause of death."

"*Now-discredited.*" This was the first time a majority opinion from an appeals court of any kind had acknowledged that Hayne had been "discredited." Not only that, the opinion acknowledged that Hayne had lied about his credentials.

Unfortunately, because of what that panel did next, the acknowledgment provided no relief for the people trying to get a new trial by challenging Hayne's credibility. That's because despite the fact that this was the first time an appeals court had described Hayne as discredited, it was already too late to do anything about it.

The federal district court judge who first ruled on Koon's petition determined that despite the evidence that Hayne had been discredited, "Dr. Hayne's expertise was questioned by the Mississippi Supreme Court in an opinion published in May 2007; Justice Diaz's Special Concurrence relied upon a magazine article published in 2006. In the absence of any evidence to the contrary, it is safe to conclude that a habeas petitioner exercising due diligence *should have discovered this information well before the fall of 2011*. . . . In other words . . . this petition is clearly time-barred." The Fifth Circuit panel agreed. The panel noted that several media outlets had first begun to criticize Hayne between 2006 and 2008, that the Innocence Project had filed its complaint against Hayne in 2009, and that Mississippi Supreme Court Justice Oliver Diaz had criticized him in his concurring opinion in the Edmonds case in 2007.

"Koon's assertion that he could not have learned of *Edmonds* from information in the Louisiana State Penitentiary law library is both implausible and immaterial in the light of the public information about Dr. Hayne that was available for several years prior to July 2011," the court wrote. Because Koon could have discovered these criticisms of Hayne much earlier, he had missed his deadline. He was out of luck.

With a single short opinion, the Fifth Circuit admitted that the medical examiner Mississippi had been using for two decades was no longer a credible witness, but then slammed the door on anyone he had helped convict. Under a precise reading of federal law and the relevant case law, this was arguably correct. It was also incredibly unfair and a stark illustration of just how ill-equipped the federal courts and federal law are to catch and correct quackery disguised as expertise.

Since the onset of DNA testing in the 1990s, the legal system has slowly been coming to terms with the fact that forensic analysts aren't nearly as accurate and reliable as they've often claimed to be. The problem has been documented in countless studies, reports, and law review articles, but the most damning evidence is the most straightforward: according to a 2007 study of the first two hundred post-conviction exonerations, over half involved flawed forensic evidence. In the majority of those cases, the state's forensic witnesses gave inaccurate and unreliable testimony.

And even as the criminal justice system can't seem to keep bad science out of its courtrooms, once someone is convicted, the same system then shifts to protect the "finality" of the verdict. Federal lawmakers have only made it worse with laws like AEDPA, altering federal code to make it ever more difficult to challenge state verdicts in federal court. The courts *still* let these witnesses testify at trial—as experts. But years later, when science proves them wrong, or the defendant finally finds funds to hire an expert to say as much, the system is all about protecting the verdict. At that point, it no longer wants to hear from experts.

But science doesn't operate on deadlines. It's a process. DNA has shown us that defendants who expert witnesses said without equivocation were guilty were unquestionably innocent. Unfortunately, the fact that unproven expertise caused a wrongful conviction in some cases hasn't been enough for the courts to reconsider other convictions in which the primary evidence came from those same disproven fields (or in a disturbing number of cases, even from the same expert) but for which post-conviction DNA testing isn't dispositive of guilt.

Most of these more subjective forensics fields have largely avoided exposing themselves to scientific scrutiny. It's easy to see why. There's no incentive for them to do so. The purpose of forensics is to solve crimes. The end game is to testify in court and persuade a judge or jury. Once the courts begin accepting analysts from a new area of forensics as experts, there's no upside to those analysts then subjecting their methods and analysis to scientific scrutiny. They already have the only approval they need: that of the courts. If the science affirms their methods, they're no better off than they were before. At best, they get the benefit of telling the jury that their field is backed by scientific research. (As we've seen with West, anyone can claim as much, regardless of whether it's true.) But if their field doesn't withstand scientific scrutiny, it's free material for opposing attorneys. It could put their entire livelihood at risk—or at least it ought to.

Because so many of these forensic specialties haven't sought out scientific validation, and because of the pervasive tension between science and law, scientists have been slow to scrutinize their claims. That began to change after the first DNA exonerations in the early 1990s. But full-fledged scientific scrutiny of forensics didn't really get going until the last decade or so.

The scientific process is slow and deliberate. A study will get submitted for peer review. It might then be published. Other studies come along to verify that study, contradict it, or refine it in some way. There's no set point in time at which science officially declares a theory to be proven or disproven. It's about the process itself. It's about the gradual accumulation of knowledge.

Courts operate under entirely different rules. Statutes of limitations toll. Procedural rules impose deadlines. And there's all of that emphasis on finality. With science, no theory is final. Revision and correction are encouraged. Judges and prosecutors, on the other hand, seem to feel that the very integrity of their system demands the certainty of a closed tomb. Institutionally, the two systems operate in fundamentally different ways. We've known this since lawyers and medical doctors first began quarreling about death investigations in the early twentieth century. Yet we still haven't figured out how to reconcile these differences.

Imagine that defendant "Johnny" is convicted based on handwriting analysis evidence. This particular variety of expert testimony has been criticized for many years but has only been acknowledged as invalid by government agencies in the last few years. Johnny now wants to file a post-conviction petition for a new trial based on the scientific consensus that the evidence used to convict him isn't scientifically reliable. At what point does the year-long window in which Johnny had to file his petition begin to take effect? Should it be after the first critical study? The second? Is it once the scientific community has reached a consensus? What defines a "consensus"? How does one define the field of scientists among which such a consensus must arise? It isn't as if scientists take an annual vote on these things.

These are critical questions, and they're essentially impossible to answer. The courts and Congress have set a trap for these defendants, and absent DNA evidence, there's really no escaping it. File your claim too soon—say, after the first few studies—and the courts could rule that you haven't presented enough evidence that the expertise used to convict you has been discredited. You now risk being barred from ever raising the issue again. But if you wait for a stronger scientific consensus before filing, the courts could rule that your deadline passed a year after those first few studies were published. Your window has closed. Here, too, you're now barred from raising that claim again.

And that's all just for the suspect *fields* of forensics. With individual experts, it gets even trickier. Michael West is a good example. Mississippi's courts, prosecutors, and attorneys continued to uphold and defend West's credibility well into the mid-2000s, despite the fact he had been repeatedly criticized and exposed going back to the mid-1990s. As previously noted, Mississippi attorney general Jim Hood finally conceded in 2008 that West wasn't a credible witness, telling the *Jackson Free Press* that West "is someone we have investigated, and I don't support him in any manner." But while Hood's office had by then stopped explicitly defending the substance of West's analyses in court, his office *still* continues to defend convictions won primarily on West's testimony. Instead of arguing that West is a credible witness, the office now argues that defendants are procedurally barred from raising West as an issue again, because most of them already challenged West's credibility and lost. It doesn't matter that even Hood acknowledges now that the courts back then were wrong.

For the purpose of challenging West in a post-conviction petition in federal court, then, at what point should a defendant have known that West had been discredited? When did the one-year window begin? Was it the first time West's testimony was thrown out in the early 1990s? When he was suspended or ousted from forensics groups in the mid-1990s? Was it after the video from the early 2000s when West erroneously matched an uninvolved individual's teeth mold to the photograph in Ray Krone's case? Has it even happened yet?

James Koon wasn't challenging the credibility of forensic pathology in general, but of a specific medical examiner. That's even more difficult. Forensic pathology is a particularly tricky area of forensics, because while its general precepts are widely accepted in the medical and scientific community, the line between objective and subjective opinions is often hard to discern. So is the line between informed expert opinions and opinions unsupported by science. "There are four bullet holes in the victim's heart" is an objective statement. Rarely will two medical examiners argue over such a point. "The bullet's trajectory suggests that the killer shot the victim while standing" is far more subjective. It may be true, but it's confounded by variables. "There were two hands on the gun that fired this bullet" isn't valid testimony. But there are countless degrees of gradation in between.

The Mississippi Supreme Court tossed Hayne's "two-hands-on-the-gun" testimony, but it didn't let his outrageous opinions in that case affect how it evaluated his testimony in other cases. When Hayne was subsequently challenged after *Edmonds*, the courts evaluated the validity of his testimony in those cases in isolation, on their own merits. But why should that be? Once an expert witness has shown himself willing to give preposterous testimony, why should the court defer to him in cases where his testimony might be scientifically plausible but is still subjective? Why should the court allow future juries in murder trials to give a medical examiner whose previous testimony was found to be reversible error the same consideration they would give a medical examiner whose previous testimony has consistently shown meticulous care for accuracy?

In cases in which forensic analysts have been clearly exposed as frauds—such as crime lab technicians shown to have faked test results—it's usually clear when the clock should start running on the window to file a petition for relief. It might be when the analyst was fired or when a newspaper series or inspector general's investigation was first published.

But in cases like that of Hayne, the situation is more nuanced. The information trickles out over time. The gradual discrediting of Hayne took place over more than a decade. In November 2014, the Fifth Circuit Court of Appeals ruled that Steven Hayne had earned the label of "discredited." But exactly when did the court reach that conclusion? And how was James Koon supposed to have known? There was no announcement. There was no press release. There was no notice given to those who may have been convicted by Hayne's testimony that said, "Hey, you now have one year to file your claims."

The added indignity for someone like Koon is that Louisiana offers post-conviction indigent legal help only to those who have been sentenced to death. Koon was sentenced to life in prison, so once he lost his appeal, he lost his lawyer. He filed his post-conviction petition himself. The Fifth Circuit ruling in his case essentially states that from his prison cell, an indigent defendant like Koon should not only have been following each revelation about Hayne's credibility as it happened but should have been able to discern the precise moment when those revelations tipped the scales to make Hayne "discredited" in the eyes of the court—even though the court itself couldn't or wouldn't say precisely when that occurred. And Koon should have then filed his petition within a year of that magical moment.

But it's even worse than that. Not only do the courts expect these defendants to abide by these dizzying rules to the letter, the courts refuse to hold themselves to the same standard. The *Flaggs* ruling that *affirmed* Hayne's credibility as an expert witness came in March 2013. That would be nineteen months *after* July 2011, which the same court declared was the *very latest* by which Koon should have already discovered the evidence that Hayne was *not* credible. There's just no way Koon could have gotten it right.

Lastly and perhaps most importantly, as this book has now thoroughly documented, this is all the more unfair given that Mississippi officials tried desperately to keep information about Hayne, his autopsies, and his arrangements with the state from public view. Mississippi's open records laws are among the worst in the country. When Innocence Project attorneys requested autopsy reports from district attorneys' offices to look for other cases possibly corrupted by Hayne or West, those requests were unanimously rejected. The criminal defense systems in both Louisiana and Mississippi are also underfunded and overworked. Even if Koon *had* an attorney, the idea that a lawyer appointed to a capital case and handed a $1,500 check should or could have spent hours looking into Hayne's credentials, researching his background, fighting with state officials to see how many autopsies he'd done, and soliciting other forensic pathologists to review his work—sometimes with no additional funding from the court—has never jibed with reality. Even if an intrepid attorney were willing and able to take all of that on, the simple fact of the matter is that the courts had qualified Hayne as an expert witness thousands of times. Though he was often challenged, no trial judge ever refused to let him testify. Not a single time. At some point, it becomes clear that any attorney who spends hours and hours chasing down material in an effort to discredit this particular expert would be doing a disservice to his client. That time would be better spent on matters more likely to have an impact on the case.

Moreover, the notion that the defendants in such cases would now be punished for their attorneys' failure to investigate or challenge Hayne (a failure that the courts also consistently ruled did not rise to the level of ineffective assistance of counsel, anyway) is anathematic to any concept of justice. And it's all the worse for those inmates who didn't have an attorney to help with their appeals.

Koon was convicted based on testimony from an expert that the Fifth Circuit now considers discredited. For the same court to nevertheless uphold his conviction because he missed a deadline he had no way of knowing existed is yet another example of keeping a person in prison on a technicality. The fact that the ruling in *Koon* wasn't necessarily wrong under the law is only more evidence that the system values process far more than justice.

Finally, it's worth noting that the "discredited" acknowledgment in the ruling did not prevent Hayne from testifying in future cases in the Fifth Circuit—or anywhere else. It did not prevent Louisiana prosecutors from using him if they so desired, or even Mississippi prosecutors should the state change its laws. Ironically (or perhaps not), the *only* real consequence of the Fifth Circuit's acknowledgment that a longtime expert witness for the state was now discredited was to prevent criminal defendants from challenging that expert in federal court.

For years, Steven Hayne had claimed that he wasn't certified by the American Board of Pathology (ABP) because he found the test questions insulting and walked out. For years, the courts bought that line. He rode it to an appointment as the interim state medical examiner, aided by his claims to be certified by a number of other, less accepted groups.

It took a while, but in 2012 a more plausible explanation finally emerged. Back in 2008 the *Clarion-Ledger* had contacted the ABP to inquire about the exam Hayne took in 1989. "I pulled the text of this examination from our files," Dr. Betsy Bennett, the group's executive director, told the paper. "There was no question on that examination that was remotely similar to Dr. Hayne's description."

But Hayne stuck to his story. He told the paper he was certain that the question was on his test. Not only that: he said he'd stake his reputation and career on it. "She is flat wrong," he said of Bennett. "She doesn't know what she's talking about. It's like remembering where you were when men landed on the moon."

In a deposition four years later, Hayne was confronted with a copy of the exam, provided by the ABP. There was no "colors of death" question. When asked why for two decades he had peddled the story about storming out over a bogus question, Hayne posited that perhaps more than one test had been given that year (the ABP said this wasn't the case), before finally saying he had "no explanation."

If Hayne did "walk out" as he had claimed, his scores offer an explanation of why: At the time he quit, Hayne was failing every section of the test. On every section, he was in the bottom decile of test takers. According to the American Board of Pathology, about 80 percent of candidates pass the exam on the first try.

Hayne has never really explained why he didn't just try to take the test again. Perhaps he felt it was beneath him. Perhaps he wasn't sure he could pass it. Instead he continued to testify about his certifications as he always had. He got away with it for twenty years.

Within just the last few years, more challenges to Hayne and West have come before appellate courts. Several are cases in which Hayne and West have introduced to the criminal justice system ever more novel methods of forensic analysis. In one such case, the murder trial of John Ross, the two men fired bullets they had made themselves into "freshly harvested canine skins" in an attempt to boost the prosecution's theory that a woman had been murdered by her husband and hadn't committed suicide as her husband had claimed. The two experts testified that when they replicated the powder burns seen on the woman's head on the dog skins, the gun was two to three inches from the skins, a distance more consistent with homicide than suicide. Ross was convicted.

But only four in five gun suicides are from that distance, meaning there was still a 20 percent chance this wasn't a murder. Hayne also claimed in his testimony that women shoot themselves in the chest instead of the head at a rate of "four, five, to one." But the research on women, guns, and suicide doesn't ultimately support Hayne's contention. In fact, one expert on guns and suicide has said not only that "there's no scientific evidence" to support the notion, but that the notion itself is based on a sexist assumption that women are vain and don't want to leave behind a disfigured corpse. And yet the verdict was upheld on appeal.

Perhaps the oddest Hayne case to hit the appellate courts in recent years involves his use of a "death mask." Joseph Osborne was accused of killing his girlfriend's son in 2002 by smothering the boy as he slept. The family initially believed that the boy had died after accidentally ingesting some drugs. But after an autopsy, Hayne concluded that the cause of death was murder by suffocation. Five months later, the boy's young brother gave some information in a police interview that was vaguely incriminating of Osborne. The authorities exhumed the boy's body and took it to Hayne for a second look. Hayne requested the services of a forensic odontologist (this time, someone other than Michael West), who created a plaster cast—a "death mask," according to Hayne's terminology—of the boy's face. Hayne then marked on the mask the sites of injury that purportedly corresponded with previous marks he'd made on his autopsy diagram. From all of this, Hayne claimed that he could determine the approximate size of the hand that inflicted the injuries. He said his calculations were consistent with the size of Joseph Osborne's hand.

At trial, Hayne testified that the boy was suffocated and that his injuries were consistent with an adult person having covered the child's nose and mouth with a hand. He further declared that his death mask demonstrated that it was a "large hand," which would "favor a male's hand," that caused the child's injuries.

When asked by the *New York Times* in 2013 to comment on Hayne's testimony, Dr. Andrew M. Baker, a previous president of the National Association of Medical Examiners and the chief medical examiner for Hennepin County, Minnesota, told the paper, "I saw a very similar case like that on 'Law & Order: SVU.' I've never heard of it in real life." Baker said not only was the technique itself unprecedented, so was the ability "to speculate from those sorts of wounds about hand size or gender." (Interestingly, the prosecutor in the case preemptively explained to the judge that Hayne was "no Michael West," and that the death mask technique was in no way as ridiculous as West's ultraviolet light technique.)

The judge allowed the death mask testimony, and after six hours of deliberation, the jury found Osborne guilty of depraved-heart murder. His conviction was then affirmed by the state's appellate courts.

By the time both John Ross and Joseph Osborne went back to court in 2014, Hayne and West had come under fire. The Mississippi Supreme Court also seemed to finally be giving more scrutiny to expert testimony. It had recently overturned a number of verdicts because of witness statements it had ruled were scientifically unreliable. In one case, the court even reminded trial judges that their gatekeeping duty under *Daubert* "includes making sure that the opinions themselves are based on sufficient facts or data and are the product of reliable principles and methods."

The timing seemed right. And yet the Mississippi Supreme Court refused to grant either defendant relief. Without addressing the merits of the claims in either case, the majority wrote only that any evidence about Hayne or West was "reasonably discoverable at the time of trial," and that even if it had been barred at trial, it would not "have caused a different result in the conviction or sentence."

There is one critical difference between cases like *Osborne* and *Ross* and those in which the Mississippi Supreme Court had recently been more skeptical of expert testimony: the other cases were civil cases. The other cases pitted two private parties against one another. In those cases, both parties had access to devoted and competent counsel—or even entire firms—who had taken the cases voluntarily and were presumably handling manageable caseloads. In those cases, the court was deciding between two private parties, not between the state and the criminally accused. The parties who mounted the challenges to expert testimony in such cases also tended to be large companies that were being sued. That meant they had more resources to support those challenges, but in a conservative state, the justices also had some political cover should they decide to uphold them.

A vote to throw out the unscientific evidence in a criminal case could result in an overturned conviction. It could anger state officials. And it could subject the justices who voted that way to attack ads when they were up for reelection.

In fact, legal scholars have consistently pointed out that *Daubert* challenges are far more likely to be successful in civil cases than in criminal cases. This despite the fact that in criminal cases the consequences of a verdict tainted by junk science are obviously quite a bit more profound.

John Ross had no more luck in federal court. Like the Mississippi Supreme Court, the federal district court found that he should have discovered the existing criticisms of Hayne and West before his trial.

～

At the end of the day, the courts' refusal to grant a new trial in these cases is understandable—still outrageous, but understandable. On some level, these defendants were asking for much more than their right to a fair trial. They were asking a court, whether the Mississippi Supreme Court or a federal court, to repudiate years—an entire era, really—of what had passed for the fair and just application of criminal law in the state of Mississippi. Every judge who considered the claims from defendants like Ross and Osborne had come of age in that era. The federal judge who denied Ross's claim had been a prosecutor for much of the 1980s and later a circuit court judge during Hayne and West's heyday. Of the nine Mississippi Supreme Court justices at the time, only one had any extensive criminal defense experience. To the extent that the others had any, they were former prosecutors. None gained their seats because they exhibited skepticism of the criminal justice system. All were cultivators and beneficiaries of the status quo.

What makes it all especially cynical, though, is that no one really believed what the courts were saying. Not even the courts themselves. By the time Shannon Rayner was prosecuted for killing his wife in 2013, Hayne had already been fired and was now freelancing for defense attorneys. At Rayner's trial, Hayne not only testified for the defense, but testified in opposition to the physicians in the state medical examiner's office—an office that for all intents and purposes he and his supporters had worked to keep vacant.

During a lunch break, Hayne and the prosecutor exchanged pleasantries. After the break, Hayne resumed his testimony. During cross-examination, the prosecutor asked Hayne: "You told me during lunch the reason you have to carry around that big notebook with you is you have to defend yourself nowadays for all the reversals you've had in the Mississippi Supreme Court. Is that correct?"

Rayner's lawyer objected. The trial court overruled, finding that the question spoke to Hayne's credibility. The prosecutor proceeded to question Hayne about those former cases, including the fact that in many of them the basis for the reversal was that Hayne had testified outside his area of expertise. In his closing argument, the prosecutor then referred to Hayne as "discredited." Rayner appealed his conviction, arguing that the state's questioning of Hayne was improper, particularly given that the state was still defending Hayne's credibility in countless other cases. The Mississippi Court of Appeals didn't agree. The court found the questioning entirely proper.

That was probably the correct ruling under the law. But it was also another indication that the system is utterly incapable of distinguishing good expertise from bad, and the protocols in place for making those decisions are a farce.

When defense attorneys would simultaneously argue that the practice of bite mark matching was illegitimate while citing their own bite mark analyst's specific criticisms of West, the appeals court would smack their hands. You could argue one or the other, but not both. Yet they had no problem when the state of Mississippi simultaneously took the position that Steven Hayne was both credible and not credible, depending whether he was testifying for the state or for the defense.

~

"I'm happy," says Levon Brooks. He's sipping from a Sprite bottle filled with rum. "For the first time since I can remember, I'm happy."

It's a cool afternoon in December 2015. Levon and Dinah Brooks live in a trailer home between Brooksville and Columbus. They met while he was in prison. She worked in the cafeteria. Brooks had proposed years ago, but he never seemed interested in setting a date. Dinah ribbed him for that.

Behind their house a menagerie of hunting dogs, chickens, rabbits, and other animals bark, cluck, bay, and scurry around in their coops. Friends and neighbors stop by, sometimes stay a while to chat. The place bustles with life.

Most who meet Brooks are immediately struck by his presence. Ed Blake, the DNA analyst in California who worked on Brooks's and Brewer's cases, recalls the first time he met Brooks. "He's not a big man," Blake says. "There are some people that simply have a look about them that commands one's attention, and Levon Brooks is one of those individuals. He hardly has to talk to you before you're drawn to him to engage in a conversation—and then once you engage in that conversation his charisma, his dignity simply flow."

Brooks's declaration of happiness becomes all the more poignant a few minutes later, when he lifts his shirt to reveal the pump that's sending chemotherapy through his body. He was diagnosed with stomach cancer in 2014. But he has good doctors in Mississippi, and the Innocence Project put him in touch with a leading oncologist in New York. His prognosis is good.

On this chilly afternoon, Brooks is dressed in a T-shirt and camouflage pants, and his hair is in braids. He offers his guests some deer jerky, then shows off his new rifle.

"Did you hear about Allgood?" he asks. "I campaigned for the new guy. I think I like him," he says. He flashes a Cheshire smile.

When asked if he holds any resentment for the men who convicted him, Brooks points out that Allgood apologized to him on the day he was released. But the two haven't spoken since. Not that they necessarily would have been friends under different circumstances.

Noxubee County is a small, close-knit community, but it's also largely segregated.

So what about former Deputy Eichelberger. Has he apologized?

"Not in words," Brooks says. "But he doesn't talk much. He gave me a huntin' dog after I got out. I think it was his way of saying he's sorry. We hunt deer together sometimes."

Within about ten minutes of meeting Brooks, odds are pretty good that he'll ask if you'd like to go hunting with him. He just assumes you'll love it as much as he does.

Since he got out, Brooks has also been on the receiving end of more than a few such invitations. One came from his old childhood friend Boswell "Bos" Stevens, the foreperson of the jury that convicted him, who lets Brooks hunt and fish on the family farm. Stevens has since come full circle. In a way, so has the plantation where he and Brooks grew up. Stevens's mother died a few years ago. Since then, the farm has been rented out to contract farmers.

In an interview several years earlier, just before Christmas, Stevens pondered his role in Brooks's trial. He stood in his yard, just outside the cabin that Brooks's aunt and uncle called home, back when they were some of the last tenant workers on the farm. For certain, he said, he regretted what happened. He was happy that he and Brooks were on friendly terms again, though he wishes there were some way to make things whole. Asked to reflect on his heritage, the trial, and what had happened since, he leaned up against his pickup truck and thought for a moment.

"I'm not my grandfather, I guess," he said. He added after a pause, "And he wasn't me."

Shortly after Brooks was released, Ashley Smith apologized to him too, for identifying him as the man who abducted her sister. She didn't need to, of course. He never blamed her. Courtney Smith's father, Rocky Allen, also apologized, though he too had no real reason to. "It troubled me all this time," he told Brooks.

Some twenty-five years ago, Brooks left the job he loved at the Santa Barbara Club to clear up any misunderstanding with the Noxubee County Sheriff's Department. He told his friends he'd be right back. He never returned. Now, with some of his wrongful conviction money, he's back in the entertainment business: he and Dinah opened a café behind his house. They named it D&T's Hill City Hide Away. The modest, cozy spot serves up fried foods, sodas, and beer. Baseball caps and saggy pants aren't allowed. On Saturday afternoons they show college football. At night, they dance.

Early last summer the Hill City Hide Away hosted a wedding— that of its owners. Levon had finally come around. A photographer from New York who had become a good friend drove down to shoot the affair. The weather was hot. The dress was casual. Dinah wore a peach chiffon dress. Levon wore white, head to toe—a white hat, white linen shirt, white jeans, and white leather cowboy boots. There was a lot of dancing.

Michael West seems to have given up. He gave up on bite mark analysis. In 2012, he said in a deposition, "I no longer believe in bite mark analysis," and then later said to a reporter, "The science is not as exact as I had hoped." West also gave up his private dental practice.

But West has hardly been chastened. In the years since the Mississippi Supreme Court's *Howard* decision in 2006, Eddie Lee Howard's attorneys were able to get DNA testing done on the knife allegedly used to kill Georgia Kemp. The tests revealed male DNA but excluded Howard as the source. That meant that not only was Michael West's bite mark testimony the only physical evidence linking Howard to the crime scene, but there was also DNA from another man on the murder weapon. That wasn't enough to get Howard a new trial, but it was enough to get him an evidentiary hearing. In preparation for that hearing, Howard's attorneys with the Innocence Project deposed West in April 2016. It was a confrontation that had been years in the making. And West put on quite a show.

During questioning by Chris Fabricant from the Innocence Project of New York, West was belligerent, profane, and petulant. He declined to prepare for the deposition at all. He was asked to bring reams of case records and other documents. He brought a Diet Coke, which he used to produce a loud belch before answering a question.

West at first answered Fabricant's questions with pouty, one-word responses, as if he were a child angry at his parents. But he soon loosened up, and those one-word answers turned into insults, defiant accusations, and meandering soliloquies. West frequently told Fabricant that he couldn't remember cases and had no interest in trying. When Fabricant asked West about the Leigh Stubbs case, he replied, "Was that the case of the two lesbians that bit the girl's vagina lip off?"

When Fabricant asked West about fellow bite mark analysts—people West once called colleagues—he described them with words like "idiot," "whore," and "fool."

When Fabricant continued to ask West about his testimony in old cases, West got angry. "Why are you beating me to death with this?" he demanded. "I told you if it's in the transcript, I stand by it. If I remembered it—I don't remember what the fuck I had for breakfast two years ago, but I do believe I ate eggs."

West reiterated his belief that both Levon Brooks and Kennedy Brewer were guilty. He speculated, as he did any time DNA testing had proven him wrong, that the tests only proved they didn't commit the rapes, not that they weren't involved. Fabricant next asked West why in so many of his cases he found that the assailant only bit the victim with his upper teeth. West answered, "That's funny—y'all like to cum on that," referring to the crude term for ejaculation.

When the deposition finally came to a close, Fabricant asked West if he had any questions. He did. "How do you sleep at night?" West asked. Fabricant answered that he slept very well. West replied, "You're a sociopath. It's amazing to me they don't care what their clients do. They will do anything to get them off, no matter how heinous murdering their clients are. . . . You're sitting next to a sociopath. You work for Innocence Project. Every attorney I've met with the Innocence Project lies, cheats, steals, and tries to obfuscate the evidence in front of the court. I have no respect for y'all."

Fabricant replied, "I see. And so that makes me a sociopath?" West answered, "No. That makes you an ass-wipe. You make yourself a sociopath." Thus ended the deposition.

One might think that the attorneys in the Mississippi Attorney General's Office would be embarrassed by the behavior of their star witness in a death penalty case. But Hood's office had no comment about West's antics, and the state even asked the trial judge for a hearing to assess the competency of Howard's legal team.

It was a brazen move. The motion was based on a rule in Mississippi's rules of criminal procedure. The intent behind that rule is sound: it gives the state's courts a mechanism to ensure that defendants in capital cases are getting adequate legal representation in their appeals. But the original language of the rule was vague and sloppily drafted.

Hood's office had been using the rule as a weapon. While Hood and his subordinates claim in briefs that they're merely fulfilling their obligation to protect the rights of criminal defendants, they aren't filing these motions as a matter of course in every capital case. The sense in Mississippi—a notion backed up by an affidavit filed by the American Bar Association—is that they've been using the rule to hassle out-of-state law firms and nonprofit legal aid groups taking Mississippi capital cases on a pro bono basis.

The attorneys at these firms and aid groups have extensive experience in capital cases. In other words, instead of using the rule to keep unqualified attorneys out of death penalty cases, Hood's office has been using the rule to attack the *most* qualified attorneys.

In the case of Eddie Lee Howard, Hood's decision to invoke the rule when he did was the legal equivalent of trolling. The particular attorneys had already been representing Howard for years. Three of them had helped win the exonerations of Kennedy Brewer and Levon Brooks. Moreover, less than a year earlier, Hood's office had *defended* the qualifications of Howard's same attorneys in response to a separate motion.

A few days after Hood filed his motion, the Mississippi Supreme Court revised the rule to fix the vague language and sloppy drafting. The new language renders the motion from Hood's office moot. It isn't clear if the court's decision to revise the rule was a direct response to the state's motion, but the timing is certainly suggestive.

The actual court hearing for Eddie Lee Howard followed a few months later. West was as prickly and pugnacious as ever. As of this writing, the court has yet to rule on the matter, and Eddie Lee Howard still sits on death row.

~

All of the criticism and fallout from these cases has isolated Hayne and West from the powerful institutions that once embraced them. They rose up together and are now falling together, although West's descent began a bit sooner and followed a steeper arc. West still reveres Hayne. He has regularly described him as one of the smartest men he knows. Both saw themselves as victims of unjust persecution, perpetrated mainly by "Project Innocence." West stopped doing bite mark analyses in 2006. He gave up his private dental practice in 2009 to work for the South Mississippi Correctional Institution near Leakesville. When West's brother died in February 2016, he called Hayne and told him, "Well, it's official. You are my number one friend now."

Some of their enablers have hit hard times too. Ed Peters, a longtime former district attorney who frequently used Hayne and was among his most vocal defenders (Peters helped lead the charge to oust Emily Ward), was caught up in a statewide bribery scandal. Peters escaped formal charges by striking a deal to cooperate against others.

In recent years, Forrest Allgood has been chastised by two courts for prosecutorial misconduct. In the November 2015 elections, he was finally defeated at the polls. Scott Colom, a thirty-two-year-old black criminal defense attorney, beat Allgood by 54 percent to 46 percent. Colom ran on a platform of ending mass incarceration and finding alternatives to prison for nonviolent drug offenders. Allgood had been in office for twenty-nine years.

Life has been better for Jim Hood. In 2014, Hood's fellow attorneys general elected him president of the National Association of Attorneys General. Hood has also received national press for taking on corporate heavyweights like State Farm, Google, and Facebook. He continues to be one of the few Democrats to win statewide elections in the deep South, largely as a result of his tough-on-crime positions and enthusiasm for the death penalty. In 2015 he was comfortably reelected to his fourth term—by over ten percentage points. He is frequently mentioned as a potential candidate for governor.

Eddie Lee Howard, Jimmie Duncan, Jeff Havard, and Devin Bennett all remain on death row.

"I can talk for a while, but I gotta go to work pretty soon," says Kennedy Brewer. It's early afternoon in early 2015, but at three p.m., he needs to begin his shift at the chicken plant in Brooksville. Now forty-five, he's wearing his trademark stocking cap and leaning up against his prized possession, the one thing to which he treated himself with his wrongful conviction money. It's a late-model Mercury Grand Marquis. It's parked under a carport next to his house, just down the road from his mother and his sister.

When Brooks and Brewer were first released, Mississippi did not yet have a law to compensate the wrongly convicted. So when Brewer was released on bail in 2007, a family friend got him a job at the chicken plant. The state finally passed a compensation bill in 2009. It provides for an annual payment of $50,000 for each year of wrongful imprisonment, with a cap at $500,000. All things considered, the payout seems paltry, and the payments stop once the exoneree passes away—the benefit isn't heritable. To receive compensation, the wrongly convicted must also agree not to sue the state. (Brewer and Brooks sued Hayne and West as private citizens.)

The money is helpful, but Brewer says he'll never quit his job at the plant. "I work because I want to," he says. Already a quiet man, Brewer's time on death row made him more solitary still. "I'd watch TV and write letters," he says. "You're in a one-man cell. You get one hour outside a week. You think a lot. I just spent a lot of time praying the truth would come out."

Brewer has a son, twenty-five, and a daughter, twenty-six. When asked what he missed most about his life, after mentioning his kids, Brewer says, "Real food. And cold beer." For his first meal as a free man, he went to Cracker Barrel.

Neither Brooks nor Brewer ever knew Justin Johnson, though both knew of him. In February 2012 Brooks and Brewer rode together to attend his sentencing hearing. Brewer initially planned to ask that Johnson be given the death penalty. Brooks talked him out of it. He cited Johnson's untreated mental illness.

"I told Kenny that after all that happened to us, we should be merciful," Brooks says. "There was no point in being mad anymore."

Johnson pleaded guilty to both crimes. At the sentencing hearing, he told district court Judge Lee Howard, "I wasn't in my right mind when I did it." Howard sentenced him to two terms of life without parole.

"I don't hate him now," Brewer says, referring to Johnson. "But I do feel bad for him."

Forrest Allgood has never apologized to Brewer. Neither have any of the state officials involved in his prosecution. Despite Justin Johnson's confession that he committed both crimes alone, Allgood still insists that Brewer had something to do with Christine Jackson's death. So does Michael West.

When asked what he'd say to Allgood, West, or Hayne if he had the chance, Brewer draws a slow smile.

"I really don't know what I'd say. I'm glad Allgood is gone. But I ain't mad at any of them anymore. The system's gonna do what the system's gonna do."

ACKNOWLEDGMENTS

RADLEY BALKO

I got married while writing this book. So thanks first to my brilliant and beautiful wife Liliana Segura—for her love, support, and suggestions, but also just for making me lucky enough to have found a partner who *enjoys* daily conversation about aggressive prosecutors, wrongful convictions, and autopsy reports. Thank you to my parents, Terry and Patricia Balko for all of their support over the years. For similar reasons, thank you to Bobbie Murphy, and to Ed Welsh and the late Margaret Welsh. More gratitude to my family in general, who were so wonderfully enthusiastic about my first book.

I'd also like to thank people who, in various different ways, made this particular book possible: David Menschel, Howard Yoon, Colleen Lawrie, Clive Priddle, the Reason Foundation, Jamie Downs, Peter Neufeld, Barry Scheck, Vanessa Potkin, Michael Bowers, Harry Bonnell, Chris Fabricant, André de Gruy, Bob Evans, Abe Pafford, Ben Vernia, Jess Cino, Julie Ford, Louisa Ely, Lynn Wilkins, and John Grisham.

I want to credit *Reason* magazine and two of its former editors, Nick Gillespie and Matt Welch. Nick published my first expose about Hayne in 2007. It was no small risk for a small magazine to publish a hard-hitting piece about a public figure with a reputation for litigiousness. Matt then published my numerous follow-ups over the years, including a cover story. Thanks also to my subsequent editors at the *Huffington Post* (Ryan Grim) and the *Washington Post* (James Downie) for continuing to publish my reporting on all of this, which can sometimes involve obscure cases and get deep into the weeds of forensics and the legal system. I've been pursuing this story for more than a decade, and that's been in large part because I've been fortunate enough to have editors who understand why it's important.

Thank you to our dogs, Wally and Daisy, for being good dogs. (Aside to the dogs: You are good dogs. Yes, yes, you are.) Also, undying gratitude to our unfailingly dependable dog sitter, Kathy Townsend. She makes our lives much, much easier. Thanks to my co-author Tucker Carrington, for nudging us to write this book, and who for a long while was the only other person on earth who grasped the full enormity of what went down in Mississippi. I wasn't sure about co-writing a book. Tucker made it easy. Mostly.

As you'll soon read, there were a handful of people who tried to blow the whistle about the events in this book. Some spoke out publicly. Some worked behind the scenes. Some spoke to me, both on and off the record. Many did so at the risk of litigation, or damage to their own careers. Some endured both. So thank you to the people who speak up. On this story. On other stories. And just in general. It matters.

Finally, we'd both like to thank Kennedy Brewer and Levon Brooks, for insisting on their innocence, for their courage, and for allowing and helping us to tell this story.

TUCKER CARRINGTON

This book took years—not only to write, but for the story to reveal itself. I join in Radley's thanks to those who made this book possible. In addition, for their constancy, I owe an enormous debt of gratitude to the University of Mississippi, the Robert C. Khayat Law Center and its faculty and staff, as well as to the George C. Cochran Innocence Project, particularly the clinic staff and students who have supported and joined in this work ever since we took on our first case. The Grisham Library at the Law School and its generous and indefatigable staff deserve my everlasting gratitude. For their unflagging research and insistence on meticulous rigor above all else, we were fortunate to have, among many others, Lynn Wilkins and Louisa Ely on our team. For their forbearance in all things, especially my absences—physical and otherwise—as I worked on this book, I offer my biggest thanks to my wife and children. In truth, their devotion was as much a sign of their support for the project as it was a gesture of kindness to me. And for that, not only do I love them beyond all measure, but I am proud to be a part of such a wonderful family.

NOTES

AUTHORS' NOTE

xiv **a moving human being:** Cory Jermine Maye v. State of Mississippi, No. 2007-KA-02147-COA (Miss. 2007).

xv **before or after her death:** Robert Evans, interview by Radley Balko; see Dr. Dean A. Hawley, "Forensic Medical Findings in Fatal and Non-Fatal Intimate Partner Strangulation Assaults," Department of Pathology and Laboratory Medicine, Indiana University School of Medicine, http://tinyurl.com/y9xmann8. Cathi Carr, "Jury Acquits Man in Slaying of Teen in Jefferson Davis," *Hattiesburg* (MS) *American*, Feb. 4, 1999.

xv **"in the manner they should be done.":** Ken Winter, interview by Radley Balko.

xv **"trace evidence at the scene.":** Former state official, interview by Radley Balko.

xv **"some on death row.":** J. D. Sanders, interview by Radley Balko.

xv **accompanying essay in the *Wall Street Journal*:** Radley Balko, "CSI Mississippi," *Wall Street Journal*, Oct. 6, 2007.

xvi **replied that he couldn't remember:** Jon Kalahar, "'Wall Street Journal' Questions Hayne's Ethics," *MS News Now*, Oct. 8, 2007.

xvi **Mississippi Supreme Court affirmed:** Danny Jones v. State of Mississippi, 962 So.2d 1263 (Miss. 2007).

xvii **"law school is impugning our integrity.":** Letter from Laurence Y. Mellen, District Attorney, to Tucker Carrington, Director of the Mississippi Innocence Project, Oct. 4, 2007.

xvii **"the guilty bastard got off scott free project.":** Letter from James H. Powell III, District Attorney for the 21st Circuit Court District, to Tucker Carrington, Director of the Mississippi Innocence Project, Sept. 17, 2007. In spite of the position Powell took in his letter, Powell later proved to be a cooperative partner in revisiting some former convictions in his jurisdiction.

xvii **increased by 80 percent:** Steven Levitt and Stephen J. Dubner, *Freakonomics: A Rogue Economist Explores the Hidden Side of Everything* (New York: William Morrow, 2005), 119.

xvii **"society has ever known.":** See William Bennett, John DiIulio, and John P. Walters, *Body Count: Moral Poverty—and How to Win America's War Against Crime and Drugs* (New York: Simon and Schuster, 1996), 26.

xviii **Oklahoma City bombing:** In 1996, Congress passed the Antiterrorism and Effective Death Penalty Act (AEDPA) as part of Newt Gingrich's "Contract with America." The bill was signed into law with overwhelming bipartisan support after the 1995 Oklahoma City bombing.

xviii **difficult for convicted prisoners:** Liliana Segura, "Gutting Habeas Corpus: The Inside Story of How Bill Clinton Sacrificed Prisoners'

Rights for Political Gain," *Intercept*, May 4, 2016, https://theintercept
.com/2016/05/04/the-untold-story-of-bill-clintons-other-crime-bill.

xviii   **"the capital of capital punishment.":** Mac Gordon, "Execution Goes
Back on Agenda," *Clarion-Ledger* (Jackson, MS), Aug. 13, 1994.

xviii   **642 were black:** Donald A. Cabana, "The History of Capital Punishment in Mississippi: An Overview," *Mississippi History Now*, Oct. 2004, www.mshistorynow.mdah.ms.gov/articles/84
/history-of-capital-punishment-in-mississippi-an-overview.

xviii   **where Brewer and Brooks lived:** Brewer's trial actually occurred in an
adjoining county after his lawyers moved for and were granted a change
of venue.

xviii   **state led the country in lynchings:** See Project HAL: Historical American Lynching Data Collection Project, http://people.uncw.edu/hinese
/HAL/HAL%20Web%20Page.htm.

xix   **married for a short time to a black detective:** Of course, being married
to a spouse of a different race doesn't prove someone isn't racist. But it's
certainly suggestive.

xix   **hundreds of innocent prisoners:** See "DNA Exonerations in the United
States," Innocence Project, www.innocenceproject.org/dna-exonerations
-in-the-united-states, last accessed July 26, 2017.

xix   **subjected to DNA testing:** See Brandon L. Garrett, "Judging Innocence,"
Columbia Law Review 108 (2008): 55, citing Nina Martin "Innocence
Lost," *San Francisco Magazine* (Nov. 2004): 78 and 105; Brandon L. Garrett, *Convicting the Innocent: Where Criminal Prosecutions Go Wrong* (Cambridge, MA: Harvard University Press, 2011); Brandon L. Garrett and
Peter Neufeld, "Invalid Forensic Science and Wrongful Convictions," *Virginia Law Review* 95, no. 1 (2009).

xix   **"It is an unreal dream.":** United States v. Garsson, 291 F. 646, 649
(S.D.N.Y. 1923).

xix   **around the nation is worse:** Garrett and Neufeld, "Invalid Forensic Sci-
ence," 147; see also M. Chris Fabricant and Tucker Carrington, "The
Shifted Paradigm: Forensic Science's Overdue Evolution from Magic to
Law," *Virginia Journal of Criminal Law* 4 (2016).

CHAPTER 1: THE MURDER OF COURTNEY SMITH

3   **an alibi wouldn't save him:** Levon Brooks, interviews by Radley Balko
and Tucker Carrington; State of Mississippi v. Levon Brooks, No. 5937
(Noxubee Cnty. Circuit Ct. Jan. 13, 1992); Aaron McCoy, statement, Jan.
1, 1992; Sonya Smith, affidavit, Jan. 15, 1992.

3   **"softened by an even spread of shade.":** Federal Writers' Project of the
Works Progress Administration, *Mississippi: A Guide to the Magnolia State*
(1938), 376.

3   **Mississippi State Bulldogs play football:** Ernest and Lucille Brown, Jack-
son Hotel, the Rebel & the Doodlebug, Mississippi Oral History Project,
Center for Oral History and Cultural Heritage, University of Southern
Mississippi.

3   **scrawled across the top:** Transcript of record, *State of Mississippi v. Levon
Brooks* (hereinafter "Brooks trial transcript"), 691, 929.

4   **before returning home:** Brooks trial transcript, 575–576, 585–586.

4   **flickered from the television:** Sources for Sept. 15 Smith family narrative: ibid., 516–536, 544–563, 570–588.

5   **just a few hours later:** State of Mississippi v. Justin A. Johnson, No. 14,738 (Noxubee Cnty. Justice Ct. Nov. 5, 1990).

5   **and drove away:** Sources for Justin Johnson narrative: Justin Albert Johnson, statement, Sept. 23, 1990; Justin Johnson, interview by Ronnie Odom, Investigator, Mississippi Attorney General's Office, Public Integrity Division, Feb. 5, 2008; State of Mississippi, County of Lowndes, Cause No. 12385, to the commissioner of the Department of Corrections, May 21, 1992.

6   **"her mamma or something.":** Brooks trial transcript, 581–582.

6   **moseyed toward morning:** Ibid., 516–536, 544–563, 570–588.

6   **inextricably entwined:** Statement of T. C. Phillips, Aug. 24, 1991, in Brooks trial transcript, 903–905.

6   **But she wasn't:** Brooks trial transcript, 946.

7   **they alerted police:** Ibid., 515–541.

7   **returned to his squad car and fell asleep:** Ibid., 594–607.

7   **around the girl's body:** Ibid., 599.

8   **Take notes:** Investigative Plan Outline and Management System, Sept. 16, 1990.

8   **the state's go-to medical examiner:** Brooks trial transcript, 612–613.

9   **killer had forced intercourse:** Ibid., 691–692; Courtney Lashondra Smith autopsy report, Sept. 17, 1990.

9   **but was not sure, were human bite marks:** Brooks trial transcript, 687–688.

9   **or shortly thereafter:** Ibid., 703.

9   **might be animal bites:** Ibid., 697.

9   **jack-of-all-trades:** Ibid., 687, 711–717.

9   **embalmed Courtney Smith's body that same night:** Ibid., 717–718.

9   **extremely difficult, if not impossible:** Ibid., 717–718, 746. But see Karen Greist, *Pediatric Homicide: Medical Investigation* (Boca Raton, FL: CRC Press, 2009), 144, which states that victims should not be embalmed because the process tends to "wash out" bite marks and should not be autopsied before suspected bite marks are photographed.

9   **no ordinary bite mark analyst:** Brooks trial transcript, 682–757; Smith autopsy report.

9   **made by human teeth:** Brooks trial transcript, 731–732.

9   **skin from Courtney Smith's wrist:** Ibid., 699–701.

9   **should have been a red flag:** Ibid., 711–757. As for why it should have been a red flag, see Declaration of J. C. Upshaw Downs, MD, Dec. 1, 2011, 14–15, Steven Hayne v. the Innocence Project, No. 3:09-CV-218-KS-LRA (S.D. Miss. 2011) (Referring to West's failure to apply a retainer: "This is not the accepted procedure to preserve such tissue. Rather, accepted general procedure typically involves stabilizing the section by means of casting the skin surface at the site and/or utilizing a 'retainer' of some type to reduce artifact due to tissue shrinkage. . . . Adherence to this practice requires minimal effort and can be critical in the determination of identification information in a homicide case"); *American Board of Forensic Odontology 2016 Bitemark Methodology Standards and Guidelines*, 3 (stating "the bite site may be excised and preserved using proper stabilization techniques prior to removal").

10   **embalming can actually preserve the skin:** Brooks trial transcript, 717–718.

10   **retaining the integrity of the bite:** Ibid., 699–701, 717–718, 734–737.

10   **of a happy coincidence:** Declaration of Downs, 14–15; *Bitemark Methodology Standards and Guidelines*, 3.

10   **had identified a suspect:** Letter from Dr. Michael West to Willie Willie, Sept. 21, 1990; Dr. Michael West bill, Court Order, *State of Mississippi v. Levon Brooks*, Feb. 4, 1992. West was paid $1,690.04.

10   **truth to come out:** Peter Neufeld and Vanessa Potkin, interviews by Tucker Carrington.

11   **believed Courtney Smith was murdered:** William Mickens statement, Sept. 26, 1990.

11   **the first of many:** William Nelson McCarthy, William Dean Mickens, Tony Smith, and William Smith arrest warrants, Noxubee County, Mississippi, Sept. 19 and 21, 1990; William Dean Smith, interview by Ernest Eichelberger, Sept. 20, 1990.

11   **Courtney's great-grandfather:** Funeral program for Courtney Lashondra Smith, Sept. 16, 1990.

11   **Slick Mickens's arrest:** Tom Wilemon, "Brooksville Man Faces Charges in Child's Death," *Clarion-Ledger* (Jackson, MS), Sept. 20, 1990.

12   **it made him feel useful:** Ibid.; Betty Mickens, interview by Tucker Carrington; Marion Smith, interview by Tucker Carrington.

12   **"teddy bear and a Bible.":** Ron Williams, "Robert 'Uncle Bunky' Williams: A Local Living Legend Reflects on His Storied Career," *Columbus* (MS) *Packet*, March 8, 2012.

12   **in Mississippi to do so:** Slim Smith, "So Long Uncle Bunky," *Columbus* (MS) *Packet*, Aug. 26, 2015.

12   **as a beloved icon:** Ibid.

12   **who would prosecute Levon Brooks:** "Robert 'Uncle Bunky' Williams," *Columbus* (MS) *Packet*, undated.

13   **"comes to something like abuse.":** Billy Watkins, "Uncle Bunky: Still Drawing for Kids," *Clarion-Ledger* (Jackson, MS), Aug. 25, 1998.

13   **"in getting any case started.":** Ibid.

13   **is a complex undertaking:** See Margaret Talbot, "The Devil in the Nursery," *New York Times Magazine*, Jan. 7, 2001; Stephen J. Ceci and Maggie Bruck, *Jeopardy in the Courtroom: A Scientific Analysis of Children's Testimony* (Washington, DC: American Psychological Association, 1995).

13   **background in psychiatry or therapy:** See Hollida Wakefield, "Guidelines on Investigatory Interviewing of Children: What is the Consensus in the Scientific Community?" *American Journal of Forensic Psychology* 24, no. 3 (2006): 57–74; "Breaking the Cycle of Violence: Recommendations to Improve the Criminal Justice response to Child Victims and Witnesses," *United States Department of Justice* (1999).

13   **"draw a few cartoons.":** Watkins, "Uncle Bunky."

13   **No further explanation was necessary:** Sources for Uncle Bunky narrative: ibid.; Smith, "So Long Uncle Bunky"; "Ask Rufus"; Ron Williams, "Robert 'Uncle Bunky' Williams: A Local Living Legend Reflects on His Storied Career," *Columbus* (MS) *Packet*, March 8, 2012; Carol Mason, "Just Say 'No' for Uncle Bunky," *Tupelo* (MS) *Daily Journal*, June 29, 1990; Tim Hollis, *Hi There, Boys and Girls!: America's Local Children's TV Shows* (Jackson: University Press of Mississippi, 2001), 161–162.

14   **fled on an airplane:** Ashley Smith, interview by Deputy Sheriff Robert Williams, Sept. 21, 1990.

14   **"had a quarter in his ear.":** Ibid.
14   **"Yeah, a earring and a quarter.":** Ibid.
14   **"Slick" Mickens sometimes did:** Brooks trial transcript, 941–942, 948.
14   **"whiskers on his face.":** Ashley Smith, interview.
15   **clearly referring to a mask:** Ibid.
15   **"Stocking.":** Ibid.
15   **and put it over her sister's head:** Ibid.
15   **often played with Travon's son:** Ibid.
15   **earring in the first place:** Ibid.
16   **"Suspicion of murder.":** See assorted police reports, *State of Mississippi v. Levon Brooks*, Jan. 13, 1992.
16   **"They call him Ta Tee," she said again:** Sonya Smith, interview by Ernest Eichelberger, Sept. 21, 1990.
17   **he could hold him for up to seventy-two hours:** Levon Brooks, statement, Sept. 22, 1990.
18   **Brooks sported an afro:** Photo array, *State of Mississippi v. Levon Brooks*, Jan. 13, 1992.
18   **no indication that she suspected him:** Sonya Smith, affidavit, Jan. 15, 1992.
18   **even when the two were dating:** Ibid.; Sonya Smith, interview by Ernest Eichelberger, Sept. 21, 1990, and Nov. 5, 1990; Sonya Smith statement, Nov. 5, 1990.
18   **that included Levon Brooks:** Brooks trial transcript, 638–640.
19   **"had a bag of money in his hand.":** Ashley Smith, interview by Deputy Sheriff Robert Williams, Sept. 23, 1990.
19   **and ignored the rest:** Ibid.
19   **"get children to say anything":** Mason, "'Just Say No' for Uncle Bunky."
19   **"not long ago.":** Justin Albert Johnson, statement, Sept. 23, 1990.
20   **source of the bite:** Letter from Michael West to Forrest Allgood, Aug. 16, 1991.
20   **they weren't human bite marks:** See Declaration of Downs; Declaration of David Senn, DDS, Nov. 30, 2011; Declaration of Michael M. Baden, MD, Nov. 30, 2011, *Hayne v. Innocence Project*. Justin Albert Johnson, interview by Ronnie Odom, Feb. 5, 2008.
20   **no mention of biting the girl:** Justin Albert Johnson, interview by Danny Welch, Feb. 5, 7, 2008.
20   **he "exonerates" many more:** Jerry Mitchell, "Forensic Dentist Defends Work He's Done in Autopsies," *Clarion-Ledger* (Jackson, MS), Feb. 28, 2009.
20   **exonerated a dozen people:** Ibid.; letter from West to Allgood, Aug. 16, 1991.
21   **"to take the test tomorrow.":** Brooks, statement.
21   **scratches and bruises:** "Consent to Search" form, Sept. 25, 1990.
21   **weren't a match for Brooks's:** Mississippi Crime Lab, Supplementary Report, MCL No. 90-3736.
21   **which were suspended:** Levon Brooks, guilty plea document and arrest records, State of Alabama v. Levon Brooks, no. CC-81-20 (April 6, 1981).
21   **stolen from a gas station:** Levon Brooks, guilty plea document and arrest records, State of Mississippi v. Levon Brooks, no. 5527 (Noxubee Cnty. Circuit Ct. Sept. 22, 1981).
22   **molds of his teeth:** Sources for Brooks arrest narrative: Levon Brooks, guilty plea document and arrest records, *State of Alabama v. Levon Brooks*;

Brooks, guilty plea document and arrest records, State of Mississippi v. Levon Brooks, no. 5527; Statement of Levon Brooks, Sept. 25, 1990; Mississippi Crime Laboratory Certified Laboratory Report, case no. 90-3736, Dec. 16, 1991; letter from West to Allgood, Aug. 16, 1991; letter from West to Harry Alderson, Oct. 18, 1990.

22   **"found on the body of Courtney Smith.":** Letter from West to Alderson.

22   **confirmed by the FBI:** Letter from John Hicks to Edward Brennan, Oct. 18, 1990.

22   **"not being number #1 suspect.":** Recognizance Bond, Sept. 28, 1990.

23   **died a broken man:** Betty Mickens, interview by Tucker Carrington, 2008.

23   **lost contact with his family:** Sources for Mickens/Smith passage: Offense Report for William Dean Mickens, Sept. 19, 1990, signed by Ernest B. Eichelberger; Marion Smith, interview; Betty Mickens, interview.

24   **girls were asleep inside?:** Marion Smith, interview; Interim Index Sheet, case #90-3736.

24   **bonded out a few days later:** Petition to Enter Plea of Guilty, Sentencing Order, Notice to Commissioner Department of Corrections, no. 12385, May 20, 1992; Victim Impact Statement, Nov. 25, 1991; Criminal Affidavit, June 18, 1991, and Indictment, no. 12385, 12551, Nov. 4, 1991; Arraignment and Guilty Plea, no. 12385, Sept. 12, 1996; Presentence investigation, no. 12551 and 12385, Feb. 10, 1992.

CHAPTER 2: THE MURDER OF CHRISTINE JACKSON

25   **the only game in town:** Transcript of record, State of Mississippi v. Kennedy Brewer, No. 94-16-CR1 (Lowndes Cnty. Circuit Ct. March 21, 1995) (hereinafter "Brewer trial transcript"), 409, 411.

25   **check on the children's welfare:** Annie Brewer, interview by Tucker Carrington, 2008.

25   **fed and bathed:** Ibid.

26   **in order to get Brewer's attention:** Brewer trial transcript, 541–546.

26   **to watch television:** Ibid., 541–547.

26   **before midnight:** Ibid., 541–546.

26   **at the foot of the bed:** Ibid., 420–432.

27   **already washed downstream:** Justin Albert Johnson, interview by Mississippi Law Enforcement, Feb. 7, 2008.

27   **"I'm not a pervert.":** Ibid.

27   **told him to go home:** Ibid.

28   **"Christine is missing.":** Annie and Ruby Brewer, interview by Tucker Carrington, 2008.

28   **to help with the search:** Annie Brewer, interview.

28   **split mostly along family lines:** Ibid.

29   **There was no trace of her:** Brewer trial transcript, 28.

29   **on a pallet on the floor:** Ibid., 31.

29   **worried about their safety:** Ibid., 579.

29   **broken one in the bedroom:** Ibid., 35, 576.

29   **lower section was broken:** Ibid., 541, 575–579, 620–622.

29   **obvious evidentiary value:** Ibid., 573–578.

30   **away from the window:** Ibid., 617–619.

30   **tiring in the heat:** Ibid., 641–646.

30   **scent from Christine Jackson's clothes:** Ibid., 646.

30   **"we couldn't see nothing.":** Ibid., 647.

30   **search was called off:** Ibid., 647–650.

30   **dogs the day before:** Ibid., 594.

31   **floated to the surface:** Ibid., 591–592.

31   **sent it to Steven Hayne for an autopsy:** Ibid., 628–631.

31   **Christine Jackson's disappearance:** Ibid., 119–120.

31   **it had not:** Ibid., 119–120.

31   **Department of Corrections:** Ibid., 119–120.

31   **mile from where Christine Jackson lived:** André de Gruy, interview by Radley Balko.

32   **any lacerations or bruising:** Emergency Room Records for Justin Albert Johnson, James Patrick Clayton, Leshone Williams, and Dwayne Graham, Noxubee General Hospital, May 6, 1992.

32   **he said they were "self-inflicted.":** Emergency Room Record for Justin Albert Johnson, Noxubee General Hospital, May 6, 1992.

32   **clear him of any blame:** Brewer trial transcript, 44.

32   **Graham, Williams, and Gloria Jackson:** Ibid., 44, 57, 731.

32   **Jackson had been manually strangled:** Ibid., 505.

32   **vagina to her rectum:** Ibid., 501.

32   **penetration by a "male penis.":** Ibid., 501–505; Report of Post Mortem Examination: Christine Jackson, May 9, 1992.

32   **Christine's arm, forearm, hand, and fingers:** Brewer trial transcript, 494–495; Report of Post Mortem Examination.

32   **about five-eighths of an inch long:** Brewer trial transcript, 494–495.

32   **to conduct additional analysis:** Ibid., 507–508; Report of Post Mortem Examination.

32   **throughout the autopsy and examination:** Letter from Michael West to Diane Brooks, May 14, 1992; Brewer trial transcript, 519–521.

32   **"indeed and without doubt inflicted by Kennedy Brewer.":** Letter from West to Brooks.

33   **six years before he was released:** Lowndes County, Mississippi, Notice to Commissioner of the Department of Corrections, no. 12,385 (May 21, 1992). (Note: A clerical error listed the sentence as four years with six suspended.)

33   **announced that he would seek the death penalty:** Brewer v. State of Mississippi, 725 So.2d 106 (Miss. 1998).

33   **phrase "indeed and without doubt.":** Letter from West to Brooks.

33   **"the teeth that inflicted the bites.":** Letter from West to Brooks; letter from Dr. Michael West to Forrest Allgood, Sept. 21, 1993; Brewer trial transcript, 782–786.

CHAPTER 3: INVESTIGATING THE DEAD

35   **presented his findings before a public forum:** Sources for Caesar assassination narrative: Suetonius, *De Vita Caesarum, Divus Iulius,* in *Suetonius,* 2 vols., translated by J. C. Rolfe (Cambridge, MA: Harvard University Press; London: William Heinemann, 1920), 1:3–119; Plutarch, *The Life of Julius Caesar,* in *Plutarch's Lives,* vol. 4, translated by John Dryden, edited by A. H. Clough (Boston: Little, Brown, 1906), 323–329; Suzanne Bell, *Encyclopedia of Forensic Science,* rev. ed. (New York: Facts on File, 2008), 22; Barry Strauss, *The Death of Caesar: The Story of History's Most Famous Assassination* (New York: Simon and Schuster, 2016), 39–141.

36   **the Qin Dynasty of the third century BCE:** Anthony Barbieri-Low, "Model Legal and Administrative Forms from the Qin, Han, and Tang and Their Role in the Facilitation of Bureaucracy and Literacy," *Oriens Extremus* 50 (2011): 125–156; Anthony Barbieri-Low and Robin D. S. Yates, *Law, State, and Society in Early Imperial China: A Study with Critical Edition and Translation of the Legal Texts from Zhangjiashan Tomb No. 247* (Leiden: Brill, 2015); "The First Monographic Works on Forensic Medicine—Xiyuan Jilu," China Culture, Aug. 2005, http://en.chinaculture .org/created/2005-08/01/content_71484_2.htm.

36   **separate and independent investigation:** P. Saukko and S. Pollack, "Autopsy: Procedures and Standards," in *Encyclopedia of Forensic and Legal Medicine*, edited by Jason Payne-James and Roger W. Byard (Boston: Elsevier Academic, 2015), 304–410.

36   **the first forensics manual ever published:** Sung Tz'u, *The Washing Away of Wrongs*, translated by Brian E. McKnight (Ann Arbor: University of Michigan Center for Chinese Studies, 1981).

37   **the sickle's owner confessed:** Richard S. Michelson, "History of Forensics," chapter 2 in *Crime Scene Investigation: An Introduction to CSI* (San Clemente, CA: LawTech Publishing Group, 2015); Sung Tz'u, *The Washing Away of Wrongs*, 69–70.

37   **feature of most criminal investigations:** Werner U. Spitz and Daniel J. Spitz, eds., *Spitz and Fisher's Medicolegal Investigation of Death: Guidelines for the Application of Pathology to Crime Investigation* (Springfield, IL: Charles C. Thomas, 2006), 4.

37   **testified in criminal courts:** Ibid., 5–6.

37   **an advisor to King Richard I:** Some historians have pointed out that there are records of a "crowner" office in some parts of England prior to 1194, but it was likely an official with much different responsibilities. Clifton D. Bryant and Dennis L. Peck, eds., *Encyclopedia of Death and the Human Experience* (Los Angeles: Sage Publications, 2009), 226.

39   **"treasure troves.":** Sources for the narrative of English coroner history: Bernard Knight, "Origins of the Office of the Coroner," "The Medieval Coroner's Duties," "The Coroner's Inquest," "The Right of Sanctuary," "Trial by Ordeal, Injuries Outlaws," and "Treasure Trove & Shipwrecks," Britannia History, www.britannia.com/history/coroner1.html; R. F. Hunnisett, *The Medieval Coroner* (Cambridge, UK: Cambridge University Press, 1961); Bryant and Peck, eds., *Encyclopedia of Death and the Human Experience*, 226; Henry William Carless Davis, *England Under the Normans and Angevins: 1066–1272* (London: Methuen, 1905), 324–326; Cecil Greek, "Drug Control and Asset Seizures: A Review of the History of Forfeiture in England and Colonial America," in *Drugs, Crime, and Social Policy: Research, Issues, and Concerns*, edited by Thomas Mieczkowski (Boston: Allyn & Bacon, 1992), 109–137; "History," The Coroners Society of England & Wales, www.coronersociety.org.uk/history; Coroners and Justice Act, 2009, chapter 25 (United Kingdom); Rudolph Eyre Melsheimer and Sir John Jervis, *The Coroners Act, 1887: With Forms and Precedents* (H. Sweet & Sons, 1888).

40   **a tradition that persists today:** See Indiana, for example, where in 2010 Hancock County sheriff C. K. "Bud" Gray was arrested for embezzlement by the coroner, "the only local official who can arrest a sitting sheriff." Richard Essex, "Hancock Co. Sheriff Arrested, Jailed," WTHR Eyewitness News, Aug. 6, 2010, www.wthr.com/article/hancock-co-sheriff

-arrested-jailed. In Mississippi, however, multiple officials are permitted to arrest the sheriff. See MS Code Section 19-25-11.

40   **to reach their conclusions:** Jeffrey M. Jentzen, *Death Investigation in America* (Cambridge, MA: Harvard University Press, 2009), 9.

40   **"demanded of potential coroners.":** Julie Johnson-McGrath, "Coroners, Corruption, and the Politics of Death," in *Legal Medicine in History*, edited by Michael Clark and Catherine Crawford (New York: Cambridge University Press, 1994), 268–288.

40   **entree into political life:** Jentzen, *Death Investigation in America*, 18.

41   **modern forensic pathology:** Ibid., 16.

41   **advocated abolishing of the coroner's office:** Ibid., 36–37.

41   **steered clear of the criminal justice system:** Ibid., 67–70.

42   **loot personal belongings from corpses:** Ibid., 16, 23–30; Johnson-McGrath, "Coroners, Corruption, and the Politics of Death."

42   **save a fortune in claims:** Jentzen, *Death Investigation in America*, 26.

43   **"physician would care to join.":** Johnson-McGrath, "Coroners, Corruption, and the Politics of Death," 277.

43   **Jennings was hanged:** People v. Jennings, 96 N.E. 1077 (1911); Jessica M. Sombat, "Latent Justice: Daubert's Impact on the Evaluation of Fingerprint Identification Testimony," *Fordham Law Review* 70, no. 6 (2002): 2819–2868; Richard C. Lindberg, *To Serve and Collect: Chicago Politics and Police Corruption from the Lager Beer Riot to the Summerdale Scandal* (New York: Praeger, 1991), 79–80.

44   **relative ratios of various body parts:** Greg Allen, "'Living Exhibits' at 1904 World's Fair Revisited," National Public Radio, May 31, 2005; "Interview with Robert Rydell," Public Broadcasting Service, 2003, www.pbs .org/race/000_About/002_04-background-02-11.htm; Jose D. Fermin, *1904 World's Fair: The Filipino Experience* (Diliman, Quezon City: University of the Philippines Press, 2006); Peter Komarinski, *Automated Fingerprint Identification Systems (AFIS)* (Boston: Elsevier Academic, 2005).

44   **he coined the term:** Sources for Galton narrative: "Bertillon System of Criminal Identification," National Law Enforcement Officers Memorial Fund, Nov. 2011, www.nleomf.org/museum/news/newsletters/online -insider/november-2011/bertillon-system-criminal-identification.html; Sir Francis Galton, *Memories of My Life* (London: Methuen, 1908), 311; "Origins of Eugenics: From Sir Francis Galton to Virginia's Racial Integrity Act of 1924," Historical Collections at the Claude Moore Health Sciences Library; Peter Komarinski, *Automated Fingerprint Identification Systems (AFIS)* (Boston: Elsevier Academic, 2005), 39–33. See also Galton biography, history, and collection of works and personal correspondence at http://galton.org.

45   **a focus on nascent forensic science:** William J. Tilstone, Kathleen A. Savage, and Leigh A. Clark, *Forensic Science: An Encyclopedia of History, Methods, and Techniques* (Santa Barbara, CA: ABC-CLIO, 2006), 17–21. See also Samuel J. Walker, *Popular Justice: A History of American Criminal Justice*, 2nd ed. (New York: Oxford University Press, 1998), 112–144.

45   **"witnesses were actually claiming.":** Jonathan Koehler, interview by Radley Balko.

46   **reformers all over the country:** "Norris Succeeds Riordan," *New York Times*, Feb. 1, 1918.

46   **followed in the next decade:** Jentzen, *Death Investigation in America*, 23.

46   **deaths from accidents and negligence:** Ibid., 138–141.

46   **only made things worse:** Ibid., 24.

47   **qualified forensic pathologists:** Ibid., 33–40.

47   **any meaningful legal reform:** Ibid., 45.

47   **Childs's model policies:** Sources for Richard Childs narrative: Ibid., 54–70; Bernard Hirschhorn, "Richard Spencer Childs (1882–1978): His Role in Modernization of Medicolegal Investigation in America," *American Journal of Forensic Pathology* (Sept. 1983).

48   **a formidable lobby:** Jentzen, *Death Investigation in America*, 61.

48   **"particular field in which it belongs.":** Frye v. United States, 293 F. 1013 (D.C. Cir. 1923).

48   **"content of a witness's testimony.":** Jonathan Koehler, interview by Radley Balko; see Alan W. Tamarelli, "Daubert v. Merrell Dow Pharmaceuticals: Pushing the Limits of Scientific Reliability—The Questionable Wisdom of Abandoning the Peer Review Standard for Admitting Expert Testimony," *Vanderbilt Law Review* 47 (1994): 1175–1203.

48   **entirely different ways of thinking:** Jonathan Koehler and Michael Saks, interviews by Radley Balko; Jentzen, *Death Investigation in America*, 24.

49   **class of candidates was certified in 1959:** W. G. Eckert, "The Forensic Pathology Specialty Certifications," *American Journal of Forensic and Medical Pathology* (March 1988).

49   **for the position at all:** "Coroner Training Requirements," Center for Disease Control, updated Oct. 26, 2016, www.cdc.gov/phlp/publications/coroner/training.html.

CHAPTER 4: AT THE HANDS OF PERSONS UNKNOWN

51   **"to the jury is rendered":** Ida B. Wells, "Lynch Law," from "The Reason Why the Colored American Is Not in the World's Columbian Exposition," 1893, http://digital.library.upenn.edu/women/wells/exposition/exposition.html.

51   **"to keep down public clamor.":** "Inaccurate Reports on Lynchings," *Afro-American* (Baltimore, MD), Jan. 7, 1932.

52   **already illegal under state law:** Robert Siegel, "Anti-Lynching Law in U.S. History," National Public Radio, June 13, 2005.

52   **"'party or parties unknown.'":** Stewart E. Tolnay and E. M. Beck, *A Festival of Violence: An Analysis of Southern Lynchings, 1882–1930* (Urbana: University of Illinois Press, 1995), 212.

52   **publications like the *Chicago Defender*:** Ethan Michaeli, "'Bound for the Promised Land,'" *Atlantic*, Jan. 11, 2016.

52   **"at the hands of persons unknown.":** See, for example, *Report of the NAACP for the Years 1917 and 1918* (1919); "Lynching, Whites and Negroes—1882–1968," Tuskegee University Archives, http://archive.tuskegee.edu/archive/bitstream/handle/123456789/511/Lyching%201882%201968.pdf?sequence=1&isAllowed=y.

52   **history of lynching in America:** See Philip Dray, *At the Hands of Persons Unknown: The Lynching of Black America* (New York: Modern Library, 2003).

53   **or pieces of the rope used for the hanging:** Amy Louise Wood, *Lynching and Spectacle: Witnessing Racial Violence in America, 1890–1940* (Chapel Hill: University of North Carolina Press, 2009), 30; see also James Allen, *Without Sanctuary: Lynching Photography in America* (Santa Fe, NM: Twin Palms, 2010).

53   **"rope that strung him up, too.":** Anna Bard Brutzman, "100 Years Later, Notorious Honea Path Lynching Remembered," *Independent Mail* (Anderson, SC), Oct. 9, 2011.

53   **"a party to help lynch the brute.":** Tolnay and Beck, *A Festival of Violence,* 26, quoting the *Crisis,* Dec. 1911, 56.

53   **Willis Jackson died "at the hands of parties unknown.":** Brutzman, "100 Years Later."

54   **rendering the crime unsolvable:** Dray, *At the Hands of Persons Unknown,* 226–229.

54   **"not conducting his own investigation":** William Wilbanks, *Forgotten Heroes: Police Officers Killed in Dade County, 1895–1995* (Paducah, KY: Turner, 1996), 30.

55   **the president of the United States himself:** See Laura Wexler, *Fire in a Canebrake* (New York: Scribner, 2004); Kathy Lohr, "FBI Re-Examines 1946 Lynching Case," National Public Radio, July 25, 2006.

55   **"The Best People Won't Talk.":** "The Best People Won't Talk," *Time,* Aug. 5, 1946; Dray, *At the Hands of Persons Unknown,* 382.

55   **"stain our national record.":** Wexler, *Fire in a Canebrake,* 81; Lohr, "FBI Re-Examines 1946 Lynching Case."

55   **"from the law enforcement standpoint":** Dray, *At the Hands of Persons Unknown,* 378–383.

55   **led the country in lynchings, with 577:** Jessie P. Guzman and W. Hardin Hughes, *Negro Year Book: A Review of Events Affecting Negro Life, 1944–1946* in The Making of African American Identity: Vol. III, 1917–1968, National Humanities Center Resource Toolbox, http://nationalhuman itiescenter.org/pds/maai3/segregation/text2/text2read.htm.

56   **was accidental or coerced:** Hilton Butler, "Lynch Law in Action," *New Republic,* July 22, 1931, 256–257.

56   **shotgunned him to death:** "Report: Negro Who Shot Man Shoots Self," *Leader-Call* (Laurel, MS), March 25, 1935.

56   **case is unsolved:** Michael Newton, *Unsolved Civil Rights Murder Cases, 1934–1970* (Jefferson, NC: McFarland, 2016), 103; "Report: Negro Who Shot Man Shoots Self."

56   **coroner called that a suicide, too:** Jessie Ames, *The Changing Character of Lynching* (Atlanta: Commission on Interracial Cooperation, 1942), 44.

56   **"to be chronicled in the dispatches.":** "The Week in Crime," *Clarion-Ledger* (Jackson, MS), May 16, 1904.

57   **coroner wrote simply: "no doctor.":** Patricia Schroeder, *Robert Johnson, Mythmaking, and Contemporary American Culture* (Urbana: University of Illinois Press, 2004), 42.

57   **But that too was never confirmed:** Sources for Robert Johnson narrative: Elijah Wald, *Escaping the Delta: Robert Johnson and the Invention of the Blues* (New York: Amistad, 2004); Tony Hays, "Robert Johnson: Murder or Bad Whiskey?" CriminalElement.com, Oct. 26, 2012, www.criminalelement .com/blogs/2012/10/robert-johnson-murder-or-bad-whiskey-tony -hays-true-crime-historical-bottoms-up-music; Joe Kloc, "Fact-Checking the Life and Death of Bluesman Robert Johnson," *Mother Jones,* June 21, 2010; Tom Graves, *Crossroads: The Life and Afterlife of Blues Legend Robert Johnson* (Spokane, WA: Demers Books, 2008), 39–43.

58   **ill-equipped to bring killers to justice:** Jay Milner, "'Heart Failure' or Stabbing?" *Clarion-Ledger* (Jackson, MS), March 20, 1955.

59   **"actual practice of pathology":** Ibid.

59   **responded with defiance:** Carole Cannon, "Black Monday: Mississippi's Ugly Response to the 'Brown v. Board' Decision," *Jackson* (MS) *Free Press*, May 12, 2004; Myrlie B. Evers, with William Peters, *For Us, the Living* (Jackson, MS: Banner Books, 1967), 109–114.

61   **"Negro Leader Dies in Odd Accident.":** "Negro Leader Dies in Odd Accident," *Clarion-Ledger* (Jackson, MS), May 9, 1955.

61   **"quite a ladies' man":** Newton, *Unsolved Civil Rights Murder Cases*, 17.

62   **The manner: "murder by persons unknown.":** Ibid.

62   **"could cause a deterioration of racial relations.":** Sources for George Lee narrative: Marc Perrusquia, "60 Years Later, Murder Still Bedevils Mississippi Delta Town," *Memphis Commercial-Appeal*, May 2, 2015; see also David T. Beito and Linda Royster Beito, "The Grim and Overlooked Anniversary of the Murder of the Rev. George W. Lee, Civil Rights Activist," *History News Network*, May 9, 2005; Michael Newton, *The Ku Klux Klan in Mississippi: A History* (Jefferson, NC: McFarland, 2010), 111; Newton, *Unsolved Civil Rights Murder Cases*, 17; M. Susan Orr-Klopfer, "Bloody Belzoni," Chapter 14 in *Where Rebels Roost . . . Mississippi Civil Rights Revisited* (Lulu.com, 2005); Stephanie Saul, "FBI Files Detail '55 Slaying," *Newsday*, May 9, 2000; "Who Is Rev. George Lee," Fannie Lou Hamer Civil Rights Museum; "Justice Dept. Urges FBI to Investigate Miss. Lynching," *Jet*, June 2, 1955.

62   **George Lee's murder:** "Humphreys," Mississippi Civil Rights Project, http://mscivilrightsproject.org/counties/humphreys.

63   **"wolf-whistled.":** Bryant has recently claimed that what she and others had claimed occurred that day in the store is not accurate. See Timothy B. Tyson, *The Blood of Emmett Till* (New York: Simon and Schuster, 2017); Jason Parham, "Emmett Till's Murder: What Really Happened That Day in the Store?," *New York Times*, Jan. 27, 2017.

64   **"charge those men with murder.":** Devery S. Anderson, *Emmett Till: The Murder That Shocked the World and Propelled the Civil Rights Movement* (Jackson: University Press of Mississippi, 2015), 48, citing "Negro Boy Was Killed for 'Wolf Whistle,'" *New York Post*, Sept. 1, 1955.

64   **"more of a post-mortem.":** "'Cover Up' Charged in Boy's Death," *Des Moines* (IA) *Register*, Sept. 4, 1955.

64   **"in an advanced state of decomposition.":** Emmett Till trial transcript, contained in Federal Bureau of Investigation (FBI), *Prosecutive Report of Investigation Concerning [redacted], Roy Bryant, John William Milam, Leslie F. Milam, Melvin L. Campbell, Elmer O. Kimbrell, Hubert Clark, Levi Collins, Johnny B. Washington, Otha Johnson, Jr., Emmett Louis Till, Civil Rights Conspiracy; Domestic Police Cooperation*, Feb. 9, 2006.

64   **"by murdering black children.":** Stephen J. Whitfield, *A Death in the Delta: The Story of Emmett Till* (Baltimore: Johns Hopkins University Press, 1988), 28, citing *New York Times*, Sept. 8, 1955, 10; *Memphis Commercial Appeal*, Sept. 1, 1955, 1, 4; *Daily News* (Jackson, MS), Sept. 2, 1955, 8.

64   **"hell to pay.":** Damon Root, "A Forgotten Civil Rights Hero," *Reason*, April 2009; see also David T. Beito and Linda Royster Beito, *Black Maverick: T. R. M. Howard's Fight for Civil Rights and Economic Power* (Urbana: University of Illinois Press, 2009).

65   **"all the niggers that'll be thrown into it.":** Randy Sparkman, "The Murder of Emmett Till," *Slate*, June 21, 2005.

66   **"I doubt it.":** Emmett Till trial transcript, contained in FBI, *Prosecutive Report of Investigation*, 299–300.

66   **"if it had been in the open air?":** Ibid., 300.

66   **"pressure," he said:** Gary Younge, "Justice at Last," *Guardian*, June 5, 2005.

66   **"it wouldn't have taken that long.":** "The Law: Trial by Jury," *Time*, Oct. 3, 1955.

66   **"$4,000 for their story":** Lottie L. Joiner, "How Emmett Till Changed the World," *Daily Beast*, Aug. 28, 2015.

67   **this was the body of Emmett Till:** Additional sources for Emmett Till narrative: Anderson, *Emmett Till*; Mamie Till-Mobley and Christopher Benson, *The Death of Innocence: The Story of the Hate Crime That Changed America* (New York: Random House, 2003); Davis W. Houck and Matthew Grindy, *Emmett Till and the Mississippi Press* (Jackson: University Press of Mississippi, 2008).

67   **was not true:** Richard Perez Pena, "Woman Linked to 1955 Emmett Till Murder Tells Historian Her Claims Were False," *New York Times*, Jan. 27, 2017.

68   **"I think I have killed a nigger.":** "Luther Jackson," Emmett Till Act (Cold Case Closing Memoranda), Civil Rights Division, US Department of Justice, Oct. 6, 2016.

68   **ruled the shooting a justifiable homicide:** Michael Newton, *The Ku Klux Klan in Mississippi: A History* (Jefferson, NC: McFarland, 2010), 116.

68   **again ruled the killing a justifiable homicide:** Newton, *Unsolved Civil Rights Murder Cases*, 215–216.

68   **whipped him with a belt:** See ibid., 215–216.

68   **to crack heads in the civil rights movement:** Florence Mars, *Witness in Philadelphia* (Baton Rouge: Louisiana State University Press, 1977), 76.

69   **an accidental drowning:** "Hubert Orsby," Northeastern University Project on Civil Rights and Restorative Justice, http://nuweb9.neu.edu /civilrights/hubert-orsby, last accessed July 27, 2017.

71   **"with a blunt instrument or a chain.":** Claude Sitton, "Arrests Awaited by Mississippians," *New York Times*, Aug. 8, 1964.

71   **"I'm talking about hands.":** Jerry Mitchell, "Experts: Autopsy Reveals Beating," *Clarion-Ledger* (Jackson, MS), June 4, 2000.

71   **complaint with the College of American Pathologists:** Jerry Mitchell, "Spy Agency Took Aim at N.Y. Pathologist," *Clarion-Ledger* (Jackson, MS), June 4, 2000.

72   **the coroner wrote "unknown.":** Sources for Chaney, Goodman, and Schwerner narrative: Douglas O. Linder, "'Bending Toward Justice': John Doar and the 'Mississippi Burning' Trial," *Mississippi Law Journal* 72 (2002): 731–780; Newton, *The Ku Klux Klan in Mississippi*, 140–147; Mitchell, "Spy Agency Took Aim at N.Y. Pathologist"; Jerry Mitchell, "Activist Slayings Reopened," *Clarion-Ledger* (Jackson, MS), Feb. 8, 2000; Richard D. deShazo, Robert Smith, and Leigh Baldwin Skipworth, "A White Dean and Black Physicians at the Epicenter of the Civil Rights Movement," *American Journal of Medicine* 127, no. 6 (June 2014); "Autopsy Shows Chaney Was Brutally Beaten, Shot," UPI, Aug. 11, 1964; Mitchell, "Experts: Autopsy Reveals Beating"; David Spain, "Mississippi Autopsy," *Ramparts*, Mississippi Eyewitness: Special Issue, 1964; Amy Goodman, "Mississippi Trial Begins in 1964 Civil Rights Killings" (interview with

Ben Chaney), *Democracy Now,* June 14, 2005; Walter Rugaber, "Mississippi Jury Convicts 7 of 18 in Rights Killings," *New York Times,* Oct. 21, 1967; John Dittmer, *The Good Doctors: The Medical Committee for Human Rights and the Struggle for Social Justice in Health Care* (New York: Bloomsbury, 2009), 55–60.

CHAPTER 5: SETTING THE STAGE FOR THE CADAVER KING

73   **permanent party stronghold:** Rick Perlstein, "Exclusive: Lee Atwater's Infamous 1981 Interview on the Southern Strategy," *Nation,* Nov. 13, 2012; Beth Schwartzapfel and Bill Keller, "Willie Horton Revisited," The Marshall Project, May 13, 2015 www.themarshallproject.org/2015/05/13 /willie-horton-revisited#.HOuhWlVRH; Robin Price Pierre, "How a Conservative Wins the Presidency in a Liberal Decade," *Atlantic,* July 9, 2016; Stephen D. Shaffer and David Breaux, "Mississippi Politics in the 1990s: Ideology and Performance," presented to the American Political Science Association, 1997, http://sds17.pspa.msstate.edu/research/Apsa97.html; Jere Nash and Andy Taggert, *Mississippi Politics: The Struggle for Power, 1976–2008* (Jackson: University of Mississippi Press, 2009).

73   **"Best States for a Murder.":** Kenneth Fairly, "On the Hill," *Clarion-Ledger* (Jackson, MS), June 18, 1968.

74   **instituted during Reconstruction:** Martin Zimmerman, "Dead Men Tell Few Tales to Mississippi's Good-Ole-Boy Coroners," *Clarion-Ledger* (Jackson, MS), Jan. 25, 1981; "Murder Haven," *Clarion-Ledger* (Jackson, MS), Dec. 19, 1984.

74   **when Mississippi was still a territory:** Don Hoffman, "Coroner System Gives Mississippi Killers a Break," *Clarion-Ledger* (Jackson, MS), Sept. 18, 1983.

74   **almost exclusively to lay coroners:** Fairly, "On the Hill."

74   **they found little success:** Kenneth Fairly, "State's Physician Coroner Tells Need to Upgrade Office," *Clarion-Ledger* (Jackson, MS), June 16, 1968.

74   **convene juries to investigate suspicious deaths:** Ibid.

74   **coroner at all:** Ibid.

74   **he wanted to get into politics:** Bob Zeller, "Ex-Coroner Doesn't Advise Job on a Part-Time Basis," *Clarion-Ledger* (Jackson, MS), May 8, 1978.

74   **"with very little effort.":** Ibid.

74   **recently reviewed the coroner system:** Fairly, "State's Physician Coroner Tells Need to Upgrade Office."

75   **paid to conduct investigations:** Josh Zimmer, "Race Livens Up for Hinds Coroner's Post," *Clarion-Ledger* (Jackson, MS), July 29, 1995.

75   **for embalming and funeral services:** Ibid.

75   **corrupt and broken anachronism:** Fairly, "State's Physician Coroner Tells Need to Upgrade Office."

75   **was never identified:** Charles B. Gordon, "Old Jud Is Daid, But How?" *Daily News* (Jackson, MS), Jan. 13, 1974.

75   **to fund the position directly:** "An Evaluation of Mississippi's Medicolegal Death Investigation Process," Report to the Mississippi Legislature, Joint Legislative Committee on Performance Evaluation and Expenditure Review (PEER), Sept. 16, 2008, 5; Bob Zeller, "Constant Uncertainty of Death Raises Doubts About Coroners," *Clarion-Ledger* (Jackson, MS), May 8, 1978.

75 **vacant for twenty years:** Jean Culbertson, "Medical Examiner Need in Mississippi Stressed," *Clarion-Ledger* (Jackson, MS), March 27, 1974.

76 **lobbied for an appropriation:** Zeller, "Constant Uncertainty of Death Raises Doubts About Coroners."

76 **"'X' at the bottom," he said.:** Ibid.

76 **for modernizing the office:** Ibid.

76 **named an official state medical examiner:** Anne Q. Hoy, "New Medical Examiner Is Lifeline in Death Investigations," *Clarion-Ledger* (Jackson, MS), Aug. 4, 1979.

77 **began to agitate for change:** James Dickerson, "State Coroner System 'Ludicrous,'" *Daily News* (Jackson, MS), March 7, 1980; Coleman Warner, "Examiner Empties Her Office," *Clarion-Ledger* (Jackson, MS), June 30, 1982.

77 **"and get away with it.":** Dickerson, "State Coroner System 'Ludicrous.'"

77 **"ludicrous joke.":** Ibid.

77 **to collect the $20 fee:** Ibid.

77 **"allowed into their homes.":** Ibid.

77 **possibility of an investigation:** "Coroner Reform: Part 1," *Daily News* (Jackson, MS), March 7, 1980.

77 **a model for the country:** Martin Zimmerman, "Death Investigation Can Combat Crime," *Clarion-Ledger* (Jackson, MS), Jan. 25, 1981.

78 **for each of several regional districts:** Ibid.

78 **sought a mixture of the two systems:** "Coroner Reform."

78 **the bill failed:** Ibid.; Warner, "Examiner Empties Her Office."

78 **take their jobs more seriously:** Martin Zimmerman, "Bill Could Bring Investigations of Death Out of 'Dark Ages,'" *Clarion-Ledger* (Jackson, MS), Jan. 26, 1981; "Coroner Reform"; Warner, "Examiner Empties Her Office"; "Coroner Reform: Part 1," *Daily News* (Jackson, MS), March 7, 1980; "Coroner Reform: Part 2," *Daily News* (Jackson, MS), March 10, 1980.

79 **compromise many of them could live with:** Faye Spruill, interview by Radley Balko.

79 **"unknown causes.":** Zimmerman, "Dead Men Tell Few Tales to Mississippi's Good-Ole-Boy Coroners."

79 **weren't being investigated:** Ibid.

79 **and no expense account:** Sources for Robert Martin narrative: Martin Zimmerman, "No 'Routine' Day for County's On-Call Coroner," *Clarion-Ledger* (Jackson, MS), Jan. 26, 1981; Robert D. Martin, "State Coroner System Given Explanatory Insight," Letters to the Editor, *Daily News* (Jackson, MS), March 25, 1980; but see Theresa Kiely, "Coroner's 20 Years Draw to a Close," *Clarion-Ledger* (Jackson, MS), Jan. 3, 2000.

79 **proposal into law:** Tom Clifford, "Coroner System's 'Old Bones' Hamper Monticello Inquiry," *Daily News* (Jackson, MS), Feb. 25, 1981; Spruill, interview.

79 **it had approved:** Coleman Warner, "State's 1981 Coroner Reform Law Not Yet Funded," *Clarion-Ledger* (Jackson, MS), Jan. 11, 1982.

80 **more powerful lawmakers:** Warner, "Examiner Empties Her Office."

80 **Crook had been around a long time:** Interestingly, Crook later represented Roy Bryant when Bryant was charged federally in a food stamp scam, referring to Bryant at the sentencing hearing as "a good citizen of Ruleville." See Devery S. Anderson, *Emmett Till: The Murder That Shocked*

the World and Propelled the Civil Rights Movement (Jackson: University Press of Mississippi, 2015), 278.

80   **a tough agricultural market:** Ibid., 270; "Two Delta Senators Offer Negro Relocation Measure," *Hattiesburg* (MS) *American*, Feb. 25, 1966.

80   **"what to do anymore":** Lloyd White, interview by Radley Balko.

80   **the number had been disconnected:** Warner, "Examiner Empties Her Office."

80   **refused to fund her office:** "Medical Examiner System Takes Big Step Backward," *Natchez* (MS) *Democrat*, July 22, 1983.

80   **or a phone:** Ibid.

81   **couldn't read or write:** Ruth Ingram, "No Medical Training Required for State Coroners," *Clarion-Ledger* (Jackson, MS), Jan. 17, 1988; Valeri Oliver, "State Coroners to Ask Legislature for Tougher Qualifications," *Clarion-Ledger* (Jackson, MS), Dec. 17, 1984; Dickerson, "State Coroner System 'Ludicrous.'"

81   **70 percent:** Dean Solov, "Proposed Bill Would Establish Standards for County Coroners," *Clarion-Ledger* (Jackson, MS), March 31, 1986.

81   **around 3 percent:** Jeanna Bryner, "Mystery Deaths Plague Coroners," *Live Science*, May 4, 2007; see M. J. Breiding and B. Wiersema, "Variability of Undetermined Manner of Death Classification in the US," *Injury Prevention* 12, Supp. 2 (2006): 49–54; A. M. Miniño, R. N. Anderson, L. A. Fingerhut, et al., "Deaths: Injuries, 2000," *National Vital Statistics Report* (2006).

81   **in other states were allocated:** Russell Carollo, "Medical Examiner Arrives," *Clarion-Ledger* (Jackson, MS), April 5, 1985.

81   **"have been sent a message!":** Ibid.

82   **"We're going to be hard on you,":** Ibid.

82   **the existence of a Supreme being:** Dickerson, "State Coroner System 'Ludicrous'"; Mississippi Code Section 19-21-103 (2013); Mississippi Constitution, Section 265.

82   **controversy in Mississippi:** Ingram, "No Medical Training Required for State Coroners"; Solov, "Proposed Bill Would Establish Standards for County Coroners"; Cristal Cody, "Only 1 Coroner in Miss. Qualified as Crime Analyst," *Clarion-Ledger* (Jackson, MS), Aug. 3, 1998; "Rankin County Pathologist Named Interim Mississippi Medical Examiner," *Clarion-Ledger* (Jackson, MS), June 24, 1987.

82   **"out of anybody?":** Solov, "Proposed Bill Would Establish Standards for County Coroners."

83   **they didn't like his diagnosis:** Ibid.; Ingram, "No Medical Training Required for State Coroners"; Cody, "Only 1 Coroner in Miss. Qualified as Crime Analyst"; "Rankin County Pathologist Named Interim Mississippi Medical Examiner"; Carollo, "Medical Examiner Arrives"; "A Policy Analysis of the State Medical Examiner Program," Mississippi Legislature Joint Committee on Expenditure and Evaluation Review, Aug. 11, 1988; Jimmy W. Cox, "You Should Clean Off Your Own Step First," *Columbian-Progress* (Columbia, MS), July 31, 1986; Sid Salter, "State Law Should Spell Out Duties of Coroners in Preserving Evidence," *Clarion-Ledger* (Jackson, MS), March 9, 1986.

83   **definitely been strangled:** Sid Salter, "State Law Should Spell Out Duties of Coroners in Preserving Evidence," *Clarion-Ledger* (Jackson, MS), March 9, 1986.

83   **fallen off on its own:** Dean Solov, "Coroner May Have Cut Off Head of Body," *Clarion-Ledger* (Jackson, MS), July 18, 1986.

84   **"one person can handle.":** Harvey Rice, "New State Pathologist Finds Full Workload," *Clarion-Ledger* (Jackson, MS), Aug. 21, 1985.

84   **to the witness stand:** Ibid.

84   **equipped for forensic pathology:** Lynn Watkins, "Bennett Fights Budget Crunch with $400 Autopsy Fee," *Clarion-Ledger* (Jackson, MS), July 26, 1986.

84   **support from the DPS:** Dean Solov, "Medical Examiner to Keep Post," *Clarion-Ledger* (Jackson, MS), June 28, 1986.

84   **"I'm just fried,":** Dean Solov, "State Medical Examiner Calls It Quits," *Clarion-Ledger* (Jackson, MS), Aug. 29, 1986.

84   **"with medical examiners":** Ibid. See Sid Salter, "Medical Examiner Bennett Leaving State for Iowa Job," *Clarion-Ledger* (Jackson, MS), Aug. 31, 1986.

84   **jumping ship:** Solov, "State Medical Examiner Calls It Quits."

84   **"continue to function":** Grace Simmons, "Roberts Sees No Immediate Problem with Absence of Pathologist," *Clarion-Ledger* (Jackson, MS), Oct. 27, 1986.

85   **"I'm really just heartsick.":** Dean Solov, "State Medical Examiner Due to Quit Post," *Clarion-Ledger,* June 27, 1986.

85   **in the case of *State v. Stinson*:** State v. Stinson, 397 N.W. 2d 136 (Wisconsin Ct. of Appeals 1986).

85   **"degree of scientific certainty":** Ibid.

85   **"hypothesis of innocence":** Ibid.

85   **exonerated by DNA testing:** Dinesh Ramde and Todd Richmond, "Man Freed 23 Years After Wrongful Conviction," Associated Press, Jan. 30, 2009.

86   **bite marks in a criminal trial:** William James Maloney, "The Salem Witch Trials: First Use of Bite Mark Evidence in Court," *New York State Dental Association News* 27, no. 1 (Feb. 2014): 1–2; George Lincoln Burr, *Narratives of the Witchcraft Cases, 1648–1706* (New York: Charles Scribner's Sons, 1914), 215–228, excerpting Cotton Mather, *The Wonders of the Invisible World*; John Demos, "Underlying Themes in the Witchcraft of the Seventeenth Century," *American Historical Review* 75, no. 5. (June 1970): 1323.

86   **court upheld the conviction:** People v. Marx, 54 Cal. App. 3d 101 (1975).

87   **bite mark identification testimony:** D. Michael Risinger, "Navigating Expert Reliability: Are Criminal Standards of Certainty Being Left on the Dock?" *Albany Law Review* 64, no. 1(2000): 138.

87   **a separate case:** People v. Slone, 76 California Ct. of Appeals 3d, 611 (1978).

87   **validating the field didn't exist:** M. Chris Fabricant and William Tucker Carrington, "The Shifted Paradigm: Forensic Science's Overdue Evolution from Magic to Law," *Virginia Review of Criminal Law* 4, no. 1 (2016): 41–42.

87   **admissible forensic discipline:** State v. Garrison, 585 P.2d 563 (Ariz. 1978).

87   **no longer even necessary:** State v. Armstrong, 179 W. Va. 435 (W.Va. 1988).

88   **judicial echo chamber:** Fabricant and Carrington, "The Shifted Paradigm."

88   **"it doesn't seem to matter":** Michael Saks, interview by Radley Balko.

88   **single dissenting opinion:** Robert A. De La Cruz, "Forensic Dentistry and the Law: Is Bite Mark Evidence Here to Stay?" *American Criminal Law Review* 24 (1987): 983.

88   **jurisdictions had accepted it:** Gerald L. Vale, "A Historical Perspective: 'History of Bitemark Evidence,'" in *Bitemark Evidence*, edited by Robert B. J. Dorion (New York: Marcel Dekker, 2005), 23.

88   **were nearly executed:** Chris Fabricant, interview by Radley Balko; Amanda L. Myers, "Men Wrongly Convicted or Arrested on Bite Evidence," Yahoo! News, June 16, 2013; Amanda L. Myers, "Once Key in Some Cases, Bite Mark Evidence Now Derided as Unreliable," *Denver Post* June 17, 2013.

90   **"do the load I've been doing,":** Solov, "State Medical Examiner Due to Quit Post"; "State's Medical Examiner to Quit," *Hattiesburg* (MS) *American,* June 27, 1986.

CHAPTER 6: RISE OF A FIEFDOM

91   **"the folly of the Vietnam War.":** Campbell Robertson, "Questions Left for Mississippi Over Doctor's Autopsies," *New York Times,* Jan. 7, 2013.

92   **other experts said was dubious:** Radley Balko, "CSI Mississippi," *Wall Street Journal,* Oct. 6, 2007.

93   **"a smart guy who would play ball":** Hayne has consistently denied that he would "play ball" for prosecutors. See, for example, Deposition of Dr. Steven Hayne, Hayne v. Innocence Project, 2011 WL 198128, No. 3:09-CV-218-KS-LRA (S.D. Miss. April 27, 2012), 150–151. When asked if he'll testify to whatever prosecutors need him to say, he responded, "That's absolutely false. . . . I've had prosecutors tell me that I was going to testify one way and I told them to go to hell. . . . I don't go out to curry the favor of anybody when I write an autopsy."

93   **"combination in an expert witness":** Parke Morris, interview by Radley Balko.

93   **"I liked their attitude.":** Deposition of Dr. Steven Hayne, *Hayne v. Innocence Project* (April 26, 2012), 21.

93   **Rhode Island:** Steven Timothy Hayne, curriculum vitae.

93   **"I wanted an Ivy League degree.":** Deposition of Dr. Steven Hayne, *Hayne v. Innocence Project* (April 26, 2012), 21.

94   **just east of Jackson:** Ibid., 81.

94   **American Board of Pathology soon after:** Hayne, curriculum vitae.

94   **at 1,857 autopsies:** "Number of Autopsies Performed by Dr. Hayne," document, *Hayne v. Innocence Project.*

95   **regardless of any other factors:** *Forensic Autopsy Performance Standards,* National Association of Medical Examiners, Oct. 2006, 10.

95   **he performed 375 autopsies:** Deposition of Steven Hayne, Christopher Lewis v. Dr. Nathaniel Brown et al., No. 99-0476 (Sunflower Cnty. Circuit Ct. Aug. 23, 2001), 65; see also letter from Ken Winter to L. Carl Hagwood, Nov. 30, 2001.

96   **did private autopsies and consulting:** Hayne, curriculum vitae.

96   **"I choose to work.":** Trial transcript, State of Mississippi v. Yolanda Williams (Washington Cnty. Circuit Ct. April 15, 2005), 375; trial transcript,

Devin Bennett v. State of Mississippi, No. 12,699 (Rankin Cnty. Circuit Ct., Feb. 18, 2003), 1285.

96 **"my record stands for itself.":** *Devin Bennett v. State of Mississippi*, 1286–1287.

96 **he topped** *two thousand* **autopsies:** Deposition of Dr. Steven Hayne, *Hayne v. Innocence Project* (April 26, 2012), 141–142.

96 **"barbecues and stuff.":** Deposition of Dr. Steven Hayne, *Hayne v. Innocence Project* (April 26, 2012), 135.

96 **help them win convictions:** See letter from Duane Dillon, president, Mississippi Sheriffs' Association, to Steve Simpson, April 14, 2008, calling Hayne "an invaluable tool for law enforcement"; letter from James H. Powell III to Governor Haley Barbour, Aug. 12, 2008, saying that if "Hayne's work was shoddy or unprofessional I would have complained to someone long ago."

97 **"useful to law enforcement":** Robertson, "Questions Left for Mississippi Over Doctor's Autopsies."

97 **what a great witness he had been:** Letter from Dillon to Simpson; letter from Powell to Barbour; letter from Dee Bates to Haley Barbour, Aug. 12, 2008 (claiming that in her district, Hayne's conclusions were "never challenged" by defense attorneys); letter from Forrest Allgood to Haley Barbour, Aug. 13, 2008 (claiming Hayne was not a "'shameless shill'" and Hayne "has told me [Allgood] on many occasions that he would not be able to testify to a matter, or given me information that was unfavorable to the prosecution").

97 **"claims of wrongful convictions.":** Letter from W. Dewayne Richardson to Governor Haley Barbour, Sept. 3, 2008.

97 **"several court appearances in one day.":** Letter from Mark Duncan to Governor Haley Barbour, Aug. 12, 2008.

97 **"without Dr. Hayne performing our autopsies.":** Letter from Bilbo Mitchell to Governor Haley Barbour, Aug. 12, 2008.

98 **for transporting bodies:** Mississippi coroner, interview by David Fechheimer, Feb. 26, 2012.

98 **sending Hayne autopsy referrals:** Deposition of Dr. Steven Hayne, *Hayne v. Innocence Project* (April 26, 2012), 90–91.

98 **Rankin County coroner in 1981:** "Roberts Elected County Coroner," *Clarion-Ledger* (Jackson, MS), Aug. 19, 1981.

98 **paraphrasing Roberts:** Douglas Demmons, "New Coroner Says Job Is Underrated," *Clarion-Ledger* (Jackson, MS), Aug. 26, 1991.

98 **"hauling bodies all over the state":** L. W. "Bump" Calloway, interview by David Fechheimer, Feb. 25, 2012; Mississippi coroner, interview by David Fechheimer, Feb. 26, 2012.

99 **transport of bodies:** Adam Lynch, "Shipping Off Bodies," *Jackson* (MS) *Free Press*, March 18, 2005.

99 **his impressive résumé:** "Rankin County Pathologist Named Interim Mississippi Medical Examiner," *Clarion-Ledger* (Jackson, MS), June 24, 1987.

99 **nationally recognized certifying organization:** See Mississippi Medical Examiner Act of 1986, § 41-61-55.

99 **at least on an interim basis:** "Rankin County Pathologist Named Interim Mississippi Medical Examiner."

99 **Mississippi's third state medical examiner:** Ibid.

99   **board-certified state medical examiner:** Grace Simmons, "Interim Medical Examiner Resigns," *Clarion-Ledger* (Jackson, MS), March 4, 1988.

100   **administration of justice:** J. F. Booth and B. J. Halderman, "A Policy Analysis of the State Medical Examiner Program," Mississippi Legislature Joint Committee on Performance Evaluation and Expenditure Review, Aug. 11, 1988.

100   **didn't seem to care:** Beverly Pettigrew, "Voters Aren't Demanding Money for Death Investigation System," *Clarion-Ledger* (Jackson, MS), Feb. 14, 1989.

100   **"needs to have their brain checked":** Ibid.

100   **"there was no other game.":** Mississippi coroner, interview by David Fechheimer, Feb. 26, 2012.

100   **"since Hayne didn't hold any office":** Douglas Posey, interview by Radley Balko.

101   **"what the coroners and prosecutors wanted":** Jim Ingram, interview by Radley Balko.

101   **as did many of the state's coroners:** Simmons, "Interim Medical Examiner Resigns."

101   **"was never an issue.":** Deposition of Steven Hayne, Christopher M. Lewis v. Dr. Nathaniel Brown et al., No. 99-0476 (Sunflower Cnty. Circuit Ct. Aug. 23, 2001), 29.

101   **for more money:** Deposition of Dr. Steven Hayne, *Hayne v. Innocence Project* (April 26, 2012), 123.

101   **"endangers public safety.":** Louisa Dixon, "Death Investigations Lax," *Clarion-Ledger* (Jackson, MS), March 30, 2008.

102   **wanted to be doing them:** Beverly Pettigrew and Sydney Cearnal, "Many Coroners Struggle Without State Medical Examiner," *Clarion-Ledger* (Jackson, MS), Feb. 13, 1989.

102   **"because that was his first love.":** Simmons, "Interim Medical Examiner Resigns"; Grace Simmons, "Assistant Medical Examiner Can't Work Outside Office," *Clarion-Ledger* (Jackson, MS), Jan. 25, 1988.

103   **by prosecuting elderly Klansmen:** See, for example, United States v. James Ford Seale, 600 F.3d. 473 (5th Cir. 2010).

CHAPTER 7: THE WEST PHENOMENON

106   **"what we're trying to do":** Sharon Wertz, "Taking a Bite Out of Crime," *Hattiesburg* (MS) *American*, Oct. 9, 1983.

106   **bite mark specialists for confirmation:** Janet Braswell, "Experts Examine Rape Evidence," *Hattiesburg* (MS) *American*, Feb. 16, 1983; Betty Mallett, "Dentist Testimony Links Bite Mark to Don Horn," *Hattiesburg* (MS) *American*, Dec. 2, 1983; Harvey Rice and Roscoe Nance, "USM Senior and NFL Hopeful Surrenders; Charged with Rape," *Clarion-Ledger* (Jackson, MS), Feb. 18, 1983; "Victim Compared Rapist to Horn," *Clarion-Ledger* (Jackson, MS), Dec. 1, 1983.

106   **was suspended from the school:** Rice and Nance, "USM Senior and NFL Hopeful Surrenders."

106   **wielded a box cutter:** Betty Mallet and Janet Braswell, "Horn Found Innocent," *Hattiesburg* (MS) *American*, Dec. 4, 1983.

107   **at her brother's wedding:** Ibid.

107   **photographs of the upper marks:** Mallet, "Dentist Testimony Links Bite Marks to Don Horn."

107 **inconsistent with Horn's teeth:** Betty Mallet, "Experts in Horn Case Conflict," *Hattiesburg* (MS) *American*, Dec. 3, 1983.

107 **testify about the bite:** Mallet and Braswell, "Horn Found Innocent."

107 **and continued to do so:** See "Seen & Heard," *Hattiesburg* (MS) *American*, Nov. 29, 1982; "Local Prosecutors Attend Conference Held in Jackson," *Hattiesburg* (MS) *American*, Dec. 3, 1982.

107 **Forensic Sciences conference:** Sharon Wertz, "Taking a Bite Out of Crime," *Hattiesburg American*, Oct. 9, 1983.

107 **"it will be very useful":** Mallet and Bramwell, "Horn Found Innocent."

108 **ninety miles southeast of Jackson:** Dr. Michael West, curriculum vitae, March 30, 2006; deposition of Michael West, Steven Hayne v. the Innocence Project, 2011 WL 198128, No 3:09-CV-218-KS-LRA (S.D. Miss. March 13, 2012), 24.

108 **when it comes to expert testimony:** Mark Hansen, "Out of the Blue," *American Bar Association Journal*, Feb. 1, 1996; Andrew Murr, "A Dentist Takes the Stand," *Newsweek*, Aug. 19, 2001.

108 **in common sense and folksy humility:** Hansen, "Out of the Blue"; Murr, "A Dentist Takes the Stand."

108 **"I've just got to get the pope to read it.":** Deposition of Michael West, *Hayne v. Innocence Project*, 166.

108 **"Colonel Callaway would assign it to me":** Ibid., 13–15, 20, 149, 165.

108 **from a New Orleans airport:** Ibid., 46–47; Janet Braswell, "Local Dentists Tell of Work to Identify Kenner Plane Crash Victims," *Hattiesburg* (MS) *American*, Sept. 21, 1982.

108 **to cowrite numerous articles:** See M. West, R. Barsley, J. Frair, and M. Seal, "The Use of Human Skin in the Fabrication of a Bite Mark Template: Two Case Reports," *Journal of Forensic Sciences* 35, no. 6 (1990): 1477–1488; Michael West and Robert Barsley, "Ultraviolet Forensic Imaging," *FBI Law Enforcement Bulletin* 65, no. 5 (May 1992); West, curriculum vitae; Robert E. Barsley, Michael H. West, and John A. Fair, "Forensic Photography: Ultraviolet Imaging of Wounds on Skin," *American Journal of Forensic Medicine and Pathology* 11, no. 4 (1990): 300–308; Russell E. Schneider, Mary Ann Cimrmancic, Michael H. West, Robert E. Barsley, and Steve Hayne, "Narrow Band Imaging and Fluorescence and Its Role in Wound Pattern Documentation," *Journal of Biological Photography* 64, no. 3 (1996): 67–75.

109 **$50 to do the biting:** Deposition of Michael West, *Hayne v. Innocence Project*, 89–90.

109 **"an hour after it was inflicted":** Ibid., 84.

109 **duplicated by other researchers:** Ibid., 79–82; Dr. Michael Bowers, interview by Radley Balko.

109 **with a police officer's gun:** West and Barsley, "Ultraviolet Forensic Imaging"; West, curriculum vitae.

109 **over and over again:** Barsley, West, and Fair, "Forensic Photography."

109 **Dental Disaster Squad:** West, curriculum vitae.

109 **American Board of Forensic Odontology:** Ibid.; deposition of Michael West, *Hayne v. Innocence Project*, 33.

109 **"coroner pro tem" for Forrest County, Mississippi:** Deposition of Michael West, *Hayne v. Innocence Project*, 48; West, curriculum vitae.

110 **"as an individual in forensics":** Deposition of Michael West, *Hayne v. Innocence Project*, 52–56.

110 **an assistant coroner:** West, curriculum vitae; Deposition of Michael West, *Hayne v. Innocence Project*, 59.

110 **"hotbed of scientific research":** Janet Braswell, "City Gets New View on Crime," *Hattiesburg* (MS) *American*, Sept. 6, 1988.

110 **killed by a lone gunman:** Janet Bramwell, "Area Researchers: President Killed by Lone Assassin," *Hattiesburg* (MS) *American*, Nov. 22, 1988.

110 **all over the world:** Transcript of Record, State of Mississippi v. Ken C. Strickland, No. 8315 (Leake Cnty. Circuit Ct. Jan. 22, 1992), 7.

110 **"Among the Mentally Retarded":** West, curriculum vitae, referencing "A New Method for Trace Metal Verification," submitted for publication to the *Journal of the California Division of the International Association for Identification*; "A Study of Surface Topography of Footwear and Automobile Pedals," presented at the 43rd Annual Convention of the American Academy of Forensic Sciences, Feb. 22, 1991; "Confirmation of the Single Bullet Theory," presented at the Midwest Symposium on Assassination Politics, Chicago, Illinois, April 3, 1993; "Protecting Children: The Hidden Danger of Scalding," *Mississippi VOICES*, Mississippi Committee for the Prevention of Child Abuse, Volume 11, No. 2, March–April 1996 and in *Sheriff's Star*, First Quarter 1996; "Peanut Butter Aspiration Deaths Among the Mentally Retarded," presented at the 43rd Annual Convention of the American Academy of Forensic Sciences, Feb. 22, 1991.

110 **nighttime autopsy sessions:** Deposition of Dr. Steven Hayne, *Hayne v. Innocence Project*, 2011 WL 198128, No. 3:09-CV-218-KS-LRA (S.D. Miss. April 26, 2012), 315.

110 **he put the figure at 16,000:** Deposition of Michael West, *Hayne v. Innocence Project*, 144.

111 **analysis, and photo enhancement:** Murr, "A Dentist Takes the Stand"; Hansen, "Out of the Blue"; Eddie Lee Howard v. State of Mississippi, 853 So.2d 781 (Miss. 2003) (McRae, J., dissenting).

111 **struck by a ruler:** West, curriculum vitae.

111 **in arson investigations:** Ibid.; Radley Balko, "Leigh Stubbs, Mississippi Woman, Serving 44-Year Sentence Despite Discredited Testimony," *Huffington Post*, Aug. 9, 2011; Flynn McRoberts and Steve Mills, "From the Start, a Faulty Science: Testimony on Bite Marks Prone to Error," *Chicago Tribune*, Oct. 19, 2004.

111 **serial killer Ted Bundy:** "Rolling's Confession to Shreveport Murders Before His Death," Associated Press, Oct. 28, 2006; Jeff Schweers, "Gainesville Student Murders: 25 Years Later," *Gainesville Sun*, Aug. 22, 2015.

111 **"little ol' dentist from Hattiesburg,":** Jerry Mitchell, "Forensic Dentist Defends Work He's Done in Autopsies," *Clarion-Ledger* (Jackson, MS), Feb. 28, 2009.

111 **the panel of a silk tent:** Eddie Lee Howard v. State of Mississippi, 487.

112 **"the West Phenomenon":** Hansen, "Out of the Blue."

112 **a freelance investigator:** Tom Lyons, "Florida Killer's Work Gruesome, But Not Sloppy, Specialist Says," *Gainesville Sun*, Sept. 9, 1990.

112 **New York dentist Lowell Levine:** McRoberts and Mills, "From the Start, a Faulty Science"; see George R. Dekle Sr., *The Investigation, Prosecution and Execution of Ted Bundy* (New York: Praeger, 2011).

112 **experience in crime scene investigations:** Lyons, "Florida Killer's Work Gruesome"; Emily J. Minor, "Thousands Back at UF; Police ID Another Suspect," *Palm Beach Post*, Sept. 5, 1990.

112 **"you'll be shocked and amazed.":** Lyons, "Florida Killer's Work Gruesome."

113 **"whatever suspicions the police have.'":** Hansen, "Out of the Blue."

113 **his thirteen years investigating murders:** Jean Dubail and Barbara Walsh, "Detectives Haven't Lost Confidence," *South Florida Sun Sentinel* (Fort Lauderdale, FL), Nov. 25, 1990.

113 **such as *Vanity Fair*:** West, curriculum vitae.

113 **Gainesville residents arm themselves:** "'Donahue' Survives Sabotage in Gainesville," *Clarion-Ledger* (Jackson, MS), Sept. 8, 1990; Jeff Brazil, "The Show Does Not Have to Go On, Gainesville Says," *Orlando Sentinel*, Sept. 8, 1990.

113 **"My favorite: *Playboy*.":** Deposition of Michael West, *Hayne v. Innocence Project*, 106.

113 **"most notable" investigations:** West, curriculum vitae; see Brazil, "The Show Does Not Have to Go On"; "Crime Expert Says Humphrey Probably Not Serial Killer," United Press International, Sept. 7, 1990.

113 **hair-trigger temper:** Deposition of Dr. Steven Hayne, *Hayne v. Innocence Project* (April 26, 2012), 148–150, 186, 257, 261–262, 281–282.

113 **"who paid him the most to say it":** Butch Benedict, interview by David Fechheimer, Feb. 28, 2012.

113 **"my savior, Jesus Christ.":** Hansen, "Out of the Blue"; "Forensic Evidence; Skepticism Surrounding Dr. Michael West's Use of Bite Mark Analysis in Murder Cases," *60 Minutes*, Feb. 17, 2002.

114 **by definition, completely wrong:** See Tyler Edmonds v. State of Mississippi, 955 So.2d 787 (Miss. 2007); Danny Jones v. State of Mississippi, 962 So.2d 1263 (Miss. 2007); David W. Parvin v. State of Mississippi, 113 So.3d 1243 (2013).

114 **"indeed and without a doubt.":** Letter from Dr. Michael H. West to Don English, Sept. 14, 1992; letter from Dr. Michael H. West to Michael D. Vick, Sept. 13, 1990; Opinion, State of Mississippi v. Larry Costell Maxwell, Cause No. 5139 (Kemper Cnty. Circuit Ct. Dec. 4, 1992); Transcript, Blind Proficiency Test, Oct. 2001.

114 **his forensic wizardry:** Hansen, "Out of the Blue."

114 **"plausible deniability":** André de Gruy, interview by Radley Balko.

114 **"Should I explain that to you?":** See, for example, Michael West deposition, *Hayne v. Innocence Project*, 150, 182; Michael West deposition, Eddie Lee Howard v. State of Mississippi, No. 2000-0015-CV1H (Lowndes Cnty. Circuit Ct. May 4, 2016), 40, 44–45, 83.

115 **rounds of drinks:** Tommy Ferrell, interview by Radley Balko.

115 **legislators, and coroners:** De Gruy, interview.

115 **made campaign contributions:** Deposition of Cecil McCrory, Hayne v. Innocence Project, 2011 WL 198128, No. 3:09-CV-218-KS-LRA (S.D. Miss. April 24, 2012), 90.

115 **couldn't be said about West:** Mississippi coroner, interview by Radley Balko.

115 **"adoring idiots.":** L. W. "Bump" Calloway, interview by David Fechheimer, Feb. 25, 2012.

CHAPTER 8: ENTRENCHMENT

117 **certification exam in forensic pathology:** Deposition of Dr. Steven Hayne, Hayne v. Innocence Project, 2011 WL 198128, No. 3:09-CV-218-KS-LRA (S.D. Miss. April 26, 2012), 253.

117   **or not exactly, anyway:** Jerry Mitchell, "Doctor's Autopsy Abilities Targeted," *Clarion-Ledger* (Jackson, MS), April 27, 2008.

117   **commonly associated with death:** Ibid.

117   **"I said that was enough.":** Deposition of Steven Hayne, Vessel v. Alleman, No. 99-0307-CI (Warren Cnty. Circuit Ct. June 26, 2003), 56–57.

117   **a different set of colors:** Ibid., 56–57; Deposition of Steven Hayne, Bennett v. City of Canton Swimming Pool, No. C1-96-0176 (Madison Cnty. Circuit Ct. June 2, 2001), 48–49; Transcript of record, State v. Townsend, No. 2000-127-CR (Montgomery Cnty. Circuit Ct. March 20, 2001), 19; Transcript of record, State v. Williams, No. 2004-048 (Washington Cnty. Circuit Ct. Oct. 18, 2004), 367–368.

118   **"answer this type of material.":** Transcript of trial, State of Mississippi v. Yolanda Williams, No. 2004-048 (Washington Cnty. Circuit Ct. Oct. 18, 2004), 368.

118   **"with crap like that":** Jerry Mitchell, "Innocence Project: Delicense Hayne," *Clarion-Ledger* (Jackson, MS), April 9, 2008; Mitchell, "Doctor's Autopsy Abilities Targeted."

118   **they think of certification:** Mitchell, "Doctor's Autopsy Abilities Targeted."

118   **to the marks on Oppie's body:** Ross Parker Simons, affidavit, Oct. 6, 2010; letter from Dr. Michael West to Lieutenant Jim McAnally, June 18, 1990.

118   **do some additional tests:** Simons, affidavit; letter from West to McAnally.

119   **on Mark Oppie's skin:** Simons, affidavit; see letter from West to McAnally.

119   **discredit West's conclusions:** Marcia Coyle, "Daubert v. Frye: A Defense Lawyer's Crusade Discredits a Busy Forensic Dentist in Mississippi," *National Law Journal*, July 11, 1994, 4; Simons, affidavit.

119   **plead guilty to manslaughter:** Mark Hansen, "Out of the Blue," *American Bar Association Journal*, Feb. 1, 1996; Simons, affidavit; Coyle, "Daubert v. Frye," 4.

119   **then consulted with West:** Letter from Michael West to Michael D. Vick, Sept. 13, 1990; Toni Lepeska, "Hattiesburg Dentist to Help in Slaying Probe," *Clarion-Ledger* (Jackson, MS), Sept. 10, 1990.

119   **"the butcher knife in question":** State of Mississippi v. Larry Costell Maxwell, opinion, Cause No. 5139 (Kemper Cnty. Circuit Ct. Dec. 4, 1992); Appellant's Opening Brief, Larry C. Maxwell v. Lauderdale County et al., no. 96-60525 (U.S. Ct. of Appeals for the Fifth Circuit Nov. 4, 1996).

120   **"particular knife wound.":** Affidavit of Robert H. Kirschner, MD, *Larry C. Maxwell v. Lauderdale County et al.*, April 20, 1992; Appellant's Opening Brief, *Larry C. Maxwell v. Lauderdale County et al.*

120   **"was used in the murders.":** Appellant's Opening Brief, *Larry C. Maxwell v. Lauderdale County et al.*, 35–36.

120   **"would have been of great intensity.":** Letter from Michael West to Michael D. Vick, Sept. 17, 1990.

120   **relying only on his memory:** Ibid.; letter from Michael West to Michael D. Vick, Sept. 21, 1990; *State of Mississippi v. Larry Costell Maxwell*, opinion; Appellant's Opening Brief, *Larry C. Maxwell v. Lauderdale County et al.*; Hansen, "Out of the Blue."

121   **submitted affidavits denying that:** Appellant's Opening Brief, *Larry C. Maxwell v. Lauderdale County et al.*, 37–38.

121   **"regional police circular,":** Affidavit of Thomas Krauss, April 21, 1992.

121   **"accepted by most of his peers":** *State of Mississippi v. Larry C. Maxwell*, opinion.

121   **"West was a fraud,":** John Holdridge, interview by Radley Balko; *State of Mississippi v. Larry C. Maxwell*, opinion; affidavits of Robert H. Kirschner, April 20, 1992; William E. Alexander, April 14, 1992; Thomas C. Krauss, April 21, 1992; Appellant's Opening Brief, *Larry C. Maxwell v. Lauderdale County et al.*

122   **in support of West's claims: Steven Hayne:** Appellant's Opening Brief, *Larry C. Maxwell v. Lauderdale County et al.*

122   **"to do them effectively,":** Beverly Pettigrew Kraft, "Texan Chosen to Face 'Challenge' of State Medical Examiner Post," *Clarion-Ledger* (Jackson, MS), April 14, 1989.

122   **"It simply is not physically possible.":** "State's New Medical Examiner to Face Same Problems His Predecessors Did," *Meridian* (MS) *Star*, April 21, 1989, reprinted, *Clarion-Ledger* (Jackson, MS), April 22, 1989.

122   **"fix something that is broken,":** Kraft, "Texan Chosen to Face 'Challenge' of State Medical Examiner Post."

122   **"more wrong than that, could I?":** Lloyd White, interview by Radley Balko.

122   **he was general manager:** "Mississippi Mortuary Services," Mississippi Better Business Bureau, www.bbb.org/mississippi/business-reviews/funeral-related-services/mississippi-mortuary-services-in-pearl-ms-183142889/reviews-and-complaints.

123   **nothing of the sort:** Deposition of Dr. Steven Hayne, *Hayne v. Innocence Project* (April 26, 2012), 91–92; see Adam Lynch, "Shipping Off Bodies," *Jackson* (MS) *Free Press*, March 18, 2005.

123   **"no safety precautions.":** Former Mississippi official, interview by Radley Balko.

123   **"sausage factory.":** J. D. Sanders, interview by Radley Balko.

123   **"barely bend his fingers.":** Ken Winter, interview by Radley Balko.

123   **"that is just outrageous.":** Deposition of Dr. Steven Hayne, *Hayne v. Innocence Project* (April 27, 2012), 134.

124   **"concerned about cross contamination":** J. D. Sanders, interview by David Fechheimer, Oct. 27, 2011; Sanders, interview by Balko.

124   **"claims to have followed.":** L. W. "Bump" Calloway, interview by David Fechheimer, Feb. 25, 2012.

124   **by Jimmy Roberts's wife:** Deposition of Michael West, *Hayne v. Innocence Project* (March 13, 2012), 174.

124   **"the Stinker Room.":** Ibid., 178–179.

124   **advertisement for their services:** Grace Simmons, "Special Photo Technique Can Expose Child Abuse," *Clarion-Ledger* (Jackson, MS), Dec. 8, 1991.

124   **West resigned instead:** Andrew Murr, "A Dentist Takes the Stand," *Newsweek*, Aug. 19, 2001.

125   **"outside the field of forensic odontology.":** ABFO Ethics Committee Report, Complaint 93-B, March 25, 1994, contained in letter from Dr. Richard Souviron, chairman ABFO Ethics Committee, to Gary L. Bell, president American Board of Forensic Odontology, March 25, 1994.

125   **suspended him for one year:** Ibid.

125   **"in order to support his testimony":** AAFS Ethics Committee Report, Case No. 143, April 13, 1994; Murr, "A Dentist Takes the Stand."

125   **before he could be expelled:** AAFS Ethics Committee Report, Case No. 143; ABFO Ethics Committee Report, Complaint 93-B; Murr, "A Dentist Takes the Stand."

125   **"draw these kinds of distinctions.":** Sources for Larry Maxwell narrative: Larry Maxwell v. Lauderdale County, 119 F.3d 3 (5th Cir. 1997); Hansen, "Out of the Blue"; letter from John Holdridge to Arkansas Post Prison Transfer Board (undated); Levon Brooks v. State of Mississippi, 748 So.2d 736 (Miss. 1999) (McRae, J., dissenting); Holdridge, interview.

125   **"which one they believe.":** Holdridge, interview.

125   **strap on the victim's purse:** Arnold Lindsay, "Coldwater Slaying Victim, 28, Raped, Strangled, Officials Say," *Clarion-Ledger* (Jackson, MS), May 27, 1991; letter from Dr. Michael West to Robert Williams, District Attorney (May 29, 1991); law enforcement notes, capital murder investigation, Grace Ford Wiseman, May 24–25, 1991.

126   **used to threaten the victim:** Stacie Lynn Waltman v. State of Mississippi, 734 So.2d 324 (1999).

126   **which exonerated his client:** Simons, affidavit; Amanda L. Myers, "Men Wrongly Convicted or Arrested on Bite Evidence," Yahoo! News, June 16, 2013; Hansen, "Out of the Blue."

126   **openly about killing his wife:** *Traces of Guilt*, BBC, Oct. 8, 1995; Hansen, "Out of the Blue."

127   **"by the teeth of Tony Keko":** Keko v. Hingle, 1999 WL 508406.

127   **"where he had bit her at.":** John Stossel, "Junk Science: What You Know That May Not Be So Scientific: Theories That May Be Wrong," ABC News, Aug. 28, 1997.

127   **"such a nice guy?'":** Murr, "A Dentist Takes the Stand."

127   **judge ordered a new trial:** Judgment, Defense Motion #55, Motion for New Trial for Newly Discovered Evidence, State of Louisiana v. Anthony Keko, case no. 92-3292, Twenty-Fifth Judicial District Court, Parish of Plaquemines, Louisiana (Dec. 14, 1994); "Reasons for Judgment," State of Louisiana v. Anthony Keko, case no. 92-3292, Twenty-Fifth Judicial District Court, Parish of Plaquemines, Louisiana (Nov. 27, 1996).

127   **only dental mold West analyzed:** Steve Cannizaro, "Murder Witness' Fairness Questioned," *Times-Picayune* (New Orleans), May 10, 1996.

127   **Louise Keko's murder remains unsolved:** Judgment, Defense Motion #55, Motion for New Trial for Newly Discovered Evidence, *State of Louisiana v. Anthony Keko*; "Reasons for Judgment," *State of Louisiana v. Anthony Keko*.

128   **on *ABC News*:** Murr, "A Dentist Takes the Stand"; Hansen, "Out of the Blue"; Coyle, "Daubert vs. Frye"; *Traces of Guilt*; Stossel, "Junk Science."

128   **"one heck of a witness.":** Hansen, "Out of the Blue."

128   **"ACLU types.":** James Gill, "Was the Right to a Fair Trial Denied?" *Times-Picayune* (New Orleans), June 12, 1994. Sources for Anthony Keko narrative: Hansen, "Out of the Blue"; Anthony G. Keko v. I.F. Hingle, 318 F.3d 639 (5th Cir. 2003); "Judgment, Defense Motion #55, Motion for New Trial for Newly Discovered Evidence," *State of Louisiana v. Anthony Keko*; "Reasons for Judgment," *State of Louisiana v. Anthony Keko*; letter from Michael West to Chuck Bowles, Oct. 12, 1992; Cannizaro, "Murder Witness' Fairness Questioned"; Gill, "Was the Right to a Fair Trial Denied?"; Stossel, "Junk Science"; *Traces of Guilt: The Verdict*, BBC, Jan. 4, 1996; Coyle, "Daubert vs. Frye"; Joanna Weiss, "Forensic Tests Are Questioned

in Murder Trial," *Times-Picayune* (New Orleans), Sept. 30, 1994; Carlos Campos, "Buras Oysterman Heading to Trial in Wife's Murder," *Times-Picayune* (New Orleans), April 17, 1993; Carlos Campos, "Husband Is Guilty in Killing—Jury to Decide Keko's Sentence," *Times-Picayune* (New Orleans), Oct. 11, 1993; Steve Cannizaro, "Buras Man May Beat Murder Rap a Second Time," *Times-Picayune* (New Orleans), Dec. 21, 1996; Appellant's Brief, Anthony G. Keko v. I.F. Hingle et al., case no. 01-30622 (U.S. Ct. of Appeals for the Fifth Circuit, Sept. 4, 2001).

128   **disciplined him were a "joke":** Coyle, "Daubert vs. Frye."

128   **"vastly ignorant.":** Ibid.

128   **since perfected the technique:** Ibid.

128   **"ahead of his time.":** Ibid.

129   **different law enforcement publications:** Dr. Michael West, curriculum vitae, March 30, 2006.

129   **address and phone number:** Dr. Michael H. West and Dr. Steven Hayne, "Alternative Light Sources for Trace Evidence Can Lead to Higher Conviction Rates," *Kodak Publications* 1 (1992): 911.

129   **"what the state told us.":** Tommy Ferrell, interview by Radley Balko.

130   **they have often gone unenforced:** Lloyd White, interviews by Radley Balko; Radley Balko, "CSI: Mississippi," *Reason*, Oct. 8, 2007.

130   **quickly embalmed and buried:** Lloyd White, interviews by Radley Balko; Lloyd White, "'Nightmare' in the Mississippi Medical Examiner's Office," letter to the editor, *Advocate* (Jackson, MS), July 8–14, 1993.

130   **"roughshod over people's civil rights.":** Balko, "CSI Mississippi."

130   **fight-the-battles-you-can-win approach:** White, interviews by Balko; Lloyd White, interview by Tucker Carrington, Sept. 2016.

131   **it was an internal matter:** Grace Simmons, "State Medical Examiner Placed on Leave," *Clarion-Ledger* (Jackson, MS), April 1, 1992.

131   **fired the following month:** Grace Simmons, "Ex-Medical Examiner Says 'Disagreement' Cost Him His Job," *Clarion-Ledger* (Jackson, MS), May 6, 1992.

131   **wanted Hayne to have White's job:** Lloyd White, Jim Ingram, and unnamed former state officials in Mississippi, interviews by Radley Balko.

131   **"banish him from the state.":** Charles Tisdale, editor's note to White included in, "'Nightmare' in the Mississippi Medical Examiner's Office."

131   **"the most firebombed newspaper in America.":** Jocelyn Y. Stewart, "Charles Tisdale, 80; Used Mississippi Newspaper to Fight Bias," *Los Angeles Times*, July 14, 2007; Hazel Trice Edney, "Charles Tisdale, Black Publisher, Passes at 80," *St. Louis American*, July 19, 2007.

131   **"None.":** Peter Applebome, "Death in Jailhouse: The Ruling, a Suicide; The Fear, a Lynching," *New York Times*, Feb. 21, 1993.

132   **"state employees and officials.":** White, "'Nightmare' in the Mississippi Medical Examiner's Office."

132   **black man who had died in police custody:** Beverly Pettigrew Kraft, "Ex-Medical Examiner: Method of Probing Jail Deaths 'Sham,'" *Clarion-Ledger* (Jackson, MS), Aug. 18, 1994.

132   **$125,000 per year in salary and benefits:** Letter from Jim Ingram, Mississippi Public Safety commissioner, to Ronald Crowe, executive director, Mississippi Ethics Commission, July 2, 1992.

132   **the certification requirement:** White, "'Nightmare' in the Mississippi Medical Examiner's Office."

133   **just on state-referred autopsy fees:** Letter from Ingram, to Crowe. According to Ingram's letter, Hayne was doing about 80 percent of the state's autopsies at the time, at $500 per autopsy. Ingram wrote that there were 1,263 autopsies in the state in 1991. If Hayne did 80 percent, he performed over 1,000. At $500 each, he grossed over $500,000.

133   **"state and local government.":** Ronald Crowe, executive director, Mississippi Ethics Commission, "Advisory Opinion No. 92-132-E," Mississippi Ethics Commission, July 10, 1992.

133   **"perform the public duty.":** Ibid.

CHAPTER 9: THE TRIAL OF LEVON BROOKS

135   **birthed a black, loamy soil:** Roy B. Van Arsdale and Randel T. Cox, "The Mississippi's Curious Origins," *Scientific American* (Jan. 2007): 75–82B; John A. Barone, "Historical Presence and Distribution of Prairies in the Black Belt of Mississippi and Alabama," *Journal of the Mississippi Academy of Sciences*, April 1, 2005.

135   **any other county in the belt:** Barone, "Historical Presence and Distribution of Prairies."

136   **the Delta or the Black Prairie Belt:** Stuart Bruchey, *Cotton and the Growth of the American Economy, 1790–1860* (New York: Harcourt, Brace & World, 1967), Table 3-C; see *Report on the Statistics of Agriculture, Eleventh Census: 1890* (Washington, DC: Census Office, Department of the Interior, 1895).

136   **three times the size of its white population:** Dunbar Rowland, ed., *Mississippi: Comprising Sketches of Counties, Towns, Events, Institutions, and Persons, Arranged in Cyclopedic Form* (Atlanta: Southern Historical Publishing Association, 1907); Eugene R. Dattel, "Cotton in a Global Economy," Mississippi History Now, Oct. 2006, http://mshistorynow.mdah.state.ms.us /articles/161/cotton-in-a-global-economy-mississippi-1800-1860.

136   **"negro problem.":** David M. Oshinsky, *Worse Than Slavery: Parchman Farm and the Ordeal of Jim Crow Justice* (New York: Free Press, 1996), 20.

136   **labor in the form of prison inmates:** Ibid., 20–21.

136   **meant returning to the plantation:** Douglas Blackmon, *Slavery by Another Name: The Re-Enslavement of Black Americans from the Civil War to World War II* (New York: Anchor, 2008), 66.

136   **worked for decades:** Levon Brooks, interviews by Tucker Carrington.

137   **"Just old enough.":** Tom Blake, transcriber, "Largest Slaveholders from 1860 Slave Census Schedules and Surname Matches for Native Americans on 1870 Census in Noxubee County, Mississippi," 2001, http: //freepages.genealogy.rootsweb.ancestry.com/~ajac/msnoxubee.htm; Levon Brooks, Annie Brewer, and Kennedy Brewer, interviews by Tucker Carrington.

137   **"followed by their murder.":** United States Congress, *Report of the Joint Select Committee to Inquire into the Condition of Affairs in the Late Insurrectionary States*, 73 (2d Sess. 1872).

137   **murders in Noxubee County alone:** Ibid.

137   **"outside world would at least care":** Daniel J. Singal, *Guide to the Microfilm Edition of the Southern Tenant Farmers' Union Papers, 1934–1970* (Glen Rock, NJ: Microfilming Corporation of America, 1971).

137   **"cutting the whole sack off":** Letter from J. R. Butler to Walter White, March 27, 1940, microfilmed on Southern Tenant Farmers' Union Papers 1934–1970, Fiche 14, University of Southern Mississippi.

138   **Their names are lost to history:** John R. Steelman, "A Study of Mob Action in the South" (PhD diss., University of North Carolina, 1928), 203, 263.

138   **swelled to become a thriving plantation:** Boswell Stevens Papers, 1918–1986, Mississippi State University Library Special Collections.

138   **president of the state bureau:** John Anderson Tyson, *Historical Notes of Noxubee County, Mississippi,* 90. These historical notes were originally published by John Tyson in the *Macon* (MS) *Beacon* and then collected in 1928. A copy of *Historical Notes of Noxubee County* is on file in the Special Collections of the J. D. Williams Library, University of Mississippi.

138   **state's defenses against integration:** Pete Daniel, *Lost Revolutions: The South in the 1950s* (Chapel Hill: University of North Carolina Press, 2000), 195, 216.

138   **supporter of the agency's goals:** Letter from John Satterfield to Erle Johnston, Sept. 20, 1963, Mississippi Sovereignty Commission Digital Collection, Mississippi Department of Archives and History.

138   **"keep them under control":** Memorandum from Zack J. Van Landingham to director of the State Sovereignty Commission (April 6, 1959), Mississippi Sovereignty Commission Digital Collection.

139   **same amount of NAACP activity:** Noxubee County Report from Tom Scarbrough, Aug. 29, 1960, Mississippi Sovereignty Commission Digital Collection.

139   **child beauty pageants:** Tyson, *Historical Notes of Noxubee County.*

139   **"something beautiful about it.":** Boswell Stevens, interview by Tucker Carrington.

140   **150 black tenants:** Ibid.

140   **him after his second:** Letter from Robert B. Prather to Levon Brooks, Jan. 13, 1992; Transcript of record, State of Mississippi v. Levon Brooks, No. 5937 (Noxubee Cnty. Circuit Ct. Jan. 13, 1992) (hereinafter Brooks trial transcript), 69–73.

141   **as well as two probable witnesses:** Letter from Prather to Brooks; Brooks trial transcript, 69–73.

141   **unrelated burglary charge:** Letter from Prather to Brooks; Brooks trial transcript, 69–73.

141   **"over the weekend.":** Letter from Prather to Brooks; Brooks trial transcript, 69–73.

141   **And that was that:** Letter from Prather to Brooks; Brooks trial transcript, 69–73.

142   **school's conservative students:** "Ox Hunts Doves," *Mirror* (S.D. Lee High School, Columbus, MS), Feb. 6, 1971.

142   **fast becoming a small minority:** Ibid.

142   **"throwing human excrement at cops.":** Ibid.

142   **assassination of Martin Luther King Jr.:** Ibid.

142   **"then you are out.":** Ibid.

142   **freshman football team:** "Ole Miss Frosh, LSU Vying Today," *Delta Democrat Times* (Greenville, MS), Oct. 8, 1971.

142   *Fun Time* **with Uncle Bunky:** Ron Williams, "Robert 'Uncle Bunky' Williams: A Local Living Legend Reflects on His Storied Career," *Columbus* (MS) *Packet*, March 8, 2012.

142   **others began to question their credibility:** Brent E. Turvey and Craig M. Cooley, *Miscarriages of Justice: Actual Innocence, Forensic Evidence, and the Law* (Oxford, UK: Academic, 2014), 245; Josie Duffy Rice, "Good News: Mississippi Votes Out Notoriously Aggressive Prosecutor," Daily Kos, Nov. 5, 2015, www.dailykos.com/story/2015/11/5/1445335/-Good -news-Mississippi-replaces-notoriously-aggressive-prosecutor-with -advocate-for-reform; Peter Neufeld, "Keynote Address," *Southwestern Law Review* 37 (2008): 1051; "District Attorney Offers Comments on Brewer, Brooks Cases," *Macon* (MS) *Beacon*, Aug. 7, 2008; Nina Martin, "A Stillborn Child, a Charge of Murder, and the Disputed Case Law on Fetal Harm," *ProPublica*, March 18, 2014.

143   **"recall him laughing.":** Anonymous defense attorney, interview by Radley Balko.

143   **"It always has been,":** "Candidate Profiles: District Attorney," *Starkville Insider*, July 14, 2015, www.starkville.org/candidate-profiles-district -attorney.

143   **"for the John Birch Society.":** J. D. Sanders, interview by David Fechheimer, Oct. 27, 2011.

143   **"he often acted from there.":** Former Mississippi state official, interview by Radley Balko.

143   **planting the pot:** Isabelle Altman, "Macon Woman, 70, Serving Decade Prison Term for Pot," *Columbus* (MS) *Dispatch*, April 23, 2016.

143   **cocaine isn't what caused the miscarriage:** Hart, "A Stillborn Child."

144   **too savvy to get caught:** Andrew Hazard, "Allgood Believes His Process Works," *Columbus* (MS) *Dispatch*, Oct. 28, 2015.

144   **"he'd have been successful at it.":** André de Gruy, interview by Radley Balko.

144   **dangerous or evil:** Years after Kennedy Brewer was exonerated and freed, Allgood still insisted he was guilty of something. See the transcript of his interview with documentarian Joe Jork: "Now let me pose you a question, you really think she'd be the first child that was ever sold for a crack rock or the first child that was ever sold for even 50 bucks with which to purchase a crack rock." Transcript from interview of Forrest Allgood by Joe York for the film *Mississippi Innocence*, 2011.

144   **pleading guilty in that case or another:** See deposition of Dr. Steven Hayne, *Hayne v. Innocence Project* (April 26, 2012), 170. When asked about criticism of his testimony in the case with the skeletonized body, Hayne noted that the suspect pleaded guilty to manslaughter. About Kennedy Brewer and Levon Brooks, he said, "I don't think they were guilty. That doesn't mean they weren't involved in some aspect." *Hayne v. Innocence Project*, (April 27, 2012), 19. West speculated that in spite of Levon Brooks's exoneration, Brooks might still have kidnapped the victim and traded her to Johnson in exchange for drugs; see deposition of Michael West, Eddie Lee Howard v. State of Mississippi, No. 2000-0015-CV1H (Lowndes Cnty. Circuit Ct. May 4, 2016), 88–89.

145   **commission of the crime:** Lee V. Robinson, case no. 121543, Mississippi State Hospital.

145   **suggestive of a sexual predator:** Ibid.

145   **The report stated that he was:** Ibid.

145   **"in the shape of a man":** Brooks trial transcript, 461.

145   **"left his mark,":** Ibid., 461.

145   **"that man . . . is Levon Brooks":** Ibid., 460–462.

145   **based solely on the bite mark evidence:** Carol S. Steiker, "*Gideon* at Fifty: A Problem of Political Will," *Yale Law Journal* 122 (2013): 701.

145   **without a rebuttal:** Brooks trial transcript, 462.

146   **"go to the devil.":** Ibid., 472–473.

146   **was named "Titee.":** Ibid., 492.

146   **"my momma boyfriend.":** Ibid., 492.

146   **and then "I forgot.":** Ibid., 498–499.

147   **played together "all the time.":** Ibid., 499.

147   **(She had.):** Ibid., 500.

147   **a gun or a knife:** Ibid., 505.

147   **eating potato chips:** Ibid., 504.

147   **a bag of money:** Ibid., 504.

147   **"to tell these people?":** Ibid., 509.

147   **she replied, "I forgot.":** Ibid., 509.

147   **"Yes," she replied:** Ibid., 512.

148   **Uncle Bunky introduced into evidence:** Ibid., 513–514.

148   **the judge refused:** Ibid., 513–514.

148   **in his closing argument:** Ibid., 1024–1036, 1059, 1067.

148   **"the guy that took my sister.":** Ibid., 1024–1035.

148   **"doesn't mean it wasn't said.":** Forrest Allgood, email interview by Radley Balko.

148   **expert in the field of forensic pathology:** Brooks trial transcript, 682–684.

148   **He didn't:** Brooks trial transcript, 685.

149   **Michael West, who concurred:** Brooks trial transcript, 697–698.

149   **who killed the girl:** Brooks trial transcript, 695, 698, 703.

149   **made by human teeth:** Declaration of J. C. Upshaw Downs, MD, Dec. 1, 2011, *Hayne v. Innocence Project*, 18 ("It was not reasonable for Dr. Hayne to conclude that the external findings could be pre-mortem or even peri-mortem human bitemarks"); declaration of Michael Baden, *Hayne v. Innocence Project*, 5 ("[Hayne's] evaluation of the death of Courtney Smith erroneously interpreted post-mortem artifacts and decomposition changes as the result of adult human bite marks which were then, again, specifically and erroneously matched to the teeth of Mr. Levon Brooks").

149   **the skin around the marks:** Declaration of Downs, 14, *Hayne v. Innocence Project*: "Dr. Hayne's failure to personally perform these analyses abrogates one of the chief purposes of the practice of Forensic Pathology and, therefore, fails to meet the standard of accepted practice."

149   **deferred to West in his report:** Declaration of Downs, 14–15, *Hayne v. Innocence Project*: "A practitioner calling in a presumably more qualified consultant maintains a level of responsibility for the consultant's findings and failures. If, as here, Dr. Hayne knew that Dr. West failed to adhere to accepted procedure and then accepted Dr. West's opinion, he is guilty of adopting that mistake by virtue of having executed Ms. Smith's autopsy report without further inquiry into Dr. West's findings."

149   **repeat over and over again:** See Willie Earl Harris, Capital Murder Investigation Memo, Grace Ford Wiseman, victim, May 24, 1991; State v. David

Duplantis & Ken Strickland, 91-DP-1220, Newton County, MS; Duplantis v. State, 644 So.2d 1235 (Miss. 1994); Duplantis v. State, 708 So.2d 1327 (Miss. 1998); Keko v. Hingle, 1999 WL 508406; Calvin Banks v. State of Mississippi, 725 So.2d 711 (Miss. 1997); State of Mississippi v. Kennedy Brewer, 725 So.2d 106 (Miss. 1998); State of Louisiana v. Jimmie C. Duncan, No. 99-KA-2615 (La. 2001); Radley Balko, "Solving Kathy Mabry's Murder," *Huffington Post,* Jan. 17, 2013.

149   **test anything in the kit:** Brooks trial transcript, 696.

149   **tying Brooks to the crime scene:** Mississippi Crime Lab Report, Supplementary Report, MCL No. 90-376 (Dec. 16, 1991).

150   **"A broom handle for example?":** Brooks trial transcript, 691.

150   **didn't involve a broom:** In a 2017 email interview, Allgood wrote that he couldn't recall mentioning the broom handle, but that if he did, "I rather suspect, however, that I was told by the Medical Examiner that such an implement could have caused the injuries he found."

150   **bluntly pointed object:** Declaration of Downs, *Hayne v. Innocence Project,* 19: "When asked about what type weapon might have caused these injuries, Dr. Hayne excludes generic broad categories 'such things as a piece of metal and the like.' Then immediately follows when queried, 'What kind of object could have, in fact, caused those injuries doctor?' with very specific exemplars 'A finger, a penis or a similar object.' Obviously, given the nature of this case and the injuries, such a narrow proffer by the witness could rightly be considered highly biased in that both would require direct physical penetration of the victim's body by the perpetrator's body—something unknown by the Forensic Pathologist. Only when further questioned by the state was another item suggested: 'A broom handle for example?' 'Yes.' In testifying to the overly specific (finger, penis) to the specific exclusion of all other myriad possibilities of items consistent with causing such a wound (basically a blunt object capable of penetrating the damaged orifice to the requisite depth) without providing clarifying general principles does a scientific disservice to the trier of fact in that it at least subliminally (if not overtly) suggests that such specificity is possible and that the perpetrator personally violated the victim. There is no scientific basis to assert such a highly specific and potentially inflammatory as a posited weapon in deference to others."

150   **$1,950 for his testimony:** Brooks trial transcript, 682–708; Letter from Dr. Steven Hayne to Forrest Allgood, Jan. 22, 1992.

150   **in a demonstration for the jury:** Billing statement from Michael H. West to Forrest Allgood.

150   **"I wouldn't challenge his qualifications.":** Letter from Forrest Allgood to Bob Prather, Nov. 7, 1991.

151   **"senior crime scene analyst.":** Brooks trial transcript, 712.

151   **then he named each one:** Ibid., 715.

151   **"the FBI academy in Quantico, Virginia.":** Ibid., 712–713.

151   **West said that it did not:** Ibid., 715–716.

151   **"You have to eat, right doctor?":** Ibid., 716.

151   **"Yes, sir," West replied:** Ibid.

151   **after they've been extracted:** Ibid., 717–718.

151   **citing a study from the early 1980s:** Reidar F. Sognnaes, "Computer Comparison of Bite Mark Patterns in Identical Twins," *Journal of the American Dental Association* 105 (Sept. 1982): 449. For criticism of this

study, see Michael Bowers, "Arguments on the Individuality of Human Teeth," presented at the 2000 American Academy of Forensic Sciences conference ("There are experimental problems in this study. . . . This is a seriously over-stated conclusion that has been perpetuated in the odontology literature"); Erica Beecher Monas, "Reality Bites: The Illusion of Science in Bite Mark Evidence," *Cardozo Law Review* 30 (2009): 1369 (stating that the study was "flawed by being extremely small [five sets of twins], and failing to set out a detailed methodology"); see generally Michael J. Saks et al., "Forensic Bite Mark Identification: Weak Foundations, Exaggerated Claims," *Law and the Biosciences* 3 (2016): 538; Iain A. Pretty, "The Barriers to Achieving an Evidence Base for Bite Mark Analysis," *Forensic Science International* 159, no. 1 (2006): S110–S120.

152   **"or tool marks, then?":** Brooks trial transcript, 719.

152   **"Exactly," West responded:** Ibid.

152   **I can look at his teeth and tell you if it's him:** Ibid., 720.

152   **"an individual through a bite mark?":** Ibid., 722, 750.

152   **"Yes, sir," West said:** Ibid., 750.

153   **"very definite fractures and bevels.":** Ibid., 723.

153   **"a scalloped-out area with a sharp edge.":** Ibid.

153   **"some wear—what we call wear facets.":** Ibid.

153   **"back of the upper teeth,":** Ibid.

153   **"stomach or your buttocks or on your legs,":** Ibid., 724.

153   **"grab into the skin and pull across it.":** Ibid.

153   **adjust for all of these variables:** See Mary A. Bush, Peter J. Bush, and H. David Sheets, "A Study of Multiple Bitemarks Inflicted in Human Skin by a Single Dentition Using Geometric Morphometric Analysis," *Forensic Science International* 211 (2011): 1–8; Mary A. Bush, Peter J. Bush, and H. David Sheets, "Similarity and Match Rates of the Human Dentition in 3 Dimensions: Relevance to Bitemark Analysis," *International Journal of Legal Medicine* 125, no. 6 (2011): 779–784; Mary A. Bush, Peter J. Bush, and H. David Sheets, "Statistical Evidence for the Similarity of the Human Dentition," *Journal of Forensic Science* 56, no. 1 (2011): 118–123; Mary A. Bush et al., "The Response of Skin to Applied Stress: Investigation of Bitemark Distortion in a Cadaver Model," *Journal of Forensic Science* 55, no. 1 (2009): 71–76; Mary A. Bush et al., "Biomechanical Factors in Human Dermal Bitemarks in a Cadaver Model," *Journal of Forensic Science* 54, no. 1 (2009): 167–176; Mary A. Bush, Howard I. Cooper, and Robert B.J. Dorion, "Inquiry into the Scientific Basis for Bitemark Profiling and Arbitrary Distortion Compensation," *Journal of Forensic Science* 55, no. 4 (2010): 976–983.

154   **"healthy intact tissue does not.":** Brooks trial transcript, 729.

154   **alleged wound on Courtney Smith's wrist:** Ibid., 731.

155   **just to be certain:** Ibid., 726–730.

155   **"the wrist of Courtney Smith":** Ibid., 731–732.

155   **where none existed before:** See Declaration of David R. Senn, DDS, Nov. 30, 2011, *Hayne v. Innocence Project,* 9: "The method of directly placing a suspect's dental models onto the skin and repeatedly moving those models in direct contact with skin is unacceptable methodology. In fact, this action actually generates patterned injuries to the skin. The creation of postmortem artifacts is ample reason to avoid this technique."

155   **claimed came from the defendant:** See later discussion of Leigh Stubbs (chapter 12) and Jimmie Duncan (chapter 10) cases.

156   **crucial to his conclusions:** One of West's fellow bite mark analysts believes West did exactly that in the Kennedy Brewer case. See Declaration of David R. Senn, *Steven Hayne v. the Innocence Project*, 7: "Dr. West placed Kennedy Brewer's dental models directly onto Christine Jackson's body—multiple times—with sufficient force to create marks visible [*sic*], as can be seen in the videotaped examination that I reviewed."

156   **"that didn't happen.":** Brooks trial transcript, 744.

156   **"a few microns.":** Ibid., 755.

156   **"on this one.":** Ibid., 722, 727.

156   **$2,902.12 for his testimony:** Ibid., 711–757; Petition, State of Mississippi v. Levon Brooks, no. 5937, Jan. 23, 1992.

157   **her current residence on Phillips Loop:** Brooks trial transcript, 925–950.

157   **He declined:** Ibid., 950–954.

157   **"funny how that worked out, isn't it?":** Ibid., 1024–1036, 1068–1069.

157   **"guilty of capital murder.":** Ibid., 1092.

157   **"been accused of harming one":** Ibid., 1126–1222.

157   **that Levon Brooks was guilty:** Ibid., 1185–1187.

159   **"And it is.":** Ibid., 1236–1243, 1254–1261.

159   **"Thank you.":** Ibid., 1243.

160   **to err on the side of caution:** Ibid., 1243.

160   **"Department of Corrections.":** Ibid., 1264.

CHAPTER 10: KEEP THAT WOMAN UNDER CONTROL

161   **completed the previous year:** Grace Simmons, "Miss. Native to Head State Forensic Lab," *Clarion Ledger* (Jackson, MS), June 18, 1993.

161   **hard on those who took the job:** See "Medical Examiner Job Still Vacant," *Clarksdale* (MS) *Press Register*, Feb. 13, 1989.

162   **improvements were possible:** Simmons, "Miss. Native to Head State Forensic Lab."

162   **an asset to the office:** Ibid.

162   **"fifty-five-gallon drums.":** Jim Fisher, "Dr. Ralph Erdmann: The Forensic Pathologist from Hell," Jim Fisher True Crime, Dec. 26, 2015, http://jimfishertruecrime.blogspot.com/2012/02/dr-ralph-erdmann-forensic-pathologist.html.

163   **with mounting caseloads:** Sources for Erdmann narrative: Jim Dwyer, Peter Neufeld, and Barry Scheck, *Actual Innocence: Five Days to Execution and Other Dispatches from the Wrongly Convicted* (New York: Doubleday, 2000), 117–119; Robert Suro, "Ripples of a Pathologist's Misconduct in Graves and Courts of West Texas," *New York Times*, Nov. 21, 1992; Fisher, "Dr. Ralph Erdmann"; Chip Brown, "Pathologist Accused of Falsifying Autopsies, Botching Trial Evidence," *Los Angeles Times*, April 12, 1992; Welsh S. White, *Litigating in the Shadow of Death: Defense Attorneys in Capital Cases* (Ann Arbor: University of Michigan Press, 2005), 152; Richard L. Fricker, "Reasonable Doubts," *American Bar Association Journal* (Dec. 1993).

163   **"the Ralph Erdmann of Mississippi.":** Levon Brooks v. State of Mississippi, 748 So.2d 736, 750 (Miss. 1999) (McCrae, J., dissenting).

163   **in a year was 480:** Dwyer, Neufeld, and Scheck, *Actual Innocence*, 117–119.

164   **seventy years after the *Frye* decision:** Frye v. United States, 293 F. 1013 (D.C. Cir. 1923).

164   ***Daubert v. Merrell Dow Pharmaceuticals, Inc.*:** Daubert v. Merrell Dow Pharmaceuticals Inc., 113 (S.Ct. 2786 1993).

164   **"settled" science in court:** See Amici Curiae Brief, Physicians, Scientists and Historians of Science on behalf of William Daubert et ux., Doc. No. 92-102, A1-A5, and Amici Curiae Brief, Nicolaas Bloembergen et al., on behalf of Merrell Dow Pharmaceuticals, Inc.

165   **"It's mostly for show.":** Michael Saks, interview by Radley Balko.

165   **prosecutors wanted more:** Calvin Banks v. State of Mississippi, 725 So.2d 711 (Miss. 1997).

166   **in the house:** Ibid. ("Indeed, the victim had eaten a small amount of bologna, consistent with the amount bitten off the sandwich, shortly before her death.")

166   **from verifying his findings:** Ibid.

166   **"and two pieces of bread,":** Nikki Davis Maute, "Pictures Should Suffice in Overturned Murder Case, Coroner Says," *Clarion-Ledger* (Jackson, MS), Dec. 10, 1997.

166   **unusable for any other analyst:** *Calvin Banks v. State of Mississippi.*

166   **violated his right to a fair trial:** Ibid.

166   **in the case of Eddie Lee Howard:** *Calvin Banks v. State of Mississippi* (Smith, J., concurring in part and dissenting in part).

167   **Kemp was buried:** Letter from Lloyd White, state medical examiner, to Chief Pete Bowen, Feb. 6, 1992; Transcript of record, State of Mississippi v. Eddie Lee Howard, 92-400-CR1 (Lowndes Cnty. Cir. Ct. May 22, 2000), 502.

167   **convicted and sentenced to death:** Eddie Lee Howard v. State of Mississippi, 697 So.2d 415 (Miss. 1997).

167   **allowed Howard to represent himself:** Ibid.

167   **questionable forensic evidence:** Ibid.

167   **several media exposés:** *Traces of Guilt*, BBC, Oct. 8, 1995; John Stossel, "Junk Science: What You Know May Not Be So," *ABC News Special Report*, Jan. 9, 1997; Marcia Coyle, "'Expert Science' Under Fire in Capital Cases," *National Law Journal*, July 11, 1994; Mark Hansen, "Out of the Blue," *American Bar Association Journal*, Feb. 1, 1996.

167   **two forensics organizations:** "Ethics Committee Report," American Association of Forensic Scientists, case no. 143 (1994); Andrew Murr, "A Dentist Takes the Stand," *Newsweek*, Aug. 19, 2001.

167   **suspended from a third:** "Ethics Committee Report," American Board of Forensic Odontology, complaint no. 93-B (1994); Murr, "A Dentist Takes the Stand."

168   **"numerous scholarly authorities":** *Howard v. State of Mississippi.*

168   **to challenge West in court:** Ibid.

168   **to tear West down:** Forrest Allgood, "District Attorney Offers Comments on Brewer, Brooks Cases," *Macon* (MS) *Beacon*, Aug. 7, 2008.

168   **"minority view nationwide,":** *Howard v. State of Mississippi* (Smith, J., dissenting).

168   **bought into bite mark matching:** See National Research Council of the National Academies of Sciences, *Strengthening Forensic Science in the United States: A Path Forward* (Washington, DC: National Academies Press, 2009), 107n81: "There is nothing to indicate that courts review bite mark evidence pursuant to *Daubert*'s standard of reliability."

168   **few had, if any:** Erica Beecher-Monas, "Reality Bites: The Illusion of Science in Bite-Mark Evidence," *Cardozo Law Review* 30 (2009): 1369; National Academies of Sciences, *Strengthening Forensic Science*, 107–108 ("Much forensic evidence—including, for example, bite marks and firearm and toolmark identifications—is introduced in criminal trials without any meaningful scientific validation, determination of error rates, or reliability testing to explain the limits of the discipline"); 176 ("Although the majority of forensic odontologists are satisfied that bite marks can demonstrate sufficient detail for positive identification, no scientific studies support this assessment, and no large population studies have been conducted. . . . The committee received no evidence of an existing scientific basis for identifying an individual to the exclusion of all others"); *Report to the President—Forensic Science and Criminal Courts: Ensuring Scientific Validity of Feature-Comparison Methods* (Washington, DC: President's Council of Advisors of Science and Technology, 2016), 87 ("Few empirical studies have been undertaken to study the ability of examiners to accurately identify the source of a bitemark. Among those studies that have been undertaken, the observed false positive rates were so high that the method is clearly scientifically unreliable at present").

169   **ran for coroner of Forrest County:** Dr. Michael West, curriculum vitae, March 30, 2006.

169   **She was told to "shut up.":** Dawn Young, "Inter Office Memo," North Louisiana Regional Forensic Laboratory, Aug. 15, 1995 (relaying a phone call with Ward in which she says she was told to "shut up"); Emily Ward, interview by Radley Balko.

169   **professional incompetence:** Letter from Kris Sperry to Richard Zumwalt, Dec. 6, 1993; Emily Ward and Jim Ingram, interviews by Radley Balko.

169   **"whether she [Ward] likes it or not.":** "County Looking for Place to Dump Its Garbage with Closing of Landfill," *Clarksdale* (MS) *Press Register*, Oct. 6, 1993.

169   **in his bid for reelection:** "Re Elect Charles Scott," *Clarksdale* (MS) *Press Register*, Aug. 7, 1995.

170   **losing business to them:** "Shop Around," *Town Talk* (Monroe, LA), Oct. 12, 1993.

170   **"a yes-man for the police.":** John Andrew Prime, "Monroe Area No Longer Uses Caddo Coroner," *Times* (Shreveport, LA), Oct. 11, 1993.

170   **just a letter to the editor:** Letter from Dawn Young to Kris Sperry, Aug. 1, 1995.

170   **didn't retain the tissue:** Letter from Steven Hayne to Joe Meng, May 16, 1994; letter from Dawn Young to John Hammons, Oct. 19, 1994; letter from Dawn Young to Steven Hanson, March 13, 1996.

170   **died three months earlier:** Letter from Hayne to Meng; letter from Young to Hammons; letter from Young to Hanson.

171   **"failed to do so.":** Letter from Young to Hammons.

171   **"unheard of in the field of pathology.":** Ibid.

171   **interview for *Reason* magazine:** Mississippi medical malpractice defense attorney, interview by Radley Balko.

171   **"from a Steven Hayne autopsy.":** Ibid.

171   **"and the medicolegal system.":** Letter from Kris Sperry to Dr. Richard Zumwalt, Dec. 6, 1993; letter from Kris Sperry to Ethics Committee of

American Academy of Forensic Sciences, Dec. 6, 1993; letter from D. M. Lucas to Kris Sperry, Dec. 17, 1993.

171 **"most obvious trespasses.":** Letter from Kris Sperry to Dawn Young, Jan. 9, 1995.

171 **"to point out the difference.":** Vincent di Maio, interviews by Radley Balko.

172 **"to review them.":** Letter from Young to Sperry.

172 **"in a false light.":** "Complaint for Libel/Slander/Defamation, Tortious Interference with and Injury to Business and Contractual Relations, and Conspiracy," Steven T. Hayne v. Dawn B. Young, George M. McCormick, and Forensic Pathologists, Inc., No. CV96–1837, July 31, 1996.

172 **"action on a national scale":** Letter from Young to Sperry.

172 **still inside and still intact:** Transcript of hearing on exhumation, *State of Louisiana v. Jimmie Duncan* (Ouachita Parish, LA, March 18, 1994), 13. (Note: Hayne responded to the accusation in the same hearing by stating that he always removes the organs in an autopsy "unless I am specifically prescribed [*sic*] during the course of a private autopsy" not to), Ibid., 52.

172 **that had nothing on them:** Transcript of hearing on exhumation, *Louisiana v. Jimmie C. Duncan*, questioning of Cecil McCormick, March 1994, 13. (Note: When asked about the allegation, Hayne responded, "I was not aware of Dr. Harlan having a problem with slides. If he had requested slides, they would have been sent off. If I reviewed a case signing it out and described the tumor of the kidney, the tumor would be there.")

172 **the summons and complaint:** Hayne v. Young et al., CV96-1837 (U.S. District Ct. Western Dist. of Louisiana, 1996); Notice of Intent to Dismiss for Failure to Prosecute Under LR 41.3W, CV96-1837, Sept. 22, 1997, *Hayne v. Young et al.*

173 **December 18, 1993, 9:35 p.m.:** Radley Balko, "Manufacturing Guilt," *Reason*, Feb. 19, 2009, http://reason.com/archives/2009/02/19/manufacturing -guilt; Haley Oliveaux autopsy video, Dec. 18, 1993.

173 **he found her in the water:** State Ex. Rel. Jimmie C. Duncan v. Burl Cain, Supplemental Petition for Post-Conviction Relief and Motion for Evidentiary Hearing Case No. 94-F0042 (Ouachita Parish, Louisiana, District Ct. 2008), 13.

173 **he was bad for Allison and Haley:** *State of Louisiana v. Jimmie C. Duncan*; Kathy Kelly, interview by Radley Balko; *Jimmie C. Duncan v. Burl Cain*, Supplemental Petition, 10–13.

173 **turned to Steven Hayne and Michael West:** *Jimmie C. Duncan v. Burl Cain*, Supplemental Petition, 15.

173 **Mississippi Mortuary Services in Pearl:** *State of Louisiana v. Jimmie C. Duncan*.

173 **witnessed the autopsy:** Ibid.; Haley Oliveaux autopsy report, Dec. 19, 1993; Balko, "Manufacturing Guilt."

174 **before conducting exams:** "Medical Examiner, Coroner and Forensic Pathologist Independence," *National Association of Medical Examiners Position Paper* 3, no. 1 (2013), https://netforum.avectra.com/public/temp /ClientImages/NAME/00df032d-ccab-48f8-9415-5c27f173cda6.pdf.

174 **come up with false positives:** See Barbara O'Brien, "Prime Suspect: An Examination of Factors that Aggravate and Counteract Confirmation Bias in Criminal Investigations," *Psychology, Public Policy and the Law* 15

(2009): 315; Michael J. Saks and D. Michael Risinger, "Baserates, the Presumption of Guilt, Admissibility Rulings, and Erroneous Convictions," *Michigan State Law Review* (2003): 1051.

174   **nearly all the parish's autopsies:** Transcript of hearing, *State of Louisiana v. Jimmie C. Duncan*, questioning of Ouachita Parish coroner Claude Smith, 28–29; questioning of Steven Hayne, 41. (Note: The questioning of Smith says the parish began contracting autopsies in 1992, but Hayne says in May 1994 that it was "six, eight months ago." Given other documentation, Hayne's estimate is likely the correct one here.)

174   **He called in Michael West:** *Jimmie C. Duncan v. Burl Cain*, Supplemental Petition, 2.

174   **with Jimmie Duncan's teeth:** Letter from Michael West to Charles Cook, Dec. 30, 1993.

174   **"positive match" to Duncan:** Ibid.

174   **indicative of sexual abuse:** *Jimmie C. Duncan v. Burl Cain*, Supplemental Petition, 18; Haley Oliveaux autopsy report, Dec. 19, 1993.

174   **copy of it in the prosecutor's file:** Kelly, interview; *Jimmie C. Duncan v. Burl Cain*, Supplemental Petition, 23.

175   **after the chest-of-drawers incident:** Haley Oliveaux autopsy video, Dec. 18 and 19, 1993; *Jimmie C. Duncan v. Burl Cain*, Supplemental Petition, 57–62.

175   **captured on video:** Haley Oliveaux autopsy video, Dec. 18 and 19.

175   **viewing the video in 2009:** Michael Bowers, interview by Radley Balko; Balko, "Manufacturing Guilt"; Haley Oliveaux autopsy video, Dec. 18.

175   **"a damn lie.":** Jerry Mitchell, "Forensic Dentist Defends Work He's Done in Autopsies," *Clarion-Ledger* (Jackson, MS), Feb. 28, 2009.

175   **affidavit for Jimmie Duncan's defense:** Michael Bowers, interview by Radley Balko.

175   **after viewing the tape:** *Jimmie C. Duncan v. Burl Cain*, Supplemental Petition, 55–56, 107–108; letter from Dr. Michael West to Charles Cook, Dec. 30, 1993; Jerry Mitchell, "Video Raises Autopsy Questions," *Clarion-Ledger* (Jackson, MS), Feb. 27, 2009.

175   **they weren't human bites:** Mitchell, "Forensic Dentist Defends Work."

176   **bite mark analyst to replace him:** *State of Louisiana v. Jimmie C. Duncan*; *Jimmie C. Duncan v. Burl Cain*, Supplemental Petition, 26 (citing state's brief acknowledging that West is "controversial" after prosecutors had replaced him with another expert).

176   **injury was weeks old:** *Jimmie C. Duncan v. Burl Cain*, Supplemental Petition, 61, 106–109; trial transcript, *State of Louisiana v. Jimmie C. Duncan*, 375.

176   **wasn't a bite mark at all:** *Jimmie C. Duncan v. Burl Cain*, Supplemental Petition, 32–35; trial transcript, *State of Louisiana v. Jimmie C. Duncan*, 667.

176   **turned out to be false:** Radley Balko, "Meet Jay Via: One Bad Cop, in One County, Who Did a Whole Lot of Damage," *Washington Post*, Dec. 11, 2015; *Jimmie C. Duncan v. Burl Cain*, Supplemental Petition.

177   **"That guy is crazy.":** Bowers, interview.

177   **"because of the death penalty.":** Mitchell, "Forensic Dentist Defends Work."

177   **including the anus:** Kelly, interview; *Jimmie C. Duncan v. Burl Cain*, Supplemental Petition, xi.

177   **inflicted near the time of death:** *Jimmie C. Duncan v. Burl Cain*, Supplemental Petition, 85–86.

177   **never sent either:** Ibid., 103–104.

177   **the records had been destroyed:** Kelly, interview; Radley Balko, "The Continuing Saga of Steven Hayne," *Reason*, Dec. 6, 2010; *Jimmie C. Duncan v. Burl Cain*, Supplemental Petition, 286–287.

178   **deaths in police custody:** Ward, interview.

178   **"often ignored in probes.":** Grace Simons, "Murder: Who Does Autopsy?" *Clarion-Ledger* (Jackson, MS), Aug. 20, 1994.

178   **"the girl who brought you.":** Ibid.

178   **she told them what she had found:** Ibid.

178   **Kitchens found this unacceptable:** Letter from John T. Kitchens to Jim Ingram, March 15, 1994.

178   **"the defendant's advantages,":** Ibid.

179   **office was prosecuting the case:** Ibid.

179   **Ingram a similar letter:** Letter from Edward J. Peters, district attorney, to Jim Ingram, commissioner of public safety, March 15, 1994.

179   **rebukes of the state's public defender system:** See *Assembly Line Justice: Mississippi's Indigent Defense Crisis*, NAACP Legal Defense and Education Fund, 2003, www.sado.org/fees/2003-02-01-assembly_line_justice.pdf.

179   **"law enforcement and prosecutors.":** Kelly M. Pyrek, *Forensic Science Under Siege: The Challenges of Forensic Laboratories and the Medico-Legal Investigation System* (Boston: Elsevier Academic, 2007), 193.

179   **"no problem talking to the defense.":** Vincent Di Maio, *Frontline*, PBS, Feb. 1, 2011.

180   **she deemed it was necessary:** Letter from Charles S. Head to Jim Ingram, Commissioner of Public Safety, March 10, 1994.

180   **"contributing to the obstruction of justice.":** Simmons, "Murder: Who Does Autopsy?"

180   **"appointed by the state.":** Ibid.

180   **"flimsy excuses":** "Medical Examiner," *Clarion-Ledger* (Jackson, MS), Aug. 29, 1994.

180   **"the practice must end.":** Ibid.

180   **"with an empty top slot":** Ibid.

180   **letters to the editor in support of Ward:** "Medical Examiner Ought to Be Impartial, Help All," *Clarion-Ledger* (Jackson, MS), Nov. 1, 1994.

181   **"I don't think that's right.":** "Bradford Signs Protest Petition Criticizing SME," *Scott County* (MS) *Times*," March 29, 1995.

181   **an affair with her:** L. W. "Bump" Calloway, interview by David Fechheimer, Feb. 25, 2012.

181   **"bull-dyke" whose do-gooderism:** Former Mississippi sheriff, interview by Radley Balko.

181   **taking orders from her:** Ibid.; Calloway, interview.

181   **but emboldened her critics:** Jim Ingram, interview by Radley Balko; Ward, interview.

181   **undermining the coroners' authority:** Coroner Petition, Jan. 27, 1995; letter from Dr. Michael West to "Fellow Coroners," Jan. 27, 1995.

181   **"how vindictive she can be.":** Coroner Petition; Letter from West to "Fellow Coroners."

181   **"we all must work and live in.":** Coroner Petition; Letter from West to "Fellow Coroners."

182   **at least publicly:** Grace Simmons, "42 Coroners Say Examiner Is Failing Post," *Clarion-Ledger* (Jackson, MS), March 24, 1995.

182   **"this woman under control.":** Ibid.

182   **Jimmy Roberts's bottom line:** Ibid.

182   **"fifth-graders had written it":** Grace Simmons, "42 Coroners Say Examiner Is Failing Post," *Clarion-Ledger* (Jackson, MS), March 24, 1995.

182   **"competent, and willing to cooperate.":** Ibid.

182   **"or been fired.":** Ibid.

182   **"she is doing a good job.":** "Medical Examiner," *Clarion-Ledger* (Jackson, MS), March 27, 1995.

182   **Emily Ward resigned:** Ibid.

183   **"money off the system.":** Grace Simmons, "State Autopsy System Ailing, Former Medical Examiner Says," *Clarion-Ledger* (Jackson, MS), June 25, 1995.

183   **"a very incompetent individual.":** Emily Wagster, "State Medical Examiner Steps Down Under Fire," *Clarion-Ledger* (Jackson, MS), June 21, 1995.

CHAPTER 11: VESSELS OF WRATH, FITTED FOR DESTRUCTION

185   **"sexually battered her.":** Transcript of record, State of Mississippi v. Kennedy Brewer, No. 94-16-CR1 (Lowndes Cnty. Circuit Ct. March 21, 1995) (hereinafter "Brewer trial transcript"), 371.

185   **little girl went missing:** Ibid., 31.

185   **came from West:** Ibid., 31–35.

186   **they went to sleep:** Ibid., 31.

186   **"That is correct,":** Ibid., 31.

186   **He said she had:** Ibid., 31.

186   **"No," Jackson answered:** Ibid., 427, 441.

187   **charges against her were dismissed:** Ibid., 444.

187   **"that I killed.":** Ibid.

187   **corroborate her claim:** Ibid., 444–445.

187   **accessory charge had been dropped:** Ibid., 443–444; Gloria Jackson, interview by James Green, Oct. 7, 1993. In a 2017 email interview, Forrest Allgood wrote that though he doesn't recall certain details of the case after twenty-plus years, he did maintain that Jackson never faced any charges. The fact that Jackson was jailed, and that she herself says in her police statement that she had been charged as an accessory to capital murder, suggests otherwise. In any case, Allgood maintains that "nothing was dropped for her testimony."

187   **under those circumstances:** Brewer trial transcript, 491.

187   **freshwater drowning:** Ibid., 499–500, 505.

187   **"they were bite wounds.":** Ibid., 507.

187   **not from insect activity:** Ibid., 508.

187   **duties as a medical examiner:** See Declaration of J.C. Upshaw Downs, M.D., Dec. 1, 2011, 14–15, Steven Hayne v. the Innocence Project, No. 3:09-CV-218-KS-LRA (S.D. Miss. 2011), 17.

188   **inflicted after Jackson's death:** Ibid., 17 ("It was not reasonable for Dr. Hayne to conclude that the external findings could be premortem or even perimortem human bitemarks"); declaration of David Senn, Nov. 30, 2011, *Hayne v. Innocence Project*, 6 ("There were no indications from the photographic and videographic images of the skin lesions seen on the body of Christine Jackson that human biting was the cause of those lesions. As there were no lesions resembling human bitemarks, there was no medical, dental, or scientific reason for Dr. Hayne to call in Dr. West to collect bite or dental evidence in the Brewer case.").

188   **"result of an adult human bite mark.":** See Declaration of Michael M. Baden, M.D., Nov. 30, 2011, *Hayne v. Innocence Project*, 5.

188   **later been dismissed:** In 1992, West matched a bite mark on an elderly rape victim to a Mississippi man named Johnny Bourn. Bourn was arrested and imprisoned for eighteen months as a result of West's findings, even though hair and fingerprint evidence pointed to someone else. Bourn was released when DNA testing on fingernail scrapings taken from the victim conclusively excluded him as the assailant. Mark Hansen, "Out of the Blue," *American Bar Association Journal*, Feb. 1, 1996; Ross Parker Simons, affidavit, Oct. 6, 2010.

188   **professional limitations:** Brewer trial transcript, 704.

188   **"So I made one mistake.":** Ibid., 788.

188   **doesn't reflect Kennedy Brewer's reaction:** Ibid., 788.

188   **hour-long documentary on BBC:** Ibid., 687; *Traces of Guilt: The Verdict*, BBC, Jan. 4, 1996.

188   **"degree of scientific certainty,":** Brewer trial transcript, 722.

189   **"an art as it is a science.":** Ibid., 722, 800.

189   **weren't bite marks:** Ibid., 865.

189   **"direct comparison":** Ibid., 875.

189   **a true "pioneer.":** Ibid., 875.

190   **"dental scientific certainty.":** Ibid., 895.

190   **"somewhat of an art.":** Ibid., 895.

191   **"class and individual characteristics":** Ibid., 735.

191   **underbite, and so forth:** Ibid., 735–736, 738–739, 744–745.

191   **"random wear and tear.":** Ibid.

191   **biting surface of a tooth:** Ibid.

192   **to show to the jury:** Brewer v. State 725 So.2d 106 (Miss. 1998), footnote 4.

192   **"to create [visible] marks.":** Declaration of David Senn, Nov. 30, 2011, *Hayne v. Innocence Project*, 7.

192   **for another two years:** Brewer trial transcript, 525–526; Stossel, "Junk Science."

192   **accessible only from the inside:** Brewer trial transcript, 30–31.

192   **she returned from the club:** Ibid., 31.

193   **on the ground underneath it:** Ibid., 34.

193   **to watch *American Gladiators*:** Ibid., 541.

193   **any sign of having done so:** Ibid., 421, 618, 541, 577–579.

193   **through the window itself:** Ibid., 577–579.

195   **"do that with you right now.":** Ibid., 991–992.

195   **"Four; no more. Four,":** Ibid., 992.

195   **retired to deliberate:** Ibid., 1039. The time was 4:10 p.m.

195   **They found Kennedy Brewer guilty:** Ibid., 1041. The time was 5:45 p.m.

195   **"atrocious and cruel.":** Ibid., 1050.

195   **much of an opening statement:** Ibid.

196   **proficient in the sentencing phase:** *Guidelines for the Appointment and Performance of Counsel in Death Penalty Cases, 2003*, American Bar Association.

196   **guaranteed by the Eighth Amendment:** For a history and discussion of mitigation and the death penalty, see Russell Stetler, "The Mystery of Mitigation," *University of Pennsylvania Review of Law and Social Change* 11 (2007–2008): 237.

196   **not to build empathy:** See Liliana Segura, "As Arkansas Prepares for Seven Back-to-Back Executions, a Victim Requests Clemency," *Intercept*, April 14, 2017. (Quoting defense attorney discussing mitigation in Arkansas in the 1990s: "I can't say we even looked for it. We had no idea what that meant.")

196   **Annie, as a witness:** Brewer trial transcript, 1059–1062.

196   **"Don't, please.":** Ibid., 1062.

196   **since her son had been locked up:** Ibid.

196   **agree that there hadn't:** Ibid.

196   **Christine Jackson's murder:** Arraignment and guilty plea transcript, State v. Justin Albert Johnson, No. 12,385 (Noxubee Cnty. Circuit Ct. May 20, 1992).

197   **"Yes, sir,":** Brewer trial transcript, 1056.

197   **"you were urged to do.":** Ibid., 1083.

197   **"we will not long exist.":** Ibid.

197   **often invoked the Bible:** For example, see Quintez Wren Hodges v. State of Mississippi, 912 So.2d 730 (Miss. 2005); Willie Jerome Manning v. State of Mississippi, 929 So.2d 885 (2006).

198   **"fit only for destruction.":** Brewer trial transcript, 1083–1084. Allgood's reference to the prophet Paul was prescient, though not in the way Allgood intended. Paul's own story is one of injustice. Facing trial and possible execution for promulgating revolt in Judea by teaching Christianity, Paul had the good fortune to land in the court of Festus, Judea's governor. Festus assured Paul that judgment would be a matter of law, not of faith. Neither Festus nor Roman consul Agrippa consented to the mob's demands that Paul be executed.

198   **"suffer the penalty of death.":** Ibid., 1088.

199   **"mercy on your soul.":** Ibid., 1089.

199   **just 4 people:** See "Mississippi and the Death Penalty," Mississippi Department of Corrections, www.mdoc.ms.gov/Death-Row/Pages/Mississippi -Death-Penalty.aspx.

199   **23 over the same period:** See "Executions," Alabama Department of Corrections, www.doc.state.al.us/Executions.aspx.

199   **166 in the 1990s alone:** See "Statistics," Texas Execution Information, www.txexecutions.org/statistics.asp.

199   **were unconstitutionally vague:** Godfrey v. Georgia, 446 U.S. 420 (1980).

199   **the word "especially,":** Maynard v. Cartwright, 486 U.S. 356 (1988).

199   **the *Godfrey* decision in 1980:** Stringer v. Black, 503 U.S. 222 (1992).

200   **finality of the gas chamber:** Leatherwood v. State, 548 So.2d 389, 403-406 (Miss. 1989) (Robertson, J., concurring) (expressing the view that there was "as much chance of the Supreme Court sanctioning death as a penalty for any non-fatal rape as the proverbial snowball enjoys in the nether regions"); Minnick v. State, 551 So.2d 77, 101 (Miss. 1988) (Robertson, J., dissenting), rev'd sub nom. Minnick v. Mississippi, 498 U.S. 146 (1990); Clemons v. State, 535 So.2d 1354, 1367 (Miss. 1988) (Robertson, J. dissenting). Robertson's dissenting opinion in *Clemons* took the position that the "heinous, atrocious or cruel" aggravating factor was unconstitutionally vague (1367–1368). Campaign advertising claimed that his decision meant that "a defendant who 'shot an unarmed pizza delivery boy in cold-blood' had not committed a crime serious enough to warrant the death penalty." Stephen B. Bright, "Political Attacks on the

Judiciary: Can Justice Be Done Amid Efforts to Intimidate and Remove Judges from Office for Unpopular Decisions?" *New York University Law Review* 308 (1997): 72.

200   **Robertson as a friend to criminals:** See Stephen B. Bright and Patrick J. Keenan, "Judges and the Politics of Death: Deciding Between the Bill of Rights and the Next Election in Capital Cases," *Boston University Law Review* 75 (1995): 759.

200   **"executions to the county seat.":** Adam Nossiter, "Making Hard Time Harder, States Cut Jail TV and Sports," *New York Times*, Sept. 17, 1994.

200   **"capital of capital punishment.":** Ibid.

200   **"zebras in Mississippi.":** Ibid.

201   **already punishable by death:** Mac Gordon, "Execution Goes Back on Agenda," *Clarion-Ledger* (Jackson, MS), Aug. 13, 1994.

201   **bipartisan support:** Ibid.; Margaret Downing, "Big Game Hunter Stalks Trophy Prey Back in Home Jungle," *Clarion-Ledger* (Jackson, MS), Aug. 7, 1994; Emily Wagster, "Who's Responsible for Crime? Depends on Whom You Ask," *Clarion-Ledger* (Jackson, MS), Oct. 29, 1995.

201   **killing her newborn daughter:** Jill Farrell King, "Teenage Mother Faces Trial in Infant Daughter's Death," *Clarion-Ledger* (Jackson, MS), April 2, 1997; Joseph Ammerman, "Investigation Continues as Newborn Baby Is Buried," *Clarion-Ledger* (Jackson, MS), Dec. 25, 1996.

201   **"penalty to be carried out.":** "Death Penalty Must Be Swift and Certain If It Is to Remain a Deterrent to Crime," *Enterprise-Journal* (McComb, MS), reprinted in *Clarion-Ledger* (Jackson, MS), Sept. 3, 1994.

201   **"carried out quickly,":** "Death Penalty: Appeal Time Should Be Shortened," *Clarion-Ledger* (Jackson, MS), Oct. 12, 1995.

201   **"to shorten the process.":** Ibid.

201   **crimes punishable by death:** "Punishment Has Not Been Given to Those Sitting on Mississippi's Death Row," *Clarion-Ledger*, (Jackson, MS), Jan. 27, 1996; Mac Gordon, "Governor Outlines His '96 Agenda," *Clarion-Ledger* (Jackson, MS), Jan. 17, 1996.

202   **"ours continues to grow.":** Joseph Ammerman, "Fordice Wants to Speed Executions," *Clarion-Ledger* (Jackson, MS), June 12, 1997.

202   **"sword of justice do its work.":** "Death Penalty: Mississippi Should Make It Work," *Clarion-Ledger* (Jackson, MS), Feb. 22, 1998.

202   **"need for the death penalty.":** "DNA Evidence: Brewer Deserves His Day in Court," *Clarion-Ledger* (Jackson, MS), July 8, 2001.

203   **autopsy totals topped 1,500:** Dr. Steven T. Hayne, autopsy data.

203   **his work in private cases:** Deposition of Cecil McCrory, *Hayne v. Innocence Project* (April 24, 2012), 33–34.

203   **conduct arson investigations:** Ibid., 35–36.

203   **and wrongful deaths:** Deposition of Dr. Steven Hayne, Hayne v. Innocence Project, 2011 WL 198128, No. 3:09-CV-218-KS-LRA (S.D. Miss. April 26, 2012), 23–25.

203   **"missed a beat without":** Thyrie Bland, "Some Say 2-Year Vacancy Proof Medical Examiner Unnecessary," *Clarion-Ledger* (Jackson, MS), June 28, 1997.

204   **"we don't have one.":** Ibid.

204   **"whenever I need him.":** Ibid.

204   **"working absolutely fine,":** "One Job Not Worth Filling," *Hattiesburg* (MS) *American*, Sept. 6, 1997.

204   **"Not one.":** Ibid.

204   **a salary of $69,000:** Ibid.

205   **West argued, but nothing more:** Butch John, "Applicants for Medical Examiner Job Tough to Find," *Clarion-Ledger* (Jackson, MS), March 22, 1999.

205   **"happened in the past.":** Ibid.

205   **exhumed and reexamined:** See depositions of Dr. Steven Hayne, Daniel Storts v. Graco Children's Products Inc., No. 95C 1007H (U.S. District Ct. Northern District of Oklahoma, 1996); deposition of Steven Hayne, Edward Dillon et al. v. Richard Rushing et al., No. 94-0040 (Lincoln Cnty. Circuit Ct. April 8, 1998), 20–30.

205   **"medical knowledge.":** Deposition of Dr. Steven Hayne, *Daniel Storts v. Graco Children's Products Inc.*, 6–7.

206   **"during the original autopsies.":** See Radley Balko, "CSI: Mississippi," *Reason*, Oct. 8, 2007.

206   **His price: $37,000:** *Edward Dillon et al. v. Richard Rushing et al.*, 25.

206   **"unsolved into police convictions.":** John Stossel, "Junk Science: What You Know That May Not Be So Scientific—Theories That May Be Wrong," *ABC News*, Aug. 28, 1997.

206   **"directed straight from God.":** Ibid.

206   **went on to kill again:** Radley Balko, "Solving Kathy Mabry's Murder," *Huffington Post*, Jan. 17, 2013.

207   **"expert in forensic odontology.":** *Brewer v. State of Mississippi*, 725 So.2d 106.

207   **"not his qualifications.":** Ibid.

207   **"and the trial itself.":** Brooks v. State of Mississippi, no. 98-KA-322, brief for the appellee (March 5, 1999), 17.

207   **"inadmissible in the present case.":** Ibid.

208   **raising them in his appeal:** Brooks v. State of Mississippi, 748 So.2d 736 (Miss. 1999).

208   **reliable as fingerprints or DNA:** Ibid.

208   **he was "elated.":** Gina Holland, "State Supreme Court Rules Bite Mark Evidence Admissible," *Clarion-Ledger* (Jackson, MS), Oct. 8, 1999.

208   **"validity of bite marks.":** Ibid., (McCrae, J., dissenting).

208   **list of transgressions:** Brooks v. State of Mississippi, 748 So.2d 736 (McRae, J., dissenting).

CHAPTER 12: PRAYERS FOR RELIEF

209   **Hayne hired him as an assistant:** Dr. Michael West, curriculum vitae, March 30, 2006; Steven Hayne v. the Innocence Project, 2011 WL 198128, No 3:09-CV-218-KS-LRA (S.D. Miss. March 13, 2012), 157.

209   **"one thing, Dr. Michael West.":** Transcript of record, State v. Howard, 92-400-CR1 (Lowndes Cnty. Circuit Ct. May 22, 2000) (hereinafter "Howard trial transcript"), 619–620.

210   **"profession as the standard.":** Ibid., 620.

210   **"So it was with Michael West.":** Ibid.

210   **"he's a leader in his field.":** Ibid., 621.

210   **"three year old child.":** Ibid., 641.

210   **sentenced him to die:** Ibid., 621, 697; sources for Eddie Lee Howard narrative: Howard trial transcript; "Teenager Acquitted of Killing Sister," Associated Press, Nov. 4, 1993; "Bleach Burns Called Deliberate,"

Associated Press, Nov. 3, 1993; "Memorandum of Authorities in Support of Answer to the Petition for Writ of Habeas Corpus," Eddie Lee Howard Jr. v. State of Mississippi, No. 3:07-CV-10-P (Jan. 20, 2010).

211   **acronyms to attorneys:** Elizabeth MacDonald, "The Making of an Expert Witness: It's Definitely in the Credentials," *Wall Street Journal*, Feb. 8, 1999.

211   **difference between them:** State of Mississippi v. David Parvin, No. CR09-135 (Monroe Cnty. Circuit Ct. June 13, 2011), 195–196; Declaration of J. C. Upshaw Downs, M.D., Dec. 1, 2011, *Hayne v. Innocence Project*, 6–7.

211   **"a problem with that.":** Radley Balko, "CSI: Mississippi," *Reason*, Oct. 8, 2007; Joseph Prahlow, interview by Radley Balko.

211   **from the American Board of Pathology:** See letter from Dawn Young to Kris Sperry, Dec. 26, 1994. ("Further, when I asked the plaintiff's attorney about this, he indicated that he was convinced that Dr. Hayne possessed the same qualifications and certifications as Dr. McCormick.")

211   **in dozens of medical fields:** Letter from John D. McLellan Jr., United States Department of Labor, to Dr. Michael Rask, Dec. 18, 1984; Ken Terry, "Visit Vegas! Get Your Boards While You're There," *Medical Economics*, Feb. 13, 1995; Jerry Mitchell, "Pathologist's Credibility on Line," *Clarion-Ledger* (Jackson, MS), Nov. 6, 2012; deposition of Dr. Steven Hayne, Hayne v. Innocence Project, 2011 WL 198128, No. 3:09-CV-218-KS-LRA (S.D. Miss. April 26, 2012), 211–213; letter from Nick Rebel to Jim Lappan, Mississippi Office of Capital Defense Counsel, May 18, 2010; letter from Barbara Schneidman, assoc. vice president of the American Board of Medical Specialties, to Emily W. Ward, assistant professor of pathology (June 18, 1996); "AFMA," American Academy of Neurological and Orthopedic Surgery, http://aanos.org/certification/afma; AFMA address found at www.directoryofassociations.com/view.asp?di=%7B 7D260A02-1D0D-4367-B8AB-427FFCB26984%7D; Mark Hansen, "Expertise to Go," *American Bar Association Journal* (Feb. 2000).

212   **"radiofrequency surgery.":** Terry, "Visit Vegas! Get Your Boards While You're There."

212   **shortly before he died:** Ibid.

212   **in 1991 for plagiarism:** Hansen, "Expertise to Go," 44; MacDonald, "The Making of an Expert Witness"; Joseph T. Wells, "The Similarities End with the Initials," *Fraud* (Sept./Oct. 2012); Leah Bartos, "No Forensic Background? No Problem," ProPublica, April 17, 2012, www.propublica .org/article/no-forensic-background-no-problem; Aaron Nesbitt, "CSI: Mississippi," letters, *Reason*, June 2008; Melody Petersen, "A Résumé Distinguished by What It Didn't Mention," *New York Times*, Sept. 6, 2001.

212   **retaliation for whistle-blowing:** Hansen, "Expertise to Go."

212   **about O'Block's credibility:** Wells, "The Similarities End with the Initials."

212   **1-800-4AExpert:** Hansen, "Expertise to Go," 44; MacDonald, "The Making of an Expert Witness."

212   **$200,000 per year:** Hansen, "Expertise to Go," 44.

213   **on an ethics test:** Ibid., 50.

213   **even that could be waived:** Ibid.

213   **name of her cat:** Bartos, "No Forensic Background? No Problem," citing Steve K. D. Eichel, "Credentialing: It May Not Be the Cat's Meow," 2011, www.dreichel.com/Articles/Dr_Zoe.htm; Steven K. Dubrow Eichel,

"Credentialing: It May Not Be the Cat's Meow," Freedom of Mind Resource Center, 2002, at http://old.freedomofmind.com/Info/articles/credentialing.php.

213   **about whom it certifies:** When Radley Balko made inquiries with the group about Hayne's accreditation, he was a told that the requested information was confidential.

213   **any of her professional references:** Bartos, "No Forensic Background? No Problem." (Note: In a posted rebuttal to the article, ACFEI argued that by joining the group, attending two conferences, enrolling in an online course, and reading enough of the materials to pass the test, she was much more qualified for her certification than she claimed. The group also argued that the purpose of its certifications is not to qualify someone as an expert witness, although plenty use the group for that purpose, and its website certainly makes that claim for a number of certifications. See https://static.propublica.org/assets/docs/ACFEI.ProPublica OfficialStmt.pdf.

213   **told Bartos in her 2012 ProPublica report:** Ibid.

214   **"or is just a diploma mill.":** Ibid.

214   **corresponding impact to the head:** See U.S. Shaken-Baby Syndrome Database, Medill School of Law, Northwestern University, www.medilljusticeproject.org/database; Jerry Mitchell, "High Court Tosses 'Shaken Baby' Conviction," *Clarion-Ledger* (Jackson, MS), Dec. 18, 2014; see also Jerry Mitchell, "Miss. Court Rejects 'Shaken Baby' Conviction," *Clarion-Ledger* (Jackson, MS), Dec. 16, 2014; Clyde Haberman, "Shaken Baby Syndrome: A Diagnosis That Divides the Medical World," *New York Times*, Sept. 13, 2015.

214   **exceptionally violent shaking:** Haberman, "Shaken Baby Syndrome."

214   **convictions have been overturned:** Ibid.

214   **there are no accidents:** André de Gruy, interview by Radley Balko; Robert Evans, interview by Radley Balko.

214   **eleven such convictions in the state:** Jerry Mitchell, "High Court Tosses 'Shaken Baby' Conviction"; see also Mitchell, "Miss. Court Rejects 'Shaken Baby' Conviction."

214   **involved in many of them:** See for example, "Baby Sitter Charged in Infant's Death," *Yazoo Herald* (Yazoo City, MS), Jan. 31, 1998; "Manslaughter Plea," *Clarion-Ledger* (Jackson, MS), Oct. 4, 2000.

215   **"leaving her employment.":** Devin Bennett v. State of Mississippi, 933 So.2d 930 (Miss. 2006).

215   **"think Devin is innocent.":** Sources for Devin Bennett narrative: Devin Bennett v. State of Mississippi, No. 2006-DR-01516-SCT (Miss. 2008); trial transcript, *State of Mississippi v. Devin Bennett*; Sylvain Metz, "Jury Hear Tape of Accused Dad," *Clarion-Ledger* (Jackson, MS), Feb. 26, 2003; "Death Row Inmate Ends His Hunger Strike After 19 Days," *Clarion-Ledger* (Jackson, MS), Aug. 24, 2012; Emily Ward, interview by Radley Balko; letter from Devin Bennett to Radley Balko.

216   **died shortly thereafter:** Jeffrey Keith Havard v. State of Mississippi, 928 So.2d 771 (Miss. 2006); see also James R. Lauridson Report, May 10, 2007.

216   **for sexual abuse:** Jeffrey Keith Havard v. State of Mississippi, 988 So.2d 322 (Miss. 2008).

216   **Shaken Baby Syndrome:** *Havard v. State of Mississippi*, 928 So.2d 771; see Chloe Britt, autopsy report, Feb. 22. 2002.

216   **when Dr. Hayne was available:** *Havard v. State of Mississippi*, 928 So.2d 771; trial transcript, State of Mississippi v. Jeffrey Keith Havard, Case No. 0141 (Adams Cnty. Circuit Ct. June 18, 2002), 44–45 (hereinafter "Havard trial transcript").

217   **they had ever witnessed:** See ibid., 307–308, 377–379, 391–393, 410; Jeffrey Keith Havard v. State of Mississippi, 988 So.2d 322 (Miss. 2008); James R. Lauridson Report, May 10, 2007.

217   **only the dilation and small contusion:** See affidavit of Dr. Janice Ophoven, Nov. 12, 2013, 2 ("There is no evidence of sexual abuse in the autopsy findings or photographs. The rectal area in the photographs is within the range of normal in a deceased infant"); affidavit of Dr. Michael M. Baden, March 13, 2013, 3–4 (no evidence of sexual abuse); Lauridson Report, May 10, 2007, (finding no evidence of sexual abuse).

217   **tears or cuts from his view:** Havard trial transcript, 546–551; Lauridson Report, May 10, 2007.

217   **an additional six times:** Havard trial transcript, 556–558.

217   **review Hayne's autopsy and trial testimony:** See James R. Lauridson affidavits of April 10, 2007, April 13, 2007, June 14, 2007, and July 23, 2007, and Lauridson Report.

217   **no evidence of sexual abuse at all:** *Havard v. State of Mississippi*, 928 So.2d 771; see Lauridson affidavits of April 10, 2007, April 13, 2007, June 14, 2007, July 23, 2007, and Lauridson Report.

218   **The ruling was unanimous:** *Havard v. State of Mississippi*, 928 So.2d 771.

218   **that suggested sexual abuse:** See Lauridson affidavits of April 10, 2007, April 13, 2007, June 14, 2007, July 23, 2007 and Lauridson Report.

218   **"was not sexually assaulted.":** *Havard v. State of Mississippi*, 988 So.2d 322.

218   **"the possibility that she was.":** Ibid.

218   **"objective evidence and are wrong.":** Lauridson Report.

218   **much more conclusive:** Lauridson Report Addendum, May 10, 2007.

218   **didn't write an opinion:** *Havard v. State of Mississippi*, 988 So.2d 322.

219   **denied Havard relief:** Jeffery Keith Havard v. State of Mississippi, 86 So.3d 896 (Miss. 2012).

219   **evidence of sexual abuse:** Ibid.

219   **"certainty that she was sexually assaulted.":** Ibid., 905.

219   **"the rectum by an object.":** Havard trial transcript, 546–551; *Havard v. State of Mississippi*, 86 So.3d 896.

219   **wasn't *technically* false:** Jamie Downs, interview by Radley Balko; Harry Bonnell, interview by Radley Balko.

219   **Havard once more:** *Havard v. State of Mississippi*, 888 So.3d 896.

219   **"*contrary to that of Dr. Hayne*":** *Havard v. State of Mississippi*, 988 So.2d 331, 332 (emphasis added).

219   **The jury obviously did, too:** *Havard v. State of Mississippi*, 888 So.3d 896.

220   **the court had rejected in 2008:** *Havard v. State of Mississippi*, 86 So.3d 896.

220   **"contrary to that of Dr. Hayne.":** *Havard v. State of Mississippi*, 988 So.2d 331, 322.

220   **reports deriding Hayne's work:** See Petition for Post-Conviction Relief, Jeffrey Havard v. State of Mississippi, Cause No. 02-KR-0141 (Adams Cnty. Circuit Ct. June 16, 2015); affidavit of Dr. Janice Ophoven, Nov. 12, 2013; and affidavit of Dr. Michael Baden, March 13, 2013.

220   **sexually assaulted at all:** Affidavit of Steven T. Hayne, July 21, 2014; Jerry Mitchell, "Capital Murder or Accidental Fall?" *Clarion-Ledger* (Jackson, MS), Jan. 19, 2014.

220   **never turned over to them:** Petitioner's Rebuttal to State's Response to Amended Motion for Relief from Judgment or for Leave to File Successive Petition for Post-Conviction Relief, Jeffrey Havard v. State of Mississippi, No. 2013-DR-01995-SCT, Oct. 13, 2014; affidavit of Steven T. Hayne, July 21, 2014; Jerry Mitchell, "Expert: Inmate Wrongfully Convicted," *Hattiesburg* (MS) *American*, August 22, 2014.

220   **"had been penetrated.":** Havard trial transcript, 300; Jerry Mitchell, "Pathologist: No Evidence Death Row Inmate Abused Child," *Clarion-Ledger*, Aug. 20, 2014; Jerry Mitchell, "Expert: Inmate Wrongly Convicted," *Hattiesburg* (MS) *American*, Aug. 22, 2014.

221   **"'That's incorrect.'":** Downs, interview; see *Ethics in Forensic Science*, edited by J.C. Upshaw Downs and Anjali Ranadive Swienton (Oxford: Elsevier Academic, 2012).

221   **he'd finally get a new trial:** Jerry Mitchell, "Science May Give Death Row Inmate New Hearing," *Clarion-Ledger* (Jackson, MS), April 23, 2015.

222   **remains on death row:** Sources for Jeff Havard narrative: Vershal Hogan, "Adams County Man on Death Row Granted Hearing That Could Lead to New Trial," *Natchez Democrat*, June 18, 2016; Affidavits of Steven Hayne in *Havard v. State of Mississippi*, April 10, 2009, July 22, 2013, July 21, 2014, and Aug. 29, 2014; Jerry Mitchell, "Facebook Post Irritates AG's Office," *Clarion-Ledger* (Jackson, MS), Sept. 1, 2013; Havard v. Mississippi, No. 2003-DP-00457-SCT (2006); Havard v. Mississippi, No. 2011-DR-00539-SCT (2012); Havard v. Mississippi, No. 2006-DR-01161-SCT (2008); Lauridson report and affidavit, May 10, 2007; Michael Baden Declaration, March 13, 2013; affidavit of Dr. Janice Ophoven, Nov. 12, 2013; *Havard v. Mississippi* trial transcripts; James Lauridson, interview by Radley Balko.

222   **family has been marshaling supporters:** Jerry Mitchell, "Capital Murder or Accidental Fall," *Clarion-Ledger* (Jackson, MS), Jan. 20, 2014; Jerry Mitchell, "Testimony in Death Row Inmate's Trial Contradicted," *Clarion-Ledger* (Jackson, MS), Jan. 30, 2012; Radley Balko, "Despite Evidence from Discredited Medical Examiner, Mississippi's Jeffrey Havard Nears Execution," *Huffington Post*, Nov. 29, 2012, www.freejeffreyhavard.org.

222   **asking for a gag order:** "Judge Denies Motion to Seal Court Files," *Enterprise-Journal* (McComb, MS), Sept. 3, 2013.

222   **"claims of innocence.":** Facebook posting regarding Jeffrey Havard case, Aug. 23, 2013.

222   **"a public spectacle.":** Motion to Seal, Jeffrey Havard v. Chris Epps, no. 5:08-cv-275-KS, Aug. 26, 2013.

222   **from the same source:** Ibid.

223   **the popular press:** The George C. Cochran Innocence Project at the University of Mississippi School of Law represents Brandon in his post-conviction litigation. Tucker Carrington is the director of that project.

223   **doesn't appear to exist:** See Reply to the State's Response to Brandon's Petition for Post-Conviction Relief, 2014-M-00596 (Lee Cnty. Circuit Ct. 2014); Vincent J. Di Maio and Dominic Di Maio, *Forensic Pathology*, 2nd ed. (Boca Raton, FL: CRC), 2.

223   **signs of neck trauma:** See Petition for Post-Conviction Relief, Christopher Brandon v. State of Mississippi, 2014-M-00596 (Lee Cnty. Circuit Ct. 2014).

223   **to review Hayne's work:** Ibid.

223   **"to be shaken baby.":** Trial transcript, State of Mississippi v. Christopher Brandon, Cause No. CR07-706 (Lee Cnty. Circuit Ct. Aug. 4, 2009), 423.

223   **"they disavow that position":** Reply to the State's Response to Brandon's Petition for Post-Conviction Relief, 2014-M-00596 (Lee Cnty. Circuit Ct. 2014).

223   **advanced case of pneumonia:** Reply to the State's Response to Brandon's Petition for Post-Conviction Relief, 2014-M-00596 (Lee Cnty. Circuit Ct. 2014); affidavit, James R. Lauridson, January 31, 2011.

224   **"that this entity exists.":** Di Maio and Di Maio, *Forensic Pathology*, 358–365.

224   **"honestly misread it.":** Radley Balko, "New Case Again Demonstrates Duplicity of Embattled Mississippi Medical Examiner," *Washington Post*, May 15, 2014.

224   **"scholarly journal article.":** See Petition for Post-Conviction Relief, *Christopher Brandon v. State of Mississippi.*

224   **"It's impossible.":** Ibid. (emphasis added).

225   **"fabricated a study,":** Response in Opposition to Application for Post-Conviction Relief, *Christopher Brandon v. State of Mississippi* (July 18, 2014).

225   **he gave in 2009:** Ibid.; Reply to State's Response, *Christopher Brandon v. State of Mississippi* (Aug. 13, 2013).

225   **what Hayne was recalling:** Response in Opposition to Application for Post-Conviction Relief, *Christopher Brandon v. State of Mississippi.*

225   **hold an evidentiary hearing:** Order, *Christopher Brandon v. State of Mississippi* (Aug. 13, 2014).

226   **Hayne's SBS testimony:** LeeVester Brown v. State of Mississippi, 152 So.3d 1146 (Miss. 2014).

227   **"if they're appointed.":** André de Gruy, interview by Radley Balko.

227   **"high-profile case.":** John Holdridge, interview by Radley Balko.

227   **"turned a killer loose.":** De Gruy, interview.

227   **Robertson wrote the opinion:** Hansen v. State, 592 So.2d 114 (Miss. 1991).

227   **over three million dollars:** Billy Corriher, "Big Business Taking Over State Supreme Courts," Center for American Progress, Aug. 2012; Billy Corriher, "Criminals and Campaign Cash," Center for American Progress, Oct. 2013.

227   **all of the candidates combined:** Corriher, "Big Business Taking Over State Supreme Courts"; "Buying Time, 2002: Mississippi," Brennan Center for Justice, Oct. 23, 2002; Robert Lenzer and Matthew Miller, "Buying Justice," *Forbes*, July 21, 2003.

227   **over the previous term:** Corriher, "Criminals and Campaign Cash."

227   **against criminal defendants:** Ibid.; see also Rachel Baye, "Secretive Group Destroys Candidates' Chances, Leaves Few Fingerprints," Center for Public Integrity, Dec. 2, 2015.

228   **surprised much of the state:** Tim Kalich, "Chief Justice's Defeat Is a Stunner," *Press Register* (Clarksdale, MS), Nov. 14, 2000.

228   **present problems for him:** Adam Liptak, "Not from a Grisham Novel, but One for the Casebook," *New York Times,* March 15, 2004; Baye, "Secretive Group Destroys Candidates' Chances"; Corriher, "Big Business Taking Over State Supreme Courts."

228   **"ad is going to look like.":** Corriher, "Criminals and Campaign Cash"; Kate Berry, "How Judicial Elections Impact Criminal Cases," Brennan Center for Justice, 2015.

229   **than a state supreme court justice:** Jerry Mitchell, "McRae's Fiery Tenure Ends with No Regrets," *Clarion-Ledger* (Jackson, MS) Jan. 5, 2004; Sid Salter, "McRae's Bright Red Bull's Eye Self-Applied," *Franklin* (MS) *County Times,* April 27, 2003.

229   **"blue jeans and lots of leather":** Lenzer and Miller, "Buying Justice."

229   **wearing only a thong:** Mitchell, "McRae's Fiery Tenure Ends with No Regrets"; Salter, "McRae's Bright Red Bull's Eye Self-Applied."

230   **a hundred miles per hour:** "McRae to Seek Reinstatement of His Driver's License," Associated Press, July 8, 1999; Ashley Elkins, "McRae Should Resign," *Tupelo* (MS) *Daily Journal,* May 21, 1999.

230   **"who supports the death penalty.":** Deborah Goldberg and Samantha Sanchez, "The New Politics of Judicial Elections 2002," Brennan Center for Justice, 2002.

230   **"McRae voted to reverse it.":** Lenzer and Miller, "Buying Justice."

230   **"murderer of a three-year-old girl.":** Goldberg and Sanchez, "The New Politics of Judicial Elections 2002."

230   **by thirty points:** "Buying Time, 2002: Mississippi," Brennan Center for Justice, Oct. 23, 2002; Lenzer and Miller, "Buying Justice"; Mitchell, "McRae's Fiery Tenure Ends with No Regrets."

231   **"have to keep your humanity.":** Levon Brooks, interview by Radley Balko.

232   **"sucking.":** Transcript of record, State of Mississippi v. Tammy Vance and Leigh Stubbs, No. 2000-362-MS-LT-2 (Lincoln Cnty. Circuit Ct. June 27–30, 2001) (hereinafter "Stubbs trial transcript"), 601.

232   **"severe oral sex.":** Ibid., 601.

233   **inflicted by Stubbs:** Ibid., 531.

233   **only that it was likely:** Ibid., 531, 601–602.

233   **"by any means.":** Ibid., 556.

233   **a human bite mark:** Ibid., 556, 601.

233   **clothing they're wearing:** See letter from David M. Hardy to Alfred M. Stubbs, Aug. 31, 2008, and attached letters from Federal Bureau of Investigation to Jerry L. Rushing, Sept. 11, 2000, and to Dunn Lampton, May 26, 2000.

233   **in Williams's injuries:** Deposition of Michael West, *State of Mississippi v. Tammy Vance and Leigh Stubbs* (Feb. 11, 2012), 50–51.

234   **obviously a body:** Stubbs trial transcript, 454–694; see letter from Hardy to Stubbs, and attached letters from Federal Bureau of Investigation to Rushing and to Lampton.

234   **"That's what I see.":** Stubbs trial transcript, 679.

234   **after having committed a crime:** Ibid., 573.

234   **"There are interpretations.":** Ibid., 569.

234   **"skin of the victim.":** Radley Balko, "Video Shows Controversial Forensic Specialist Michael West Fabricating Bite Marks," *Huffington Post,* Sept. 1, 2011. Note: As of this writing, the Bowers and Averil blog is no longer online.

235 **"is also an assault,":** Ibid.
235 **"thigh injury is 37 inches.":** Ibid., 506, 524.
235 **good scrub and some chlorine:** Ibid., 175, 578.
235 **belong to Williams:** Ibid., 175.
235 **"it wouldn't be unusual.":** Ibid., 559.
235 **"would almost be expected.":** Ibid.
235 **"Almost.":** Ibid.
235 **"the girl's vagina lip off.":** Deposition of Michael West, Eddie Lee Howard v. State of Mississippi, No. 2000-0015-CV1H (Lowndes Cnty. Circuit Ct. May 4, 2016), 16.
235 **The ruling was unanimous:** Leigh Stubbs and Tammy Vance v. State of Mississippi, 845 So.2d 656 (Miss. 2003).
236 **"area of his expertise.":** Ibid.
236 **were no longer using West:** Jerry Mitchell, "Forensic Dentist Defends Work He's Done in Autopsies," *Clarion-Ledger* (Jackson, MS), Feb. 28, 2009. (West says he "hasn't practiced forensic dentistry in three years.")
236 **West isn't a credible witness:** Lacey McLaughlin, "The JFP Interview with Jim Hood," *Jackson* (MS) *Free Press*, Oct. 12, 2011. (Quote from Hood: "Dr. [Michael] West is someone we have investigated, and I don't support him in any matter.")
236 **turn over exculpatory evidence:** Tammy Vance and Leigh Stubbs v. State of Mississippi, Cause No. 2011-388-LS-LT, June 27, 2012.
237 **The women agreed:** Ibid.; Order of expungement, Leigh Stubbs v. State of Mississippi, cause no. 200-363-MS-IT, Dec. 15, 2014.
237 **was nearly executed:** See "Ray Krone," Innocence Project, last accessed Aug. 3, 2017, www.innocenceproject.org/cases/ray-krone.
238 **"teeth did create that mark.":** Christopher Plourd video, Kim Ancona case; Paul C. Giannelli, "Bite Mark Analysis," *Criminal Law Bulletin* 43 (2007): 930, 939–940. (Dr. West, in a written and videotaped report, opined: "Finding this many patterns on this injury, I believe, can only lead an odontologist to an opinion that these teeth did create that mark.")
238 **certifying West as an expert witness:** Christopher J. Plourd affidavit, Sept. 15, 2005; James Rix affidavit (undated); *State of Mississippi v. Kennedy Brewer*, Defendant's Motion, Pursuant to M.R.E. 104(a), 702, 703, and 403 to Exclude the Expert Testimony of Dr. Michael West, D.D.S., and Request for an Admissibility Hearing with Live Witnesses, Cause No. 5999, Sept. 19, 2005.
238 **"everything the same or have anything change?":** Letter from Kennedy Brewer to Thomas Kessler, undated.
238 **"I don't want that to happen to me":** Letter from Kennedy Brewer to Thomas Kessler, undated.
239 **nor had she ever worked an appeal:** Kennedy Brewer v. State of Mississippi, Answer to Show Cause Order, No. 95-DP-0915 (Jan. 21, 1997).
239 **requested the aid of another attorney:** Ibid.
239 **limited experience practicing criminal law:** Ibid.
239 **removed from the case:** Ibid.; Kennedy Brewer v. State of Mississippi, Motion for Leave to Withdraw, No. 95-DP-0915 (Dec. 9, 1996); Kennedy Brewer v. State of Mississippi, Undersigned Counsel's Response to Court, No. 95-DP-0915 (Jan. 21, 1997).
239 **"Oldest African-American Attorneys.":** See House Resolution No. 87, 2014 Regular Session.

239   **"defense of the accused.":** Michael Lee Triplett v. State of Mississippi, 666 So.2d 1356 (Miss. 1995); see also *Kennedy Brewer v. State of Mississippi*, Answer to Show Cause Order, No. 95-DP-0915, Jan. 22, 1997; *Kennedy Brewer v. State of Mississippi*, Undersigned Counsel's Response to Court, Jan. 21, 1997; The Mississippi Bar v. Richard Burdine, No. 96-135-1, April 18, 1997; The Mississippi Bar v. Richard Burdine, No. 89-B-164, Feb. 16, 1990; The Mississippi Bar v. Richard Burdine, No. 2008-B-0930, Oct. 27, 2008; The Mississippi Bar v. Richard Burdine, No. 1999-B-1372, April 18, 2001; The Mississippi Bar v. Richard Burdine, No. 97-111-1, July 6, 1998; The Mississippi Bar v. Richard Burdine, No. 2005-B-1003, May 23, 2005; Willie Jerome Manning v. State of Mississippi, 735 So.2d 323 (Miss. 1999).

239   **the man his chance to appeal:** *Mississippi Bar v. Burdine*, No. 96-135-1, April 18, 1997.

239   **The client was sentenced to death:** *Manning v. State of Mississippi*, 735 So.2d 323.

240   **Brewer's execution date:** *Brewer v. State of Mississippi*, 725 So.2d 106.

240   **issue of testing:** Brewer v. State of Mississippi, 819 So.2d 1165 (Miss. 2000); Charles Press, interview by Tucker Carrington.

240   **was Kennedy Brewer:** Reliagene Technologies Inc., report, June 22, 2001.

240   **"indicating Brewer's involvement.":** *Brewer v. State of Mississippi*, 819 So.2d 1165.

241   **Allgood of Brewer's innocence:** Peter Neufeld and Vanessa Potkin, "Confidential Memorandum," November 23, 2007.

241   **"personal jealousy.":** Andrew Murr, "A Dentist Takes the Stand," *Newsweek*, Aug. 19, 2001.

241   **error rate of 63.5 percent:** Ibid.

241   **"stop bothering me.":** Ibid.

242   **"opinions are based on the science.":** Sherri Williams, "'60 Minutes' Focuses on Dentist," *Clarion-Ledger* (Jackson, MS), Feb. 17, 2002.

242   **"a dangerous, dangerous witness":** "Forensic Evidence; Skepticism Surrounding Dr. Michael West's Use of Bite Mark Analysis in Murder Cases," *60 Minutes*, Feb. 17, 2002.

242   **"violent confrontation with that individual.":** Ibid.

242   **"percentage rate of error,":** Ibid. It was in this interview that West compared his forensic virtuosity to the musical skills of Itzhak Perlman.

242   **or the death penalty:** Ibid.

242   **include Kennedy Brewer and Levon Brooks:** Ibid.

243   **"a state office and staff.":** Ken Winter, interview by Radley Balko.

243   **"consistent with Suffocation/Strangulation.":** Jane Doe (Rankin County), autopsy report, Sept. 28–30, 2002.

243   **"borders on criminal negligence.":** Letter from Harry J. Bonnell to Mr. Conlee, Oct. 30, 2003. Note: Bonnell was paid $570 to review the autopsy. He would later file a complaint against Hayne with the National Association of Medical Examiners.

243   **more scathing still:** When Hayne was asked about Bonnell's criticism of him in a 2012 deposition, he replied, "I had no respect for him. . . . I believe his medical license was revoked twice." The latter doesn't appear to be true. The website of the California Medical Board lists no sustained actions against Bonnell, and as of this writing, his license is

still active. Bonnell did often clash with his boss when he worked for the San Diego County medical examiner, and at times those clashes led to complaints against him with the state medical board. He was removed from the position in 2001. But he was later cleared for each accusation of wrongdoing, and at least according to the medical board, has never had his license revoked. See Deposition of Dr. Steven Hayne, *Hayne v. Innocence Project* (April 27, 2012), 137; search of Dr. Harry Bonnell via the California BreEZe Online License Search, www.mbc.ca.gov/Breeze /License_Verification.aspx; Caitlin Rother and Greg Moran, "Medical Examiner Fires His Top Aide," *San Diego Union-Tribune*, Aug. 9, 2001.

243 **"near-total speculation.":** Letter from Harry J. Bonnell to Dan W. Duggan, Nov. 24, 2004.

243 **his work in the case:** Deposition of Dr. Steven Hayne, *Hayne v. Innocence Project* (April 26, 2012), 168–170.

243 **the defendant was acquitted:** Robert Evans, interview by Radley Balko; "Jury Finds Eric Jones Not Guilty of Murder," *Prentiss* (MS) *Headlight*, Feb. 5, 1999; Jane Doe autopsy report, Feb. 15, 2008.

243 **done so in self-defense:** Tavares Antoine Flaggs v. State of Mississippi, 999 So.2d 393 (Miss. Ct. App. 2008).

243 **hadn't been defending himself:** Ibid.

244 **National Academy of Sciences:** National Research Council of the National Academy of Sciences, *Strengthening Forensic Science in the United States: A Path Forward* (Washington, DC: National Academies Press, 2009), 177; see also President's Council of Advisors of Science and Technology, *Report to the President—Forensic Science and Criminal Courts: Ensuring Scientific Validity of Feature-Comparison Methods*, Sept. 2016.

244 **only as a pathologist:** *Flaggs v. State of Mississippi*.

244 **"defensive posturing injury.":** Ibid.

244 **"whose blood it was.":** Petition for Post-Conviction Relief, Tavares Antoine Flaggs v. State of Mississippi, No. 2012-M-1848, Nov. 2012, 23.

244 **even examined those:** Ibid., 61.

244 **to find Flaggs guilty:** Response Petition for Post-Conviction Relief, *Tavares Antoine Flaggs v. State of Mississippi*, March 6, 2013, 12–13.

245 **one of Flaggs's later appeals:** Jonathan Turley, "Fifth Circuit Dismisses Challenge of Conviction Based on the Testimony of Discredited Mississippi Pathologist," Res Ipsa Loquitor, March 6, 2014, https: //jonathanturley.org/2014/03/06/fifth-circuit-dismisses-challenge-of -conviction-based-on-the-testimony-of-discredited-mississippi-pathologist.

245 **"about the law each day.":** Letter from Kennedy Brewer to Thomas Kessler (undated).

245 **"would highly appreciated.":** Letter from Kennedy Brewer to Mrs. Greene, Oct. 26, 2000.

CHAPTER 13: THE UNRAVELING

247 **to accommodate Hayne's schedule:** Former Jimmy Roberts employee, interview by Radley Balko.

247 **parted ways with Roberts:** Deposition of Dr. Steven Hayne, Hayne v. Innocence Project, 2011 WL 198128, No. 3:09-CV-218-KS-LRA (S.D. Miss. April 26, 2012), 154–158.

247 **It was invented:** See generally Deposition of Dr. Steven Hayne, *Hayne v. Innocence Project* (April 26–27, 2012).

247   **classes to coroners:** Designated Pathologist Agreement, June 19, 2006; see deposition of Dr. Steven Hayne, *Hayne v. Innocence Project* (April 27, 2012), 59–60.

247   **his private autopsy practice:** Designated Pathologist Agreement, June 19, 2006. This allows Hayne to accept fees for county autopsies, plus pay $100 to use the lab for private autopsies for parishes in Louisiana.

248   **professional life:** "Number of Autopsies Performed by Steven Hayne," calendar prepared by Mississippi Crime lab; list of cases in which Steven Hayne gave expert testimony.

248   **eighteen-month period in 2007 and 2008:** "Number of Autopsies Performed by Steven Hayne"; list of cases in which Steven Hayne provided expert testimony.

248   **in Jackson and performed four autopsies:** "Number of Autopsies Performed by Steven Hayne"; list of cases in which Steven Hayne provided expert testimony; Stewart v. City of Jackson, et al.

248   **performed three more:** "Number of Autopsies Performed by Steven Hayne"; list of cases in which Steven Hayne provided expert testimony; State of Mississippi v. Robert McKinley.

248   **and completed five:** "Number of Autopsies Performed by Steven Hayne"; list of cases in which Steven Hayne provided expert testimony; see State of Mississippi v. Johnathan Jones.

248   **four more autopsies:** "Number of Autopsies Performed by Steven Hayne"; list of cases in which Steven Hayne provided expert testimony; see State of Mississippi v. Kendal McCray; State of Mississippi v. Antonio Knowles.

248   **six more autopsies:** "Number of Autopsies Performed by Steven Hayne."

248   **Clarksdale in the Delta:** "Number of Autopsies Performed by Steven Hayne"; list of cases in which Steven Hayne provided expert testimony; see State of Mississippi v. Dewayne Earl.

248   **Magnolia:** "Number of Autopsies Performed by Steven Hayne"; list of cases in which Steven Hayne provided expert testimony, see State of Mississippi v. Eric Williams.

248   **Columbia in the far south:** "Number of Autopsies Performed by Steven Hayne"; list of cases in which Steven Hayne provided expert testimony; see State of Mississippi v. Ralph Luter Jr.

248   **Forest in central Mississippi:** "Number of Autopsies Performed by Steven Hayne"; list of cases in which Steven Hayne provided expert testimony, see State of Mississippi v. Isaac Jermaine Nelson and Craig Leshoun McBeath.

248   **knocked out seven autopsies:** "Number of Autopsies Performed by Steven Hayne."

248   **he testified in Jackson, Hazlehurst, Tunica, and Yazoo City:** "Number of Autopsies Performed by Steven Hayne"; list of cases in which Steven Hayne gave expert testimony; see State of Mississippi v. Harvey Williams; State of Mississippi v. John Ray Newell; State of Mississippi v. Jarvis Hill; and State of Mississippi v. Micah Ruffin.

248   **nine autopsies:** "Number of Autopsies Performed by Steven Hayne"; list of cases in which Steven Hayne provided expert testimony.

248   **over $100,000 per year:** Deposition of Dr. Steven Hayne, *Hayne v. Innocence Project* (April 26, 2012), 80.

248   **The victim was male:** J. Stewart Parrish, interview by Tucker Carrington.

249   **removed four years earlier:** Complaint, Estate of Randy Lynn Cheney v. Wanda Collier et al., No. 4:09-CV-00111-P-S (N.D. Miss. Oct. 26, 2009); Steven T. Hayne, final report of autopsy, AME# 8-Q5-07, Aug. 30, 2007; Northern Mississippi Medical Center, Department of Pathology, tissue examination for Randy Cheney, Nov. 28, 2003; deposition of Dr. Steven Hayne, *Hayne v. Innocence Project* (April 26, 2012), 238–239. When confronted with this discrepancy, Hayne explained in a 2012 deposition that a new spleen must have grown in place of the old. Ibid. ("Well, you know, an accessory spleen can go in the size of the original spleen. So that would be my interpretation of what occurred.").

250   **a company official said:** Elizabeth Crisp, "Camden Mother Wants Kids Back," *Clarion-Ledger* (Jackson, MS), May 28, 2008.

250   **eighteen months in jail:** Crisp, "Camden Mother Wants Kids Back"; Elizabeth Crisp, "Murder Charge Dropped Against Camden Mother," *Clarion-Ledger* (Jackson, MS), May 24, 2008; Andrew Nelson, "Woman Charged in Death of Her Baby," *Clarion-Ledger* (Jackson, MS), Aug. 10, 2006.

250   **shared with her husband, Joey:** Donna Ladd and Valerie Wells, "Rush to Judgment: Trying Kids as Adults," *Jackson* (MS) *Free Press*, Dec. 1, 2010; Tyler Edmonds v. State of Mississippi, 955 So.2d 787 (Miss. 2007); Tyler Edmonds v. State of Mississippi, 955 So.2d 864 (Miss. Ct. App. 2006).

252   **from getting the death penalty:** Tyler Edmonds v. State of Mississippi, 955 So.2d 787 (Miss. 2007); Tyler Edmonds v. State of Mississippi, 955 So.2d 864 (Miss. Ct. App. 2006); Ladd and Wells, "Rush to Judgment."

252   **"want to see me fry":** *Edmonds v. State of Mississippi*, 955 So.2d 787.

252   **"found in Mr. Fulgham?":** *Edmonds v. State of Mississippi*, 955 So.2d 864.

252   **"of anybody's expertise":** Ibid.

252   **hold a hearing:** Ibid.

253   **"with the facts that I saw.":** Ibid.

253   **"positioning of the weapon.":** Ibid.

254   **psychiatrist or social scientist:** *Edmonds v. State of Mississippi*, 955 So.2d 787 (Diaz, J., concurring).

254   **sentenced to death:** Kristi Fulgham v. State of Mississippi, 46 So.3d 315 (Miss. 2010). Fulgham was later resentenced to life in prison.

254   **Edmonds would have missed:** *Edmonds v. State of Mississippi*, 955 So.2d 864.

255   **"killed Joey Fulgham.":** Ibid. (emphasis added).

255   **evidence from Allison Redlich:** *Edmonds v. State of Mississippi*, 955 So.2d 787.

255   **testify in Mississippi's courts:** Ibid. (Diaz, J., concurring) ("this Court should not qualify Dr. Hayne as an expert in forensic pathology"; "This Court cannot qualify Dr. Hayne as an expert").

255   **Edmonds's taped confession:** Ibid.

255   **reversed their votes:** Oliver Diaz, interview by Radley Balko.

255   **quickly acquitted:** Sources for Edmonds narrative: "Edmonds Acquitted of Killing Brother-in-Law," *Enterprise-Journal* (McComb, MS), Nov. 2, 2008; Tyler Edmonds v. State of Mississippi, No. 2004-CT-02081-SCT (May 10, 2007); Tyler Edmonds v. State of Mississippi, No. 2004-KA-02081-COA (April 25, 2006).

256   **saw as a maternal figure:** Ladd and Wells, "Rush to Judgment"; Donna Ladd, "Tyler Edmonds Says He's 'Dusting Off' After 5th Circuit Loss," *Jackson* (MS) *Free-Press*, March 27, 2012.

257   **second comment:** Forrest Allgood, email interview by Radley Balko. All-good's complete answer: I have no recollection of refusing to meet with the lawyers if Brewer was present, but candidly, that sounds right. In spite of what you see on TV, meeting with the defendant is not a good idea. He can say you said anything, and the only people you can rely on to refute it is the defense lawyers who may not be your friend and have agendas of their own. It's bad practice and I rarely did it. I did so on occasion only when I knew and trusted the defense lawyer.

The conversation you relate is a case in point. I did not say, "You really believe in this science stuff, don't you?" I did say, "Everybody's got to believe in something." My recollection is that they made an initiating comment. People hear/perceive largely what they expect to hear and perceive. That's colored by their past experiences. That's why if you stand 5 people on a street corner you'll get at least 3 different versions of how the car wreck occurred. Somebody isn't always lying when there are contradictory versions of events. They just remember things differently.

I have never "disbelieved" in DNA. I used it in trials before Brooks and Brewer, if I recall correctly. At the time, it could only test the allele at DQa and wasn't much more discriminating than an ABO blood test. That said, there are different ways to interpret what you find. Just because Brooks's or Brewer's DNA wasn't found in the victim's vaginal vault doesn't mean they *didn't* participate in the kidnapping/killing. The Mississippi Supreme Court observed as much when they refused to render Brewer's case and sent it back for retrial. Then too, DNA can give you a false negative, but it can never give a false positive. That said, Justin Albert Johnson's profile was developed, and I have no doubt that he engaged in intercourse with both victims.

In short, they believed in DNA. I believed in my case. The circumstances of the child's disappearance were powerful, and I would have retried Brewer had I been able to remain in the case. When the initial post-conviction filing was made on Brewer, I could have fought the DNA testing. I didn't, something else you falsely reported about me. In fact, I agreed to it. That is not the action of a reckless, glory seeking prosecutor just seeking to convict anybody, which is how I've been painted.

257   **"he just isn't going to stop.":** André de Gruy, interview by Radley Balko; Peter Neufeld, interview by Tucker Carrington.

260   **"to the rule of law.":** Sources for James Ford Seale narrative: Donna Ladd, "I Want Justice, Too," *Jackson Free Press*, July 20, 2005; "The Dee and Moore case," Civil Rights and Restorative Justice Project, Northeastern University School of Law, www.northeastern.edu/law/academics /institutes/crrj/case-watch/dee.html; "Cold Case: James Ford Seale: A Sheriff's Election, Nine Deaths and a Silver Dollar," *Concordia* (Parish, LA) *Sentinel*, Oct. 2, 2009; FBI Memo, Nov. 6, 1964, #JN 62-5, http://lsucoldcaseproject.com/blog/tag/monroe; Donna Ladd, "James Ford Seale: A Trail of Documents Tells the Story," *Jackson* (MS) *Free Press*, Jan. 31, 2007; Trial transcript, *United States v. James Ford Seale*; Shaila Dewan, "Push to Resolve Fading Killings of Rights Era," *New York Times*, Feb. 3, 2007; Reply Brief for Appellant, United States v. James Ford Seale, 2008 WL 7909282 (5th Cir. March 31, 2008); Harry N. Maclean, *The Past Is Never Dead: The Trial of James Ford Seale and Mississippi's Struggle for Redemption* (New York: Basic Civitas Books, 2009); United States v. James

Ford Seale, No. 07-60732 (Fifth Circuit Ct. of Appeals March 12, 2010) (DeMoss, J., dissenting and concurring in part).

CHAPTER 14: REDEMPTION AND INSURRECTION

261   **"hurt him with a jury,":** André de Gruy, interview by Radley Balko.

261   **mentally disabled:** Motion to Preclude from Seeking the Death Penalty Due to Mental Retardation, State of Mississippi v. Kennedy Brewer, Cause No. 5999 (May 11, 2005).

261   **"given it up a long time ago?":** de Gruy, interview.

262   **never apologized to Brewer:** Ibid.

262   **"to grieve for that little girl":** Ibid.

263   **"then he may be released.":** Transcript of record, State of Mississippi v. Kennedy Brewer, No. 94-16-CR1 (Lowndes Cnty. Circ. Ct. March 21, 1995) (hereinafter "Brewer trial transcript"), 1081–1082.

263   **thinking about oligonucleotides:** Kary B. Mullis and Michael Smith, "The Polymerase Chain Reaction," Nobel Prize Lecture, Dec. 8, 1993.

264   **"Ed Blake is Ted Williams.":** Peter Boyer, "DNA on Trial," *New Yorker,* Jan. 17, 2000.

264   **consistent, conclusive results:** See Kelly M. Pyrek, *Forensic Science Under Siege: The Challenges of Forensic Laboratories and the Medico-Legal Investigation System* (Boston: Elsevier Academic, 2007).

264   **starving him to death:** Stephen G. Michaud, "DNA Detectives," *New York Times,* Nov. 6, 1988.

264   **two other men had raped Christine Jackson:** Reliagene Technologies Inc., report, June 22, 2001.

265   **"killing ground.":** Brewer trial transcript, 991–993.

265   **finished having sex:** Forensic Science Associates, report (July 17, 2007), 72–75.

265   **There was only one:** Ibid., 72–75.

265   **DNA couldn't therefore exonerate him:** Shaila Dewan, "Despite DNA Test, a Case Is Retried," *New York Times,* Sept. 6, 2007.

265   **up and running for years:** Ibid. In a 2017 email interview, Allgood again said that the state did not have its own state DNA database at that time, but he was able to access the FBI's, though he was unaware of this at the time.

265   **took over as special prosecutor:** Forrest Allgood, "District Attorney Offers Comments on Brewer, Brooks Cases," *Macon* (MS) *Beacon,* Aug. 7, 2008.

266   **belonged to Justin Johnson:** Dr. Edward Blake, interview by Joe York and Tucker Carrington, June 26, 2009.

266   **and took a left:** See Justin Albert Johnson, interview by Danny Welch, Feb. 7, 2008; interview by Ronnie Odom, Feb. 5, 2008.

266   **green clapboard cottage:** Johnson, interview by Danny Welch.

266   **knocked on the front door:** Ibid.

266   **to the crime scene:** Ibid.

266   **still alive, into the creek:** Ibid.

266   **parking near a pond:** Ibid.

266   **entering the bedroom:** Ibid.; Justin Albert Johnson, interview by Ronny Evans, Clay Baines, and Danny Welch, Feb. 4, 2008.

266   **never bit either girl:** Johnson, interview by Evans, Baines, and Welch, Feb. 4, 2008.

267   **"Without DNA, He'd Be Dead":** Jerry Mitchell, "Brewer Cleared in '92 Slaying of Child," *Clarion-Ledger* (Jackson, MS), Feb. 16, 2008.

267   **"back the time and loss.":** Ibid.

267   **"free to go.":** Jerry Mitchell, Ibid.

267   **without the possibility of parole:** State of Mississippi v. Justin Albert Johnson, No. 2008-026 (Noxubee Cnty. Circuit Ct. April 9, 2012).

267   **"had to be done":** Blake, interview.

267   **"strength of our system.":** Ibid.

268   **"daughter of time.":** Allgood, "District Attorney Offers Comments on Brewer, Brooks Cases."

268   **"truism, not a revelation":** Kansas v. Marsh, 548 U.S. 163 (2006) (Scalia, J., concurring); Joshua Marquis, "The Myth of Innocence," *Journal of Criminal Law & Criminology* 95 (2005): 501.

268   **"Just go on with your life.":** *Mississippi Innocence*, directed by Joe York, Center for Media and Documentary Projects at the University of Mississippi, 2011.

268   **"in the kidnapping/killing":** Forrest Allgood, email interview by Radley Balko.

269   **"remain in the case":** Ibid.

269   **"No one died.":** *Mississippi Innocence.*

269   **NASCAR-themed license plates:** Richard Fausset, "Mississippi Moves to Fix Autopsy System," *Los Angeles Times*, Aug. 6, 2008.

270   **autopsies in the state lab:** Steve Simpson, letter to Steven Hayne, Aug. 4, 2008.

270   **"he has not been terminated.":** Radley Balko, "Mississippi Official Fires Dr. Hayne, Then Praises Him," *Reason*, Aug. 5, 2008.

270   **he'd be doing none:** Jerry Mitchell, "State to Hire Autopsy Expert," *Clarion-Ledger* (Jackson, MS), Aug. 6, 2008.

271   **National Association of Medical Examiners:** Ibid.

271   **false evidence in a number of cases:** Mark Hansen, "Crime Labs Under the Microscope After a Sting of Shoddy, Suspect, and Fraudulent Results," *American Bar Association Journal* (Sept. 1, 2013).

271   **as many as 134 people:** Paul C. Giannelli and Kevin C. McMunigal, "Prosecutors, Ethics, and Expert Witnesses," *Fordham Law Review* 76 (2007): 1493.

271   **on drug charges:** Brian Haas, "Dr. Levy Moves Beyond Arrest," *Tennessean*, Dec. 12, 2010.

272   **respected medical examiner:** Ibid.

272   **and a state lab in Ohio:** Brian Rogers, Cindy George, and Keri Blakinger, "Crime-Scene Errors Put 65 Cases Under Review, Audit Finds," *Houston Chronicle*, April 12, 2017; Tony Plohetski, "2,200 Convicted Persons to Be Notified of Austin DNA Lab Problems," *Austin American-Statesman*, Feb. 9, 2017; Caitlin Doornbos, "Personnel File Shows Extent of Orange County Fingerprint Examiner's Alleged Mistakes," *Orlando Sentinel*, March 19, 2017; Jonathan Quilter, "Questions About Ex-BCI Scientist May Cast Doubt on Convictions," *Columbus* (OH) *Dispatch*, Oct. 30, 2016; "Another Oregon State Police Crime Lab Is Under Investigation," Associated Press, March 10, 2016; Justin Zaremba, "Lab Tech Allegedly Faked Result in Drug Case; 7,827 Criminal Cases Now in Question," *NJ Advance Media for NJ.com*, March 2, 2016; Vic Lee, "Whistleblower: San Francisco Crime Lab Scandal Dates Back Years," *ABC 7 News*, April 6, 2015; Tracey

Kaplan, "Santa Clara County: Doubts About Forensic Test Could Undermine Dozens of Sex Cases," *San Jose Mercury-News*, Dec. 3, 2016; R. Scott Moxley, "Orange County's Crime Lab Accused of Doctoring DNA Analysis in Murder Cases," *OC Weekly*, Sept. 27, 2017; Antonia Noori Fazan, "Approximately 2,000 Closed Cases Could Be Reopened Due to BSO Crime Lab Flaws," *Broward–Palm Beach* (FL) *New Times*, Sept. 30, 2016; Lynh Bui, "Pr. George's Police Investigating DNA Lab Operations, Suspended Employee," *Washington Post*, April 1, 2017.

272   **faking results for years:** Bob Salsberg, "Lawyers: Dismissed Drug Convictions Mostly for Freed Inmates," *Seattle Times*, April 21, 2017.

273   **"may have been convicted.":** Radley Balko, "Solving Kathy Mabry's Murder," *Huffington Post*, Nov. 7, 2013.

273   **"themselves in those positions.":** Vincent Di Maio, interview by Radley Balko.

273   **lone dissenter in that case:** Jones v. State, 962 So.2d 1263 (Miss. 2007) (Diaz, J., dissenting).

274   *The Appeal:* Scott Horton, "Justice in Mississippi," *Harper's Magazine*, Sept. 18, 2007.

274   **ad was referring to Jeffrey Havard:** Viveca Novak, "The Case of the Sleeping Justice," FactCheck.org, Nov. 26, 2008, www.factcheck.org /2008/11/the-case-of-the-sleeping-justice.

274   **run statewide for at least a week:** Ibid.

275   **"sent baselessly to their deaths.":** Doss v. State of Mississippi, No. 2007-CA-00429-SCT (Dec. 12, 2006) (Diaz, J., dissenting).

276   **complaints against him:** Deposition of Dr. Steven Hayne, Steven Hayne v. Innocence Project, 2011 WL 198128, No. 3:09-CV-218-KS-LRA (S.D. Miss. April 26, 2012), 168–170; letter from Robert L. Breckenridge, Chair, Inquiry Committee to Steven T. Hayne (May 22, 2008); letter from Robert L. Breckenridge, Chair, Inquiry Committee to Jared N. Schwartz (Aug. 20, 2008).

276   **revoke Hayne's license:** Ibid.; Ronni Mott, "Hood Responds to Hayne Criticism," *Jackson* (MS) *Free Press*, April 7, 2010; Jerry Mitchell, "Group Recommends No Action on Hayne," *Hattiesburg* (MS) *American*, Aug. 22, 2008.

276   **"It's malpractice.":** Radley Balko, "President of Mississippi State Medical Association Denounces Dr. Hayne," *Reason*, Feb. 15, 2008.

276   **cases in which Hayne had testified:** "Pathologists Work Should Be Probed," editorial, *Hattiesburg* (MS) *American*, March 8, 2008.

276   **full staff and a dramatic overhaul:** Louisa Dixon, "Death Investigations Lax," *Clarion-Ledger* (Jackson, MS), March 30, 2008.

277   **"the death of their loved ones.":** "Attorneys Seek Documents on State Pathologist's Work," *Clarion-Ledger* (Jackson, MS), March 6, 2008.

278   **lived to see his name cleared:** Letter from Jon Mark Weathers to Gabriel S. Oberfield, March 20, 2008; Campbell Robertson, "Thirty Years Later, Freedom in a Case with Tragedy for All Involved," *New York Times*, Sept. 16, 2010.

278   **"limits of the discipline.":** National Research Council of the National Academy of Sciences, *Strengthening Forensic Science in the United States: A Path Forward* (Washington, DC: National Academies Press, 2009), 3–18.

278   **"the exclusion of all others.":** Ibid., 5–37.

278   **Texas Forensic Science Commission:** *Justice Through Science,* Texas Forensic Science Commission, April 12, 2016.

278   **"scientifically valid method to be low.":** President's Council of Advisors of Science and Technology, *Report to the President—Forensic Science and Criminal Courts: Ensuring Scientific Validity of Feature-Comparison Methods,* Sept. 2016, 9.

279   **never implemented at the DOJ:** Kyra Lerner, "Attorney General to Ignore New Report Finding That Commonly-Used Forensics Are Bogus," *ThinkProgress,* Sept. 21, 2016; "The President's Role in Advancing Criminal Justice Reform," *Harvard Law Review* 130 (2017): 811.

279   **theory was bogus:** Jules Epstein, "Preferring the 'Wiseman' to Science: The Failure of Courts and Non-Litigation Mechanisms to Demand Validity in Forensic Matching Testimony," *Widener Law Review* 20 (2014): 81.

280   **from the air:** See Ryan Gabrielson and Topher Sanders, "Busted," ProPublica, July 7, 2016; Ed Lavandera, "Dogs Sniff Out Wrong Suspect; Scent Lineups Questioned," CNN, Oct. 5, 2009; Eyder Peralta, "Report: Drug-Sniffing Dogs Are Wrong More Often Than Right," National Public Radio, Jan. 7, 2011.

280   **get sober, objective analysis:** Roger Koppl and Meghan Sacks, "The Criminal Justice System Creates Incentives for False Convictions," *Criminal Justice Ethics* 32 (2013): 126.

280   **to help win convictions:** Mandy Locke and Joseph Neff, "Witness for the Prosecution: Part 3: Lab Loyal to Law Enforcement," *Raleigh* (NC) *News & Observer,* Aug. 12, 2010.

280   **any action against him:** Jimmie E. Gates, "Pathologist Accepts Settlement," *Clarion-Ledger* (Jackson, MS), May 20, 2012.

281   **would take no further action:** Letter from Breckenridge, to Hayne; letter from Breckenridge, to Schwartz.

281   **"wild accusations.":** Jerry Mitchell, "Panel: No Action Taken Against Miss. Pathologist," *Clarion-Ledger* (Jackson, MS), Aug. 22, 2008.

281   **He chose to resign:** Anonymous official, email to Radley Balko.

281   **so he resigned:** Deposition of Dr. Steven Hayne, *Hayne v. Innocence Project* (April 26, 2012), 168.

281   **contract with its insurer:** Jeff Clark, "Forensic Expert Hayne Settles Defamation Suit," *Dispatch* (Columbus, MS), June 6, 2012.

281   **the DNA from their cases:** Jimmie E. Gates, "Pathologist Accepts Settlement," *Clarion-Ledger* (Jackson, MS), May 20, 2012.

281   **go for it:** Letter from James Y. Dale to Ricky Shivers, June 26, 2009.

281   **sympathetic coroners around Mississippi:** Ricky Shivers, interview by Radley Balko; unnamed Mississippi coroner, interview by Radley Balko.

281   **new independent districts:** Shivers, interview; unnamed Mississippi coroner, interview.

282   **"board of supervisors.":** Shivers, interview.

282   **"allowed to use the state lab.":** Radley Balko, "The Coroners Revolt," *Jackson* (MS) *Free Press,* Aug. 4, 2009.

282   **"to defend the results in court.":** Ibid.

282   **"invaluable tool to law enforcement.":** Letter from Dwayne Dillon, president, Mississippi Sheriffs' Association, to Commissioner of Public Safety Steve Simpson, April 14, 2008.

283   **"we all have to do more.":** Letter from Forrest Allgood to Governor Haley Barbour, Aug. 13, 2008.

283   **affiliation with the University of Mississippi:** Letter from James H. Powell to Governor Haley Barbour, Aug. 12, 2008.

283 **defense attorneys solved it in 2012:** Radley Balko, "Solving Kathy Mabry's Murder: Brutal 15-Year-Old Crime Highlights Decades-Long Mississippi Scandal," *Huffington Post*, Jan. 17, 2013.

283 **"Forensic Pathology.":** Steven T. Hayne, letter (undated).

CHAPTER 15: NO RECKONING

285 **cherry-picking:** Memorandum of Authorities in Reply to Defendants' Motion to Dismiss Plaintiff's First Amended Complaint, Steven Hayne, M.D., v. Innocence Project, No. 3:09cv218 DPJ-JCS, (S.D. Miss. April 26, 2010); Dr. Steven Timothy Hayne's Memorandum of Authorities in Support of His Motion to Dismiss, or Alternatively, for Summary Judgment, Kennedy Brewer v. Steven Timothy Hayne and Michael H. West, No. 4:09-cv-19 HTW-LRA, U.S. District Ct. Southern District of Mississippi, June 3, 2009.

286 **signed off on autopsies he didn't do:** Robert D. Felder, "A Coroner System in Crisis: The Scandals and Struggles Plaguing Louisiana Death Investigation," 69 *Louisiana Law Review* 627 (2009); Statements Allege Fmr. Caddo Coroner Did Not Perform Autopsies, *KSLA 12 News*, April 23, 2006.

286 **in Iowa and Montana:** Leila Szpaller, "Forensic Pathologist Will No Longer Do Work for Montana County Coroners," *Missoulian*, July 11, 2015.

286 **over a four-year period:** Alan Judd, "Outside Work Challenges Medical Examiner's Credibility, Judgment," *Atlanta Journal-Constitution*, Oct. 3, 2015; Alan Judd, "'Embarrassed' Medical Examiner Abruptly Retires," *Atlanta Journal-Constitution*, Oct. 9, 2015.

286 **implicated the accused:** Dr. Steven Timothy Hayne's Memorandum of Authorities in Support of His Motion to Dismiss, or Alternatively, for Summary Judgment, *Kennedy Brewer v. Steven Timothy Hayne and Michael H. West*; see Deposition of Dr. Steven Hayne, *Hayne v. Innocence Project*, No. 3:09-CV-218-KS-LRA (S.D. Miss. Apr. 26–27, 2012.)

286 **"beyond my expertise.":** Deposition of Dr. Steven Hayne, *Hayne v. Innocence Project* (April 27, 2012), 182.

286 **bite marks on the girl:** Autopsy report, Courtney Smith, September 17, 1990.

287 **"they were insect bites.":** Brewer trial transcript, 508.

287 **"a little excessive.":** Deposition of Dr. Steven Hayne, *Hayne v. Innocence Project* (April 26, 2012), 330. Note: the "West Phenomenon" is referred to as the "West Effect."

287 **"can show error rates.":** Ibid., 241.

287 **directly into the victim's skin:** Ibid., 231–232. Note: Hayne also defended West's use of the "direct comparison" method in the Jimmie Duncan case. See Jerry Mitchell, "Forensic Dentist Defends Work He's Done in Autopsies," *Clarion-Ledger* (Jackson, MS), Feb. 28, 2009.

287 **"It's not DNA.":** Deposition of Dr. Steven Hayne, *Hayne v. Innocence Project* (April 27, 2012), 174.

288 **to defeat it:** Ronni Mott, "Hood Responds to Hayne Criticism," *Jackson* (MS) *Free Press*, April 7, 2010; Sid Salter, "It Costs to 'Get Tough' on Crime," *Clarion-Ledger* (Jackson, MS), March 24, 2010; Radley Balko, "Mississippi AG Jim Hood Still Actively Supporting Steven Hayne," *Reason*, March 12, 2010; unnamed Mississippi coroner, interview by Radley Balko; "Medical Examiner Bill Advances," *Hattiesburg* (MS) *American*,

March 18, 2010 (Lawmaker says, "Some resistance came from Attorney General Jim Hood, who asked county coroners and others to oppose the bill").

288   **"potentially harmful legislation.":** Hood's email reported in Balko, "Mississippi AG Jim Hood Still Actively Supporting Steven Hayne."

288   **lobbied to kill it:** Balko, "Mississippi AG Jim Hood Still Actively Supporting Steven Hayne."

288   **signed it into law:** Ward Schaeffer, "Medical Examiner Bill Sent to Barbour," *Jackson* (MS) *Free Press*, March 17, 2010.

288   **"important court cases.":** Letter from ACFEI to Steven Hayne, May 12, 2010.

288   **cost for the new certification: $869:** Certified Forensic Physician Program, www.acfei.com/forensic_certifications/cfp.

288   **requirements of the new law:** Letter from Steven T. Hayne to Michael Langford, May 6, 2010.

288   **by the Department of Public Safety:** Letter from James Y. Dale to Steven T. Hayne, May 24, 2010.

289   **"and that culture.":** Edwin L. Pittman, interview by Tucker Carrington.

289   **Mississippi National Guard:** Chief Justice Edwin L. Pittman announces retirement, March 8, 2004, https://courts.ms.gov/news/2004/030804 pittman.pdf.

289   **"prosecutors and expert testimony.":** Pittman, interview.

289   **"more than I do now.":** Ibid.

290   **"that they're impossible.":** Ibid.

290   **criticism longer than West:** Ibid.

290   **"all downhill from there":** Ibid. Once, Pittman's opponent in a judicial campaign excoriated him in a series of television ads for his vote to reverse a death sentence. Pittman told his constituents that if they wanted a judge who would be cavalier in a review of a death sentence and find joy in doing it, then they shouldn't vote for him. He was reelected.

290   **unanimously rejected the petition:** Derek Brandon Conway v. State of Mississippi, 48 So.3d 588 (Miss. Ct. App. 2010). Specifically, Pittman and Conway's other attorneys argued that Conway's trial counsel was ineffective for not challenging Hayne's qualifications. The Mississippi Court of Appeals unanimously rejected that argument, and rejected the argument that Hayne wasn't qualified. The Mississippi Supreme Court then declined to hear Conway's appeal in Dec. 2010. Derek Brandon Conway v. State of Mississippi, 49 So.3d 1139 (Miss. 2010).

290   **"to the finances.":** Deposition of Dr. Steven Hayne, Steven Hayne v. Innocence Project, No. 3:09-CV-218-KS-LRA (S.D. Miss. April 26, 2012), 11.

291   **claims for possible arson:** Deposition of Cecil McCrory, *Hayne v. Innocence Project* (April 24, 2012), 17, 22, 35.

291   **McCrory was on the committee:** "McCrory Elected PEER Chairman," *Clarion-Ledger* (Jackson, MS), Feb. 25, 1993; Jay Eubank, "Watchdog: Auditor Used Funds Improperly," *Clarion-Ledger* (Jackson, MS), Feb. 11, 1993; see deposition of Cecil McCrory, *Hayne v. Innocence Project*.

291   **consulting in civil cases:** Both Hayne and McCrory have provided different dates in answer to when Hayne started working for the company.

291   **defer to McCrory:** See generally deposition of Dr. Steven Hayne, *Hayne v. Innocence Project*; Edward Dillon et al. v. Richard Rushing et al., No. 94-0040 (Lincoln Cnty. Circuit Ct. April 8, 1998), 19; Cedric Webb v.

MS. Carrier, Inc., No. C1-09-0017 (Washington Cnty. Circuit Ct. Feb. 24, 2001), 35–36.

291   **particular interest to Hayne:** Emily Le Coz, "McCrory's Connections Vast, Deep," *Clarion-Ledger* (Jackson, MS), Nov. 9, 2014.

292   **had to go through McCrory:** Deposition of Cecil McCrory, *Hayne v. Innocence Project*, 8–9, 47–48, 66–67, 70–71, 81–82; deposition of Dr. Steven Hayne, *Hayne v. Innocence Project* (April 26, 2012), 10–11, 28–29, 36–7, 43, 58.

292   **$50,000 to $60,000:** Deposition of Cecil McCrory, *Hayne v. Innocence Project*, 21.

292   **partner at the firm:** See Depositions of Steven Hayne, *Edward Dillon et al. v. Richard Rushing et al.*, 25; Christopher M. Lewis v. Dr. Nathaniel Brown et al., No. 99-0476 (Sunflower Cnty. Circuit Ct. Aug. 23, 2001), 22–23; *Hayne v. Innocence Project*, 27; Jeffrey Harrell et al. v. Waqar Syed et al., No. 2000-0571 (Sunflower Cnty. Miss. Feb. 17, 2001); *Cedric Webb v. MS. Carrier, Inc.*; Charles Vessel v. Anthony Alleman, et al. No. 99-0307-CI (Warren Cnty. Miss. June 26, 2003); Christopher M. Lewis v. Dr. Nathaniel Brown et al., No. 99-0476 (Sunflower Cnty. Miss. Aug. 2001); Daniel Storts v. Graco Children's Products Inc., No. 95C-1007H (U.S. Dist. Ct. for the Northern District of Oklahoma Sept. 15, 1996); Carolyn Gail Hand v. Colbert County–Northwest Health Care et al., No. CV-03-234 (Franklin Cnty. Alabama Circuit Ct. March 8, 2005); Pam McVeyk v. Jimmy C. Havard, No. CI 99-0183 (Forrest Cnty. Circuit Ct. Nov. 11, 2003); Deposition of Dr. Steven Hayne, *Hayne v. Innocence Project*; Deposition of Michael West, *Hayne v. Innocence Project* (March 13, 2012); Deposition of Michael West, Leigh Stubbs v. State of Mississippi, No. 2011-288-LS-LT (Lincoln Cnty. Circuit Ct. Feb. 11, 2012); Deposition of Cecil McCrory, *Hayne v. Innocence Project*; Ross Adams, "Prison Bribery Case Now Up to $800 Million, Prosecutors Say," WAPT.com, April 12, 2016; Jeff Amy, "Ex-Prison Boss Admits Guilt," *Hattiesburg* (MS) *American*, Feb. 26, 2015; assistant to Jimmy Roberts interviewed by Radley Balko; Steven Hayne v. Ann Hayne, Final Judgement of Divorce, no. 55-239 (Rankin Cnty. Chancery Ct. July 19, 2004); Steven Hayne v. Tonia Hayne, Divorce Agreement, no. 2007-459-B (Madison Cnty. Chancery Ct. July 14, 2008); Le Coz, "McCrory's Connections Vast, Deep"; Transcript of trial, State of Mississippi v. Yolanda Williams, No. 2004-048 (Washington Cnty. Circuit Ct. Oct. 18, 2004).

292   **had been mistaken:** Deposition of Dr. Steven Hayne, *Hayne v. Innocence Project* (April 26, 2012), 26–28; see deposition of Steven Hayne, *Cedric Webb v. MS. Carrier, Inc.*, 35–36.

292   **"Cecil McCrory and myself.":** Deposition of Cecil McCrory, *Hayne v. Innocence Project*, 104–105.

292   **a stake in the company:** Ibid., 17–18.

292   **billing half that much:** Deposition of Steven Hayne, *Hand v. Colbert County–Northwest Health Care et al.*, 29.

292   **"zero percent":** Deposition of Steven Hayne, *Edward Dillon et al. v. Richard Rushing et al.*, 29; see deposition of Steven Hayne, *Cedric Webb v. MS. Carrier, Inc.*, 35.

292   **"5, 7, 8 percent":** Deposition of Steven Hayne, *Edward Dillon et al. v. Richard Rushing et al.*, 29.

292   **as a hobby:** See depositions of Steven Hayne, *Edward Dillon et al. v. Richard Rushing et al.*, 26, 36; *Cedric Webb v. MS. Carrier, Inc.*, 36; *Hayne v. Innocence Project*, 31.

292   **"what he's talking about.":** Deposition of Cecil McCrory, *Hayne v. Innocence Project*, 82.

292   **had been letting him use:** *Cedric Webb v. MS. Carrier, Inc.*, 33–36.

293   **"recollection of why I did that.":** Deposition of Cecil McCrory, *Hayne v. Innocence Project*, 70–73, 75.

293   **"early part of two thousand.":** Deposition of Dr. Steven Hayne, *Hayne v. Innocence Project* (April 26, 2012), 10.

293   **Hayne left in 2008:** Deposition of Cecil McCrory, *Hayne v. Innocence Project*, 4.

293   **and various charities:** See deposition of Steven Hayne, *Cedric Webb v. MS. Carrier, Inc.*, 35; *Edward Dillon et al. v. Richard Rushing et al.*, 26, 36; *Christopher M. Lewis v. Dr. Nathaniel Brown et al.*, 22–23; Bennett v. City of Canton Swimming Pool, No. C1-96-0176 (Madison Cnty. Circuit Ct. June 2, 2001), 90–91.

293   **or to his ex-wife:** Deposition of Dr. Steven Hayne, *Hayne v. Innocence Project* (April 26, 2012), 29, 60.

293   **leaves no public record:** Deposition of Cecil McCrory, *Hayne v. Innocence Project*, 9–16, 87.

293   **"kids going to college.":** Ibid., 87.

293   **"more requests than he had money.":** Ibid., 87–88.

293   **"supportive of that,":** Ibid., 97.

293   **couldn't recall their names:** Ibid., 89–90; Deposition of Dr. Steven Hayne, *Hayne v. Innocence Project* (April 26, 2012), 28, 35.

293   **he didn't trust them:** Deposition of Dr. Steven Hayne, *Hayne v. Innocence Project* (April 26, 2012), 119.

294   **putting a student through college:** Ibid., 24–27.

294   **assisting him with his autopsies:** Deposition of Cecil McCrory, *Hayne v. Innocence Project*, 47–49; Butch Benedict, interview by David Fechheimer.

294   **sent his staff their tax forms:** Deposition of Dr. Steven Hayne, *Hayne v. Innocence Project* (April 26, 2012), 28, 29, 39.

294   **"let that happen again.":** L. W. "Bump" Calloway, interview by David Fechheimer.

294   **"even if you couldn't see him.":** Butch Benedict, interview by David Fechheimer.

294   **"15 years.":** Deposition of Dr. Steven Hayne, *Hayne v. Innocence Project* (April 26, 2012), 29.

294   **"I looked.":** Ann Hayne, interview by David Fechheimer.

295   **when he left:** Deposition of Dr. Steven Hayne, *Hayne v. Innocence Project* (April 26, 2012), 80–81.

295   **from his consulting work on private cases:** Deposition of Steven Hayne, *Hand v. Colbert County–Northwest Health Care, et al.*, 29.

295   **$1 million per year from those:** If Hayne did 1,800 autopsies in a year at $500 per autopsy, he'd have made $900,000, not counting his hourly rate for trial preparation and testimony.

295   **acres in Rankin County:** Steven Hayne v. Tonia Hayne, Divorce Agreement, No. 2007-459-B (Rankin Cnty. Chancery Ct. July 16, 2008).

295   **Lee Michaels jewelry store:** *Steven Hayne v. Tonia Hayne.*

295   **per year in alimony:** Steven Hayne v. Ann Hayne, Final Judgment of Divorce—Irreconcilable Differences, No 55–239 (of Rankin Cnty. Chancery Ct. July 19, 2004).

295   **to the state crime lab:** Deposition of Dr. Steven Hayne, *Hayne v. Innocence Project* (April 26, 2012), 3, 6–7, 13–14.

295   **thrown out by his wife:** Michael West deposition, *Hayne v. Innocence Project* (S.D. Miss. March 13, 2012), 11–17.

296   **"see the world *accountant*.":** Deposition of Michael West, *Hayne v. Innocence Project*, 6–10, 185; deposition of Michael West, Eddie Lee Howard v. State of Mississippi, Nos. 2000-0115-CV1 2010-DR-01043-SCT (Lowndes Cnty. Circuit Ct. April 16, 2016), 126–130.

296   **paid for Hayne's services:** Deposition of Cecil McCrory, *Hayne v. Innocence Project*, 5, 9–12, 21.

296   **including Investigative Research:** Le Coz, "McCrory's Connections Vast, Deep"; Jimmie E. Gates and Geoff Pender, "Ex Rep's Wife Charged in Epps Case," *Clarion-Ledger* (Jackson, MS), July 26, 2016.

296   **in the massive scheme:** Adams, "Prison Bribery Case Now Up to $800 Million."

296   **eight and a half years in prison:** Jimmie E. Gates, "McCrory Sentenced to 8.5 Years," *Hattiesburg* (MS) *American*, Feb. 4, 2017.

296   **"sick to my stomach.":** Le Coz, "McCrory's Connections Vast, Deep."

297   **"played it by the rules.":** Radley Balko, "Mississippi AG Jim Hood: Forrest Allgood a 'Straight Arrow,'" *Reason*, March 3, 2008; "Hood: Allgood a 'Straight Arrow,'" *Commercial-Dispatch* (Columbus, MS), March 2, 2008.

297   **separate death penalty trial:** See Quintez Wren Hodges v. Christopher Epps, 2010 WL 3655851 (N.D Miss. 2010) (stating that "the testimony of Mr. Kitchens at Petitioner's trial and in this Court is factually at odds with what is contained in the record, and DA Allgood should have known that the testimony given by ADA Kitchens was false").

297   **Hood had personally prosecuted:** Radley Balko, "Progress and Challenges in Mississippi," *Reason*, March 29, 2010; "Hood Opposes Limit on Those Who Do Autopsies," *Sun-Herald* (Biloxi, MS), March 11, 2010; Lacey McLaughlin, "The JFP Interview with Jim Hood," *Jackson* (MS) *Free Press*, Oct. 12, 2011.

297   **no one responded:** Radley Balko calls to Hood's press office.

297   **"support him in any matter.":** Lacey McLaughlin, "The JFP Interview with Jim Hood," *Jackson* (MS) *Free Press*, Oct. 12, 2011.

297   **"requesting at this time.":** Email from Jim Hood's office to Radley Balko.

298   **Google search:** Transcript of Motion Hearing, Leigh Stubbs v. State of Mississippi, No. 2011-388 (Lincoln Cnty. Circuit Ct. Oct. 25, 2011), 91.

298   **Buffalo, New York:** Lacey McLaughlin, "Mississippi Hires First Medical Examiner in 15 Years," *Jackson* (MS) *Free Press*, Nov. 5, 2010.

298   **"become a campaign issue.":** Radley Balko, "Steven Hayne, Michael West 'Expert' Witness Scandal Could Affect Mississippi Attorney General Race," *Huffington Post*, Aug. 29, 2011.

298   **two years earlier:** Robbie Ward, "DuPree Campaigns Against the Tide," *Jackson* (MS) *Free Press*, Oct. 26, 2011; Jerry Mitchell, "Hood Says Political Foe Abused His Office," *Clarion-Ledger* (Jackson, MS), Oct. 25, 2011.

298   **twenty-two points:** Lacey McLaughlin, "Jim Hood Eases into Third Term," *Jackson* (MS) *Free Press*, Nov. 9, 2011.

298   ***Gause v. State:*** Curtis Wayne Gause v. State of Mississippi, No. 2010-KA-00127-SCT, June 23, 2011.

298   **"expert testimony.":** Ibid.

298   **challenged Hayne's credibility at trial:** Ibid.

299   **David Parvin's story:** David Parvin v. State of Mississippi, 113 So.3d 1243 (Miss. 2013).

299   **"requirements for admissibility.":** Ibid.

299   **before a jury:** Ibid.

299   **"related scientific tests.":** Ibid.

299   **called him on it:** Ibid.

299   **wasn't his responsibility:** For example, see Cory Maye v. State of Mississippi, No. 2007-KA-02147-COA (Nov. 17, 2009), 7–10 (discussed in Authors' Note); Danny Jones v. State of Mississippi, No. 2006-KA-00343-SCT (Aug. 16, 2007) (Diaz, dissenting) (Hayne testified that wounds in decedent were "consistent with" buckshot coming from a spot across the road from where the State argued the defendant had shot her. Diaz pointed out that Hayne wasn't a ballistics expert and had no information about other variables that could have affected the wound pattern); State of Mississippi v. Levon Brooks, No. 5937 (Noxubee Cnty. Circuit Ct. Jan. 13, 1992) (aforementioned Hayne testimony about wounds being consistent with penetration by a broom handle); State of Mississippi v. Jeffrey Keith Havard, Case No. 0141 (Adams Cnty. Circuit Ct. June 18, 2002) (aforementioned Hayne testimony about wound consistent with "penetration by an object"); Tyler Edmonds v. State of Mississippi, 955 So.2d 787 (Miss. 2007); Tyler Edmonds v. State of Mississippi, 955 So.2d 864 (Miss. Ct. App. 2006) (aforementioned Hayne testimony about victim's wounds being consistent with defendant's confession that he and his sister held the gun simultaneously when firing the fatal shot).

300   **"accuracy of Hayne.":** *David Parvin v. State of Mississippi.*

300   **four-paragraph opinion:** In re Tavares Antoine Flaggs, No. 13-60896, Motion for an Order Authorizing the United States District Court for the Southern District of Mississippi to Consider a Successive 28 U.S.C. § 2254 Application, Jan. 31, 2014.

300   **"Innocence Project's letter.":** Ibid.

301   **"Hayne's opinion testimony.":** Ibid.

301   **for killing an infant:** James Koon v. Burl Cain, No. 3:13-CV-2538, Appeal from the United States District Court for the Western District of Louisiana, Nov. 6, 2014.

301   **"the cause of death.":** Ibid. (emphasis added).

302   **"clearly time-barred.":** Judgment, James Koon v. Warden Burl Cain, 2014 WL 120894, United States District Court for the Western District of Louisiana, Jan. 13, 2014 (emphasis in original).

302   **"prior to July 2011,":** *James Koon v. Burl Cain.*

303   **involved flawed forensic evidence:** See Brandon L. Garrett, "Judging Innocence," *Columbia Law Review* 108, no. 55 (2007): 59–60, 76.

303   **inaccurate and unreliable testimony:** Brandon L. Garrett and Peter J. Neufeld, "Invalid Forensic Science Testimony and Wrongful Convictions," *Virginia Law Review* 95, no. 1 (2009): 2.

305   **"in any manner.":** McLaughlin, "The JFP interview with Jim Hood."

308   **less accepted groups:** See Deposition of Steven Hayne, Vessel v. Alleman, No. 99-0307-CI (Warren Cnty. Circuit Ct. June 26, 2003), 56–57;

Deposition of Steven Hayne, *Bennett v. City of Canton Swimming Pool*, 48–49; Transcript of record, State v. Townsend, No. 2000-127-CR (Montgomery Cnty. Circuit Ct. March 20, 2001), 19; Transcript of record, State v. Williams, No. 2004-048 (Washington Cnty. Circuit Ct. Oct. 18, 2004), 367–368.

308 **"Hayne's description.":** Jerry Mitchell, "Doctor's Autopsy Abilities Targeted," *Clarion-Ledger* (Jackson, MS), April 27, 2008.

308 **"when men landed on the moon.":** Ibid.

308 **"no explanation.":** Deposition of Dr. Steven Hayne, *Hayne v. Innocence Project* (April 26, 2012), 244–245, but see extended questioning of Hayne on the matter on pages 245–275.

308 **decile of test takers:** Mitchell, "Doctor's Autopsy Abilities Targeted"; Deposition of Dr. Steven Hayne, *Hayne v. Innocence Project* (April 26, 2012), 255–256.

308 **on the first try:** Jerry Mitchell, "Pathologist's Credibility on Line: Expert Admits He Failed to Complete Certification Exam," *Clarion-Ledger* (Jackson, MS), Nov. 13, 2012.

309 **chance this wasn't a murder:** Ralph Riviello, *Manual of Forensic Emergency Medicine* (Sudbury, MA: Jones & Bartlett Learning, 2009), 13.

309 **"four, five, to one":** Transcript of record, State of Mississippi v. John Ross, No. 200-109 (Sunflower Cnty. Circuit Ct. May 1–4, 2002), 282.

309 **support Hayne's contention:** See I. C. Stone, "Observations and Statistics Relating to Suicide Weapons," *Journal of Forensic Science* 32, no. 3 (May 1987); Valerie J. Callanan and Mark S. Davis, "Gender and Suicide Method: Do Women Avoid Facial Disfiguration?" *Sex Roles* 65, no. 11 (Aug. 2011): 867–879; V. Strajina, V. Zivkovic, and C. Nikolic, "Forensic Issues in Suicidal Single Gunshot Injuries to the Chest: An Autopsy Study," *American Journal for Medical Pathology* 33, no. 4 (2012): 373–376.

309 **disfigured corpse:** Kate Masters, "A Psychiatrist Debunks the Biggest Myths Surrounding Gun Suicides," TheTrace.com, Nov. 2, 2015.

309 **was upheld on appeal:** John Ross v. State of Mississippi, 883 So.2d 1181 (Miss. Ct. App. 2004), reh'g denied (Miss. Ct. App. Aug. 3, 2004). The Mississippi Innocence Project represented Ross in his post-conviction litigation.

310 **"about hand size or gender.":** Campbell Robertson, "Questions Left for Mississippi over Doctor's Autopsies," *New York Times*, Jan. 7, 2013. The Mississippi Innocence Project represented Osborne in his post-conviction litigation.

310 **state's appellate courts:** Source for Osborne narrative: Trial transcript, State of Mississippi v. Joseph Eugene Osborne, No. 499-03 (Lauderdale Cnty. Circuit Ct. April 5, 2004).

310 **"principles and methods.":** Sherwin Williams Co. v. Gaines, 75 So.3d 41 (Miss. 2011).

311 **"in the conviction or sentence.":** Joseph Eugene Osborne v. State of Mississippi, 20212-M-08145, Order (Miss. 2013).

311 **quite a bit more profound:** See for example, Paul C. Giannelli, "*Daubert* and Criminal Prosecutions," *Criminal Justice* 26, no. 3 (Fall 2011); Deirdre Dwyer, "(Why) Are Civil and Criminal Expert Evidence Different?" *Tulsa Law Review* 43 (2007): 381; Peter J. Neufeld, "The (Near) Irrelevance of *Daubert* to Criminal Justice and Some Suggestions for Reform," *American Journal of Public Health* 95, no. S1 (Sept. 1, 2005).

311   **before his trial:** John A. Ross Jr. v. Christopher B. Epps et al., No. 14-cv-87-SA-JMV, Report and Recommendation, United States District Court for the Northern District of Mississippi, July 30, 2015; John A. Ross Jr. v. Marshall L. Fisher, No. 15-60776, Appeal from the United States District Court for the Northern District of Mississippi, April 10, 2017.

312   **"Is that correct?":** Rayner v. State, 186 So.3d 881 (Miss. 2015).

312   **"discredited.":** Ibid.

312   **entirely proper:** Ibid.

314   **"And he wasn't me.":** Bos Stevens, interview by Tucker Carrington.

315   **a lot of dancing:** Levon Brooks, interview by Radley Balko.

315   **"I had hoped.":** Deposition of Michael West, Leigh Stubbs v. State of Mississippi, No. 2011-387-LS-LT (Lincoln Cnty. Circuit Ct. Feb. 11, 2012), 37; Jerry Mitchell, "Dentist Now Doubts Science of Bite-Analysis," *Clarion-Ledger* (Jackson, MS), Aug. 6, 2012.

315   **private dental practice:** Michael West deposition, *Hayne v. Innocence Project*, 10–11.

315   **before answering a question:** Chris Fabricant, interview by Radley Balko. Tucker Carrington also represents Howard and participated in the deposition.

315   **"vagina lip off?":** Deposition of Michael West, Eddie Lee Howard v. State of Mississippi, Nos. 2000-0115-CV1 2010-DR-01043-SCT (Lowndes Cnty. Circuit Ct. April 16, 2016), 16.

316   **"I ate eggs.":** Ibid., 75.

316   **"cum on that":** Ibid., 91.

316   **"I have no respect for y'all.":** Ibid., 140–141.

316   **"yourself a sociopath.":** Ibid., 142.

316   **Howard's legal team:** Motion to Determine Qualifications of Counsel, *Eddie Lee Howard v. State of Mississippi*, April 26, 2016.

317   **pro bono basis:** Affidavit of Emily Olson-Gault, American Bar Association, Nov. 9, 2015.

317   **"Project Innocence":** See e.g., Deposition of Dr. Steven Hayne, *Hayne v. Innocence Project* (April 26, 2012), 191, 194, 211, 234, 238.

317   **near Leakesville:** Deposition of Michael West, *Hayne v. Innocence Project*, 11.

317   **"my number one friend now.":** Deposition of Michael West, *Eddie Lee Howard v. State of Mississippi*, 96.

318   **a deal to cooperate against others:** Peters did not prosecute the case; his office did, and Bobby DeLaughter (later a judge and convicted in the same bribery scandal) was the line prosecutor; see Paul Quinn, "Federal Prosecutor Wished He Could Go After Former Hinds DA," *Hattiesburg* (MS) *American,* Aug. 16, 2009; Peter Boyer, "The Bribe," *New Yorker,* May 19, 2008.

318   **for prosecutorial misconduct:** Holliman v. State, 79 So.3d 496 (Miss. 2011) ("The prosecutor essentially requested that each juror put himself or herself in the place of Laura during the fatal altercation, which was an egregious display of prosecutorial misconduct"); Quintez Wren Hodges v. Christopher Epps, 2010 WL 3655851 (N.D. Miss. 2010) ("the testimony of Mr. Kitchens at Petitioner's trial and in this Court is factually at odds with what is contained in the record, and DA Allgood should have known that the testimony given by ADA Kitchens was false"); Nerissa Young,

"Holliman Murder Conviction Overturned," *Columbus* (MS) *Dispatch*, Dec. 2, 2011.

318   **finally defeated at the polls:** Jimmie E. Gates, "Scott Colom Ousts Longtime DA Forrest Allgood," *Clarion-Ledger* (Jackson, MS), Nov. 6, 2015.

318   **National Association of Attorneys General:** "Jim Hood Elected President of National Association of Attorney Generals," *NewsMS*, June 7, 2014.

318   **enthusiasm for the death penalty:** "Mississippi AG Wants "State" to Mull Firing Squad, Nitrogen Gas as Execution Options," *New Orleans Times Picayune*, Jan. 27, 2016; "Attorney General Jim Hood Applauds Senate Passage of Senate Bill 2237," Office of Mississippi Attorney General Jim Hood, March 1, 2016.

318   **ten percentage points:** "All Statewide Incumbents Re-Elected with Ease," *Jackson* (MS) *Free Press*, Nov. 4, 2015.

318   **candidate for governor:** For example, see Charlie Mitchell, "Strange But True: Trump Win Boosts Hood for Governor," *Clarion-Ledger* (Jackson, MS), Dec. 14, 2016.

319   **"what the system's gonna do.":** Kennedy Brewer, interview by Radley Balko.

Radley Balko is an investigative journalist and reporter at the *Washington Post*. He currently writes and edits The Watch, a reported opinion blog that covers civil liberties and the criminal justice system. He is the author of the 2013 book *Rise of the Warrior Cop: The Militarization of America's Police Forces*, which has won widespread acclaim, including from the *Economist*, the *New Yorker*, the *Wall Street Journal*, and *Publishers Weekly*, and was named one of the best investigative journalism books of the year by the Nieman Foundation at Harvard University. Since 2006, Balko has written dozens of pieces on Steven Hayne, Michael West, and Mississippi's forensics disaster. His January 2013 investigation, "Solving Kathy Mabry's Murder: Brutal 15-Year-Old Crime Highlights Decades-Long Mississippi Scandal," was one of the most widely read *Huffington Post* articles of 2013. In 2015, Balko was awarded the Innocence Project's Journalism Award, in part for his coverage in Mississippi.

Tucker Carrington is the director of the George C. Cochran Innocence Project at the University of Mississippi School of Law. He has worked as a criminal defense lawyer for his entire legal career, most of it as a public defender in Washington, DC.

© Kevin Bain

PublicAffairs is a publishing house founded in 1997. It is a tribute to the standards, values, and flair of three persons who have served as mentors to countless reporters, writers, editors, and book people of all kinds, including me.

I. F. STONE, proprietor of *I. F. Stone's Weekly*, combined a commitment to the First Amendment with entrepreneurial zeal and reporting skill and became one of the great independent journalists in American history. At the age of eighty, Izzy published *The Trial of Socrates*, which was a national bestseller. He wrote the book after he taught himself ancient Greek.

BENJAMIN C. BRADLEE was for nearly thirty years the charismatic editorial leader of *The Washington Post*. It was Ben who gave the *Post* the range and courage to pursue such historic issues as Watergate. He supported his reporters with a tenacity that made them fearless and it is no accident that so many became authors of influential, best-selling books.

ROBERT L. BERNSTEIN, the chief executive of Random House for more than a quarter century, guided one of the nation's premier publishing houses. Bob was personally responsible for many books of political dissent and argument that challenged tyranny around the globe. He is also the founder and longtime chair of Human Rights Watch, one of the most respected human rights organizations in the world.

·   ·   ·

For fifty years, the banner of Public Affairs Press was carried by its owner Morris B. Schnapper, who published Gandhi, Nasser, Toynbee, Truman, and about 1,500 other authors. In 1983, Schnapper was described by *The Washington Post* as "a redoubtable gadfly." His legacy will endure in the books to come.

Peter Osnos, *Founder*